HUMANITARIANIS

Humanitarian sentiments have motivated a variety of manifestations of pity, from nineteenth-century movements to end slavery to the creation of modern international humanitarian law. While humanitarianism is clearly political, *Humanitarianism and Suffering* addresses the ways in which it is also an ethos embedded in civil society, one that drives secular and religious social and cultural movements, not just legal and political institutions. As an ethos, humanitarianism has a strong narrative and representational dimension that can generate humanitarian constituencies for particular causes. The emotional nature of compassion is closely linked to visual and literary images of suffering and innocence. Essays in this volume analyze the character, form, and voice of private or public narrative themselves and explain how and why some narratives of suffering energize political movements of solidarity, whereas others do not. *Humanitarianism and Suffering* explores when, how, and why humanitarian movements become broadly popular. It shows how public sentiment moves political and social elites to action and, conversely, how national elites appropriate humanitarian ideals for more instrumental ends.

Richard Ashby Wilson is Gladstein Distinguished Chair of Human Rights, Professor of Anthropology, and Director of the Human Rights Institute at the University of Connecticut. He is the author or editor of numerous works on human rights, truth commissions, and international criminal tribunals, including *Maya Resurgence in Guatemala, The Politics of Truth and Reconciliation in South Africa, Low Intensity Democracy, Human Rights, Culture and Context, Culture and Rights, Human Rights in Global Perspectives,* and *Human Rights and the "War on Terror."* He has been a visiting professor at the University of Oslo, Norway; the New School for Social Research; and the University of the Witwatersrand, South Africa. He is a member of the Committee for Human Rights of the American Anthropological Association. In addition, he serves on the editorial boards of *Critique of Anthropology,* the *Journal of the Royal Anthropological Institute,* the *Journal of Human Rights,* the *Journal of Transitional Justice,* and the *Journal of Social Justice.*

Richard D. Brown is a Board of Trustees Distinguished Professor of History and Director of the University of Connecticut Humanities Institute. He specializes in the cultural and political history of early America and is the author of *The Hanging of Ephraim Wheeler: A Story of Rape, Incest, and Justice in Early America* with Irene Quenzler Brown; *The Strength of a People: The Idea of an Informed Citizenry in America, 1650–1870; Knowledge Is Power: The Diffusion of Information in Early America, 1700–1865;* and *Major Problems in the Era of the American Revolution, 1760–1791,* among other works. Past President of the Society of Historians of the Early American Republic, he has held fellowships from the John Simon Guggenheim Foundation, the National Endowment for the Humanities, the Social Science Research Council, and the Woodrow Wilson Foundation. Currently, he serves on the editorial board of the *New England Quarterly.*

For Helene and Irene

Humanitarianism and Suffering
The Mobilization of Empathy

Edited by

RICHARD ASHBY WILSON
University of Connecticut

RICHARD D. BROWN
University of Connecticut

CAMBRIDGE UNIVERSITY PRESS

CAMBRIDGE UNIVERSITY PRESS
Cambridge, New York, Melbourne, Madrid, Cape Town,
Singapore, São Paulo, Delhi, Tokyo, Mexico City

Cambridge University Press
32 Avenue of the Americas, New York, NY 10013-2473, USA

www.cambridge.org
Information on this title: www.cambridge.org/9780521298384

© Cambridge University Press 2009

First published 2009
First paperback edition 2011

A catalog record for this publication is available from the British Library

Library of Congress Cataloging in Publication data
Humanitarianism and suffering: the mobilization of empathy / edited by Richard
Ashby Wilson and Richard D. Brown.
p. cm.
Includes bibliographical references and index.
ISBN 978-0-521-88385-6 (hardback)
1. Humanitarianism. 2. Suffering. 3. Empathy. 1. Wilson, Richard, 1964–
11. Brown, Richard D. 111. Title.
BJ1475.3.H86 2008
361.2–dc22   2008023734

ISBN 978-0-521-88385-6 Hardback
ISBN 978-0-521-29838-4 Paperback

Contents

Contributors

Rony Brauman, Associate Professor of Humanitarian Studies, Institut d'Études Politiques (Paris, France); Research Director, Médecins Sans Frontières (France)

Ron Dudai, Visiting Lecturer, Centre for Applied Human Rights, University of York (UK)

David P. Forsythe, Charles J. Mach Distinguished Professor, Department of Political Science, University of Nebraska (Lincoln)

Elizabeth Jelin, Senior Researcher, CONICET (National Council of Research) and IDES (Institute for Social and Economic Development) (Buenos Aires, Argentina)

Margaret M. R. Kellow, Associate Professor, Department of History, University of Western Ontario

Flora A. Keshgegian, independent scholar, Providence, Rhode Island

Thomas W. Laqueur, Helen Fawcett Distinguished Professor, Department of History, University of California, Berkeley

Michael R. Marrus, Chancellor Rose and Ray Wolfe Professor Emeritus of Holocaust Studies, University of Toronto

Kristin Bergtora Sandvik, SJD candidate, Harvard Law School, Cambridge, Massachussetts

Joseph R. Slaughter, Associate Professor of English and Comparative Literature, Columbia University New York, New York

Susan Slyomovics, Professor of Anthropology and Near Eastern Languages and Cultures, University of California, Los Angeles

Laura Suski, Ph.D., Instructor, Sociology and Global Studies, Vancouver Island University (previously Malaspina University-College), Nanaimo, BC, Canada

Lars Waldorf, Director and Lecturer, Centre for International Human Rights, Institute of Commonwealth Studies, University of London (UK)

Acknowledgments

This edited volume arises out of a conference on Humanitarian Narratives of Inflicted Suffering, co-organized by the Human Rights Institute and the Humanities Institute of the University of Connecticut, and held on October 13–15, 2006. Funding for the conference came from a five-year grant from the University of Connecticut Provost's Competition, and we acknowledge the generous support of Provost John Petersen, Interim Provost Fred Maryanski, Provost Peter Nicholls, and Vice-Provost Suman Singha. We thank Dean Ross Mackinnon of the College of Liberal Arts and Sciences for his generous support of this teaching and research program. In thinking through the issues raised by our discussion of humanitarianism, we benefited greatly from conversations with Eleni Coundouriotis, David Forsythe, Wiktor Osiatynski, Nigel Rapport, and John R. Wallach. Human Rights Institute Administrator Rachel Jackson and Humanities Institute Administrator Jo-Anne Waide provided superb organizational skills during the conference and for the wider program. Copy editors Aaron Paterson, Katharine Hawkins, and Sally Nicholls showed meticulous attention to detail. Finally, thanks to John Berger, Senior Editor at Cambridge University Press, for his support and encouragement.

Introduction

RICHARD ASHBY WILSON AND RICHARD D. BROWN

Though our brother is on the rack, as long as we ourselves are at ease, our senses will never inform us of what he suffers. . . . It is by the imagination only that we can form any conception of what are his sensations. . . . It is the impressions of our senses only, not those of his, which our imaginations copy.

Adam Smith (1759/2002: 11–12)

The Boundaries of Humanitarianism

Why have individuals been concerned with the suffering of others, especially distant others who are not members of their own family, race, gender, social class, or religious community, people with whom they share no apparent social connections or moral obligations? Historically, a number of world religions have encouraged assisting others in dire need; Judaism, Christianity, and Islam, for example, justify helping others based on charity and their belief that all humans are created in God's image. That people have joined in large numbers on expressly secular[1] grounds to alleviate the suffering of others near and far, and sought to coordinate relief by establishing local, state, and transnational institutions, is recent in world history, a phenomenon that only emerged fully in Europe and the Americas in the late eighteenth century.

[1] A rigorous distinction between secular and religious often breaks down empirically, and has been extensively criticized as the basis of Western exclusion by writers such as Talal Asad (2003). Nevertheless, it ought to be recognized that secular liberal humanism's approach to suffering, particularly in the eighteenth century, does have unique attributes that distinguish it from religious doctrine up to that point.

Thanks are due to those who commented on earlier drafts of this Introduction: Eleni Coundouriotis, Ilana Feldman, David Forsythe, and Helene Kvale. Wiktor Osiatynski deserves thanks for helping the editors distinguish between humanitarianism and human rights. Any errors are the sole responsibility of the editors.

1

This volume is drawn from a University of Connecticut conference on "Humanitarian Narratives of Inflicted Suffering" that charted the history of secular and religious humanitarian and human rights movements from the late eighteenth century to the present day in order to comprehend the ethical principles that propel them forward, the political interests they attempt to realize, and the narratives and representations they employ to mobilize empathy for distant others. The conference and this volume aim to promote comparative and interdisciplinary insights into the operation of the ethic of humanitarianism in modern history by bringing together anthropologists, historians, humanitarian practitioners, lawyers, political scientists, sociologists, and scholars of comparative literature.

We begin by explaining our understanding of this fundamental shift in public consciousness as it emerged in the eighteenth century and by describing the boundaries between humanitarianism and the adjacent, overlapping concept of human rights. Faced with the suffering of others, humanitarians maintain that their ethical response arises from emotions: compassion, sympathy (in the nineteenth century), and, more recently, empathy.[2] In its secular form, humanitarianism usually asserts the ideal of the realization of individual potential, often derived from Immanuel Kant's moral philosophy.[3] For Richard Rorty (1993: 124–5), Kant's foundational argument for respect between rational agents and against the domination of one human being by another amounted to a secularizing of the Christian doctrine of universal brotherhood.

Humanitarian sentiments have motivated a variety of manifestations of pity, from nineteenth-century movements to end slavery to the creation of international humanitarian law. While humanitarianism is clearly political in its implications of solidarity, this volume addresses the ways in which it is also an ethos embedded in civil society, one that drives secular and religious social and cultural movements, not just legal and political institutions. As an ethos, humanitarianism has a strong narrative and representational dimension that can generate humanitarian constituencies for

---

[2] Sympathy refers to the recognition of another's emotional state, in this discussion, a state of suffering. Empathy inhabits a site further along on the emotional register and refers to a projection of one's own mental state into that of another. Whereas in a state of sympathy one says "I recognize your pain," in empathy one says "I feel your pain." For a discussion of the cognitive aspects of empathy, see Monroe (2004: 248–50). See Richard Rorty (1993: 128–9) for a discussion of sympathy in the context of human rights stories and sentimental education.

[3] Berlin (2000: 71) indicates that there is not a great deal before the eighteenth century and before Kant that maintains that the exploitation of one human by another is an evil.

particular causes. The emotional nature of compassion is closely linked to visual and literary images of suffering and innocence, as we explore in a later section of this Introduction and throughout this collection of essays.

In Chapter 2 in this volume, David Forsythe defines international humanitarianism as "the transnational concern to help persons in exceptional distress," and argues that humanitarianism's declaration of secular universalism allows it to transcend boundaries such as race, class, religion, gender, and nation. As the director of the World Food Program Josette Sheeran declared, "When you see a hungry child, you feel you represent all humanity" (Rosenthal 2007: A4). We are not dealing here with hesitant values characterized by passive contemplation, but a belief that promotes immediate action to end suffering across the globe. As Luc Boltanski (1999: xv) writes, "when confronted with suffering all moral demands converge on the single imperative of action. Commitment is commitment to action, the intention to act and orientation towards a horizon of action. But what form can this commitment take when those called upon to act are thousands of miles away from the person suffering?"

Advocates of humanitarianism express profound indignation towards those who renounce responsibility for the fate of others, especially state officials who reject concerted action to end suffering. There are many modern instances of state calculation of interest that leads to inaction or disregard for the suffering of distant others. The 1994 British television documentary on East Timor, called *The Death of a Nation*, included an interview regarding the sale of ground attack aircraft to the Suharto regime with the minister responsible for defense procurement in Margaret Thatcher's cabinet. The notoriously controversial Alan Clarke remarked, "Does anyone know where East Timor is?" adding, "I don't really fill my mind much with what one set of foreigners is doing to another" (Pilger 2007). Yet hundreds of millions of pounds of British-made arms, the documentary reported, were used by the Indonesian military in the invasion of East Timor and the massacre of approximately 200,000 Timorese.

The late Alan Clarke, one of the more grandiloquent antihumanitarians, is not alone in his forthright defense of state interests, narrowly defined. German foreign minister Volker Rühe declared in December 1992, "I am not willing to risk the lives of German soldiers for countries whose names we cannot spell properly."[4] The USA's Clinton Administration studiously avoided a humanitarian campaign to end "distant

---

[4]   As cited in David Edgar's *Pentecost* (1994: 55).

suffering"[5] when it repudiated applying the term "genocide" to the mass slaughter of Tutsis in Rwanda in 1994. Instead it referred to "acts of genocide"[6] in order to evade its obligations to prevent genocide under the terms of the 1948 Convention on the Prevention and Punishment of the Crime of Genocide. Samantha Power (2002: 362–3) maintains that in Rwanda "the case for a label of genocide was the most straightforward since the Holocaust," yet the US State Department shirked the concomitant obligation to intervene and put an end the killing.[7] Ironically, by their selective use of language, US government officials implicitly recognized the compelling nature of the humanitarian duty they chose to evade.

In defining what humanitarianism stands for and against, we must be careful not to oversystematize this loosely bounded ethic of moral and political action. While secular humanitarianism has clear roots in the politics and philosophy of eighteenth-century liberalism, humanitarian movements are remarkably diverse and may be motivated by radically different principles. Some have favored a rights-based approach that asserts that all individuals are, for example, entitled to an education by right, whereas others hold the colonial idea that non-Westerners are to be educated as part of a Kipling-like "white man's burden." Such competing views can be found within the same humanitarian organizations, as we see in Kellow's discussion of the United States' anti-slavery movement in Chapter 5 in this volume. Humanitarianism, as an ethic, cuts across political orientations and can be associated with religious and political projects as diverse as Quaker pacifism, Protestant evangelicalism, Great Power imperialism, Catholic social democracy, and grassroots democratic socialism. The array of activities included under the label "humanitarian practices" are similarly diverse and range from food aid to refugee resettlement from immigration reform laws to full-scale military intervention.

Humanitarianism and Human Rights

In addition to the internal diversity of humanitarianism, there are moral-political concepts that lie alongside and interact with it, the most

---

[5] A term used extensively by Boltanski (1993).

[6] See Power (2002: 363).

[7] Recognizing that, while US military intervention might have ended the immediate killing, it might also have had other damaging and unintended consequences.

fundamental of which is human rights. Human rights and humanitarianism share many attributes and emerged from the same intellectual origins in liberal political philosophy of the eighteenth century. Both have common origins in natural law thinking[8] and Ruti Teitel (2004: 225) weaves these strands into a common category of "humanity law" – "an amalgam of natural law, the law of human rights, and the law of war." Human rights and humanitarian law share a view of humanity as a unified legal community when crimes are committed that offend not only a nation or country, but the entire human race.

Human rights and humanitarianism share a common view of the essential characteristics of human welfare and human dignity. When individuals experience the same abject conditions, they suffer in more or less the same way, regardless of their gender, cultural or religious identity, or political persuasion. As a rule, humanitarians, like human rights advocates, reject the relativist view that suffering is acceptable when it is part of an established way of life. At certain junctures they have advanced a vision of a universal human subject protected by the universal juris-diction of the "law of humanity." The idea of humanity can furnish the legal grounds and legitimacy for a new type of political sovereignty – one that can be exercised across national borders. Without this idea of humanity, humanitarians cannot advocate laws with universal jurisdiction or prohibit crimes so heinous that they violate the sensibility of all humanity.

While the modern human rights system arose in the same post–World War II moment as key international humanitarian conventions (notably the 1949 Geneva Conventions), the modern human rights system we see in place today is an extension of an older framework of humanitarian law that sought to limit the exercise of violent state power and, more specifically, the amount and type of damage that could be inflicted in war. The concept of "crimes against humanity" that appeared in the Nuremberg trials drew legal sustenance from nineteenth-century conventions that invoked the

---

[8]   Hugo Grotius (1625/1949: 277) in *On the Law of War and Peace* made extensive use of natural law to justify the legal regulation of war "from motives of interest of humanity," arguing that prisoners of war may not be put to death. See Neff (2005: 224) on the connection between natural law and sympathy towards the concept of humanitarian intervention. See Michael Freeman (2002: 14–26) on the natural law origins of human rights. Janis (2005:767) notes that, in the famous antislavery case in Britain of *Somerset v. Stewart.* June 22, 1772, "Francis Hargreave and Alleyne, attorneys for Somerset, argued not only that slavery was illegal in England but that it violated natural law."

forbid

"laws of humanity."[9] These and other conventions sought to proscribe the
"excessive" cruelty of modern war and gained legitimacy from emerging
understandings of the "laws of humanity," the "law of nations" and the
customary practice of "civilized nations."[10] Human rights law rests on the
same conventions, and restricts how states treat accused persons in their
custody, though it generally binds rights more closely to individuals than
states. One thinks of the recent US detention of suspected terrorists in
Guantanamo Bay and the concerns expressed by human rights organizations regarding torture, habeas corpus, the right to counsel, and other
common due process standards.[11]

Human rights and humanitarian law have taken a similar course in
recent years, with the bearer of rights increasingly shifting away from states
and towards the individual. While the right to humanitarian intervention
was originally a right asserted by the intervening *state*,[12] in the post–Cold
War era this right became progressively transferred to the victims of
abuses. In the 1990s, international human rights and humanitarian law
moved even more closely together and, in the NATO military operation in
Kosovo, it became difficult to distinguish between them, especially as the
liberal conception of military humanitarian interventions was often
grounded in the human rights of innocent persons.[13] In this way, modern
humanitarianism has come to draw increasingly from the model of human

interveners
to
victims
SHIFT

---

[9] Including the 1864 Geneva Convention for the Amelioration of the Wounded, the 1868
St. Petersburg Declaration Renouncing the Use, in Time of War, of Certain Explosive
Projectiles, and perhaps most famously, the "Martens Clause" contained in the 1899
Convention With Respect to the Laws and Customs of War on Land (Hague II). The
clause, drafted by Hague subcommittee chair Frederic de Martens, extended protections
to those who did not clearly conform to standard criteria of the time for combatant status
(See Neff 2005: 210). It states: "Until a more complete code of the laws of war is issued,
the High Contracting Parties think it right to declare that in cases not included in the
Regulations adopted by them, populations and belligerents remain under the protection
and empire of the principles of international law, as they result from the usages
established between civilized nations, from the laws of humanity and the requirements of
the public conscience." See Teitel (2004: 226) for additional references to "laws of
humanity" in nineteenth-century humanitarian law.
[10] For a discussion of how Nuremberg's understanding of crimes against humanity drew
upon the concepts of civilization and civilized practice, see Douglas (2001: 83–4).
[11] See Duffy (2005) and Wilson (2005).
[12] Drawing here from the work of legal historian Stephen Neff (2005: 223). Neff later (224)
refers to the military action taken by Britain, France, and Russia on behalf of the Greeks in
their struggle against the Ottoman Empire as arguably the first major instance of
humanitarian intervention.
[13] See Fernando Tesón (2003: 114–15) for a lucid discussion of humanitarian intervention,
human rights and the rights of innocents.

rights in its conferral on individuals of rights hitherto reserved for states. The two aspects, state and individual, are integrated in Holzgrefe's (2003: 18) definition of humanitarian intervention as the "threat or use of force across state borders by a state (or group of states) aimed at preventing or ending widespread and grave violations of the fundamental human rights of individuals other than its own citizens, without the permission of the state within whose territory force is applied."

And yet, there are ways in which human rights and humanitarianism are historically distinct and require careful disentangling from one another.[14] In their earliest historical manifestation, they arose in diametrical opposition to one another. Legal historian Stephen Neff (2005: 223) cites the August 27, 1791, Declaration of Pillnitz by Emperor Leopold II of Austria and King Frederick-William III of Prussia in response to the revolutionary events in France as the first articulation of the modern principle of humanitarian intervention, insofar as it contained two conceptual elements that continue to characterize it: "a statement that seemingly internal or domestic events could be a matter of common concern to the world at large even in the absence of any direct material interest; and a willingness to use force to set the situation aright." While the Pillnitz Declaration failed to sway the British and was never acted upon, it was a clarion call to European powers to stem the tide of republicanism and human rights and to shore up the monarchical system.

We can identify other conceptual discrepancies that emerge from the disparate legal justifications for human rights and humanitarianism. Whereas human rights are pre-existing legal protections of individuals, humanitarian action by states is often justified less by a legal claim than a moral one. This is in part because humanitarianism is less firmly grounded in international law than is human rights. The principle of humanitarian military intervention by states has never been decisively or unambiguously accepted in international law, and weaker states are often wary of the ways in which stronger states have appropriated and pursued this right, especially because humanitarian military interventions often occur without permission from the governments within whose territory the intervention is taking place.[15]

Even when considering humanitarian assistance that stops short of military intervention, such as a right to humanitarian assistance in the form

---

[14] See Moyn (2007) for a critical view of humanitarianism and a statement of the view that human rights and humanitarianism have completely different historical lineages.

[15] The editors thank David Forsythe for emphasizing this point to them. See Farer (2003) for a discussion of how the debate on humanitarian military intervention has shifted since 2001.

of refugee resettlement, such a claim is not widely recognized. According to Kristin Sandvik in this volume, officials of the United Nations High Commission for Refugees make clear to African refugees that "resettlement is not a right." A state or international institution defining its actions as humanitarian may not accept an inalienable right to resettlement that would compel it to assist refugees. Within the human rights system, some victims of human rights violations can expect their cases to be taken up by an array of international criminal tribunals, including the International Criminal Court.[16] But there is no obvious legally constituted international setting for those in dire need of humanitarian assistance to pursue their claims against a potential state provider, even if such a claim could be acknowledged as a right. Consequently, potential recipients are more reliant upon the moral impulses of those who provide assistance or aid, often as a gift without the implied reciprocity of many forms of gift-giving.

These distinctions result from a different view of the "agency" of recipients of human rights or humanitarian assistance. Writers have commented upon the antipathy of human rights activists to the language of humanitarianism, a language often perceived as laden with outmoded notions of charity, protection, sentiment, and neocolonial paternalism.[17] Human rights, it is argued, confer a modern inventory of entitlements, where the obligation to victims arises not from the heart, but from the head – from legal-bureaucratic duties. Pursuing or defending one's human rights presupposes an assertive political agency on the part of rights-holders. Individuals may require assistance in order to claim their rights, but the assumption is still one of self-directed individuals vigorously pursuing their claims, immunities, privileges, and liberties.

In the context of humanitarian assistance, on the other hand, the recipients are less likely to actively determine their own fate. Because beneficiaries of humanitarian aid are more likely to appear as passive recipients, critics have asserted that humanitarianism may, in its quest to be seen as "apolitical," draw attention away from the political reasons for victimization, disempower individuals, and strip them of agency.[18] Cultural anthropologists such as Miriam Ticktin (2003: 41) have been among the

---

[16] And including the International Criminal Tribunals for Rwanda and for the former Yugoslavia, and the Special Court for Sierra Leone.

[17] See Rajaram (2002).

[18] See Wilson (1997: 148). More recently, Miriam Ticktin (2003), writing about the treatment of *les sans-papiers* in France, refers to the "violence" of the humanitarian framework, and see Ruti Teitel (2004), writing about the depoliticizing consequences of international humanitarian law.

most critical of modern humanitarianism's creation of new "political subjects, albeit with limited political choices." Such arguments resonate with Flora Keshgegian's account in Chapter 6 of this volume of early twentieth-century American Christian groups and their portrayal of Armenians subjected to genocide by the Ottoman Empire as powerless and backward, and with Laura Suski's chapter on the denial of the agency of children by humanitarian organizations (Chapter 9).[19]

Clearly, there is no easy resolution to the tension between rights-based and humanitarian approaches; this is one rationale for this book, which explores directly how human rights and humanitarianism connect, overlap, and disconnect in specific historical, political, and cultural contexts of suffering.

Historical Origins of Humanitarianism and Human Rights

Compassion is a natural feeling, which, by moderating the love of self in each individual, contributes to the preservation of the whole species. It is this compassion that hurries us without reflection to the relief of those who are in distress; it is this which in a state of nature supplies the place of laws, morals and virtues.

Jean-Jacques Rousseau (1754/1973: 68)

Long ago, biblical prophets proclaimed the equality of humans before God. But in their time and ever after, inequalities have characterized human societies. In the biblical era, claims to rights depended on hierarchies within and among families as well as rankings of power and privilege among ruling and subordinate groups. As the overlapping connection between rights and privileges suggests, the unequal distribution of rights was integral to the structure of ancient, medieval, and early modern politics in the West. The idea that here on earth human beings should actually possess rights equally – not as fathers, not as heirs, not even as citizens – is recent. To suppose that all humans may claim "their" rights as equals, and that state and society are bound to recognize and defend human rights, is a radical departure from most of history.

Enlightenment human rights ideology came into its own in the eighteenth-century Atlantic world when the United States' "Declaration of Independence" (1776) and the French "Declaration of the Rights of Man and of the Citizen" (1789) proclaimed as fact the universality of inherent, inalienable, natural rights (Hunt 2007). For revolutionaries, these assertions were inspiring, though defenders of monarchy responded

---

[19] Susan Sontag (1993: 9) sees Virginia Woolf's abhorrence of war as a way of avoiding a political engagement with Spanish history, and states baldly, "It is to dismiss politics."

furiously to their challenge to traditional, prescribed, and inherited "rights and liberties." Even nineteenth-century reformers like the utilitarian Jeremy Bentham ridiculed "the Rights of Man" as "simple nonsense ... rhetorical nonsense, nonsense upon stilts."[20] And since the eighteenth-century era of revolutions, although there have been other proclamations of human rights, culminating in the United Nations' "Universal Declaration of Human Rights" (1948), such claims have been contested. Rights have been defended more often and more successfully based on nationality or group membership – as rights belonging to citizens or members of ethnic and religious groups – not as the inalienable possession of each person as an individual human being.

Practical arguments support this older national- and group-based view of rights because, as individuals, people are seldom capable of defending their rights outside the framework of standing law. "How many legions has the Pope?" tyrants have asked dismissively, and world history has reinforced the presumption that it is meaningless to assert rights without the threat of force to back up those rights.[21] Yet there have been moments and movements in times past when the rights of individuals have won recognition even without their own state to defend them. The abolition of the slave trade by Britain in 1807, and the permanent abolition of slavery in the British (1833), Swedish (1843), Danish (1847), French (1848), and Dutch (1863) colonies demonstrates that, under certain conditions, the recognition of a human right to personal liberty could be won by enslaved persons who had no "legions" and who were nominally powerless.[22] Moreover, the abolition movement in the British Empire, in Europe, and in some measure in the United States, reveals that men and women, even children, whose own rights were assured by their governments could mobilize effectively to assert what they took to be universal human rights. In the case of slaves and abolition, reformers succeeded in arousing sympathy and in awakening moral qualms so powerfully as to mobilize political action which, though certainly colored by self-interest, actually won rights for people who were "other" in the fullest sense.

Arousing sympathy and awakening moral qualms, and connecting them to real and imagined self-interest, appears to be the proven method for the realization of human rights. This process has brought "legions" to enlist on behalf of powerless ethnic and religious groups, and for children and

[20] As quoted in Hunt (2007: 125).
[21] Attributed to Napoleon and to Josef Stalin.
[22] See D. B. Davis (2006), P. Kolchin (1987), and J. P. Rodriguez, ed. (2007).

women, thereby transforming what might have seemed "nonsense upon stilts" into a commonsense imperative. Today the legitimacy of human rights is so widely established that nations, singly and collectively, routinely profess commitment to these rights, even as many abuse them.

Here the historical divergence between "humanitarianism," the wish to promote human welfare, and human rights is critical. As noted, the humanitarian seeks to assist fellow human beings and to alleviate suffering, and does not necessarily act to defend violated rights. In British colonial America, for example, in the name of humanitarianism some slaveholders acted to improve the conditions of slave life, never imagining that the enslaved Africans enjoyed rights that forbade their enslavement (Chaplin 1990). The latent conflict between humanitarianism and human rights is vividly illustrated in Margaret Kellow's chapter, "Hard Struggles of Doubt: Abolitionists and the Problem of Slave Redemption." Kellow shows the willingness of such human rights advocates as the abolitionist William Lloyd Garrison to compromise principle when he assisted in purchasing the freedom of individual slaves. Here, the humanitarian desire to alleviate individual suffering in the 1840s and 1850s overrode the rights-based claim to freedom. Humanitarian payments to the slave owner tacitly recognized a legitimacy for slavery that abolitionists simultaneously repudiated. This conflict between the urgent desire to relieve immediate suffering – even when relief may reinforce the denial of rights – is persistent and chronic.[23]

Often the distinction between the humanitarian alleviation of suffering and the vindication of human rights has, as with the purchase of a slave's freedom, meant the difference between immediate action to achieve individual results and unrelenting, generations-long efforts to establish new

---

[23] Reference to "purchase" of East Germans by West German government from Prof. Anke Finger, University of Connecticut, who writes in a letter of 28 June 2007: "At first, it was the West German protestant church who sought to free political prisoners in the early sixties, not more than twenty at first, all of whom were active in the GDR churches and had come under suspicion. They offered the GDR government payment in forms other than money, but soon the 'transfer' was too much to handle and they handed the 'business' over to the West German Government. According to Wolfgang Mayer, *Flucht und Ausreise: Botschaftsbesetzungen als wirksame Form des Widerstands und Mittel gegen die politische Verfolgung in der DDR* (Berlin: A Tykve, 2002), between 1963 and 1989 about 34,000 prisoners were bought by the West, providing the GDR with appr. 3,6 billion D-Mark (a very low estimate, there is evidence of a much higher sum). Between '65 and '89, about 250,000 citizens who cited political reasons for their desire to leave the GDR were bought as well. The GDR government soon included these 'revenues' in their annual budget. The price of a prisoner at first was about 45,000 D-Mark, around 1982 it was already 95,700. Family reunions could cost somewhere around 100,000 per person. These are just the numbers, and they may vary, depending on whom you consult."

legal and political arrangements for whole classes of people. Because a commitment to humanitarianism can frequently be fulfilled and rewarded more promptly in the here and now than can a commitment to human rights, humanitarianism more reliably delivers emotional rewards. Because suffering is a universal human experience, potentially all individuals can connect emotionally to specific people and their woes. In contrast, in order to empathize with the deprivation of the rights of others one must possess a vivid sense of one's own rights. Until Westerners articulated a keen commitment to their own rights, they could never conceive a transnational human rights movement.

The way that liberal Europeans and Americans came to internalize their belief in the natural rights of individuals and to empathize with others, the historian Lynn Hunt explains, was tied closely to the rapid rise of the novel in the late eighteenth and early nineteenth centuries. Novels, whose galloping expansion in popularity and reach depended on their readers' belief in individual autonomy, appealed to their audiences by evoking feelings of empathy for the novels' subjects – often vulnerable young women. Authors like Samuel Richardson, who created *Pamela: Or, Virtue Rewarded* (1740) and *Clarissa: Or the History of a Young Lady* (1748), Jean-Jacques Rousseau, whose *Julie, or the New Héloise* appeared in 1761, and Johann Wolfgang von Goethe, author of *The Sorrows of Young Werther* (1774), not only "equalized" servants and others of modest station but went beyond sympathy to cultivate empathic sentiments in the minds of genteel readers (Hunt 2007: 35, 38–40).[24] As Hunt explains, to feel the pain of others closed the distance between the parties and encouraged readers to project onto others the rights they cherished for themselves in an era when a universal idea of "mankind" prevailed. Once these "others," whether characters in novels or in slave narratives, could be imagined as individual persons, their rights sprung to life as worth defending.

The emergence of this new sensibility and the blurred boundary between humanitarianism and human rights was evident in the movement to end torture and to revise penal codes just as sentimental novels were proliferating. In 1761 and 1762, while Rousseau's *Julie* swept into genteel salons

[24] The titles of Rousseau's and Goethe's novels are, here, obviously, translated to English. *Julie* went through 115 French and 10 English editions before 1800. *Sorrows of Young Werther* not only saw numerous German editions, but six in France from 1775 to 1778 and twenty in Britain from 1779 through 1799, in addition to five in the USA, and others in Italy and Russia. Compilations of British editions from British Library Catalog and United States editions from American Antiquarian Society catalog. On Continental publication, see Unseld (1996: 23).

and drawing-rooms, the Calas affair shocked the same articulate, politically connected classes. In the city of Toulouse, France, the authorities convicted Jean Calas, a bourgeois French Protestant, for murdering his son so as, it was said, to prevent the young man's conversion to Catholicism. After an appeal to a higher court in early 1762, judges condemned Calas to public execution by being "broken on the wheel," that is, each limb to be broken by the executioner so that the convict could be strapped face-up to a wheel, there to remain until he expired (Bien 1960: 22).

To gain a confession from Calas and testimony that would reveal accomplices, the judges ordered that he be questioned under torture before execution. Accordingly, they brought Calas to the torture room to be stretched on the rack and forced to swallow gallons of water. Still, the 64-year-old cloth merchant denied any part in his son's death and refused to implicate anyone else. Eight times he denied his interrogator before being taken to the Place St. George where he was broken on the wheel. His agonies were limited only because, as an act of mercy, the judges had secretly directed the executioner to strangle Calas after two hours on the wheel. Finally, the executioners burned the Protestant's corpse and scattered his ashes to the winds (Bien 1960).

Voltaire turned the narrative of the Calas affair into an Enlightenment *cause célèbre*. He raised money for Calas' suffering family and published such a powerful history of the case (1762), followed by a treatise on tolerance (1763), that the judicial establishment in Paris ultimately reversed the Toulouse verdict, belatedly acquitting the dead Protestant in 1765 (Silverman 2001: 158). Consequently, when Count Cesare di Beccaria's essay on crimes and punishments (1764) was translated from Italian into French in 1766, it found eager readers in precisely those salons where Rousseau's and Voltaire's works won applause. Quickly translated into English (1767) with an approving commentary by Voltaire, Beccaria's arguments against torture and cruel physical punishments won adherents across the Western world, from St. Petersburg and Vienna, to London, Madrid, Stockholm, and Philadelphia.

Voltaire began by remarking that he had read Beccaria's "little book ... with infinite satisfaction," and then supplied comments that ran almost half the length of *An Essay on Crimes and Punishments*. Opening with the figure of a vulnerable female who is more acted upon than acting, Voltaire followed the style of an epistolary novel: "I was informed, that, within a few miles of my abode, they had just hanged a girl of eighteen, beautiful, well made, accomplished, and of a very reputable family." Her crime, after "having suffered herself to be got with child," was abandonment of her infant who subsequently perished. To execute this anguished mother, Voltaire declared, was utterly disproportionate to her "crime," an abandonment committed only to hide her shame (Beccaria 1767: i, ii, 191). Underlying this response of Voltaire and Beccaria's multinational audience was a sense of the legal system's unfeeling violation of equal rights to justice, though their rhetoric appealed to the humanitarian principle of ending unnecessary human suffering.

Not everyone shared Beccaria's views and the fashionable humane sensibility, but few were ready to rebut the Italian *philosophe*. One who did, in 1767, was the notable French jurist Pierre François Muyart de Vouglans, who not only defended France's punishment regime – including the treatment accorded Calas – but also defended the morality and efficacy of interrogation accompanied by torture. According to Muyart de Vouglans, both preparatory torture to elicit a full confession prior to final judgment and sentencing ("*la question préparatoire*"), and torture after sentencing but before execution ("*la question préalable*"), as in Calas' case, so as to obtain a full confession and evidence against accomplices, were necessary and efficacious. The protection of social order, he argued, deserved the highest priority; so if there was reasonable cause, the individual must be sacrificed. As to the possibility of abuse, Muyart de Vouglans assured his readers that French procedures as recodified in 1670 barred abuses: torture was employed only in capital cases; it must be ordered and witnessed by several senior judges; and it was applied only after multiple evidences assured the guilt of the subject (1781: II: 291–93, 312–13).[25]

Muyart de Vouglans sat on the King's Great Council (*Grand-Conseil*), but even among the leaders of the *Ancien Régime* arguments like his were losing favor. In fact, both torture and the most brutal and horrific punishments were, if not exactly lapsing into disuse, at least diminishing decade by decade (Silverman 2001: 73–8, 182). In 1781, when Muyart de Vouglans published a standard edition of the French criminal code with his own commentaries, he included – ironically – King Louis XVI's declaration of August 24, 1780, wherein the monarch abolished preparatory torture because, he proclaimed, great and experienced judges had decided that such torture rarely produced truthful responses from the accused. Six days later, the King announced humanitarian reforms of French prisons – also printed in Muyart de Vouglans' book – with the goal of destroying all underground jail cells, "not wishing to risk that men accused or unjustly suspected, and later recognized as innocent by the courts, should have in advance met with severe punishment from being held in unhealthy

[25] See also Silverman (2001: 42, 43).

and dark places." Evidently the old view, that society came before the individual, was being revised.

In 1788, the year before the fall of the Bastille, Louis XVI took the final step in overturning France's judicial torture regime by abolishing *la question préalable*, torture preceding execution.[26] Though the victory of Beccaria and Voltaire was far from complete, when the monarchs of Austria, France, Prussia, and Russia embraced the humanitarian message of Beccaria's *Essay on Crimes and Punishments*, the new presumption of a human right to be protected from unjust or, in the words of the 1791 United States Bill of Rights, cruel and unusual punishment had become part of mainstream policy in the West.

Thomas Laqueur's chapter on "Mourning, Pity, and the Work of Narrative in the Making of 'Humanity'" (Chapter 1) reveals further dimensions of this process as it came to flourish in the nineteenth century. Once more, the key ingredient was recognition of the value of the individual and of the individual body, even in death. Whereas, Laqueur points out, common soldiers had fought and died anonymously in past centuries, and they, like other poor people, had been buried in unmarked graves, now every life became worthy of remembrance. Governments and communities inscribed the names of common soldiers on monuments, and the families of the poor placed grave markers over their dead. No one explicitly proclaimed a human right to be remembered, but by acknowledging the value of each ordinary person such a right was implied.

A further dimension of the emergent mobilization of empathy was the recognition of the common soldier's horrific battlefield agony. In the past – for example, Germany's seventeenth-century Thirty Years' War – elites expressed sympathy for the suffering of peasants, a suffering so extreme and extensive that it cast a deep shadow across the German population and found expression in arts such as painting and music. But in that era, Grotius and Vattel notwithstanding, violations of human rights were not invoked, nor were soldiers' casualties assigned special importance. By the mid-nineteenth century, however, Joseph Slaughter shows how battlefield misery could become a human rights cause. His chapter, "Humanitarian Reading" (Chapter 3), shows how Jean-Henry Dunant's *A Memory of Solférino* (1862) led directly to the formation of the International Committee of the Red Cross in 1863 and to the first Geneva Convention to aid wounded armies a year later. Though soldiers came to the battlefield

---

[26] In Muyart de Vouglans, *Les lois criminelles*, I, 428 (translated by Richard D. Brown); Silverman, *Tortured Subjects*, 180.

expressly to kill and to be killed on behalf of their nations, their nationality vanished once they were wounded. They became suffering humans whose natural right to succor must be defended by all. In Slaughter's view, Dunant's battlefield narrative prepared readers for an emerging humanitarian consciousness.

Over the past two centuries the tension between the humanitarian impulse and the drive to assert human rights has been so often intertwined as to seem intrinsic. For generations, abolitionists in Britain, France, and the United States wavered between the two orientations, as did aid societies of nearly every description, from the romantic Philhellenic groups of the 1820s, who ardently supported the Greek struggle for independence from Ottoman rule – a precursor of pro-Armenian efforts nearly a century later – to advocates for women's emancipation and enfranchisement. Perhaps the only strictly humanitarian efforts where rights did not come into play were nineteenth-century societies for the prevention of cruelty to animals and children.

Obviously, human rights claims as such cannot extend beyond the boundary of our species, although the concept of animal rights, in which legal personhood would include the great apes and extend to them the rights of life, liberty, and protection from torture, is now well developed.[27] The rights of children, however, have been proclaimed in the United Nations' Universal Declaration of Human Rights (1948), although not without ambiguity because family governance, however harsh it may be for children, is a protected right (article 16, sec. 3). The complexity of children's rights is further manifested in the assertion that "motherhood and children are entitled to special care and assistance" (article 25, sec. 2). According to this widely accepted UN standard, proclaimed around the world, the human rights of children are fewer than those of adults, but their claims on humanitarian support are greater. Here, tensions between the humanitarian impulse, respect for established cultures, and the assertion of human rights are embodied in one of the fundamental human rights texts. Laura Suski's chapter, "Children, Suffering and the Humanitarian Appeal" (Chapter 9), illuminates this problem as it appears around the world in our own time. Though Suski treats the post-1948 world as one in which international recognition of children's rights is commonplace, the central impulses of those who assist children are more fully humanitarian than defense of children's rights as such. Providing immediate relief urgently – while children still remain children – is the first objective.

[27] On animal rights see Singer (1989), Regan (2001).

As difficult as it is to gain humanitarian support and to claim full human rights in the post-1948 world, all such claims were even more difficult to assert during the period between the two World Wars. In Michael Marrus's chapter, "International Bystanders to the Holocaust and Humanitarian Intervention" (Chapter 7), we see how, in the nineteenth century, humanitarianism often implied military adventures conducted by the "civilized" Great Powers of Western Europe against the actions of "barbarians" on their boundaries, and especially the Ottoman and Tsarist Russian Empires.[28] The use of humanitarianism as a cloak for imperial hypocrisy and aggression reached its pinnacle in the nineteenth century, as the British denounced Ottoman and Russian barbarism while standing unmoved while famine decimated Ireland, and U.S. diplomacy adopted a sanctimonious tone while conducting brutal wars to subordinate Native Americans.

In the twentieth century, some political philosophers pointed to the cynical misuse of "humanity" as a subterfuge for state and imperial interests. It is indeed almost impossible to identify a "pure" case of humanitarian intervention where imperial or state interest was entirely absent. The philosopher Carl Schmitt, arguably the main intellectual progenitor of modern antihumanitarianism, once proclaimed that "[w]hoever speaks of humanity is a liar" (Wheeler 2001: 179).[29] For Schmitt, moral and ethical responsibility ends at the boundaries of the collective group, and in *The Concept of the Political*, he contends that when states appeal to "humanity" (e.g., to prevent or punish "crimes against humanity"), they are usurping a universal concept against their opponent: "At the expense of its opponent, it tries to identify oneself with humanity in the same way as one can misuse peace, justice, progress and civilization in order to claim these as one's own and to deny the same to the enemy" (Schmitt 1996: 54). Here, "humanity" is little more than naked self-interest parading under the banner of altruism.

Nevertheless, though states certainly calculate self-interest and use it to explain their actions to a domestic constituency that may resist

---

[28] The link between humanism, humanitarianism and empire-building has a long pedigree. In his book on *The Ideological Origins of the British Empire*, David Armitage (2000: 51–2) comments, "There is no necessary connection between humanism and humanitarianism. However, classic humanism ... did transmit important assumptions regarding the superiority of civility over barbarism and the necessity for civilized polities to carry their civility to those they deemed barbarous." For some observers, humanitarianism and human rights advocacy are still a cloak for imperialism. See Lieven (2007).

[29] For a response from Jürgen Habermas to Schmitt's position, see Habermas in De Greiff and Cronin (2002: 204).

spending national blood and treasure on the welfare of foreigners, private organizations have room for maneuver. Moreover, a more complex account of the self-interest of states must be considered. Many states do care about their international reputation, and "moral" behavior reinforces a positive reputation at home and abroad. Indeed "moral policies" may compel further ethically motivated behavior not originally envisaged by the state. In this way, a humanitarian morality can become politically useful and can reshape state interest in unintended ways.[30]

Marrus proceeds to chart the decline of humanitarianism in Great Power politics in the early twentieth century. In the wake of 1918, not only were the emerging British and French imperial and international humanitarian movements of the pre-war era spent, but the League of Nations was largely ineffective. National sovereignty and self-interest, both as principle and for reasons of expedience, dominated policymaking and public opinion in Europe and the Atlantic world. Post-1948 and more recent expectations concerning what should have been done to rescue European Jewry before 1945, Marrus points out, are anachronistic. The narrative that would emerge from the Nazi death camps and work its way through international politics, he reminds us, only became fully articulated in 1945 and thereafter. That narrative, of course, would become a fundamental justification for the creation of the Universal Declaration of Human Rights.

Humanitarian Narratives and the Mobilization of Empathy

Maybe what we need isn't better laws but more troubled consciences – pricked perhaps, by a Darfur puppy with big eyes and floppy ears. Once we find such a soulful dog in peril, we should call ABC news ...

If President Bush and the global public alike are unmoved by the slaughter of hundreds of thousands of fellow humans, maybe our last, best hope is that we can be galvanized by a puppy in distress.

Nicholas Kristof (2007: 33)

Since 1990, an impressive literature on the international politics of humanitarian intervention has emerged.[31] These studies primarily address the rise of international humanitarian law and the pursuit of political interest by states, and we seek to complement their insights by focusing on the narratives of suffering accompanying humanitarian endeavors, and especially

---

[30] The editors thank David Forsythe for emphasizing this aspect of state interest to them.

[31] Perhaps the most influential books being Holzgrefe and Keohane (2003), Kennedy (2004), and Wheeler (2000).

on victims' voices of suffering and their representation in media, literature, human rights reports and in legal contexts. While writers from political science and international affairs often refer to the "new humanitarianism," much can be gained by thinking about the time-honored techniques used to generate compassion, what we call "the mobilization of empathy." From the eighteenth century to the present day, humanitarian campaigns seemingly as disparate as the antislavery movement, modern children's rights activism, and efforts by nation-states to achieve societal reconciliation exhibit some remarkably similar characteristics.

What becomes apparent from examining the history of humanitarian campaigns over the last 200 years is that laws, state and international humanitarian institutions, and the cold light of reasoned justification are not sufficient to explain why movements spring to life to end some instances of suffering and not others. In his discussion of the Red Cross network, David Forsythe (Chapter 2) notes the "spasmodic condition" of multilateral humanitarianism that emanates from the lack of a thick transnational morality and corresponding local attitudes of compassion and sympathy, particularly in the USA. If sheer numbers and reliable statistics and evidence of harm were adequate in and of themselves, we could not so easily list the humanitarian tragedies that have largely gone unnoticed outside of the country in which they occurred. The most recent egregious example would be the approximately four million killed in the Democratic Republic of the Congo between 1998 and 2006, a massive loss of civilian life that is greater than the estimates for the conflicts in the Balkans, Rwanda, Iraq, and Darfur combined (Szabo 2006).

While a full consideration of the differences between the Congo and the other examples would require more space than is allowed, a crucial aspect to consider is the dearth of any well-publicized narratives of suffering by Congolese victims.[32] This compels us to be more attentive to the emotive power of humanitarian narratives that generates indignation at the suffering of others and channels it towards a wide array of humanitarian acts, from charitable food assistance to physical resettlement to military intervention. A number of essays in this volume seek to analyze how, exactly, arousing sympathy and awakening moral qualms have operated to support humanitarian assistance and human rights claims. The use of narratives,

---

[32] This is partly related to Congo's location in Africa, which receives significantly less media coverage than other world regions. The Rwandan conflict is an exception, as it did receive significantly more media coverage, and coverage in films such as *Hotel Rwanda* and *Sometimes in April*.

"humanitarian narratives," seems crucial for the mobilization of empathy. For, as the abolition movement demonstrated, the narrative form not only prompts emotional engagement, sympathy, and guilt; it can also promote a remarkable variety of types of action. In particular, we note that individual victims' narratives seem to be a necessary component in the mobilization of empathy, and in the formation of global political constituencies to end the suffering of others.

These observations appear to be borne out by recent studies in cognitive and social psychology on altruism and affect in relation to politically inflicted suffering. For Slovic, "the statistics of mass murder or genocide, no matter how large the numbers, fail to convey the true meaning of such atrocities. The numbers fail to spark emotion or feeling and thus fail to motivate action" (2007: 2). Indeed, exposure to the full numbers and overall picture of suffering has a numbing effect on individuals and their capacity to experience an affective response. Research indicates that attention is greater with respect to individual suffering and loses intensity when oriented towards entire groups of people. In one experiment, participants were given the opportunity to contribute $5 to Save the Children in three different conditions: first, an identifiable victim with a life story, an African girl from Mali called "Rokia"; second, statistical victims; and third, an identifiable victim, "Rokia," combined with statistical information (Slovic 2007: 10). Researchers found, perhaps unsurprisingly, that donations were highest for the identified individual, Rokia. They were, however, surprised to find that that combining Rokia's story with wider statistical information about poverty in Africa significantly reduced donations.

The role of emotions in human rights campaigns is a central part of the liberal vision of the philosopher Richard Rorty (1993). Drawing inspiration from Scottish Enlightenment thinkers such as Adam Smith and David Hume, Rorty locates his commitment to a humanitarian project less in reason and democratic deliberation, than in a shared "moral capacity" that sympathizes with the position of the other, and imagines oneself in their place (Rorty 1993: 129). Affect binds us together as much as laws and political institutions, and Rorty wishes to extend the commitment to human rights, not by appealing to rationality, but to our humanitarian feelings: "let us concentrate our energies on manipulating sentiments, on sentimental education" (1993: 122). The primary means of sentimental education Rorty espouses is the "long, sad, sentimental story" (1993: 133). As a result of the public telling of narratives of suffering over the past two hundred years, there has occurred "an astonishingly rapid progress of sentiments, in which it has become much easier for us to be moved to action by sad and sentimental stories" (1993: 134). Such comments have a whiggish tone to them and do not sufficiently recognize that, as with the heroines of eighteenth-century novels, the key is innocence, not suffering, per se. Rorty is writing here about human rights and yet his observations apply more convincingly to humanitarianism. The moral tone of humanitarian campaigns is more explicit, as inhumane behavior is considered evil and condemned more on moral than legal or rights grounds, because brutal acts may be both legal and culturally sanctioned within some states.

The recounting of stories of suffering is not only beneficial for the moral and emotional education of the listener, but, it is argued, for the victim and teller also. The late twentieth century was a period when the benefits of public narration and recognition of psychological pain became widely touted. Veena Das (2000) and Arthur Kleinman (2001) have examined the aftermath of political violence and documented how narrative plays a central role in the reconstitution of the self and the remaking of a social world. They argue that if pain and suffering destroy people's capacities to speak and explain themselves, then the resuscitation of narrative can be the first step towards recreating functioning social selves. The idea of the restorative power of narrative has played a central role in the establishment of truth and reconciliation commissions in places such as Argentina, Chile, and South Africa, where victims are given a public platform to recount their experiences of suffering, usually at the hands of state agents.

Truth commissions are conventionally seen as a reaction to the limits of legal and bureaucratic processes in accepting and valuing subjective victim testimony.[33] This seems to be a feature of legally constituted approaches more generally and, in this volume, Ron Dudai (Chapter 11) examines the reports of Israeli human rights organizations, which are characterized by moral minimalism and a stark lack of emotionalism. Their authority arises from the carefully maintained objectivity and ideological neutrality on the part of the speaker. Dudai is critical of the rhetorical style of human rights reporting, but he is also sanguine, insofar as he recognizes that it may be necessary for realizing other commendable goals: namely, furnishing information that states can use to pressure other states, and presenting actionable evidence that could stand up in a court of law and facilitate legal and political redress.

Perhaps the most prominent argument against emotionalism in political life comes from Hannah Arendt, who in *Eichmann in Jerusalem* (1965) and

---

[33] See Martha Minow (1998: 144).

On Revolution (1990), sustained a principled position against emotions such as compassion and sympathy and "their 'disastrous' effects on politics in public discourse" (Nelson 2004: 224). For Arendt, the politics of pity led not to greater human freedom, but to mendacity and romantic excess, including Rousseau's delusional self-introspection and Robespierre's "Terror" (Nelson 2004: 236–8). In *Eichmann in Jerusalem*, Arendt uses ironic detachment to argue that sad, sentimental stories of victimhood, such as prosecutor Gideon Hausner's recalling of the persecution of Jews by the Egyptian Pharaohs, run counter to the requirements of justice and due process. For Arendt, facing up to reality means looking at tragedy without looking through the prism of victims' narratives of suffering (Nelson 2004: 224).

One need not fully embrace Arendt's austere realism to see the benefits of moving beyond a sentimental examination of human tragedy to an approach that is informed by historical and contextual analysis and less encumbered by perspectivism, rhetoric, and distortion. For a start, as Susan Sontag (1993: 13) reminded us, images of atrocities can give rise to the opposing responses of both peace and violent revenge. We can never be sure how a sentimental story will be received by its intended audience. Second, it is valuable to consider how nation-states, multilateral institutions and nongovernmental organizations elicit narratives of suffering for their own instrumental ends. Kristin Sandvik's chapter (Chapter 10) documents how UN High Commission for Refugees officials sometimes exclude displaced individuals who utilize a rights language that does not correspond to a humanitarian relief image of authenticity, of unvarnished and spontaneous emotions and "deserving victimhood." By tackling the actual process whereby refugees achieve permission to resettle in a new country, she shows us the extent to which classic humanitarian appeals continue to operate.

In Sandvik's account, to win access to a safe country, the candidate and her or his narrative must achieve a high level of credibility in a competition where only a tiny fraction of the candidates and their stories pass muster. Simply telling one's unvarnished victimization story will rarely suffice; the story must be told so as to fulfill bureaucratic criteria while also winning points for candor and authenticity. Here, as in eighteenth- and nineteenth-century novels, gender plays a role – women and children are more credible as victims than are men. In addition, Sandvik explains, the humanitarian plea for relief can trump demanding one's rights. As a result refugees employ rhetorical strategies that are made to appear authentic and persuasive.

Sandvik's observations are echoed in other ethnographic studies, for instance in Miriam Ticktin's (2006) analysis of the effects of the "illness clause" in French law, which was passed by the government in an ostensibly humanitarian gesture. This legislation had unexpected consequences, however. In her work in French hospitals, clinics, and medical offices, Ticktin found immigrant women refashioning their narratives of illnesses such as HIV/AIDS to position themselves more favorably within the new "humanitarian" immigration legal framework.

For humanitarian sympathies to be elicited, it seems imperative that the narrative of suffering strongly testify to the innocence of the sufferer. Few feel an obligation to assist those who appear to have actively provoked, exacerbated, or seemingly deserve their own torment. As Rony Brauman demonstrates in his chapter on the global media response to the 2004 tsunami (Chapter 4), the innocence of the victim explains the overwhelming public responses to natural disasters, rather than to civil wars, where, of course, the victims may be no more or less deserving of their fate. For Brauman, this is linked to a range of other preconceived assumptions on the part of the media, which create disaster myths (e.g., the idea that corpses create epidemics, when, in fact, only the reverse is true) and various moral panics that distort the actual needs of the affected population.

In Flora Keshgegian's chapter on "Starving Armenians" (Chapter 6), theological motifs shaped the perception of American Christians of the 1915–18 Armenian genocide. Armenians were innocent Christians martyred by Muslim Turks, much as Christ was the innocent son of God sacrificed to redeem the sins of humankind. Keshgegian's chapter recalls the narrative themes of late eighteenth-century novels, where injured innocents are victimized by cruel men – Muslim in this case. Moreover the Armenians, viewed as feminized and helpless, she explains, were understood more as subjects of condescending humanitarian sympathy than as equals who deserved empathy, even though, unlike their persecutors, they were fellow Christians. In this case, Christian humanitarianism relies heavily on the place of innocence in biblical ideas of sin, martyrdom, and redemption.

Laura Suski's chapter (Chapter 9) explores the link between innocence, vulnerability, and the humanitarian impulse towards children expressed by a Canadian nongovernmental organization. An emotive appeal based upon childhood innocence is central to the sponsorship programs of humanitarian organizations and to the development of an attachment between the sponsor and the distant suffering child. The appeal and the delivery of aid obstruct the process of empowering children within a more politically engaged framework and so hinder the global project for social justice. The narratives deployed on the children's behalf utilize the same themes of innocent vulnerability that recall the heroines of eighteenth-century novels.

As in those novels, sympathetic condescension can be blended with the more egalitarian feeling of empathy; the children can become "ours" metaphorically, so we can empathize as we do with our literal children. To be effective, Suski explains, children's narratives must portray injured innocence.

While the extent of a humanitarian response depends heavily upon the assumed innocence of the victim, human rights activists insist upon the rights of those accused or convicted of even the most heinous crimes. We have already referred to the human rights campaigns for the basic due process rights of Guantanamo Bay detainees regardless of their blameworthiness, and there are many other examples such as the Amnesty International campaign to prevent the execution of confessed juvenile murderers and rapists in the USA.[34]

Humanitarian and human rights approaches to victims' narratives diverge in identifiable ways, yet they share an underlying commonality in that public narratives of suffering are seldom, if ever, unmediated. While the suffering of refugees in exile or detainees being tortured is actual enough as a realm of personal experience, certain issues arise when their stories are represented in public, bureaucratic, or media settings, when the performance of suffering is linked to access to services and real resources, such as resettlement and housing and financial compensation. Susan Slyomovics' chapter on financial reparations and state restitution in Morocco and Algeria grapples with the complexities arising from the commoditization of victims' narratives. For many victims, telling their stories as part of a reparations claim puts them in a moral quandary – whether their suffering was being measured in monetary terms, whether or not they were accepting "blood money," and whether human lives and money really were fungible or not.

Given the stakes involved for often marginal and vulnerable individuals and populations, it is problematic to separate "true" and "authentic" narratives of suffering from "manufactured" and "artificial" narratives in every instance. At the same time, the imperative to measure and gauge suffering will no doubt continue because governments and multilateral aid agencies, like courts considering financial compensation, cannot proceed without such distinctions. At the same time, their procedures can seem capricious and based upon arbitrary hierarchies of victimhood.

[34] "USA: Time to Stop Executing Juvenile Offenders and Join the Modern World," AI Index AMR 51/121/2001-News Service Nr. 145, http://web.amnesty.org/library/index/engAMR511212001?open&of=eng-usa, August 16, 2001, last accessed July 12, 2007.

Narratives of suffering draw upon surrounding cultural and political codes and are constituted by them. While ostensibly universal and based upon an idea of humanity without boundaries or distinctions, in practice narratives of suffering are often bound up with particularist and communitarian projects, usually of a religious or nationalist nature. In Elizabeth Jelin's chapter (Chapter 8), the narratives of victims of Argentina's conflict in the 1970s are closely associated with the national politics of the family (which she terms "familism") and, more specifically, with the *Marianismo* (the cult of the Virgin Mary) of traditional Catholicism. The suffering mother image legitimates the speaker's voice and her claims and grants the stamp of authenticity to the victim as a mother or sister or grandmother of a victim. She sees the politics of familism as allowing a location from which to speak, but also as constraining in similar terms as Laura Suski's critique of children's organizations (Chapter 9): it impedes a more active and politicized view of citizenship. While this is an obvious interest on the part of authoritarian states, Jelin points out how civilian democracies also join in perpetuating a politically quiescent population. Lars Waldorf's chapter on Rwanda's *gacaca* trials (Chapter 13) exposes an even more cynical state project of calling forth narratives of perpetrators and victims as part of a wider attempt by the nation-state to shore up its declining authority and legitimacy by imposing collective guilt on all members of one ethnic group, the Hutu.

As these essays demonstrate, one is presented with a number of complex options in listening to and responding to the suffering of others. Despite the best intentions, many narratives are prey to realpolitik, hypocrisy, and political manipulation. One insight of this volume is that, if audiences for narratives of suffering appreciate the historical, political, and cultural contexts of those narratives, they can gain greater awareness of the distortions, misrepresentations, and unintended political usages of humanitarian narratives. This should provide a much-needed counterweight to Rorty's assumptions about the power of "sad sentimental stories" devoid of relevant contextual and historical information.

In this volume, we develop a position that occupies a middle ground between Schmitt's cynicism and Rorty's credulity. The essays encourage us to see how story-telling is central to humanitarian action and how narratives of suffering are vulnerable to appropriation and misrepresentation by political institutions. The chapters foreground the element of context that cognitive studies have shown is problematic in humanitarian appeals, and furnish a comprehension of the suffering of individuals within a global political context, without reducing individual subjectivity to the conventional patterns of history and Great Power politics. The challenge is to apprehend actual conflicts by simultaneously holding in view narratives of suffering and the political and legal contexts. In this way, we combine humanitarianism's capacity to generate compassion for others with the promise of the assertion of human rights and the defense of individual liberties.

REFERENCES

Arendt, H. (1965). *Eichmann in Jerusalem: A Report on the Banality of Evil.* New York: Viking Press.

———. (1990). *On Revolution.* New York: Penguin Books.

Armitage, D. (2000). *The Ideological Origins of the British Empire.* Cambridge: Cambridge University Press.

Asad, T. (2003). *Formations of the Secular: Christianity, Islam, Modernity.* Stanford: Stanford University Press.

Beccaria, C. (1767). *An Essay on Crimes and Punishments, Translated from the Italian; with a Commentary attributed to Mons. De Voltaire, Translated from the French.* London: J. Almon.

Berlin, I. (2000). *The Roots of Romanticism.* Edited by Henry Hardy. London: Pimlico, Random House.

Bien, D. (1960). *The Calas Affair: Persecution, Toleration, and Heresy in Eighteenth-Century Toulouse.* Princeton: Princeton University Press.

Boltanski, L. (1993). *Distant Suffering: Morality, Media and Politics.* Cambridge: Cambridge University Press.

Chaplin, J. E. (1990). "Slavery and the Principle of Humanity: A Modern Idea in the Early Lower South." *Journal of Social History,* Winter, pp. 299–315.

Davis, D. B. (2006). *Inhuman Bondage: The Rise and Fall of Slavery in the New World.* New York: Oxford.

Douglas, L. (2001). *The Memory of Judgment: Making Law and History in the Trials of the Holocaust.* New Haven: Yale University Press.

Duffy, H. (2005). *The "War on Terror" and the Framework of International Law.* Cambridge: Cambridge University Press.

Edgar, D. (1994). *Pentecost.* Stratford-upon-Avon: Royal Shakespeare Company.

Farer, T. J. (2003). "Humanitarian Intervention Before and After 9/11: Legality and Legitimacy." In J. L. Holzgrefe and R. O. Keohane, eds., *Humanitarian Intervention: Ethical, Legal and Political Dilemmas.* Cambridge: Cambridge University Press, pp. 53–89.

Freeman, M. (2002). *Human Rights.* Cambridge: Polity Press.

Grotius, H. (1949). *The Law of War and Peace (De Jure Belli ac Pacis).* Translated by L. Loomis. Roslyn, NY: Walter J. Black.

Habermas, J. (2002). "On Legitimation Through Human Rights." In P. De Greiff and C. Cronin, eds., *Global Justice and Transnational Politics: Essays on the Moral and Political Challenges of Globalization.* Cambridge: MIT Press, pp. 197–214.

Holzgrefe, J. L. (2003). "The Humanitarian Intervention Debate." In J. L. Holzgrefe and R. O. Keohane, eds., *Humanitarian Intervention: Ethical, Legal and Political Dilemmas.* Cambridge: Cambridge University Press, pp. 15–52.

Holzgrefe, J. L. and Robert O. Keohane, eds. (2003). *Humanitarian Intervention: Ethical, Legal and Political Dilemmas.* Cambridge: Cambridge University Press.

Hunt, L. (2007). *Inventing Human Rights: A History.* New York: Norton.

Janis, M. (2005). "Dred Scott and International Law." *Columbia Journal of Transnational Law,* vol. 43, no. 3, pp. 763–810.

Kennedy, D. (2004). *The Dark Sides of Virtue: Reassessing International Humanitarianism.* Princeton: Princeton University Press.

Kolchin, P. (1987). *Unfree Labor: American Slavery and Russian Serfdom.* Cambridge, MA.: Harvard University Press.

Kristof, N. (2007). "Save the Darfur Puppy." *New York Times,* May 10, p. A33.

Lieven, A. (2007). "Humanitarian Action Can Mask an Imperial Agenda." *Financial Times,* Aug 21.

Minow, M. (1998). *Between Vengeance and Forgiveness: Facing History after Genocide and Mass Violence.* Boston MA: Beacon Press.

Monroe, K. R. (2004). *The Hand of Compassion: Portraits of Moral Choice During the Holocaust.* Princeton: Princeton University Press.

Moyn, S. (2007). "On the Genealogy of Morals." *Nation,* April 16, pp. 25–31.

Muyart de Vouglans, P. F. (1781). *Les Lois Criminelles de France, dans Leur Ordre Naturel.* 2 vols. Paris.

Neff, S. (2005). *War and the Law of Nations: A General History.* Cambridge: Cambridge University Press.

Nelson, D. (2004). "Suffering and Thinking: The Scandal of Tone in *Eichmann in Jerusalem.*" In L. Berlant, ed., *Compassion: The Culture and Politics of an Emotion.* London: Routledge.

Pilger, J. (1994). "The West's 'Dirty Wink' ". www.johnpilger.com/, Feb 12. Last accessed March 26, 2007.

Rajaram, P. K. (2002). "Humanitarianism and Representations of the Refugee." *Journal of Refugee Studies,* vol. 15, no. 3, pp. 247–64.

Regan, T. (2001). *Defending Animal Rights.* Urbana: University of Illinois Press.

———. (2004). *Empty Cages: Facing the Challenge of Animal Rights.* Lanham, MD: Rowman & Littlefield.

Rodriguez, J. P., ed. (2007). *Encyclopedia of Emancipation and Abolition in the Transatlantic World.* Armonk, NY: M. E. Sharpe.

Rorty, R. (1993). "Human Rights, Rationality and Sentimentality." In S. Shute and S. Hurley, eds., *On Human Rights: The Oxford Amnesty Lectures 1993.* New York: Basic Books, pp. 112–34.

Rosenthal, E. (2007) "A Desire To Feed the World and Inspire Self-sufficency," *New York Times,* August 11, p. A4.

Rousseau, J.-J. (1754/1973). *The Social Contract and Discourses.* London: Everyman.

Schmitt, C. (1996). *The Concept of the Political.* Chicago: University of Chicago Press.

Singer, P. (1989). "All Animals are Equal." In T. Regan and P. Singer, eds., *Animal Rights and Human Obligations.* New Jersey: Prentice Hall, pp. 148–62.

Silverman, L. (2001). *Tortured Subjects: Pain, Truth, and the Body in Early Modern France.* Chicago: University of Chicago Press.

Smith, A. (1759/2002). *The Theory of Moral Sentiments.* Edited by Knud Haakonssen. Cambridge: Cambridge University Press.

Slovic, P. (2007). " 'If I Look at the Mass I Will Never Act': Psychic Numbing and Genocide." *Judgment and Decision-Making*, vol. 2, no. 2, pp. 1–17.

Sontag, S. (1993). *Regarding the Pain of Others*. New York: Picador.

Szabo, L. (2006). "Humanitarian Tragedies the World Has Forgotten: Aid Group Lists Underreported Global Crises." *USA Today*, Jan 16, p. 7D.

Teitel, R. (2004). "For Humanity." *Journal of Human Rights*, vol. 3, no. 2, pp. 225–37.

Tesón, F. (2003). "The Liberal Case for Humanitarian Intervention." In J. L. Holzgrefe and R. O. Keohane, eds., *Humanitarian Intervention: Ethical, Legal and Political Dilemmas*. Cambridge: Cambridge University Press, pp. 93–129.

Ticktin, M. (2006). "Where Ethics and Politics Meet: The Violence of Humanitarianism in France." *American Ethnologist*, vol. 33, no. 1, pp. 33–49.

Unseld, S. (1996). *Goethe and his Publishers*. Chicago: University of Chicago Press.

Wheeler, B. R. (2001). "Law and Legitimacy in the Work of Jürgen Habermas and Carl Schmitt." *Ethics and International Affairs*, vol. 15, no., 1, pp. 173–83.

Wheeler, N. J. (2000). *Saving Strangers: Humanitarian Intervention in International Society*. Oxford: Oxford University Press.

Wilson, R. A., ed. (1997). *Human Rights, Culture and Context: Anthropological Perspectives*. London: Pluto Press.

———, ed. (2005). *Human Rights in the "War on Terror."* Cambridge: Cambridge University Press.

PART I: HISTORIES AND CONTEXTS

1. Mourning, Pity, and the Work of Narrative in the Making of "Humanity"

THOMAS W. LAQUEUR

Richard Rorty in his Oxford Amnesty Lecture of 1993 gave the clearest and most cogent philosophical exposition we have of the "sentimentalist thesis": the view that narratives of suffering generate fellow feelings that are – and historically were – crucial to the origins and continuing success of an ever widening struggle for human rights. In the first place, he argues against a competing tendency that any effort to ground human rights on an accepted, essential, characteristic of humanity – reason, for example – is hopeless. To claim that we should care for others because they are the same species as we are and share what defines us as such begs the question: why would one believe that mere species being is the foundation for treating someone else morally; why accept the Platonic idea that there is something special that we share with all featherless bipeds that gives each and every one of them a claim on us? But that does not mean, Rorty continues, that we have to agree with Nietzsche that the idea of inalienable rights is a joke, a ploy by the weak to resist the strong. Mercifully, we have moved beyond this either-or choice. The answer to "why should we care for a stranger," Rorty says, is "the sort of long, sad, sentimental story which begins 'Because this is what it is like to be in this situation ... because her mother would grieve for her'" (Rorty 1993: 133).[1]

Put more abstractly, Rorty argues that David Hume, more specifically Annette Baier's version of Hume, is right: "corrected (sometimes rule corrected) sympathy, not law discerning reason, is the fundamental moral capacity" (129). We have enjoyed two hundred years of moral progress, the advent and coming to maturity of a "human rights culture," because – to put it crudely – we have given up on Plato and embraced Hume.

---

[1] Lynn Hunt (2007) provides the most recent, historically inflected, statement of this thesis but now Rorty's views have become so much the common coin that he goes uncited.

31

These two centuries are most easily understood not as a period of deepening understanding of the nature of rationality or of morality, but rather as one in which there occurred an astonishingly rapid progress of sentiments, in which it has become easier for us to be moved to action by sad and sentimental stories (134).

Once we get past the uncomfortable irony of speaking about the "astonishingly rapid progress of sentiments" and the ideological and institutional elaboration of a "human rights culture," in a post-Holocaust age – in the shadow of Darfur, the Terrorism Act, and so much more – we recognize that there is a great deal to be said for Rorty's claim, both philosophically and historically. We are, in fact, more likely today to have sympathy for, and even to do something to alleviate, the suffering of people and animals distant from ourselves – geographically, culturally, in their species being – than were men and women three centuries ago. The displaced and dishonored dead have been called into "the circle of the we"[2] as never before as part of the same process that led to its expansion among the living. Laws and norms that mandate human rights as well as the mechanisms that make their violation exigent were and are rooted in "sad and sentimental stories" even if they are at the same time justified, and come to have efficacy, by other means (Hollinger 1993). In the end, one needs to care in order to legislate and to act.

That said, a "rapid progress of sentiments" is too elastic and historically ungrounded a rubric to describe the origins and progress of human rights cultures and norms. I want first to suggest why this is the case, that is, to lay out briefly the limitations of Rorty's insight, and of the "sentimentalist thesis" generally. I want then to align myself with its fundamental insight by showing how, in the late eighteenth century, the "human" in "human rights" – both in life and in death – came to take on new moral urgency; how in new ways it came to demand our attention and our power of imagination; how it became "easier for us to be moved to action by sad and sentimental stories."

First, limits. There is no reason to believe that sympathy with a character in a fictional work or nonfictional narrative would make us more rather than less likely to treat kindly a real live person. To the contrary, as Elaine Scarry points out, flesh and blood people are seldom as uncomplicatedly sympathetic as their literary models. Disappointment at confronting this disjuncture, the reality of human neediness and human weakness, in

---

[2] I take this suggestive phrase from David Hollinger (1993) for as far as I can tell he is the first to use it in print.

relation to the stripped down purer humanity of narrative, is just as likely to harden as to soften the heart (Scarry 1999). Already in the early nineteenth century it was clear that sympathy and fellow feeling for the suffering of others produced a strange moral geography. The contemplation of distant pain could just as well produce more pleasure, or in any case merciful blindness to more local misery, for the ostensible humanitarian than it did relief for the subjects of "sad and sentimental tales." "Humanity is in fashion – it's Popular ... the subject is sublime," the Liverpool antiquarian Matthew Gregson pointed out, suggesting that it might have no greater moral consequence than viewing a deep torrent-filled ravine – a sublime sight.[3] In any case, his fellow citizens were perfectly capable of ignoring the squalor in which Irish immigrants lived. It was a standard trope of the northern English working-class movement that sensitive people were oblivious to the suffering of "factory slaves" while they gushed over the evils of black slavery. The very term "humanitarianism" has long been suspect precisely because sentiments for humanity generally did not translate easily into care for humanity at hand: Dickens' Mrs. Jellyby in *Bleak House*, who worried about children in Africa but neglected her own, is the paradigmatic fictional case. It is, and was, far easier to be moved than to be moved to action, far easier to see clearly at a distance than near by. This strange optic may indeed have enabled, as much post-colonial history writing suggests, an ever mounting level of imperial violence against imperial subjects beyond the limits of sentiment: touching stories of the violation of women and children seemed almost to justify in the hearts if not the minds of contemporary Englishmen the brutality of the repression of the Mutiny or the Mau Mau rebellion. One is reminded of Gandhi's bon mot when asked by a reporter what he thought of Western civilization: "I think it would be a good idea."

It is also not the case that there was an "astonishingly rapid progress of sentiments" if by that is meant something about the quality of the narratives through which sentiments were nourished in the hearts of readers and hearers. The striking fact is that, like violins in the age of Stradivarius, "sad and sentimental tales" as a form reached perfection very early in their history; there has been little progress over the centuries. Their capacity to move anyone to action is certainly no greater today than it was in the nineteenth century. An American journalist, J. A. MacGahan, for example, writing about Turkish atrocities in Bulgaria for the *London Daily Mail* during the early 1870s would have little to learn from present-day

---

[3] As quoted in Mackenzie-Grieve (1941/1968: 295).

narratives of suffering: "We looked again at the heap of skulls and skeletons before us, and we observed that they were all small and that the articles of clothing intermingled with them and lying about were all women's apparel. These, then, were all women and girls. From my saddle I counted about a hundred skulls" (MacGahan 1874). Shortly after this discovery he came upon the shattered walls of peasants' houses along which sat some women who had survived. The air was full of lamentations, he reported. "I had a home now I have none," cried one of them: "I had a husband, now I am a widow; I had a son, now I have none; I had five children and now I have only this one." Another "shrieks with agony and beats her head madly against the wall" where MacGahan could see the remains of her daughter, "her long hair flowing wildly among the stones and dust." Nearby he is shown the place where a little girl had "evidently been stripped to her chemise, partly in search of money and jewels partly out of mere brutality, and afterwards killed." An old man showed him where a blind boy had been burned alive. At the spot one could still see the "calcined bones." His reports, relentlessly heart-tugging and precise, left little room for narrative progress. Gashes in skulls, children spitted on bayonets, an abundance of minute horrors sound depressingly like those, to take but one example, in a recent Human Rights Watch report on military attacks on civilians in Colombia (Human Rights Watch 2005).

In the case of the Bulgarian atrocities, the wide circulation in the British press of "sad and sentimental stories," and a long-standing enmity to the Ottoman Empire did move the public and their leaders to action and it would do so again in other circumstances. "I am apparently more useful than ever," writes W. T. Stead, one of the founders of the aptly named "sensational journalism": "The Bulgarian atrocity agitation was in a great measure my work. I have received the highest compliments from Gladstone, Freeman, W. E. Forster, John Bright and Lord Hartington. ... I believe that in God's hands I have been instrumental in doing much to prevent a great national crime, a war with Russia on the side of the Turks."[4]

The audience was far broader in the age of the steam press than it was a century earlier at the beginning of the movement to abolish the slave trade, but the narrative strategies and the translation of religious conviction into political action – the seamless merger of the religious and the secular – were little changed.

---

[4] As quoted in Robertson (1952: 104).

For Stead, the Bulgarian agitation was what anti-slavery had been for Clarkson and Wilberforce or education and penal reform for other evangelicals in the eighteenth century: a part of his own, public as well as private, narrative of salvation. "I felt the clear call of God's voice," he announces. "'Arouse the nation or be damned.' If I did not do all I could, I would deserve damnation." "A sense of my prophethood returned," – and of Christ's precepts – that speak here in the new language of sentiment.[5]

Whether through divine intervention, the contingencies of high politics, or the masterful accumulation of "sad and sentimental narratives," the campaign worked. Britain did not side with Turkey. In 1885 Stead's reporting in the mass circulation *Pall Mall Gazette* about how he bought, chloroformed, and spirited out of the country a child prostitute who had been sold to him by her mother – the so called "Maiden Tribute of Modern Babylon" series – forced a legislative change of the age of consent. Sensationalism was very close to the "sad and sentimental," a new twist on an old form. It was certainly not "progress" over the narratives of the 1780s and little has happened since except perhaps that new media has enabled stories of distant suffering to reach a wider audience swiftly.

It almost goes without saying that the success rate of "sad and sentimental stories" was, and still is, discouragingly low. A cornucopia of such stories did not prevent the killings of hundreds of thousands of Armenians by the soldiers of Sultan Abdul-Hamid II, nor the great genocide of 1915–1916 by the regime of the young Turks.

But, more importantly, narratives, sentimental or otherwise, do not come with built-in moral gyroscopes and they are no more likely to do so now than in the past. In that sense there has been no progress either. The essence of Rorty's claim is that an "astonishingly rapid progress of sentiments" has lowered the threshold of alterity: it is now easier and more common to include strangers in the "circle of the we," that category of creatures to whom we ascribe rights and whom we feel obligated to treat decently and to help if their rights have been abrogated. Even if this proposition is generally true, as I think it is, it is also the case that sad and sentimental narratives can raise just as readily as lower the alterity threshold. The divide between who is in and who is out, between neighbor and stranger, is terrifyingly vulnerable and is secured by exactly the same means as it is breached in the name of humanity.

Consider, for example, the words "they are not human, they are animals," perhaps the most common formula for why one does not need to, indeed

[5] Robertson (1952: 102).

should not, extend the moral franchise to another person or group. It is supported not by an argument for a switch of species being – Rorty is right that such arguments are largely irrelevant – but by a "sad and sentimental tale," that is meant to make the hearer treat someone as radically other. One finds, for example, wrenching accounts of the murder of the American businessman Nick Berg combined with taunts to liberals that if they cannot watch the video with eyes open they should not even begin to talk about the rights of Al Qaeda detainees. The killers of Berg are called "savage beasts" precisely because the sort of narrative, individual, intimate familial details that would move humans to compassion did not move them: "My name is Nick Berg, my father's name is Michael, my mother's name is Suzanne, I have a brother and sister. ... " Family as the locus of sentiment was crucial to the advent of antislavery, and to compassion for the dead. Berg's words, embedded in the Web's sad and sentimental tale, are meant to lead right-thinking people to want to shoot the perpetrators and their allies on sight.

These limitations of the "sentimentalist thesis" will surprise no one. We must hold in view the more "political" understanding of empathy and narratives of suffering that emphasize political factors external to the narratives themselves, as Richard Brown and Richard Wilson remind us in their Introduction to this volume. That is, narratives work through, or more precisely constitute, motivate, and authorize political action – or fail to do so – only under certain conditions and not under others. One can argue whether this or that context is relevant: it may or may not be the case, for example, as Christopher Brown has recently claimed, that the moral legitimacy of the slave trade abolition movement depended on the new circumstances of the post–American Revolutionary era and specifically on the moral reassessment of national purpose that Britain's loss engendered. But something mediates between the sad and sentimental tale and the action of states upon which human rights ultimately exists (Brown 2006).

That something can be "politics" in its multiplicity of forms: the many ways in which nongovernmental agencies force governments to act, that is, translate moral into political imperative. But equally important in sustaining "human rights culture" is law in its relationship to narratives of suffering. Brown and Wilson suggest that legal processes are often the institutional bridge between private stories – this person suffers – on the one hand and public actions on the other.

No one would question the centrality of a robust legal mandate for human rights. One of the terrible things we have learned from the twentieth century is that neither intimacy, nor familiarity, nor similarity assures that one group of people will treat another ethically. Elaine Scarry has suggested precisely the opposite: knowing another may well enable, rather than disable, the capacity to inflict pain on that person (Scarry 1999). Divorce battles are a small-scale case in point. The purpose of the Geneva Conventions from 1864 to 1949, the 1948 Convention on the Prevention and Punishment of the Crime of Genocide and Declaration of Human Rights, the Helsinki Conventions – to invoke some obvious examples – is to prescribe how one may or may not treat one's fellow human beings regardless of how well one may understand them. They affirm the norm that humans are to be treated in certain ways because they bear rights, not by virtue of some essential feature of being human, possessing reason or being the subject of a sentimental narrative, but because of positive law.

The original sin of National Socialism was not the sporadic murder of Jews and others that escalated into the bureaucratic monstrosity of genocide, or the tens of thousands of local acts of cruelty and murder that, in league with industrial methods, constituted the crime, but rather it was the stripping of rights from, first, citizens and then from conquered people. It was the stroke of the pen by which a burger became less than a burger; a citizen, a "friend," became an enemy – "out-law" – someone beyond the law and outside culture, to use Carl Schmitt's terms (Schmitt 1976). This was the giant necessary first step in the slaughter of the merely biological beings in camps and marches who disappeared unnoticed into the air or the ground.

But law as the bulwark of human rights is not independent of narrative or of the norms that give sad and sentimental tales their resonance. "No set of legal institutions or prescriptions exists apart from narratives that locate and give it meaning," the legal scholar Robert Cover argues. And vice versa. Narratives give prescriptions – norms, laws – meaning; they transform them from a set of rules into "a world in which we live." The two are mutually constitutive: "Every prescription is insistent in its demand to be located in discourse – to be supplied with history and destiny, beginning and end, explanation and purpose. And every narrative is insistent in its demand for its prescriptive point, its moral" (Cover 1983: 4–5). Prescription, a normative guarantee of rights, in law is thus less the mediator of narrative than the condition for its existence, and vice versa.

My account of the problems of the "sentimentalist thesis" is not meant as a rejection. The fact that sympathy for characters in literature does not necessarily translate to sympathy for real live people; that sentimental feelings for distant strangers can blind us to suffering at home for all sorts of self-serving reasons; that sad and sentimental as a genre have made little progress in the forms of narrative; that narratives of suffering can work against just as they can work for human rights; and that human rights as a history narrative tends to short change the history of political and legal change – these facts do not, however, diminish the core insight of the thesis. Limits ought not to diminish the importance of what happened: in the late eighteenth century the ethical subject was democratized. More and more people came to believe it was their obligation to ameliorate and prevent wrongdoing to others; more and more people were seen as eligible to be members of "the circle of the we." My story is about how this happened. I take two cases that stand together at the beginning of human rights culture and that have sustained their power – their grip over the moral imagination – for three centuries. The first concerns the living. It is the story of how "human," not as shorthand for "reason" or for some other essence of a species or as the bearer of abstract rights, but as the word for the ethical subject – the protagonist – of humanitarian narrative, came into being in the late eighteenth century. The other concerns the dead who no longer felt pain and who were thus not literally pitiable. Their claims were very much part of the sensibility – the imagination – that brought forth human rights.

In the late eighteenth century, at roughly the same time as "human" and "life" took on new meanings, so did "death" and the "dead." Dying unknown, dying unmarked or uncommemorated or unnamed or even unnumbered came to be a sign of abjection, of being nonhuman. (For Adam Smith, an imaginative identification with the dead was the paradigmatic case of sympathy.[6]) To die and be simply shoveled under constituted the deepest "Vernichtung," that is eradication, or making into nothing. This is where the popular radicalism of my title comes in. I want to suggest that the popular fear of a pauper funeral is part of the same cultural constellation that produced monuments naming the ordinary dead of war and disaster and the great uncovering projects of modern human rights: the bringing to public recognition of the dead who had been made nothing because they had been regarded as nothing – in any case as not fully human – the accounting for them, and incorporating them again into a remade world of the living. In this period, sympathy – the story of the "human" – and mourning have a joint history, not causally connected necessarily, but part of the same cultural constellation and indeed of the same political moment.[7]

---

[6] "We sympathize even with the dead" (Smith 1759: sec. 1, ch. 1). See also Esther Schor (1994) for an exposition of this point.

[7] The photo obituaries in the *New York Times* of the victims of 9/11 are in a tradition whose history I trace in "Memory and Naming in the Great War" (1993). For an instance of naming in commemoration of the Holocaust see my essay "The Sound of Voices Intoning Names" (1998).

A specific instance of this is the British officer, in 1775, who came upon the grave of John Jack, a freed slave, whose epitaph had been written by a loyalist lawyer. He copied what he read, and sent a report of his feelings to a magazine back in London:

> The grave of this forgotten African is in a retired spot surrounded by a cluster of beautiful young locust trees – where his ashes will quietly repose, till the grand inquest of this world shall be summoned and its decisions proclaimed. It will then be known by what right this son of immortality was torn from his mother's arms, his native land, his home, and upon this soil of the free reduced to the condition of the beast that perisheth. It will then be known by what right millions of the race have been stolen from their father-land and here converted into beasts of burden, into goods and chattels and retained in that condition of sorrow by human legislation from mere reasons of state.

Some thirty years later antislavery activists found and rehabilitated the grave that had by then fallen into disrepair. And in 1838 an abolitionist journal published this whole story with praise for the author of the epitaph "who, doubtless, harbored that old-fashioned idea, that *all* men have 'inalienable rights.'"[8]

Narratives of suffering and of vanishing – of pain and dying unremembered – constituted a claim to be regarded, to be noticed, to be *seen* as someone to whom the living have ethical obligations. They are insistent and, in that sense, work like art, facts transformed through craft, that demand what the critic Jed Perl calls "slow seeing," seeing that takes place in time, that is not, he says, just "a matter of imaging a narrative," but "involves rather the more fundamental activity of relating part to part" (Perl 2000: 312). "We need to see particular elements," he continues, "and see that they add up in ways that become more complex – and sometimes simpler" (312). To understand the subject of humanitarian narratives in such a way as to make a difference is not so far from what the philosopher Alexander Nehamas says about aesthetic engagement: "To understand the beauty of something we need to capture it in its particularity, which calls for knowing how it differs from other things and that, in turn, is to be able to see, as exactly as possible, what these things are and how each one of them, too, differs from the rest of the world" (Nehamas 2007). The humanitarian narrative demands, indeed it is constituted by, this sort of engagement. In a sense it transforms the longing and desire for beauty into a duty to engage

---

[8] As quoted in the *Emancipator*, July 26, 1838; see also the *Concord Freeman*, June 20, 1835. I am grateful to Professor Robert Gross of the University of Connecticut for sending me this material after discussing an earlier version of this essay with me.

ugliness, to elevate ourselves above the moral status of passersby who pass
without noticing. Exact, slow, active, engaging seeing is central in the creation of sentiment, in keeping someone else within ethical range.

This is what Thomas Clarkson demanded with his arresting and wholly
original diagrammatic engraving of the slave ship *Brookes*, the first image
of slave suffering to be reproduced for a mass audience and the first
secular image to change the world. The astonishing fact is that there were
very few images of slavery as an evil before Clarkson's appeared in 1789.
(The famous Wedgwood medallion "Am I not a Man and a Brother" was
1787.) There were of course depictions of slaves as servants in aristocratic
family portraits and even, on rare occasion, as subjects of portraiture
themselves (Gainsborough's 1768 portrait of Ignatius Sancho, for example); they appear as figures in landscapes and as workers in drawings of
sugar or tobacco cultivation and processing – all images about something
other than the wrongs of slavery. Slaves as captives and as chattel were
largely invisible with a few exceptions; refined images – there are hints
of change in the 1760s – generally depicted their existence as morally
unproblematic. All the famous pictures of horrendous punishment
come after 1789 even if, as in the case of William Blake's illustration of
J. G. Stedman's *Narrative of a Five Year Expedition Against the Revolted
Negroes of Surinam*, they depict earlier events. Quite literally, slavery as an
evil – and simply as a fact – was largely invisible. And largely unspoken.
William Fox's 1791 *Address to the People of Great Britain on the Propriety
of Abstaining from Sugar* was printed in the hundreds of thousands; no
tract printing before had managed more than a few thousand.[9]

Clarkson's image insists that we – and in the first instance all members of
Parliament – *see* the middle passage for what it was: something other than
an exercise in the mere transport of goods. It does so with the precise
enumerative strategy that was in this period just coming into being. Exactly
482 captives are packed into the hold with an inhuman geometric precision.
Each and every *body* suffers. How the enumerative representation of suffering became linked to individuated suffering will be treated later. It was
basically a matter of facing the demands of the Kantian arithmetic sublime:
too many numbers gave the overpowering sense of the massiveness but lost
the particular; and conversely, the particular lost the scale of the whole.

[9] On the diagram of the *Brookes* and its impact, see the account in Adam Hochschild (2005:
     155–9). On the circulation of images and antislavery pamphlets, see William St Clair
     (2004: 258, Appendix 7, 561–2). On the visual history of slaves, see Hugh Honor (1984:
     27–8), and specially on the slave ship *Brookes*, see pp. 65–7. See also the excellent collection
     of images at http://hitchcock.itc.virginia.edu/Slavery/search.html.

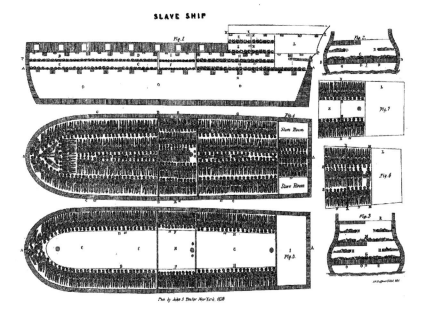

SLAVE SHIP

Figure 1. Thomas Clarkson's *The Slave Ship* Brookes was first published on a broadsheet in 1789.

Not or *no longer* seeing – vanishing, disappearing, looking the other way – is the ubiquitous other side in the history of human rights. Germans, we are told, "looked the other way" when their Jewish neighbors disappeared. German civilians, fleeing west in front of the advancing Russian army, reported in their diaries a great deal about their own suffering and those of fellow refugees on the road but they rarely reported seeing the tens of thousands of concentration camp inmates in far worse condition being driven to their death along the same road. "We did not know" was, and is, the way we say we did not see.

I will begin my brief history of regarding – seeing – someone as human through humanitarian narrative beginning with three senses of the word or its cognates, each of which expands its cultural resonance. First, "human" itself as in the title of the most famous of antislavery tracts, Thomas Clarkson's *Essay on the Slavery and Commerce of the Human Species, Particularly the African* (1785). Second, "humane" as a variant of "human" in the sense of showing qualities proper to person, to a human – "he was very human and sent the poor seamen presents" – a sense which by the early 1700s was specified in English by the addition of an "e." And finally, "humanity," as in J. G. Stedman's, *Narrative of a Five Year Expedition Against the Revolted*

Negroes of Surinam (1760): "Why I ask in the Name of Humanity should they [slaves] undergo the most cruel Racks and tortures entirely depending upon the despotic Caprice of their proprietors and overseers. ... "

In Clarkson's book we seem to be invited in the first instance to understand "human" biologically as an inclusive, universal category, which contains within it another more circumscribed group that merits our special attention: "human species" equals "particularly African." This is the sense of "genre humain" – the most common seventeenth- and eighteenth-century French sense of the word "human," and it is one that goes back at least to Aristotle and to the notion that, at a minimum, it is at the level of our bodies that our species is defined: some of this and some of that, a peculiar position or arrangement and so on. This biological sense of human constitutes a minimum position: their bodies, as a matter of physiological fact, suffer just as ours suffer; no metaphysical claim about the status of the human soul is required.

But Clarkson and his colleagues are far more Rousseauist than Aristotelian: their efforts are directed towards showing how the human as animal becomes the human as ethical subject. "Human species – particularly African" thus refers to those who *suffer* – not just feel pain but feel wrongs – in and through bodies that are like ours and in the context of cultural expectations like ours. Slaves have feelings; they do not just feel.

This is why so much effort is made not just to document violations of the flesh: a "whip ... that erases the skin;" or "branded upon the breast with a hot iron" (Clarkson 1785: 155, 130). Of course, in the first instance, wrong is done to bodies, to "inviolable rights of man," to property in itself. But the greater part of Clarkson's and most other antislavery texts demand insistently that we see these bodies embedded in exactly the sort of nexus of social relations as those of their readers and auditors. African mothers nurse, and suffer when their children are taken from their breasts; African parents suffer when their children are beaten and taken from them; African husbands and wives suffer when they are forcibly separated; African women feel the shame of sexual humiliation. In short, Africans feel their wrongs.

It is this rhetoric of cultural and not just physical violence that brings religious and secular sentiments together. It mobilizes the Christian obligation to the human body of Christ as never before: "Verily I say unto you, inasmuch as ye have done it to one of the least of these my brethren, ye have done it unto me" (Matthew 25:40.) But more importantly it echoes the fiercer imperatives of the Old Testament. The evangelical Granville Sharpe warns of God's vengeance for the violence done to black families in the words of the prophet Ezekiel to the Hebrews against the "VIOLENCE of them that dwell" among them. The analogy is the point of more than 350 pages.

([M]ark this, ye British Slave-dealers and Slave Holders; "in thee have they vexed the fatherless and the Widow ... "in the midst of thee they commit lewdness – One has committed abomination with his Neighbor's wife; another defiled his Daughter-in-law ... What a "bloody crime" among the Jews was more notorious, and more wickedly premeditated, than the late Invasion and Conquest of the poor innocent Carribees at St. Vincent ... "Destruction Cometh." (Sharp: 1776: 31–5)

"Human" in the sense of "humane" has a long history and reminds us that, in some very general sense, belonging to a common species – human – has long entailed an obligation to treat fellow humans as family. Precisely to whom we owe these courtesies was of course much controverted; broader interpretations have long jostled with narrower ones. The rise of efforts to educate humans to treat the so-called lower animals in a humane way is a major eighteenth-century expansion of the circle of moral inclusion but could also be traced back to its Franciscan pre-history and on through seventeenth-century Puritan texts. It was not even limited to the living and embraced solicitude for the nearly, apparently, or really dead: beginning in the 1770s organizations to teach and research strategies of revivifying the seemingly inanimate victims of drowning, seizures, or fumes were called in English "Humane Societies."

Humane behavior, the exercise of humanity, certainly did not entail a commitment to human equality, social or juridical. Clearly acts of charity, hospitality, and courtesy were as often practiced by social superiors to their inferiors as to their equals or superiors. Indeed, in an aristocratic society such acts of humanity were meant to produce the nexus of hierarchically ordered attachments, the mutual obligations and rewards that constituted the social order predicated on inequality. In the context of slavery this was precisely the sense in which Christopher Codrington hoped to do good when he left two sugar plantations in Barbados to the Anglican Society for the Propagation of the Gospel with the profits of which they would support physicians, scholars, and divines who would by their "apparent usefulness" to "all mankind" "endear themselves to the people" by ministering to their bodies and souls. An early nineteenth-century slaveholder in South Carolina declared himself pleased that the treatment of slaves had become more inclined toward "tenderness and humanity."[10] But the point is

---

[10] See Bennett (1958: 1). These plantations came to be notorious for slave breeding during the abolitionist movement. On the question of "humane" slavery more generally, see Joyce Chaplin (1990).

that "human" in the sense of "humane," broadened its reach during the eighteenth century, particularly at its end.

"Human" and "humane," resonated in a third word: "humanity." We have already seen it function as a placeholder for "God" in Stedman's question: "why in the Name of Humanity. ... " The great Whig orator and supporter of Wilberforce's, Charles James Fox, expanded it further. "He was glad," he said in a speech to the House of Commons on the abolition of the slave trade, "to see that these tales affected the House. Would they then sanction enormities, the bare recital of which make them shudder?" But revulsion was not enough. "Let them remember that *humanity* did not consist in a squeamish ear" (Fox 1824). It did not consist in shrinking and starting at such tales, but in a disposition of the heart to remedy the evils they unfolded. *Humanity* belonged rather to the mind than to the nerves. But, if so, it should prompt men to charitable action. The crucial point here is that Fox wants to mobilize the heart and the mind, sentiment or the imagination on the one hand, and reason on the other, in characterizing *humanity.*

The tales to which he referred were a series of horror stories : "the shrieks from the outhouse" as a female slave, stark naked, tied by the wrists to a beam, was tortured by a lighted faggot held to her feet; a master who caught a slave running away and brought him to a surgeon demanding that he cut off one leg to prevent another escape; the surgeon refused; the master broke the slave's leg and said to the surgeon "Now you must cut it off or the man will die." Fox insists that mere sympathy – the faculty of the body of the hearer or the beholder to be affected by another's screams – is not enough. Humanity belonged in the heart and the mind, in the sustained capacity of heart and mind to understand and to insist on a remedy for wrongs against distant people.

The sense of humanity both as the quality of being humane, of treating others with kindness and civility, and as the human disposition towards benevolence are old. The connection of humanity to feeling and sentiment is novel in our period. And so is its expanded range. The ethical requirement of humane behavior or humanity in both their biblical and early modern European contexts was confined to the stranger in our midst – the poor, the leper, the sojourner – who is present before us and whom we are enjoined to treat as a guest, as part of our community, instead of as a stranger, an "other." This is the fragile humanity of the face to face encounter that was easily shattered by expulsion beyond the limits of a parish boundary or city wall. The remarkable creation of the eighteenth century is the vastly expanded ethical category of the "human(e)" to include animals as a limit case, but more centrally humans unseen and unheard, those who suffer across what would seem to be unimaginable distances, geographical and cultural, those who are in the old sense already excluded.

Few members of the British Parliament had ever seen a black slave other than, perhaps, as a servant in an aristocratic household. (In any case, they had not seen a slave *as* a slave.) Fewer still had been to Africa or the Caribbean where they might have seen a slave beaten, or captured, or packed on a ship for the middle passage. The subjects of Clarkson's pamphlet, "Slaves, the Human Species, particularly African," and of Fox's speech calling for "humanity" and "charity" were thus largely abstractions that could go unnoticed or be coolly debated. These new pleas for humanity called for sympathy, for fellow feeling, and for action across great distances. They, in turn, were predicated on the imagination, on the heart, and on reason that contrived to render the abstract real and ethically present.

Aesthetics – or, more precisely, new forms of the "humanitarian narrative" – that demanded new ways of seeing were the instruments for this exercise in moral magic. In the beginning was the fact, the detail, as the sign of truth. Pain, as a necessary if not sufficient condition for suffering, had, *in fact*, happened. Pictures reproduced in the hundreds of thousands, the realistic novel, the autopsy, the clinical report, the accounts of how slaves, climbing boys, factory workers, seamstresses, miners, and many many others of the oppressed were made to feel pain made that pain and the consequent suffering real to audiences that spread well beyond the sentimentally inclined aristocracy and evangelical middle class. People were exposed to unprecedented quantities of facts rendered into artifacts and articles as well as seemingly endless minute observations about people who had before been below or beyond notice. Out of sight out of mind would not erase facts.[11]

But the two questions remain: even if it is admitted that culturally and geographically distant people feel pain just as we do, how do we come to feel that they suffer as we would under similar circumstances and, more pointedly, how do we come to feel that we should care? In what might seem to be an unlikely or even an undesirable reversal of what appears so natural, one must actually come to feel that the suffering of strangers matters in some measure akin to one's own suffering or to that of those

---

[11] I have spelled out more fully how "humanitarian narratives" came into being in "Bodies, Details, and the Humanitarian Narrative" (1989).

near and dear to us. It is an extraordinary demand whose challenges
Adam Smith understood with fine precision: "If he were to lose his little
finger tomorrow," he says, he "would not sleep to-night. But, provided he
never saw them, he will snore with the most profound security over the
ruin of a hundred millions of his brethren, and the destruction of that
immense multitude seems plainly an object less interesting to him, than
this paltry misfortune of his own" (Smith 1759: ch. 3 p. 4). Two centuries
later, after Auschwitz, Primo Levi says almost the same thing:

> There is no proportion between the pity we feel and the extent of the pain by
> which pity is aroused. ... If we were able to suffer the sufferings of everyone,
> we could not live. Perhaps the dreadful gift of pity for many is granted only to
> saints. ... and to all of us there remains in the best of cases only the sporadic
> pity addressed to the single individual, the Mitmensch, the co-man: the
> human being of flesh and blood standing before us, within the reach of our
> providentially myopic senses. (Levi 1989: 56)

Humanity in the first instance begins at home, in our own community.[12]

Only a very devoted Kantian or hard core utilitarian would believe that
anything else is actually possible, and few today would think it desirable.
Ethics is about making human communities not about abstract claims, and
of course the suffering of those near us means more than the suffering of
strangers. As Bernard Williams has argued, there is something very odd
about the calculus that one ought to save many strangers even if to do so
would cost the life of one's child. But this is not my point. In the first place,
no one was being asked to sacrifice their own children for African ones,
although the demand that slavers abandon their livelihood may have
seemed to be asking almost as much. (The central move of the antislavery
movement was to make the choice less stark; in eating sugar, the proponents of boycott argued householders and their children were literally
taking in the blood of slaves who died producing it.) And the rubric that
charity begins at home did not go unspoken. The important point is that
the antislavery campaign – as with subsequent human rights campaigns –
was not engaged in philosophy but in the crafting of narratives that would
convince hearers that owning a person was wrong, that the system in which
this was possible inflicted untold amounts of pain, and that living in a
country that engaged in buying, selling, and transporting slaves made one
immediately culpable.[13]

---

[12] Adam Smith's problem was also Diderot's. For an exposition of his formulation and of the
general question, see Carlo Ginzburg (1994).

[13] On interpretations of slave bodies and the sugar boycott, see Charlotte Busman (1994).

What Fox told the House of Commons suggests how the awful gap between the here of England and the there of the distant slave might be bridged. Neither for him, nor for any of the humanitarians of the eighteenth century whom I am considering, would it be through the application of utilitarian rules or of reason alone: one did not act kindly towards slaves or foundlings out of a strict respect for a Benthamite calculus or Kantian precepts. Theirs was a more discursive, affective humanity. Recall that Fox claimed it "belonged rather to the mind than to the nerves"; it does not consist of the "shrinking and starting," the "shudders," the discomfort of the "squeamish ear" that horror stories engender. That said, he was clearly assuming – or in any case nurturing – a facility for "sympathy" and for the "heart" in his audience. But more was needed than an almost physiological response to another's pain. The party of humanity in the eighteenth century was built on the assumption that humans had an inbuilt capacity to feel beyond themselves, but that this natural gift required training.

By the late eighteenth century the capacity for outreach was generally localized in the nerves but crucially their responses had to be rendered at the service of the imagination and also of reason. Malebranche, in the late seventeenth century, had already hinted at how a physiology of compassion might work. A loud cry quite literally stirs us as if by mechanical action; we are, as if by some miracle, affected by the distress of others and will offer them succor. A cry "pierces the ears;" it penetrates our heads. And, "it makes them [the ears] understand it, let them be of what nation or Quality soever; for 'tis a Cry of all nations and all Conditions, as indeed it ought to be. It makes a Commotion in the Brain, and instantly changes the whole disposition of the Body in those that are struck with it; and," here is the most breathtakingly optimistic leap of all, "makes them run to give succor, without so much as knowing it ... " (Malebranche 1997: 332). Malebranche's own unwillingness to see the writhing of animals in pain as evidence for their suffering demonstrates again the centrality of culture in expanding the "circle of the we."[14]

By the early eighteenth century the body's capacity to respond to "sad and sentimental stories" was commonplace. William Wollaston, for example, whose widely quoted *Religion of Nature Delineated* sold over 10,000 copies in the 1720s, thought that "human nature" was constituted with a generic disposition that "renders us obnoxious to the pains of others, causes us to sympathize with them, and almost comprehends us in their case" (1722/2003: 258). The reaction, he says, is direct and comes in response, it

---

[14] For more on animals not feeling their pain, see Malebranche (1997: 323–4).

seems, to an actual, present distress: "It is grievous to hear (and almost to hear of) any man, or even any animal whatever, in torment" (258).

This explains the necessary foundation of the squeamish, uncomfortable response of Fox's audience to stories of the horrors of slavery. But there is still distance to be closed, the question of how we come to "comprehend" the case of someone who is not actually present to our senses: the problem of the absent sufferer. The answer implicit in Rorty and made explicit by Adam Smith is that we do it through the imagination:

> By the imagination we place ourselves in his situation, we conceive ourselves enduring all the same torments, we enter as it were into his body, and become in some measure the same person with him, and thence form some idea of his sensations ... His agonies, when they are thus brought home to ourselves, when we have thus adopted and made them our own, begin at last to affect us, and then tremble and shudder at the thought of what he feels. (Smith 1759: 3)

Imagination – both of pain and of cultural embeddedness – substitutes for the sound of cries, the sight of blood and mangled flesh, the look of suffering, the awareness of social similarity.

But there remains the problem of why "a disposition of the heart," if not a direct signal from the nerves, should "prompt men to charitable action." "Humanity" demands action – the cry of humanity need be heeded – only if it could be represented as stemming from something that could be helped; someone or something did something that caused pain, suffering, or death that could have been avoided or mitigated. Natural disasters or cruelty supposedly rooted so deeply in history that it may as well be natural – the European analysis of the Bosnian genocide – cannot be abolished or prevented. In the eighteenth century the argument was made that the conditions of Africans in Africa was so terrible and so beyond repair that slavery, therefore, was but a continuation, perhaps even an improvement, of an unshakable status quo that might be lamented but could not be helped. An analysis of causation was needed to link sentiment, obligation, and action.

This was precisely what the sugar boycott did; it is one of the first examples of how "sad and sentimental stories" came to have consequences. It brought the family table full square up against the body of a beaten slave. Buying sugar, William Fox made clear in a tract that circulated in hundreds of thousands of copies, is – in a literal sense – serving as the accessory to crime: "The slave-dealer, the slave-holder, and the slave-driver, are virtually the agents of the consumer, and may be considered as employed and hired by him to procure the commodity." And conversely, if a family that uses five pounds of sugar per week abstains for twenty-one months they "prevent the slavery or murder of one fellow creature"; eight such families abstaining for nineteen years save 100, and so on (Fox 1792: 4–5). Robert Southey makes the same analytic point in his poetry, as he draws a picture of a slave mangled by the whip:

> .... O ye who at your ease
> Sip the blood-sweetened beverage! thoughts like these
> Haply ye scorn (1860: 66).

Opponents of slavery insisted that their countrymen look "carefully and unflinchingly" at the nexus of such facts. The English poet William Cowper contemplates the precise causal links between his world and slavery in the context of the 1788 bill before Parliament that was meant to "protect the lives and limbs of slaves from wanton cruelty" by limiting the number of slaves that could be transported on ships of any given tonnage. It was this bill that Clarkson's picture mocked: it allowed the 482 slaves to be squeezed into every space. The sheer bureaucratic calculation of the enterprise is evidence to Cowper that: "The enormity cannot be palliated; we can no longer plead either that we were not aware of it or that our attention was otherwise engaged, and shall be inexcusable therefore ourselves if we leave part of it un redressed."[15] A shiny glazed porcelain black man or woman, gesturing toward the refined product of their bodies, was a common figure on sugar bowls in the early eighteenth century. The sugar boycott specifically demanded new ways of seeing such figures.

The dead too – through those living who spoke for them – came to insist on being seen as never before. The humanitarian narrative, I suggest, broadened the "circle of the we" to include those whose death in earlier times would have gone unnoticed. Antislavery and an imaginative recuperation of lost bodies were, of course, linked in the contemporary sensibility. I have already offered one example: the grave of the freed slave John Jack that became an abolitionist site. One could make the connection biographically and visually: J. M. W. Turner's 1840 *Slavers Overthrowing the Dead and Dying*, with its bodies about to be lost in the depths or devoured by monsters. But it is the careful new sort of visual, literary, and topographical accounting of the dead in his 1817 *Field of Waterloo* that points to an expansion of who counts as human. On the right of this large canvas is the burning farmstead; in the center, in the white cold light of the moon, and warmed by a few torches are masses of dead soldiers. Modestly dressed women are looking for their dead and ministering to the wounded. In his

---

[15] Taken from J. King & C. Rykskamp, eds. (1983).

Figure 2. *The Field of Waterloo*, J. M. W. Turner, Oil on canvas (Tate, London / Art Resource, NY).

sketches for the painting, Turner noted every detail of the landscape and of the battle's military positions to a remarkable degree. But more to the point is his interest in numbers and locations: 4,000 killed here, 1,500 killed there, he notes.

The dead of this battle, as Tennyson puts it, may have been shoveled under and soon forgotten. But, beginning in the late eighteenth century, more and more of the poor came to demand visibility and accountability in death. I sketch this story under three headings that are historically linked to each other and to the rise of the "human rights culture": pauper funerals and more generally the funerals of the dispossessed and displaced – slaves, freemen, immigrants; the demand to be remembered by name; and finally forensic inquiries on the bodies of the wrongly dead as an exercise intended to integrate their stories into the lives of the living. Together these constitute a great broadening of engagement with the common, as opposed to the special or elite, dead.

Poor people had of course always been buried with far fewer material and commemorative resources than the more prosperous. And communal organizations – guilds, confraternities – had long existed to bury members. But before the late eighteenth century, the pauper funeral as a symbolically freighted event simply did not exist. Burial *as a pauper* was not a category that mattered. It came to matter not as a response to a decline in the resources given to burying the poor; in fact, the actual material conditions afforded by parishes and other public bodies in early nineteenth-century England to the dead poor were more generous than they had been a century before. Coffins had become standard, where before many went into the ground wrapped only in a shroud. At least as much if not more food was provided for the mourners. And, most tellingly, there were name plates to identify the coffins of even those destined for common graves, bodies that a century earlier would have gone into the ground anonymously.[16]

It came to matter because the radical claim made at the great Putney Heath debate of 1647 at the beginning of the most radical phase of the English Revolution – that "the poorest he that is in England has a life to live as the greatest he" – started to gain cultural traction through the demand to be seen, to be noticed, if only for a moment at the time of death. Why the demand for a proper funeral became so central to the working classes of Western Europe is part of the larger story of their entry on to the main

---

[16] On the advent of the pauper funeral, see Thomas Laqueur (1983), and more generally for a later period, Julie-Marie Strange (2005).

stage of history. Why it happened among free blacks and others is another story still. And, why the funeral in particular came to be the one indispensable moment among the great transitions of life – if the poor saved for anything it was for a funeral – must be part of a different discussion. But, there is no question that being buried with a degree of public notice became a central part of the narrative of what it was to be human, to be an ethical subject with rights to be seen by a community.

There is evidence for this not only in the spectacular rise of burial societies but also in the multiplication of meanings that the funeral took on. So, for example, the radical journalist William Cobbett in his eccentric history of the Reformation argues that it was "engendered in beastly lust, brought forth in hypocrisy and perfidy, and cherished and fed by plunder, devastation, and by rivers of innocent English and Irish blood" (1824: 449). This he illustrates with a frontispiece that shows the dignified burial of the poor in a monastery compared with the beastliness of the modern pauper funeral. The pauper funeral is the central image of the Tory paternalist Augustus Pugin's attack on the inhumanity of capitalism. And, conversely, public burial became one of the grand gestures of the working class in its struggles to be seen and heard. The funeral of a Derby carpenter or a Barnsley linen operative was far grander than the grandest heraldic funeral of the sixteenth century. Between 20,000 and 50,000 saw the funeral of Samuel Holberry, "martyred" as a working-class political prisoner in 1842. The moment of the triumph – temporary of course – of the 1848 revolution in Berlin was when the working-class dead – the sacrifices of March – were *seen* by those in power. Frederick William IV is said to have taken his hat off as the coffins of the proletarian dead – identified, father of six – passed by. Adolph von Menzel's painting, *Lying in State of the March Victims*, offers an interpretation of this paradigmatic moment. These dead matter and demand to be seen.[17]

There was a related development in the commemorative use of names. Of course, names have always been understood as that marker of personhood that lives on; there is nothing new in human rights culture or commemorative practices about what names mean. But the insistence on making names visible, on bringing them before a community, of imposing them on a landscape, of giving them meaning is part of the story of how humans as ethical subjects came into being. One could talk about this quantitatively: on average 1 to 4 percent of bodies buried in

---

[17] Pugin (1841/2003: "Contrasting Residences of the Poor," n.p. following Appendix 2). For Holberry, see Gammage (1894/1969: 214).

British cemeteries were named at the beginning of the nineteenth century; between 60 and 70 percent were named by the end (Schell 2003). Names are also part of the story of the constitution of a democracy. There had been no stelae with the names of the dead of war in a public burial place between Marathon – the moment, as Pericles made so clear, where Athens was saved – and Gettysburg, a fact that figured prominently in the speech by Edward Everett, the Harvard professor of classics who gave the main oration at the dedication of the first US national cemetery. Lincoln, more economically, used the deaths of thousands of ordinary men to redefine the purpose of the Civil War and reinterpret the founding of the nation. With the cemeteries of the Great War on the battlefields of Europe and elsewhere there was a logarithmic increase in the number of individual names on the landscape and an elaboration of "sad and sentimental stories" connecting them to those left to mourn.

It would be easy to attribute all this to the state that, to be sure, had an interest in commemoration. But the demand to name the dead did not come from above. At Gettysburg a local undertaker began identifying the dead in response to the queries of their loved ones; in the Great War relatives pushed an unprepared army to account for those who were lost. Civilians did the hard work of keeping track. Naming is part of the story of how the normative claim that everyone has a life to live came to command cultural resonance.[18]

Readers of this book will recognize how widely naming has come to be adopted as a way both to make evident the great catastrophes of human rights in the past century and to heal them. There are many examples: the Yale Cambodian Genocide Project has compiled an archive of 5,000 photographs of prisoners processed by the Tual Sleng prison and asks help in identifying them; Serge Klarsfeld has painstakingly documented 75,721 Jews, named one by one, who were deported from France of whom 11,400 were under 18 and 2,500 could be remembered through pictures; the names of victims in Bosnia, South Africa, El Salvador, Argentina, and many other sites of murder have been gathered as if to resurrect them, to bring them into view both to make a mourning community whole and to establish the point yet again that to be human is to be kept in view and in memory. Naming the dead is of course not new and has deep roots in all religious

---

[18] It was a touching and even partially successful strategy of the German Jewish community to bury the Jewish dead of the Great War, one to a named grave, in special plots. This answered the scurrilous rumors that Jews shirked their patriotic duty but more to the point created a refuge of sorts: for a time Jewish veterans were spared the worst rigors of Nazi anti-Semitic legislation.

traditions; no culture precipitously cuts them off from the living. But as a social practice it has exploded in the last two centuries as if to make the claim that more and more lives are worth remembering.[19]

Exhumations and forensic human rights inquests make the dead even more manifest; they bring the bodies back into the world of the living and incorporate them in a story that, like the slave narratives, makes clear how they died, who is directly responsible for their deaths, and who is indirectly responsible through silence. At the most general level – the most abstract, the most dependent on the moral imagination for its efficacy – I might point to the gathering in of the ashes from the concentration camps and their reburial in a public place. The periphery of Pere Lachaise in Paris – the part near the *mur des fédérés* where the 1871 revolution ended – now has a row of prominently placed stelae containing the ashes of specific concentration camps along with accounts of the numbers who were buried there.

On the more specific level, the forensic inquest literally brings the body back to light and tells its story. There are huge ironies in the history of these inquests. The first large-scale human rights inquiry was conducted by the Germans in 1943 – "Mass Murder in the Forest of Katyn: A Factual Account" – in which an international team of experts examined 2,500 bodies of executed Polish officers exhumed from a mass grave and proved that these particular victims of savagery did not suffer their fate at the hands of the Third Reich. But since then, the human rights inquiry has become ubiquitous, if not in preventing, then in documenting the most horrible breaches in the fabric of human communities and laying the foundation for some future accounting and reconciliation. Physicians for Human Rights has made this a specialty and has brought the latest techniques of modern forensic anthropology to naming the dead, rendering them individuals one by one, and making evident how they died.[20]

This contemporary engine for generating human rights narratives brings us back to the beginning of this essay and to the origins of talking about human rights as we do. The historical record does not confirm "an astonishingly rapid progress of sentiments, in which it has become easier for us to be moved to action by sad and sentimental stories," as Rorty put it. But it does suggest that over the past two centuries we have seen an expansion of

---

[19] For the Yale Cambodia Project database see www.yale/cgp/edu; for Klarsfeld's project see Laqueur (1998).

[20] An English version of the German inquiry, produced by the US Congress as part of the Cold War effort to discredit the Soviet Union, is available (US Gov. Printing Office 1952). For a scholarly treatment see Zawadny (1962).

the universe about whom such moving stories might be told. "Human" as ethical subject has extended its range independently of more widespread agreement about the existence of "human rights" as shorthand for a claim to rights so fundamental – so grounded in an abstract "humanness" – that they are self-evident. In fact, and this is Rorty's great insight: "rights" – in law and practice – followed upon the sentiment and stories even though rights now enjoy the independent force of normative prescription.

The question was how stories and sentiments spread their influence to encompass distant as well as nearby people and to compel action and not just tears. Narratives that expanded the "circle of the we" – of those to whom one owes humane behavior, "humanity" – worked in ways much like beauty works in art: they came to have the power to command "slow looking," "attentive looking," an insistent regard not of a work of art but of a person and a condition in its particularity.

But they also came to be embedded in stories of causality that bound the hearer to the protagonists and in a broader cultural story that included the lives of people who had before gone unnoticed. This is where the dead did their work. A new dignity for the living was part of the same constellation of ideas as a new dignity for the dead. Human rights and the claims of the dead grew together; the dead body came to stand for the body of the living. Mourning was married to sympathy to a remarkable extent so that today the paradigmatic evil is genocide where once it had been slavery, and recovering bodies and names is a kind of action, too late, but – one hopes – a warning against future crimes and a balm for present loss.

REFERENCES

Bennett, J. H., Jr. (1958). *Bondsmen and Bishops: Slavery and Apprenticeships on the Codrington Plantations of Barbados, 1710–1838* Berkeley: University of California Press.
Brown, C. L. (2006). *Moral Capital.* Chapel Hill: University of North Carolina.
Busman, C. (1994). "Women and the Politics of Sugar, 1792." *Representations,* no. 48, Fall, pp. 48–69.
Chaplin, J. (1990). "Slavery and the Principle of Humanity: A Modern Idea in the Early Lower South." *Journal of Social History,* vol. 24, no. 2, Winter, pp. 299–315.
Clarkson, T. (1785/1804). *Essay on the Slavery and Commerce of the Human Species, Particularly the African.* (1804 edn) Philadelphia: Nathan Wiley.
Cobbet, W. (1824). *A History of the Protestant Reformation in England & Ireland.* London.
Cover, R. (1983). "Forward: Nomos and Narrative" to "The Supreme Court: 1982 Term." In *Harvard Law Review,* vol. 97, no. 1, pp. 4–5.

King, J., and C. Rykskamp, eds. (1983). *The Letters and Prose Writings of William Cowper.* Oxford: Oxford University Press, vol. 3.

Dickens, C. (1905). *Bleak House.* London: MacMillan.

Fox, C. J. (1824). *The Speech of the Rt. Hon Chas. James Fox in the House of Commons, June 10th, 1806, on a Motion Preparatory to the Introduction of a Bill for Abolition of the Slave Trade.* Newcastle: J. Clark.

Fox, W. (1792). *An Address to the People of Great Britain on the Propriety of Abstaining from West-India Sugar and Rum.* Tenth edition, with alterations. Limerick.

Gammage, R. C. (1894/1969). *History of the Chartist Movement, 1837–1854.* London: 1894; Merlin Press: 1969.

Ginzburg, C. (1994). "Killing a Chinese Mandarin: The Moral Implications of Distance." *Critical Inquiry,* vol. 21, no. 1, Autumn, pp. 46–60.

Hochschild, A. (2005). *Bury the Chains.* New York/Boston: Houghton Mifflin.

Hollinger, D. (1993). "How Wide the Circle of the We? American Intellectuals and the Problem of the Ethnos Since World War II." *American Historical Review,* vol. XCVIII, pp. 317–37.

Honor, H. (1989). *The Images of the Black in Western Art.* Vol. 4. Cambridge, MA: Harvard University Press.

Human Rights Watch. (2005). *Columbia: Displaced and Discarded. The Plight of Internally Displaced Persons in Bogotá and Cartagena.* Retrieved from http://hrw.org/reports/2005/colombia1005/, Jan 5, 2008.

Hunt, L. (2007). *Inventing Human Rights: A History.* New York: W. W. Norton.

Laqueur, T. (1983). "Bodies, Death and Pauper Funerals" *Representations,* January, no. 1, pp. 109–31.

———. (1989). "Bodies, Details, and the Humanitarian Narrative." In L. Hunt, ed., *The New Cultural History.* Berkeley/ Los Angeles: University of California Press, pp. 176–204.

———. (1993). "Memory and Naming in the Great War." In J. Gillis, ed., *Memory and Commemoration.* Princeton: Princeton University Press.

———. (1998) "The Sound of Voices Intoning Names." In F. Kermode and V. Coode, eds., *The London Review of Books 25th Anniversary Anthology.* London: Profile Books.

Levi, P. (1989). *The Drowned and the Saved.* Trans. R. Rosenthal. New York: Summit Books.

Mackenzie-Grieve, A. (1941/1968). *The Last Years of the English Slave Trade: Liverpool 1750–1807.* Originally pubd. New York: Putnam. Reprint edn., with corrections, London: Frank Cass.

MacGahan, J. A. (1876). "Dispatch." In *London Daily News.* August 22. Retrieved from http://www.attackingthedevil.co.uk/related/macgahan.php, Jan 5, 2008.

Malebranche, Nicholas. (1997). *Elucidations of the Search After Truth.* Trans. and ed. Thomas M. Lennon and Paul J. Olscamp. Cambridge: Cambridge University Press.

Nehamas, A. (2007). *Only a Promise of Happiness: The Place of Beauty in a World of Art.* Princeton: Princeton University Press.

Perl, J. (2000). *Eyewitness: Reports from an Art World in Crisis.* New York: Basic Books.

Pugin, A. W. (1841/2003). *Contrasts: And the True Principles of Pointed or Christian Architecture.* London: Spire Books.

Robertson, J. W. (1952). *The Life and Death of a Newspaper.* London: Methuen.

Rorty, R. (1993). "Oxford Amnesty Lecture." In S. Shute and S. Hurley, eds., *On Human Rights: The Oxford Amnesty Lectures, 1993.* New York: Basic Books, pp. 111–34.

Scarry, E. (1999). "The Difficulty of Imagining Other Persons." In C. Hesse and R. Post, eds., *Human Rights in Political Transitions : Gettysburg to Bosnia.* New York: Zone Books.

Schell, K. D. M. (2003). "Gravestones, Belonging, and Local Attachment in England, 1700–2000." *Past and Present,* May, pp. 97–134.

Schmitt, C. (1976). *The Concept of the Political.* Trans. George Schwab. New Brunswick, NJ: Rutgers University Press.

Schor, E. (1994). *Bearing the Dead: The British Culture of Mourning from the Enlightenment to Victoria.* Princeton: Princeton University Press.

Sharpe, G. (1776). *The Law of Retribution or a Serious Warning to Great Britain and Her Colonies Founded on Unquestionable Examples of God's Temporal Vengeance Against Tyrants, Slave Holders and Oppressors.* London: W. Richardson.

Smith, A. (1759). *The Theory of Moral Sentiments.* London.

Southey, R. (1860). *The Poetical Works of Robert Southey.* Boston: Little Brown.

St Clair, W. (2004). *The Reading Nation in the Romantic Period.* Cambridge: Cambridge University Press.

Stead, W. T. (1885). "The Maiden Tribute of Modern Babylon." *Pall Mall Gazette,* July.

Stedman, J. G. (1796). *Narrative of a Five Years' Expedition Against the Revolted Negroes of Surinam, in Guiana, on the Wild Coast of South America, from the year 1772 to 1777.* London.

Strange, J. (2005) *Death, Grief, and Poverty in Britain, 1870–1914.* Cambridge: Cambridge University Press.

U.S. Government Printing Office. (1952). *The Katyn Forest Massacre. Hearings Before the Select Committee to Conduct an Investigation of the Facts, Evidence and Circumstances of the Katyn Forest Massacre, Eighty-second Congress, first[-second] session, on Investigation of the Murder of Thousands of Polish Officers in the Katyn Forest near Smolensk, Russia . . .*

Wollaston, W. (1722/2003). *The Religion of Nature Delineated.* Kessinger Publishing.

Zawadny, J. K. (1962). *Death in the Forest.* Notre Dame, IN: Notre Dame University Press.

2. Contemporary Humanitarianism: The Global and the Local

DAVID P. FORSYTHE

One can document in the United States of America and the rest of the Western world a persistent strain of compassion that leads to concern for others, including those beyond one's national borders. Whether the same phenomenon holds with equal strength in other parts of the world I leave to other inquiries, at least for now. But the best of local feelings and intentions about foreign disasters have to be translated into transnational institutions and policies if those feelings are to be anything more than armchair musings and a *cri de coeur*. At the same time, a powerful global humanitarian response would necessarily be connected to dynamic local roots – meaning national attitudes. Otherwise, international actors and programs remain distant, subject to state manipulation and the vagaries of media coverage.

Somewhat surprisingly, most treatments of global humanitarianism focus on how to perfect the international arrangements, with scant attention to local foundations.[1] Perhaps this is because those writing about international responses to natural, political, and other disasters are international specialists. Perhaps it is because local attitudes are not now conducive to an evenhanded and powerful humanitarianism, so one is inclined to analyze something else. In any event, I propose here to fill a void by focusing on the link between the global humanitarian system and local attitudes. The basic assumption is that the global system will remain as it is as long as local views remain what they are. That is to say, global humanitarian efforts will remain uneven, with important gaps and insufficient resources, as long as popular

---

[1] See, for example, United Nations *The Humanitarian Decade* (2004). Even Hoffman & Weiss (2006), for all of their insights, pay almost no attention to public attitudes.

Parts of this essay have been previously published in Forsythe (2006), and are used here with permission.

attitudes, affected by media coverage, remain highly affected by narrow nationalism – and along with it selective inattentiveness – and morally indefensible priorities, at least from a cosmopolitan viewpoint. Even if we remain skeptical about mass public opinion per se, we can inquire about the attentive public that pays some attention to public affairs, that votes, and that supports various organizations.

There are no quick fixes to the current situation. A long-term hope for improvement in at least some grassroots attitudes stems primarily from self-interest connected to economic globalization. In this latter context, dynamic and progressive leadership might make a difference.

Overview

States themselves have produced a cosmopolitan and liberal framework by constructing an international law that mandates attention to universal human rights and humanitarian affairs, whether in peace or war (Forsythe 1995; Beetham, ed. 1995). Within this framework there are different types of mandated international arrangements for persons in exceptional dire straits. This global system entails officially states, intergovernmental organizations (IGOs), and nongovernmental organizations (NGOs). But all too often the states that drive the process choose – or feel compelled to choose – a realist policy reflecting state power politics and expedient state advantage. They preach liberalism but often practice realism. They preach cosmopolitan liberalism but often manifest indifference to "others" beyond their own state.

Contemporary international humanitarianism – the transnational concern to help persons in exceptional distress – reflects the pervasive tension between nationalism and cosmopolitanism. And because the tension is unresolved, for humanitarianism and for international relations in general, the nature and forms of humanitarian action have varied by context. The five main components of international humanitarianism today – states, the United Nations system, the NGO community, the Red Cross network, and the media – have combined in different ways at different times in different places. At the very same time that there was an unprecedented outpouring of humanitarian assistance for the victims of the tsunami disaster in Asia at the end of 2004 and the beginning of 2005, there was widespread indifference to a greater disaster in the Democratic Republic of Congo – where almost four million civilians died over the course of a few years of political conflict. Whether such inconsistencies can be leveled out in a more just and orderly world is an important question.

Because the global humanitarian challenge is so great, and because its sources are so varied, the response is usually complex and often chaotic. Typical was the response to the 2004–2005 tsunami disaster: national militaries worked side by side with NGOs and IGOs; some Asian states welcomed involvement by other states and some did not. It may be chaotic internationalism, but there is indeed a global pattern of response. As usual, questions of effectiveness and participation must be addressed. After all, the primary value is not the response per se, but the effective protection of human dignity for persons in exceptional distress, with perhaps participation of stakeholders.[2] Because the West pays for this system and mostly leads it, Western attitudes are crucial – including attitudes that would guard against neo-imperialism.

A unipolar world or, more precisely, a unipolar military situation (featuring US putative primacy), in the larger game of international relations, creates certain dilemmas but does not fundamentally alter the central and persistent tension between nationalism and cosmopolitanism, the latter entailing universal standards of human rights and humanitarian norms. This is not the place for an extended discussion of humanitarian military intervention; other authors have addressed the subject of saving foreigners by military force (International Commission 2001; Weiss 2006). I do, however, have to note coercive factors in passing. Paradoxically, while particularly Red Cross humanitarianism arose as an effort to limit the human costs of war, contemporary humanitarianism – including now even the Red Cross – recognizes that there is sometimes a role for political action to deal with the root causes of a humanitarian crisis, perhaps even entailing the use of force.[3]

This analysis stresses humanitarianism in war and other political conflict, while largely leaving to others the matter of the humanitarian response to natural and industrial disasters (International Red Cross and Red Crescent Federation 2004). I also do not address, except in passing, persons being in persistent and thus routine distress because of a failure of economic and social development.

As a general historical trend, there is now greater attention to humanitarianism in world affairs. This is certainly true for war and similar political conflict, which is easily seen if we think back to the plight of individuals, whether combatant or civilian, in situations like the Wars of the Austrian

[2] See further Keohane (2006) on the importance of three core values: human rights, democratic process, and effectiveness.
[3] I thank Ramesh Thakur for this insight.

Succession or the Crimea wars towards the middle of the nineteenth century. Compared to that time, all national military establishments in developed states now have sophisticated medical services, supplemented by a vast array of other humanitarian actors, whether public or private, national or international. Moreover, in the violence in southern Lebanon in the middle of 2006, it was striking that there were repeated demands that humanitarian agencies be given access to civilian victims, even in the midst of armed conflict, even if this meant some kind of cessation of military operations by the belligerents. The same general trend of greater attention to victims is no doubt true for natural and technological disasters, and in that regard we can note the extensive response not only to the tsunami in the Indian Ocean but to other more or less contemporary calamities, such as the 1995 earthquake that affected Kobe, Japan, and Hurricane Mitch in 1998, which affected Central America. Even with regard to Hurricane Katrina in the USA in 2005, that wealthy country was the recipient of considerable outside assistance, with the US Agency for International Development helping to link foreign aid to domestic disaster relief. The annual business of global disaster response has been estimated at about USD10 billion. As noted, however, this general trend of progress is dotted with exceptions and limitations.

The central question is whether in the world today humanitarianism, which is inherently global because of the location and size of the problems and the vast array of actors involved, can be made balanced and effective, with appropriate attention to the needs and desires of victims.

I want briefly to analyze the components of international humanitarianism today in an inductive process, with a focus on the UN system and Red Cross network, then put the pieces of the puzzle into a larger picture at the end that stresses grassroots attitudes.

The UN System

Has the United Nations been able to provide a streamlined and reliable response to humanitarian disasters, particularly in conflict situations? Has the UN been able to combine its own agencies with private groups and governmental units, in the context of media coverage, to at least coordinate meaningful multilateral humanitarianism? One overview published in 2004 provides a distressing answer:

> There exists no system for triggering and delivering international disaster assistance; there is rather a hodgepodge of public and private agencies. And the independent role of the communications media in covering or ignoring a story

is often important. Whether ... actors are motivated to act because of a concern for the human rights to food, clothing, shelter, and health care (which has been rare) or because of humanitarian compassion (more prevalent), all of these actors have proceeded with minimal central coordination – and thus with resulting overlap and confusion.

Various UN organizations have been protective of their decentralized independence. The private agencies have resisted coming under the full control of public authorities. Various agencies have competed among themselves for a slice of the action in a given situation and for credit for whatever accomplishments were achieved – said to be important for fund raising. To be sure, emergency assistance has been delivered and lives have been saved in a vast number of situations. ... (Weiss, Forsythe, & Coate 2004: 187)

As we shall see, the UN response to persons in dire straits is better than it has been even if it is not what it should be.

Some History

During the era of the League of Nations, the "Nansen Office" was created to supplement Red Cross and other private, public, and quasi-public efforts in order to deal with refugee relief – especially given the number of persons on the move in Europe following communist revolutions in places like Russia and Hungary. But the League never developed a comprehensive system of response to various humanitarian disasters (Skran 1995). An international relief union was stillborn.

Surprising as it may now seem, the United Nations system was very slow to manifest any broad responsibility for disaster response. True, the Office of the UN High Commissioner for Refugees (UNHCR) was created in 1950, as was a legal framework for refugees, which was originally designed to deal in fact with a trickle of persons fleeing from persecution by European communist countries – countries that proved very adept at sealing borders. But the UNHCR was said to be a protection agency, not a relief agency, meaning that it concentrated on diplomatic and legal representations designed to protect the rights of manageable numbers of refugees. Only in the aftermath of the Israeli-Palestinian contest for control of western British Palestine did the UN General Assembly create an early refugee relief agency – UNWRA – whose mandate was limited to one group in one part of the world.

The UN system was not utilized to help manage a systematic and multilateral response to a broad range of humanitarian disasters until about 1970. In the well-publicized Nigerian-Biafran conflict (1967–1970), the major relief players trying to get aid to civilians in secessionist Biafra were the International Committee of the Red Cross (ICRC) and its Red Cross partners, and Joint Church Aid, a faith-based private consortium. While other relief actors like the French Red Cross acted independently, no UN organ or agency was a major player in that drama.

After Biafra, and with other changes in international relations, in 1971 the General Assembly created the Disaster Relief Office (Stephens 1978). By 1992 this office had become the UN Department of Humanitarian Affairs. In 1998, this department was changed into the Office of the Coordinator of Humanitarian Affairs (OCHA), headed by an Under Secretary-General who became at the same time the UN Emergency Relief Coordinator. Other administrative arrangements were created in related developments to enhance coordination of a multilateral process involving different actors.

The UNHCR and UNRWA both continued. The former became more and more a relief agency and not just a legal protection agency.[4] This was in no small measure because Western donor states wanted refugees to be cared for "over there," rather than to become asylum-seekers in the Western states themselves. Other parts of the UN system also developed, or were given, mandates to deal with refugees, internally displaced persons, and others in emergency distress: UNICEF, the World Food Program, the UN Development Program and its Resident Representative in particular countries, the World Health Organization, and so on.

Significantly, as the Cold War wound down the UN Security Council began to concern itself more often with humanitarian affairs.[5] During the Cold War, the deployment of military force under the Security Council's aegis had led to traditional (simple or first-generation) peacekeeping missions entailing primarily observation and reporting, with only light weapons used for self-defense. The point was to show the UN flag and utilize armed diplomacy to help fighting parties reduce or avoid hostile confrontation. Humanitarian matters were excluded. But increasingly in the 1990s the UNSC began to deploy complex (or second-generation) peacekeeping missions, which entailed human rights and humanitarian mandates. The point was not just to limit or avoid conflict, but to create a humane and rights-protective situation. Further, on occasion the UNSC would assert a right under UN Charter Chapter VII to engage

[4] Loescher (2002), among others, argues that the UNHCR gave such priority to relief that its traditional protection work suffered.

[5] See Weiss (2004). According to Weiss, during the Cold War the UNSC was mostly "missing in action" regarding humanitarian affairs. The first mention of humanitarian matters in a SC resolution was in 1968 regarding Israeli-occupied territory. The ICRC was not mentioned until 1978.

in enforcement action, not just peacekeeping narrowly defined, and sometimes this was related to human rights and humanitarian affairs.

Thus, the UNSC became progressively involved in humanitarian matters because they were seen as linked to international peace and security. Either one had to protect rights and humane values in order to get peace and stability, and/or one had to use force to compel a target party to respect rights and humane standards. The previously low politics of humanitarianism became enmeshed in the high politics of peace and security.[6] The process developed inconsistently and selectively with many double standards, because at times "the unwillingness by major powers to spend money was matched by an unwillingness to run risks" (Weiss 2004). Still, in general, the notion of international peace and security in the UNSC more and more was informed by humanitarian concern – that is, by the concern for human security in conflict areas.

Unfortunately, the UNSC also played fast and loose at times with the language of human rights and humanitarian affairs. Clearly in the Balkan wars of 1992–1995, state members of the UNSC, especially the Permanent-5, and most especially the USA, used the discourse of human rights and humanitarianism to avoid a more disagreeable, if more decisive, response to atrocities. To these states on the UNSC, it was more agreeable to dispatch the UNHCR to care for those persecuted and uprooted than to commit their military forces to stop the root causes of the forced displacement and other abuses. Likewise, to them it was more agreeable in the short term to create a criminal court (the ICTY for former Yugoslavia in 1993, then the ICTR for Rwanda in 1994) than to risk blood and treasure in a forceful intervention. Only in the wake of media coverage of the massacre at Srebrenica, and media coverage of other terrible events, did powerful states finally use UN authority to help bring pressure to bear on Serb parties sufficient to end the worst Balkan atrocities by 1995. But even graphic media coverage of genocide in Rwanda failed to mobilize particularly Western states to significant intervention there (mainly because of US difficulties in Somalia and a domestic backlash against incurring costs to save "others").

In Bosnia, we were treated to the unseemly spectacle of the UN High Commissioner for Refugees, Sadako Ogata, suspending UNHCR relief in order to try to force UNSC members to deal responsibly with the situation, only to have the UN Secretary-General, Boutros Boutros Ghali, order a

---

[6] This was broadly characteristic of the situation throughout international relations that Robert Keohane and Joseph P. Nye called complex interdependence.

resumption of relief– even though he probably lacked the legal authority to do so.[7] Likewise, when Ogata brought to the attention of the UNSC the fact that Hutu militias, particularly in Zaire, had infiltrated, even had taken over, some of the UNHCR refugee camps, state members of the UNSC refused to authorize a deployment of force to deal with the situation.[8]

In places like Bosnia and the Great Lakes region of Africa, UNHCR leaders faced hard choices. They knew their role was being manipulated by various states and non-state parties for "political" purposes. They tried to carve out a zone of relatively neutral humanitarian space for the impartial benefit of innocent victims. But, in the final analysis, key states refused to take decisive action to guarantee the neutral space required for genuine humanitarian action. A few NGOs, or sections of NGOs, withdrew from the field in protest, but that meant that their efforts for victims were terminated. One may not want relief to reach belligerents, but abandoning victims has moral and material repercussions as well.

Regardless of state-driven developments within the UN system, private aid and relief agencies constituted a cumulative force to be reckoned with regarding humanitarian affairs. Some had rather long histories during which they had built up expertise, name recognition, and a donor base. The Save the Children network dates from 1919; the International Rescue Committee from 1933; Oxfam from 1942; CARE from 1945; World Vision from 1950, to give just a few examples. Others were more recent, such as Doctors Without Borders (Médecins Sans Frontières, or MSF), from 1971, but brought considerable energy and commitment to their work. Annual budgets in 2002, however small compared to national militaries, were significant relative to UN and Red Cross agencies: CARE USA, $420 million; World Vision, $820 million; Oxfam, $390 million; MSF, $400 million.

Then, too, private human rights advocacy groups such as Amnesty International and Human Rights Watch, among others, while not providing relief on the ground, provided a running commentary on humanitarian crises (that entailed human rights violations) and tried to pressure states and UN bodies into further action. Their locales, contacts, and

---

[7] Even though the High Commissioner for Refugees is nominated by the UN SG, the High Commissioner is selected by the UN GA and does not report to the SG but to the GA. Nevertheless, Ogata, having made her political point to no avail, agreed to a resumption of UNHCR relief.

[8] Some relief NGOs, or parts of relief NGOs, withdrew to protest caring for *les génocidaires*, even though this withdrawal meant that genuine refugees would suffer the consequences. Most relief NGOs stayed.

budgets (AI, \$32.5 million; HRW, \$19.5 million) also contributed often to media coverage that sometimes helped set the agenda for other actors. They constantly peppered states with reports and requests, urging more protection of human dignity. Other private actors like the International Crisis Group, an advocacy group for conflict monitoring and resolution, pushed in the same direction.

On the one hand, some of these private groups were co-opted into the UN system in a relatively systematic way. The UNHCR, which increasingly (some would say disproportionately) became a general relief agency, relied on these private groups for grassroots action. In effect, the UNHCR tried to coordinate relief in such places as the Balkans and the Great Lakes region of Africa, while the private agencies did the actual work in the field. On the other hand, at times various private relief or development groups went their own way, with little regard for any designation of "UN lead agency." In Cambodia (and Thailand) during 1979–1983, Oxfam intentionally undercut some of the principles and policies of UNICEF, the latter coordinating with the ICRC to try to provide coordinated multilateral relief in that devastated area. Oxfam wanted an independent part of the action, even if this impaired what other humanitarians were trying to do (Forsythe 2005; Shawcross 1984). In and around Rwanda in 1994, some NGO relief agencies operated completely independently, causing major headaches for both UNAMIR and UNHCR.[9]

The UN family has been highly fragmented in the matter of response to humanitarian disasters. OCHA or the UNHCR certainly has had trouble coordinating the private aid agencies that did the grassroots work in UN-sponsored programs.

Global Governance, Multilateralism, Effectiveness
Nation-states control the UN system. They get the type of United Nations they authorize and pay for. For the most part, state hypocrisy dominates, not only regarding the principle of state sovereignty but more generally as well (Krasner 1999). States profess high-sounding values, but they undercut those values daily. I noted at the outset that states preach a cosmopolitan liberalism but often practice realism or just plain indifference about "others." It is not unusual for states to provide only a fraction of what they pledge in response to various disasters.

Foundational to the evolution of this state of affairs are two factors: the weakness of a broad transnational morality despite increasing material globalization, and national elite interest in protecting a preferred

---

[9]   See Dallaire (1998: 71–86).

position.[10] On the first, even after US Secretary of State Colin Powell declared the Darfur region of the Sudan to be the locus of genocide in 2004, reaction both inside and outside the USA was muted. On the second factor, a centralized and powerful United Nations would be seen by many national officials as a threat to their preferred position, not as a primary means to deal with the distress of "others." Thus, it is not so surprising that multilateral humanitarianism associated with the United Nations remains essentially in the same spasmodic condition it was about a quarter of a century ago.

Having said that, there has been some substantive progress. As one author noted, "the prominence of the humanitarian impulse altered the ethical, rhetorical, and military landscapes of Security Council decision-making in the 1990s. The nature and scope of enforcement decisions have amounted, on occasion, to a fundamental increase in the relevance of humanitarian values in relationship to narrowly defined vital interests (Weiss 2004) Yet the process was not consolidated into systematic and sure practice. And, issues of coordination and effectiveness remained much discussed but mostly unaltered.[11]

The major donor countries to UN humanitarianism, who also channel significant funds through private relief agencies, could certainly insist on a more streamlined and effective UN system. Above all, we are talking about the US Agency for International Development (USAID) and the Humanitarian Office of the European Community (ECHO). But they do not do so. In addition to a lack of interest at high levels of governments, a serious argument can be made that a certain amount of choice in relief mechanisms is a good thing.

There is something to be said for going with UNHCR as lead agency in the field for one situation, but UNICEF or even the World Food Program in another. One may be better situated than the other for that lead role, depending upon contacts, history in-country, and so on. There is an argument to be made for coordination by consensus among leading relief actors (Minear 2002). Many times the UNHCR, UNICEF, the WFP, and others, do in fact work out rather clear divisions of labor for relief. And OCHA is there, plus associated standing committees, to facilitate such arrangements. Of course, when a UN lead agency is designated for relief,

---

[10] See Keohane (2006) about how loyalty still flows mostly to the nation state.
[11] It is striking how much the older literature on aspects of humanitarianism resembles the discussions of the contemporary world. See, for example, Stephens & Green, eds. (1979), and Nichols & Loescher, eds. (1989).

that agency should be authorized and empowered to rigorously manage the private aid agencies that contract with the UN. And the relief groups that try to act as lone rangers need to be marginalized. But if the lone ranger NGO strikes a separate deal with the host state, which is "sovereign," then what?

Can UN humanitarian bodies be independent from state strategic calculations? Many UN officials and other observers call for precisely this type of independence from politics – meaning in reality from the strategic calculations of governments (Egeland 2004; Loescher 2004; Giradet 2004). But the UN system is an intergovernmental system. OCHA, as part of the UN secretariat, can properly aspire to that independent status. Even the UNHCR can appeal to its authorizing resolutions and associated conventional instruments to seek independent, impartial, and neutral programming. But in the last analysis, UNHCR and UNICEF and WFP will not be fully independent. Their mandates and budgets come from governments. If the USA and its Western allies want UNHCR or UNICEF to become a large relief agency caring for refugees and IDPs far away from western borders, they have the political power and money to make that happen.

It is a fact of life that the USA in 2009 will provide more money for relief, reconstruction, and development in Iraq or Afghanistan, than it will provide to the Sudan, the Democratic Republic of the Congo, or northern Uganda. In Iraq and Afghanistan, there is a greater security interest, along with commitments of personal and national prestige. With regard to the African countries mentioned, and most humanitarian disasters occur in the less-developed countries, the UN system may manifest a limited humanitarian impulse, but not a neutral and impartial moral imperative.[12] Powerful states, and above all the quasi-imperial USA, will ensure that this is so. The UN Emergency Relief Coordinator may be principled and dynamic, a spokesperson for a liberal cosmopolitanism, but he or she will remain powerless to change the dominance of nationalistic decision-making in UN bodies. The two fundamental principles continue to clash; they remain unresolved on a systematic basis.

It does not help matters that the Western-based media outlets are also highly nationalistic, more interested in the fate of a few Western soldiers or journalists than in the hugely greater numbers of those in distress in non-Western poor countries. One has only to look at the lack of sustained Western media coverage of the Democratic Republic of the Congo to see

---

[12] This distinction is developed by Weiss (2006).

that this is so. And, when there is Western media attention to the humanitarian disasters of the Global South, it is mostly short lived. Even regarding the 2004–2005 tsunami in Asia, eventually the media moved on to other stories. In commercial journalism, one can only report on the disaster for so long. The follow-on problems of development and reconstruction do not make good pictures or stories with public appeal.

States acting unilaterally would do well to avoid the discourse of humanitarianism. Most of the time (but not always), such state foreign policy debases the notion of humanitarianism. One of the more egregious examples was when the USA's Reagan Administration referred to its nonlethal but nevertheless military aid to the Contras in Central America as "humanitarian." State unilateral reference to humanitarianism is most often a self-serving cover for self-interested concerns. When the USA adopted "humanitarian" policies towards the population in Afghanistan in about 2002, such as emergency food relief, its fundamental goal was strategic and self-interested – to separate the Taliban and Al Qaeda political factions from the rest of the Afghanistan people and to show to the rest of the world that its fight was with those political factions, not with Islamic peoples per se.

Moreover, a certain state reference to humanitarianism can endanger the real humanitarians. Both Colin Powell and US AID Director Andrew Natsios called for relief NGOs to get on the US team, to fully support US objectives in places like Iraq.[13] This effort is misguided.

In Iraq, Coalition forces used the same Red Cross emblem on certain military equipment and facilities while carrying out their invasion and occupation, undermining the neutrality of Red Cross projects.[14] The hard fact was that in Iraq there was no automatic neutral space for humanitarian work, and it proved extremely difficult, if not impossible, to construct that neutral humanitarian space. There were repeated violent attacks on a variety of "aid workers." When Secretary of State Powell referred to relief NGOs as force multipliers for the occupying Coalition, he helped to erase their image of neutrality, impartiality, and independence.

When the ICRC and the United Nations independently tried to improve the daily lives of Iraqis through improved sanitation and medical care, inter alia, this inadvertently contributed to what the Coalition

---

[13] See Burnett (2004).
[14] Likewise, in Bosnia, the UNHCR used the UN emblem while presenting itself as a neutral relief agency, while the UNSC and UNPROFOR acted under the same emblem while sometimes employing coercion.

sought to achieve: a satisfied Iraqi population willing to accept a Coalition-inspired government friendly to the West. The best that the ICRC could do was to try to locate and establish dialogue with the anti-Coalition forces, to convince them that the organization was not motivated to support the Coalition and its interim government. The same dilemma of how to construct neutrality plagued not only the UN in Iraq, but also NGOs like CARE in Iraq and MSF in Afghanistan, whose personnel were also attacked by radical Islamic elements. Seventeen people working for a French private humanitarian group in Sri Lanka were intentionally killed in 2006.

It is no easy thing for many NGOs to chart an independent, neutral, and impartial course in humanitarian relief, distinct from the strategic calculations of states. Care USA receives 40 to 70 percent of its annual budget from the US government; Save the Children USA may receive about 40 percent of its budget from the US government in a particular year; and the International Rescue Committee may get about 80 percent. World Vision, which receives only about 20 to 35 percent of its income from the US government in a given year, is part of the American Christian social conservative movement; it started as part of a broad anticommunist concern and worked closely with the US government during the Cold War, and it has worked hand in hand with the US government regarding food aid to North Korea. A former Vice President of World Vision was Andrew Natsios, who became the Director of the US AID under President George W. Bush, after having been the head of AID's Office of Foreign Disaster Relief under President George H. W. Bush. Such facts raise questions about the independent humanitarianism of these and other NGOs.

UN Humanitarianism Today

Space does not allow a detailed further examination of UN humanitarianism today. It is sufficient to note the continuing unevenness and unpredictability of the process. In the 2004–2005 tsunami disaster, the UN's Jan Egeland, as Emergency Relief Coordinator, played a valuable if controversial role. He was both an effective (if sometimes irritating) stimulus for greater resources and also a reasonably effective coordinator, trying to minimize overlap, duplication, and inappropriate donations in kind. Given the size of the disaster, some management and coordination problems were inevitable and did indeed occur. But on the whole, the international response, led by the UN, was good enough to prevent mass starvation and epidemics.

However, in Kosovo in 1999, the UN and particularly the UNHCR were pushed aside early on by NATO states. NATO regarded the displaced ethnic Albanians as too important to be left to the care of others – because their plight was the publicized raison d'etre of the forceful intervention by those Western states. It was also the case that early on the UNHCR was thinly staffed, unprepared, slow in response, and basically unimpressive in that particular case.[15] So, whereas particularly OCHA got reasonably high marks for effective coordination in the tsunami relief effort of 2004–2005, the UNHCR particularly was marginalized and ineffective early on in the Kosovo affair.

At the UN World Summit in September 2005, there were official promises to improve OCHA's Central Emergency Revolving Fund. Otherwise, humanitarian relief did not loom large in talk of institutional reform. There was also little attention to humanitarianism in the Secretary-General's preceding report ("In Larger Freedom"), and none in the report of the Secretary General's High Level Panel on Threats to Stable International Relations. The World Summit did pay some attention to refugees and IDPs.

Red Cross Redux

Long before the United Nations even existed, the ICRC, the lead agency in conflicts for the International Red Cross and Red Crescent Movement, was trying to organize a transnational humanitarian movement. In the ICRC's view, international humanitarianism involves not only the provision of food, water, clothing, shelter, and health care, but also the supervision of detention conditions and the protection of family cohesion in a variety of ways (the tracing of missing persons, reunification of family members, reintegration of former child soldiers into civilian society, provision for those orphaned). Since about 1970, after the Nigerian-Biafran conflict, the ICRC has been reinventing itself so as to better its performance. Where there are persons in distress because of war and other types of political conflict, the ICRC is always present – often in highly important ways. It stresses its independence from the UN system, in the name of neutrality, while cooperating with it at times according to its own decisions.[16]

---

[15] See, for example, Groom & Taylor (2000: 291–318). See further Minear, Baarda, & Sommers (2000).

[16] This section draws heavily on Forsythe (2006).

Some History

From its beginnings in 1863, the ICRC focused on persons in distress because of war – and later other forms of political conflict. Starting with a focus on wounded combatants in international war, because of the work of its founder Henry Dunant in caring for the wounded after the battle of Solferino in 1859 in northern Italy, the ICRC later took up the plight of individuals in internal conflicts, as within the Ottoman Empire. During World War I it gave great attention to prisoners of war, and immediately after that war it started visiting political prisoners in situations of internal troubles and tensions in such places as Hungary and Russia. World War II brought recognition for both civilian relief and prisoner protection, as well as the tracing of missing persons. Basic ICRC functions did not change during the Cold War or the following unipolar period.

The ICRC's original intent, not fully consistent with Dunant's direct action, was to help develop a legal framework for humanitarian action by others. It drafted the 1864 Geneva Convention (GC) for victims of war, under which wounded soldiers were neutralized, along with the medical personnel who cared for them. The wise course of action was to give public authorities the primary obligation for the care of victims of war. This was the first full treaty in international humanitarian law (IHL), with other core treaties following in 1906, 1929, 1949, and 1977. Particularly in the four interlocking GCs of 1949, the ICRC is recognized and even given certain rights – such as the right of detention visits to combatant and civilian prisoners in international armed conflict. In modern IHL there is a right to humanitarian assistance in war, although it is not clear who exactly is supposed to implement the right, and under what conditions.

From its start the ICRC also promoted the development of national relief or aid societies, which over time evolved into today's 189 National Red Cross and Red Crescent Societies.[17] But the Franco-Prussian War of

---

[17] Two emblems emerged for the Movement when the Ottoman Empire in the 1870s refused to use the Red Cross emblem for its aid society, but rather chose the Red Crescent emblem, a move supported by Persia and Egypt and a few other Islamic states. In 2005 a Diplomatic Conference adopted a Third Protocol to the 1949 Geneva Conventions, adding a Red Crystal in its international operations. This solved the problem of Israel's official society, Magen David Adom, being outside the Movement because it used the Red Star of David. MDA agreed to use the Red Crystal. It is states that designate neutral emblems in international law. Theoretically the Movement could do as it pleases, but then Movement emblems might find no recognition in international law. Moreover, many national Red Cross or Red Crescent societies are not independent from their governments when voting in Red Cross conferences.

1870 and then World War I showed the strength of narrow nationalism, the other side of which was the weakness of the cosmopolitanism envisaged by Dunant for the Red Cross. Various national aid societies were not able to rise above nationalism to practice neutral and impartial humanitarianism. They cared mostly for co-nationals. Over time these official national aid societies increasingly were nationalized and militarized by their chartering governments.[18] The ICRC, based in neutral Switzerland, became more of an actor in the field and less of a rearguard storage depot and mailbox. The ICRC was well positioned to practice independent, neutral, and impartial Red Cross humanitarianism (as long as Swiss national interests did not come into play).

After World War I the large and influential American Red Cross tried to push aside the all-Swiss ICRC by creating a League of Red Cross and Red Crescent Societies. The ICRC was not able to block the creation of the League, now the Federation, as a union of all the national societies. But the ICRC was able to limit the Federation's mandate to natural (and industrial) disasters and development of the national societies, thus preserving for itself the leadership role for Red Cross humanitarianism in conflicts. After much organizational competition and some confusion during 1920–1990, the components of the Red Cross have reaffirmed and codified this basic division of labor.

In the Seville Agreement of 1997, the Movement again stipulated that the ICRC was the network's lead actor in armed conflict for the roles of detention visits, relief, and family reunification efforts. The ICRC also maintained its lead role concerning detainees and their families in situations of internal troubles and tensions. The Federation took on work with refugees and IDPs in countries not characterized by armed conflict, as well as continuing its coordination regarding the international response to natural and industrial or technological disasters. National societies were to support both the ICRC and Federation internationally, as well as to continue a broad range of domestic social programs. A national society might even become the lead agency for the Movement in an international action, but only with the "concurrence" of the two (separate) headquarters in Geneva.

This Seville Agreement has reduced friction between the ICRC and Federation, or more accurately codified an improvement in relations that was already occurring, as well as encouraging a more orderly relationship between the ICRC and its natural "local partners," the national societies. Officials of these societies are now regularly seconded to the ICRC (and Federation) for short-term contract work.

---

[18] The best treatment is by Hutchinson (1996).

The significance of Seville is that the Red Cross network is relatively more integrated than in the past, with the ICRC better able to tap into the resources of the stronger national societies without being undercut by the Federation. A division of labor has been clarified particularly regarding refugees and IDPs, where the ICRC has ceded some ground to the Federation. The ICRC, having too often ignored the national societies in humanitarian fieldwork between about 1914 and 1990, now is relatively more interested in a better integrated Red Cross network at least for relief, but not for detention visits.[19]

The fact remains, however, that most national societies are often more aligned with their national governments than with the ICRC. Like the American, British, or French Red Cross Societies, most are more nationalistic than cosmopolitan. They are more patriotic than neutral and impartial. For example, they followed their governments into Northern Iraq in 1991 without much coordination with the ICRC. They may enthusiastically support some ICRC humanitarian operations when their governments do not object or interfere. In the Darfur region of the Sudan, for example, there is a loose coordination between the ICRC and various Western national societies that have taken an interest in that conflict.

At the international conferences of the network, which occur in principle every four years, and at which states that are parties to the Geneva Conventions also attend and vote, in addition to Red Cross and Red Crescent agencies, there is some renewed discussion of cosmopolitan neutrality for the national societies as compared to nationalistic deference to their governments. But almost 150 years of fragmented and nationalized history will be difficult for the Red Cross network to completely change, to understate matters.

Mononationality, Multilateralism, Effectiveness

ICRC statutes, reinforced by Movement statutes, establish the ICRC as a private Swiss organization ultimately governed by a Committee of not more than twenty-five Swiss citizens, which, when meeting in formal session, is called the Assembly. It is the Assembly, not the Red Cross Conference or any other body, that is responsible for ICRC governance, or the basic rules and doctrine (strategy). The ICRC is democratic internally,

---

[19] See Morehead (1998/1999). ICRC doctrine on relations with national societies regarding detention visits is that the relationship depends on the context. The ICRC may bypass, or work with, or partially involve the NS, depending on what will prove effective in protecting the dignity of detainees.

with votes in its Assembly on general policies. It also bears noting that even democratic processes often manifest undemocratic elements. In the USA, there are not only appointed judges but also a Federal Reserve System that is largely shielded from democratic pressures in the interest of effective monetary policy. In the same way, it can be said that the ICRC is shielded from outside democratic pressures manifested through the Red Cross network or the United Nations. The self-governing nature of the ICRC has been approved by votes in the Red Cross Conference, with states that are parties to the Geneva Conventions also participating.

Arguably it is ICRC mononationality that is foundational for its independence, neutrality, and impartiality. The all-Swiss Assembly, linked to permanent Swiss neutrality, in the last analysis does ensure that no member from international war, or from the factions in a civil war, or from internal troubles and tensions will be on the Assembly.

The ICRC now has a headquarters agreement with the Swiss Confederation, as if it were an international organization, making its premises and records off-limits to the Swiss government. The organization has similar agreements with dozens of states where it maintains rather permanent offices. Since 1992, the ICRC manifests an international staff, drawn overwhelmingly from the North Atlantic area. The Global South is hardly represented at all (approximately 5 percent). In the future, important ICRC officials, such as the Director-General, the Director of Operations, and the heads of various delegations and offices, may be non-Swiss. On occasions, there are joint programs with the multinational Federation, and, as noted, personnel from various national societies are seconded to the ICRC. So the ICRC is now a blend of mononationality at the top and a certain type of internationalism in its professional staff.

The all-Swiss Committee/Assembly has reduced importance today. It meets only five times a year. The daily operations are managed by the Director-General, who has personal responsibility for the Directorate, a five-person "cabinet" that coordinates the professional side of the house. However, the ICRC President and the Council of the Assembly, a subgroup of the Assembly, remain both Swiss and influential. In reality, the leadership of the organization is shared by the President and the Director-General, with the Council of the Assembly as a periodically important body. At the time of writing, all of these latter persons are Swiss. (These offices and bodies are also dominated by white males, but that is another discussion.)

The Swiss connection at the ICRC has indeed led to considerable independence, neutrality, and impartiality over time in its humanitarian endeavors, not to mention an impressive record of accomplishment that has led to three or four Nobel peace prizes.[20] No organization is perfect, and a reasoned argument can be made that the ICRC was not as independent, neutral, impartial, and effective as the organization projects, especially prior to 1970.[21] The ICRC was carefully supervised by Bern during World War II to ensure that its activities did not unduly antagonize Nazi Germany. This constitutes the major blight on its record of independence. The ICRC tilted towards Mussolini when the Italians invaded Ethiopia (then Abyssinia) in the 1930s (Baudendistel 2005). The organization was not totally neutral during the Cold War, favoring the USA in the Korean War, and France in Southeast Asia during 1947–1954. During the Cold War, indeed from 1917, the ICRC leadership, overlapping with the political elite in Bern, was almost as anticommunist as Bern. There were times, especially during its early history, when it was less than impartial in responding to human distress based on need. In World War I, it gave more attention to the Western front than to other theaters of war. In World War II, it gave more attention to Europe than to the Far East.

Still, we should not establish impossible standards of perfection for organizations, which of course are comprised of fallible human beings. Particularly since 1970, after reviewing its defects in the Nigerian-Biafran conflict, the ICRC has paid careful attention to how to establish and improve a record of independence, neutrality, and impartiality in its humanitarian work. As for independence, it now keeps a greater distance from Bern. Also, the ICRC did not hesitate to oppose the USA, a major donor, over the desirability of an absolute prohibition on the deployment of antipersonnel land mines.[22] While there are always charges of bias in any emotion-laden conflict, one example of the ICRC's neutrality is that it has worked on both sides of the Israeli-Palestinian conflict since 1948 and virtually without interruption since 1967. As for impartiality, when much of the Western press wanted to focus on Afghanistan and Iraq after September 11, 2001, the ICRC tried to remind the international community of pressing humanitarian need elsewhere, as in the Democratic Republic of the Congo.

---

[20] 1906, to Henry Dunant and Fredric Passy; 1917 to the ICRC; 1945 to the ICRC; 1963 to the ICRC and League, now Federation.

[21] See Forsythe (2006).

[22] The ICRC receives about 85% of its approximately $600 million annual budget from state voluntary contributions. The largest donors are the USA, Switzerland, the UK, and the EU. The USA provides about 30% of the total.

At the moment, there is no drive under way to change the mononationality of the ICRC.[23] This is primarily because of the reduced importance of the Committee/Assembly relative to other parts of the house, and because of the organization's mostly impressive record since about 1970.

Red Cross Humanitarianism Today

The ICRC is one of the major humanitarian actors in international relations today by any standard. It is one of the big four relief agencies (the others being the UNHCR, UNICEF, and the World Food Program), operating on a par with these major intergovernmental agencies (Natsios 1997). It achieved this status by 1979–1980 when it teamed with UNICEF, and in some ways was more dynamic than UNICEF, to run a major relief program in Cambodia (and parts of Thailand). To indicate but one aspect of its relief work, the ICRC recently won an award for its efforts regarding prostheses around the world, as it determinedly used its medical relief to cope with the physical and psychological traumas of land mines, unexploded ordinance, and the other after-effects of conflict that continued to maim long after active combat.[24] It is also the premier agency for detention visits around the world regarding international and internal armed conflict and also situations of internal troubles and tensions. And, it still does more than any other agency to restore family ties interrupted by conflict, working often in partnership with various national RC societies.

Two thumbnail sketches indicate its primary and direct contribution to international humanitarianism in conflicts.[25] In Somalia in the early 1990s, when the complexities and brutalities of that failed state led to a situation of massive malnutrition and starvation, the ICRC was central to breaking the back of that humanitarian disaster by 1994. While most UN agencies and NGOs retired to the sidelines, the ICRC stayed in-country despite the dangers and frustrations. For the first time in its long history, it accepted the role of organizing relief efforts under the protection of military forces.[26] Teaming with the Somali Red Crescent, which the ICRC itself rejuvenated and made into an important and reliable partner, it had the best access of any agency to those in dire straits in rural Somalia.

---

[23] The last major effort was after World War II.

[24] The International Society for Prosthetics and Orthotics awarded the Brain Blatchford Prize to the ICRC in 2004 for outstanding service in developing countries. ICRC news release No. 04/91, 6 August 2004.

[25] For detailed treatment, see Forsythe (2006).

[26] At about the same time, in the Balkans, it organized the release and movement of some detainees under the guns of UNPROFOR, the UN security field operation, because of snipers in that area.

It displayed enough size, resources, creativity, and expertise to save perhaps 1.5 million lives in that era. It was not bureaucratic or stodgy. It required the US military and others to keep weapons out of neutralized planes and premises, then turned around and hired local security forces to protect against theft.[27] To reduce theft of rice, which had become the currency of the nation, it provided cooked food in a network of soup kitchens. For a time, faced with kidnappings for ransom, it moved to Nairobi but ran relief convoys under the protection of local Somali groups identified as reliable partners by the Somali Red Crescent. It took journalists at its own expense on tours of the country in order to generate public pressure that could ameliorate the situation. In a setting where almost no one with a weapon had ever heard of international humanitarian law, the ICRC outperformed most others, and certainly the UNHCR, in responding to civilians in extreme distress.

In the US-led "war against terrorism," the ICRC played its usual role with regard to detention visits. The organization was faced with two contradictory policies established by the US government. First, the ICRC was allowed in principle to conduct detention visits at Guantanamo Bay, in Afghanistan, and in Iraq (but was denied access to certain prisoners held secretly either in the USA or in foreign jurisdictions). Second, the USA instituted a policy of coercive or abusive interrogation of certain prisoners deemed to be of high intelligence value (Amnesty International 2004; Hersh 2004; Danner 2004; Greenberg and Dratel, eds. 2004). This policy involved the techniques of terrifying with dogs, removal of clothing, sleep deprivation, subjection to loud noises, and other measures designed to break resistance to interrogation. Some reported measures, such as simulating drowning, clearly amounted to serious violations of human rights and humanitarian law. The other measures were clearly violations of standards against mistreatment. This policy led to the widely publicized abuses at the Abu Ghraib prison in Iraq, where abuse and humiliation occurred unrelated to interrogation. There the policy of selective abuse ran out of control because of insufficient training and supervision.

While asking repeatedly for access to those held in secret, the ICRC reported discreetly to US authorities on what its delegates witnessed. Particularly at Guantanamo, relations became strained between ICRC delegates and prison authorities, because of the ICRC's repeated challenges to prevailing practices. Regarding Guantanamo, and consistent with its doctrine, starting in mid-2003, the ICRC went public with its concern about the effect

---

[27] Contrary to some speculation, the ICRC contribution to the war economy and prolongation of conflict in Somalia was extremely slight.

of indefinite detention without charge or trial on the mental health of detainees.[28] Regarding Guantanamo and Afghanistan, ICRC President Kellenberger went to Washington, DC, and spoke privately with high officials several times. The ICRC at the time of writing had not gone public with regard to detention in Iraq, partly because the scandal about abuse erupted in 2004 through other sources, and partly because the ICRC believed US authorities had shown sufficient will to institute beneficial changes. The ICRC repeatedly commented in public about its lack of access to secret or ghost detainees.

The ICRC largely left to others the public debate about legal issues, preferring to concentrate on practical improvements "on the ground." President Kellenberger did tenaciously continue a private dialogue with various US officials about the protections afforded by IHL, some of which the ICRC believed applied to various detainees held by the USA. At the time of writing, many of these practical and legal matters remained unresolved, with US courts showing less enthusiasm for taking up many issues of prisoner rights in the US "war on terrorism." There remained room for debate about whether the Geneva headquarters had been dynamic enough in making timely representations to high Bush Administration officials about continued mistreatment of prisoners, especially in Guantanamo and Afghanistan, not to mention in the US secret or "black" sites.

There has been persistent controversy and debate about discreet Red Cross neutralism – mainly as practiced by the ICRC. MSF and other agencies have from time to time articulated a more engaged form of humanitarianism, one that, at least theoretically, expresses more solidarity with victims through more public criticism about how victims are created. Yet the ICRC, on the basis of Red Cross discreet neutralism, has carved out an enduring space in international relations. It is worth noting that in Rwanda in 1994, MSF personnel were incorporated into the ICRC delegation, under ICRC rules of engagement, in order to survive.

The Local Roots of Global Humanitarianism

The UN system and the Red Cross network ultimately depend on grassroots attitudes and beliefs, especially in liberal democracies where direct donations and pressure on governments occur. It is the wealthy liberal

---

[28] ICRC doctrine on discretion/publicity is that the organization will make representations about violations of IHL discreetly to authorities and give those authorities reasonable time to make proper changes, but the ICRC reserves the right to go public about violations if proper changes are not made and if such public comment will benefit detainees.

democracies that fund the global humanitarian programs, as well as providing through their governments the leadership and other key elements of those programs. So the real foundations for global humanitarianism are found in Western attitudes and beliefs. (Japan is included in this group for ease of analysis.)

If we focus on Americans as a first step in analysis, we find a population that is woefully ignorant about many aspects of international relations.[29] Long after September 11, 2001, about half of the American public was badly informed about Iraq's lack of weapons of mass destruction and links to Al Qaeda (Hook 2005: 203, 208). Many Americans thought that US foreign assistance was in the range of 5 to 10 percent of gross national product, when in reality development assistance was less than one-tenth of 1 percent, and overall foreign economic assistance was about 1 percent (PIPA 2001). Attitudes were often frivolous. They paid far more attention to the death of British Princess Diana (54 percent said they followed those reports closely in 1997) than Hurricane Mitch, a devastating natural disaster in nearby Central America in 1998 (36 percent) (Pew 2006). Like others, they preferred reports about their own nationals, rather than about foreigners.[30]

On the other hand, there was some good news as well. More of them said they followed reports about the 2004 tsunami in the Indian Ocean (58 percent) than said they had followed reports about Princess Di (54 percent). There was a strong and persistent support (passive support, as measured in attitudinal polls) for doing more about global hunger, poor countries, and women's inequality in those countries, among other subjects sampled (PIPA 2001). Thirty percent of them said they had donated to tsunami relief (and 30 percent more said they planned to do so) (Pew 2006), and more sizable sums of money were raised for private charities doing international relief and development than in any given year or era (Wallace 2006).

A key question was how to take this cosmopolitan compassionate streak in the American public and make it broader, more systematic, and more dependable. The central problem in this regard was that for most Americans, most foreign events, whether from natural disaster or otherwise, did not seem to affect their daily lives. They could pay

[29] This point is part of the conventional wisdom for specialists of US foreign policy. See, for example, Rosati (2004).

[30] Rossmeissl (2006). The same pattern was evident in the UK. See Robinson (2006), commenting on too much coverage of British evacuees.

attention or not, donate or not, follow up with sustained attention or not, and it did not seem to affect them directly and personally. The USA remained a large country with relatively weak and friendly immediate neighbors. Only about 25 percent of its economy was affected by trade, compared to 60 to 80 percent in the European democracies.[31] Most Americans still did not deal with foreign nationals in their daily experiences. What happened abroad might prove temporarily interesting, but it did not affect them in any concrete and meaningful way, requiring sustained attention and involvement. Even after the international terrorism of 9/11, but especially with growing frustration about the war in Iraq, there was an upswing in isolationist sentiment in the United States (Bortin 2005).

Compounding the basic problem was that the commercial communications media in the USA had cut back on international reporting after the Cold War (Moeller 1999). The media chased the financial bottom line as the all-dominating concern, and whenever the national news weeklies carried a cover focusing on international events, sales declined. Coverage of national events was cheaper, and brought in more revenue, than coverage of international events. It was one thing for independent analysts to call for the media to act like public servants and cover international affairs regardless of the bottom line. It was another thing for media executives, dependent on the bottom line, to cover the world as if they were a public corporation with a guaranteed, subsidized existence (Moeller 1999). The BBC might be able to do that, but not Time-Warner.

To the extent that the American society and economy become more globalized, more interdependent with others, both the media and the public might change. When North Americans realized their economies were affected by the SARS epidemic in China, mediated via air travel, serious and sustained attention was paid to that problem on the other side of the world. When West Coast businesses were affected by natural disasters in the Indian Ocean, because parts needed in economic production were not available, sustained attention followed in short order. Morality is nice, but economic self-interest is a very strong motivator for most.[32]

---

[31] Personal calculation by the author.

[32] Relevant is the experience of the former director of Amnesty International USA, who concluded that to get Americans interested in human rights abroad, one had to appeal to their self-interest. See Schulz (2001).

On the other hand, the USA has been interdependent with various oil-producing states for some time now, but there seems little common identity between Americans and citizens of Saudi Arabia, for example.

Still, to the extent that Western societies become economically intertwined with China, India, and other foreign places (which is indeed occurring, even if at differentiated rates and degrees), there is some hope that a stronger transnational compassion may follow. Even in places like Darfur and the Democratic Republic of the Congo, knowledgeable outside parties are interested in certain natural resources. In the Balkans in the 1990s, outside parties like the USA should have recognized certain self-interests at play – for example the fear of forced displacement disrupting allies.

To summarize, there is a compassionate streak in most Western societies. It accounts for the private funding and other civic support that goes to national Red Cross societies and various other NGOs involved in international relief and development. One can hope that the transnational morality at work in such institutions could be broadened and deepened by increased recognition of the self-interested connections linking those societies to the rest of the world.

Conclusion

The UN Secretary-General, as well as the UN Emergency Relief Coordinator, and even various UN agency heads, can articulate the cosmopolitan and liberal view of coherent and consistent global humanitarianism. They can personify the international moral imperative to help strangers. But it is even more important that national public figures make that pitch to the public.[33] The problem, in structural terms, is that top national leaders are there to advance the national interest, not to articulate a global ethic. So, the push for attention to others abroad usually comes from elsewhere – from a Henry Dunant, a Ralph Lemkin, a William Proxmire, an Elie Wiesel.[34]

---

[33] For an argument that public officials determine the national agenda, not the media, see Holm (2002). It is now generally agreed that "the CNN effect" has been generally overstated. It is reasonably clear, however, that media coverage and increased public concern spurred further action by George W. Bush re the 2004 tsunami disaster, not to mention Bill Clinton and the Balkans in 1995 and 1999. Other pressures were also at work, such as critical commentary by foreign parties. The above points are supported by Olsen, (2003).

[34] For the thesis that humanitarian progress is led by individuals who swim against the stream of conventional thought, see Power (2002).

For now at the United Nations, because of state values and power, humanitarian programs are likely to reflect more of an inconsistent humanitarian impulse, affected by political calculation, than a genuine and thus consistent moral imperative. After all, if states want to advance a genuinely neutral and impartial humanitarian endeavor, they can give more resources to the ICRC, although in that case they will lose control of the operation, given the independence of the ICRC. The ICRC remains private, even if recognized in IHL, and its Assembly does not take instruction from public authorities.

One can dwell on the defects of the one remaining superpower or hyperpower, and the USA was certainly slow to act in the Balkans and never acted constructively at the time of the genocide in Rwanda. The USA also misused the humanitarian argument in its invasion of Iraq (Roth 2005). Further, even in the 1999 case of Kosovo, US leadership for action was partially driven by concern for its own reputational costs – its shame at not having acted more effectively in Bosnia earlier (Roberts 2000).[35] Moreover, the George W. Bush administration was slow and relatively miserly in its response to the 2004–2005 tsunami crisis, until UN officials and others gave it reasons to change.[36] But we should recall that the Dutch were not eager to suffer costs for the defense of Srebrenica in the summer of 1995, nor the Belgians for staying the course in Rwanda in early 1994. And when the Japanese did help in Cambodia, or the Australians in East Timor, certain expedient national interests drove those policies as much or more than pure compassion or altruism.[37]

This record but confirms the core point about the continuing weakness of transnational morality. Thick morality reflects nationalism, in that the group of genuine and intense and sustained humanitarian concern is the

---

[35] Worth noting is the fact that even with some Western interest in trying to protect Albanian Kosovars, NATO's high altitude bombing to protect the pilots jeopardized some of the very victims it was intended to benefit.

[36] It is likely that Washington increased its assistance once it realized that it was presented with an opportunity to show Muslim Indonesia and elsewhere that its attacks on Islamic radicals did not preclude positive relations with Islamic communities. Some research shows that US contributions to relief and reconstruction did mitigate anti-American feelings in places like Sri Lanka. See Rajapakasa and Dundes (2006). In general, US decisions about disaster relief are very political. See Drury, Olson, and van Belle (2005).

[37] Among other concerns, the Japanese wanted to show that they deserved a seat on the UN Security Council, and the Australians wanted stability in East Timor in order to staunch a flow of unwanted asylum seekers.

nation, while thin morality continues to characterize reaction to the suffering of "others."

Whether a continuing material globalization will deepen social globalization in the future is an interesting question. Only if more persons identify with foreign suffering, and see that it has relevance to them, morally or expediently, is the situation likely to change. Some social science evidence suggests that when persons view foreign suffering as related to them, either for moral reasons (my own humanity is diminished) or expedient reasons (an abusive or failed state may breed terrorists that may attack me), then one might see the institutionalization of cosmopolitan liberalism through systematic and reliable humanitarianism.[38] If improvement does occur, this is not going to happen tomorrow. Self-interest is likely to be more important than appeals to altruism in effectuating this change. Paradoxically, compassion may be conditioned by self-interest.

Still, there has occurred in bits and pieces, and often at great human cost, a stronger and inherently multilateral humanitarian impulse in the world. The process can certainly be depressing in historical perspective. It took the slaughter of World War I to establish firmly the Red Cross network (even if disjointed), not to mention the 1929 Geneva Convention for Prisoners of War. It took the disaster of World War II to produce the 1949 Geneva Conventions. It took ethnic cleansing and genocide in the Balkans and Rwanda to move the international community toward further hard-headed discussion of what was needed to stop atrocities. Likewise, it took the Asian tsunami disaster to move forward the discussion about a global disaster alert system.[39]

So there has been a certain if costly humanitarian progress. The challenge is to tame the process, which is to say to manage it efficiently, and to make it responsive to the needs and sensitivities of those in dire straits in a timely way. The central challenge comes from the continuing strength of narrow nationalism, and the selfish state power on which it is based, and the inherent difficulty of coordinating diverse if often well-intentioned partners. Progressive national leadership might help strengthen transnational morality, albeit stimulated by self-interest, in the context of economic globalization.

---

[38] See further Monroe (2004); and by the same author, Monroe (1998). And see Held (2004).

[39] I subscribe to the view that it is disasters that shake us out of our routine and compel us to consider alternatives. See further Stoessinger (1994).

REFERENCES

Amnesty International. (2004). "The United States of America: Human Dignity Denied – Torture and Accountability in the 'War on Terror.' Available at http://web.amnesty.org.library/print/ENGAMR511452004.

Beetham, D., ed. (1995). *Politics and Human Rights.* Oxford: Blackwell.

Baudendistel, R. (2005). *Between Bombs and Good Intentions.* New York: Berghahn Books.

Bortin, Meg (2005). "Americans Are More Isolationist, Poll Finds." *International Herald Tribune*, November 18, www.iht.com/bin/print_ipub.php?file=/articles/2005/11/17/pew.php.

Burnett, J. S. (2004). "In the Line of Fire." *New York Times*, August 4, available at www.nytimes.com/2004/08/04/opinion/04burnett.html.

Dallaire, R. A. (1998). "The End of Innocence: Rwanda 1994." In J. Moore, ed., *Hard Choices: Moral Dilemmas in Humanitarian Intervention.* Lanham, MD: Rowan & Littlefield, pp. 71–86.

Danner, M. (2004). *Torture and Truth: America, Abu Ghraib, and the War On Terror.* New York: New York Review Books.

Drury, A. C., R. S. Olson, and D. A. van Belle (2005). "The Politics of Humanitarian Aid: U.S. Foreign Disaster Assistance, 1964–1995." *Journal of Politics*, vol. 67, no. 2, pp. 454–73.

Egeland, J. (2004). "Humanitarianism Under Fire." *Christian Science Monitor*, August 5, available at www.csmonitor.com/2004/0805/p09s01-coop.htm.

Forsythe, D. P. (1995). "Human Rights and US Foreign Policy: Two Levels, Two Worlds." *Political Studies*, vol. XLIII, special issue, pp. 111–30.

———. (2005). *The Humanitarians: The International Committee of the Red Cross.* Cambridge: Cambridge University Press.

———. (2006). "International Humanitarianism in the Contemporary World: Forms and Issues." In E. Newman, R. Chandra, and J. Tirman, eds., *Multilateralism Under Challenge.* Tokyo: UNU Press, pp. 234–58.

Giradet, E. (2004). "A Disaster for Humanitarian Relief." *International Herald Tribune*, August 2, available at www.iht.com/articles/532107.html.

Greenberg, K. J., and J. L. Dratel eds. (2004). *The Torture Papers: The Road to Abu Ghraib.* Cambridge: Cambridge University Press.

Groom, A. J. R., and P. Taylor (2000). "The United Nations System and the Kosovo Crisis." In A. Schnabel and R. Thakur, eds., *Kosovo and the Challenge of Humanitarian Intervention*, Tokyo: UNU Press, pp. 291–318.

Held, David (2004). *Global Covenant: The Social Democratic Alternative to the Washington Consensus* Cambridge: Polity Press.

Hersh, S. (2004). *Chain of Command: The Road from 9/11 to Abu Ghraib.* New York: Harper Collins.

Hoffman, P. J., and T. G. Weiss (2006). *Sword & Salve: Confronting New Wars and Humanitarian Crises.* Lanham/Boulder: Rowman & Littlefield.

Holm, H.-H. (2002). "Failing Failed States: Who Forgets the Forgotten?" *Security Dialogue*, vol. 33, no. 4, pp. 457–71.

Hook, Steven W. (2005). *U.S. Foreign Policy: The Paradox of World Power.* Washington: Congressional Quarterly Press.

Hutchinson, J. F. (1996). *Champions of Charity: War and the Rise of the Red Cross.* Boulder: Westview.

International Commission (2001). *The Responsibility to Protect: Report of the International Commission on Intervention and State Sovereignty.* Ottawa: International Development Research Centre.

International Red Cross and Red Crescent Federation (2004). *World Disasters Report 2003.*

Keohane, R. (2006). "The Contingent Legitimacy of Multilateralism." In E. Newman, R. Chandra, and J. Tirman eds., *Multilateralism Under Challenge.* Tokyo: UNU Press, pp. 56–76.

Krasner, S. D. (1999). *State Sovereignty: Organized Hypocrisy.* Princeton: Princeton University Press.

Loescher, G. (2002). *The UNHCR in World Politics: A Perilous Path.* Oxford/New York: Oxford University Press.

———. (2004). "An Idea Lost in the Rubble." *New York Times,* August 20, p. A25.

Minear, L. (2002). *The Humanitarian Enterprise: Dilemmas and Discoveries.* Bloomfield, CT: Kumarian Press.

Minear, L., T. van Baarda, and M. Sommers (2000). *NATO and Humanitarian Action in the Kosovo Crisis.* Watson Institute for International Studies, Brown University, Occasional Paper no. 36.

Moeller, S. D. (1999). *Compassion Fatigue: How the Media Sell Disease, Famine, War and Death.* New York/London: Routledge.

Monroe, K. R. (1998). *The Heart of Altruism: Perceptions of a Common Humanity.* Princeton: Princeton University Press.

———. (2004). *The Hand of Compassion: Portraits of Moral Choice During the Holocaust.* Princeton: Princeton University Press.

Morehead, C. (1998/1999). *Dunant's Dream: War, Switzerland and the History of The Red Cross.* New York: Harper Collins.

Natsios, A. (1997). *U.S. Foreign Policy and the Four Horseman of the Apocalypse: Humanitarian Relief in Complex Emergencies.* Westport, CT: Greenwood.

Nichols, B., and G. Loescher, eds. (1989). *The Moral Nation: Humanitarianism and U.S. Foreign Policy Today.* South Bend: Notre Dame University Press.

Olsen, G. R. (2003). "Humanitarian Crises: What Determines the Level of Emergency Assistance? Media Coverage, Donor Interests and the Aid Business." *Disasters,* vol. 27, no. 3, pp. 109–26.

Pew Research Center (2006). Reports: Public's Agenda Differs from President's. http:/people_pres.org/reports/display.php3?ReportID=235.

PIPA (2001). *Americans on Foreign Aid and World Hunger: A Study of U.S. Public Attitudes.* Washington: Program on International Policy Attitudes. Available at: http://www.worldpublicopinion.org/pipa/articles/btdevelopmentaidra/135. php?lb=btda&pnt=135&nid=&id&. Last visited May 15, 2008.

Power, S. (2002). *"A Problem from Hell:" America in the Age of Genocide.* New York: Perennial.

Rajapakasa, S., and L. Dundes (2006). "Can Humanitarianism Instill Good Will? American Tsunami Aid and Sri Lankan Reactions." *International Studies Perspective,* vol 7, no. 3, pp. 231–38.

Robinson, J. (2006). "As Lebanon Sinks into the Ground." *Observer,* July 23, p. 8.

Rosati, J. A. (2004). *The Politics of the United States Foreign Policy.* Third edn. Belmont, CA: Thomson/Wadsworth.

Rossmeissl, R. (2006). "U.S. Media Places Higher Value on Americans' Lives than Foreigners'." *Wisconsin Badger Herald,* February 22, p. 1.

Roberts, A. (2000). "NATO's 'Humanitarian War' Over Kosovo." In L. Minear, T. van Baarda, and M. Sommers, eds., *NATO and Humanitarian Action in the Kosovo Crisis.* Occasional Paper no. 36, Watson Institute, Brown University, pp. 121–51.

Roth, K. (2005). "Was the Iraq War a Humanitarian Intervention?" In Richard Ashby Wilson, ed., *Human Rights in the "War on Terror."* Cambridge: Cambridge University Press, pp. 143–56.

Schulz, W. F. (2001). *In Our Own Best Interest: How Defending Human Rights Benefits US All.* Boston: Beacon.

Shawcross, W. (1984). *The Quality of Mercy: Cambodia, Holocaust and Modern Conscience.* New York: Simon & Schuster.

Skran, C. (1995). *Refugees in Inter-War Europe.* Oxford: Oxford University Press.

Stephens, L. H., and S. J. Green, eds. (1979). *Disaster Assistance: Appraisal, Reform, & New Approaches.* New York: New York University Press.

Stephens, T. W. (1978). *The United Disaster Relief Office: The Politics and Administration of International Relief Assistance.* Washington, DC: University Press of America.

Stoessinger, J. G. (1994). *Nations in Darkness, Nations at Dawn.* Sixth edn, New York: McGraw Hill.

United Nations Office for the Coordination of Humanitarian Affairs (2004). *The Humanitarian Decade: Challenges for Humanitarian Assistance in the Last Decade and into the Future.* Vols. I and II, New York: United Nations.

Wallace, N. (2006). "International Groups See Revenue Jump." *Chronicle of Philanthropy,* vol. 18, no. 10, p. 17.

Weiss, T. G. (2004). "The Humanitarian Impulse." In D. Malone, ed., *The U.N. Security Council: From the Cold War to the 21st Century.* Boulder: Lynne Rienner, pp. 37–54.

———. (2006). "Using Military Force for Humanitarian Protection: What Next?" In E. Newman, R. Chandra, and J. Tirman eds., *Multilateralism Under Challenge.* Tokyo: UNU Press, pp. 376–94.

Weiss, T. G., D. P. Forsythe, and R. A. Coate (2004). *The United Nations and Changing World Politics.* Fourth edn. Boulder: Westview.

3. Humanitarian Reading

JOSEPH R. SLAUGHTER

When two elephants are fighting,
  (The grass dem' a-suffer)
Which is the position of the civilian?
      Sierra Leone's Refugee All-Stars, "Weapon Conflict"

The Rights of Man: or, What Are We Reading For?

In the early months of World War II, British novelist H. G. Wells posed the question "What are we fighting for?" in an open letter to the "Atlantic Parliamentary peoples" published in the London *Times*. Challenging Prime Minister Neville Chamberlain to give some account of British "War Aims," Wells offered his own *peace* aims, in the form of an international "Declaration of Rights" – a "broad principle[d]" plan that would constitute the "fundamental law" upon which "our public and social life is [to be] based" in a "new World Order" (1940: 29–30, 12). "[W]e need," he writes, "another fundamental assertion of the supremacy of the claims of the common man against any privilege, pre-emption or government whatever ... [that] will involve an ultimate repudiation of violence and warfare from end to end of the earth" (1940: 29). After laying out his decalogue for a "new phase" of man, Wells concluded with a general appeal to the leaders of Atlantic democracies, asking them, not wholly rhetorically: "Is this what we are fighting for? And if not, then please tell us what you imagine we *are* fighting for?" (1940: 29–30).

Wells was updating a classical ideal that seems to be native to most (if not all) human moral and cultural traditions: war should only be prosecuted in the name of, and for the ends of, peace. For Wells, this is not just any peace, but a perpetual international peace characterized and guaranteed by the universal observance and enjoyment of human rights. A version

88

of Wells' humanitarian war aims were formalized in international law with the adoption of the Universal Declaration of Human Rights (UDHR) by the United Nations General Assembly in 1948, which sought to bring about "the advent of a world in which human beings shall enjoy freedom of speech and belief and freedom from fear and want [that] has been proclaimed as the highest aspiration of the common people."

Just as that which we call human rights is the law not of individuals but of peoples, or nations (*jus gentium*), humanitarian law is the law not of peace but of war. It is the collection of international legal agreements that seek to civilize war, to make war humane. The displacement of war by peace is a humanitarian ideal that abides the logic of humanitarian reversal, whereby conditions of suffering and privation are transformed into states of tranquility and well-being. In this regard, Wells' provocation to the parliamentary peoples anticipates something of the logic of muscular humanitarianism that emerged in the wake of the Cold War and prepared the way for the cynical deployment of humanitarian rhetoric in the so-called "War on Terror." Under this militarized version of the "new humanitarianism," which authorizes the use of force in the pursuit of humanitarian aims, "avenging angels" distribute death and deliverance simultaneously (Herman and Peterson 2002).[1] "Smart bombs" alternate with "literature drops," and both promise to liberate the "common people" from fear and want.

My substitution of "reading" for "fighting" in Wells' poignant question reenacts the logic of supplementation and reversal by which humanitarianism operates, and it will prove, I hope, less capricious than it may at first seem – not merely the predictable elevation of reading, literacy, and literature to the status of warfare (or to the level of international relations) by a professional reader and teacher of comparative literature.[2] Indeed, the substitution of reading for fighting is a humanitarian displacement; it captures the liberal ideal of reading as an alternative to belligerent activity that promotes, in the language of UNESCO's *Charter of the Book*, "international understanding and peaceful cooperation" (Barker & Escarpit

---

[1] See also Rieff (2002); Kennedy (2004); Douzinas (2007). The "new humanitarianism" emerged with the decline of the welfare state in the countries of "the Atlantic parliamentary peoples." Indeed, it has a parallel in the new domestic policies of the traditional social democracies, where the welfare state has largely been replaced by what I call the humanitarian state: basic social, civil, and economic entitlements once conceived of as human rights are now construed as voluntary expressions of the state's humanitarian benevolence.

[2] I have argued elsewhere that this humanitarian substitution is a primary goal of international human rights law generally. See especially Slaughter (2007: ch. 5).

1973: 155). Time and again, over the *longue durée* of the Enlightenment (what has also been described by Richard Rorty as the period of sentimental progress), reading has been promoted as a benign alternative to fighting – reading, at both its most basic level (the acquisition of functional literacy) and at the macro-scale of *Weltliteratur*, promoted by avid readers like Goethe, Marx, and Engels to transcend "[n]ational one-sidedness and narrow-mindedness" (Marx & Engels 1975: 37–8). Twentieth-century internationalism sought to give this cosmopolitan ideal some formal, institutional expression. It spurred, for instance, the translation projects of the International Institute of Intellectual Cooperation under the League of Nations, which comprised part of a cultural program to cultivate what Paul Valéry called a "League of Minds" (1993). It also provided the spiritual force driving the mass literacy campaigns of the mid-twentieth century, which followed UNESCO's dramatic declaration in 1947 of a full-scale humanitarian "war on ignorance," a global "attack on illiteracy" necessitated, in UNESCO's judgment, by the "threat" that illiteracy posed to the "peace and security" of the literate (UNESCO 1947: 1. vii).

"To live in a library," writes Gianni Vattimo, capitalizing on the etymological link between liberty and *libri* in the Romance languages, "is perhaps the image itself of perfection, of humanism, of the experience of the truth which renders us ... free" (2001: 69). To live without a library, then, is a case for humanitarian intervention. In a globalized "information society," teaching someone to read and write may still represent the quintessential act of humanitarianism. All of these secular expressions of faith in reading share a foundational assumption about the intrinsic relation between literacy and liberty. This liberal ideal was revived and given renewed philosophical vigor during the so-called "Culture Wars" of the 1980s and 1990s by public intellectuals such as Richard Rorty, Martha Nussbaum, and K. Anthony Appiah. These thinkers advocate models of sentimental and cosmopolitan reading that ask readers to enter into imaginative relations of identification with what Rorty generically describes as "people very unlike us" (1993: 77). In this chapter, I elaborate a model of humanitarian reading that tends to be overlooked by philosophers who consistently pose the question of humanitarian sentiment as a problem of what Elaine Scarry calls "generous imagining," a problem of the reader's imaginative identification with the suffering individual. Such models "allow the fate of another person to be contingent on the generosity and wisdom of the imaginer" (Scarry 2002: 106). My model is drawn primarily from a reading of J. Henry Dunant's *Un Souvenir de Solférino* (*A Memory of Solferino*, 1862), which is one of the most objectively successful of humanitarian interventionist narratives in history, precipitating both the incorporation of the Red Cross and the first Geneva Convention for the Amelioration of the Condition of the Wounded and Sick in Armed Forces in the Field.

Imaginative Models of Sentimental Reading

[T]he average Western observer cannot be expected to "identify" with a starving African child, in the sense of being able to imagine herself in the place of the other.
(Cohen 2001: 183)

The link between literature and humanitarianism has an august, if perhaps apocryphal, place in the Greco-Judeo-Christian tradition. To impress his civility upon his vanquished subjects during his conquest of Greece in the fourth century BCE, Philip II of Macedonia, whom Demosthenes consistently characterizes as a "barbarian" in his *Philippics*, reputedly liberated prisoners of war who could recite Homer (Bennett 2005: ix). In this exemplum of humanitarian mercy, Homer's epic poems of war, suffering, rape, and the other violent events that historically constitute the making of a people (a nation) serve as a literary litmus test for distinguishing between the civilized and the barbarians, between people like and unlike the Greeks. Reading or, more precisely, recitation poses an alternative to death and a means for claiming a right of belonging to the new polity. Less spectacular connections between literature and humanitarianism are usually explained in terms of literature's salutary effects on the sympathetic imagination, what Martha Nussbaum calls the "narrative imagination." "[N]arrative art," she writes, "has the power to make us see the lives of the different with more than a casual tourist's interest – with involvement and sympathetic understanding" (1997: 88). In his Oxford Amnesty lecture of 1993, Richard Rorty commended the literary "manipulation of sentiment" as a practical way of doing international relations. Rorty invests transnational reading with the capacity "to expand the reference of the terms 'our kind of people' and 'people like us'" (1993: 74). Thus, it is through reading or "hearing sad and sentimental stories" that "sympathy" is historically cultivated ("manipulated") in such a way as to "have induced us, the rich, safe, powerful, people, to tolerate, and even to cherish, powerless people – people," Rorty clarifies, "whose appearance or habits or beliefs at first seemed an insult to our own moral identity, our sense of the limits of permissible human variation" (80).

These sentimental models of reading are imagined to have a double benefit – for the reader and for the subjects of the stories being read; thus, such reading practices are supposed to "cultivat[e] our humanity" (in Nussbaum's words), and to make us "see the similarities between ourselves and people very unlike us as outweighing the differences" (for Rorty), which in turn expands the affective and effective compass of the category of "humanity" itself (Nussbaum 1997: 10; Rorty 1993: 77). These paeans to the power of literature construct what Scarry calls "a framework of cosmopolitan largesse that relies on the population to spontaneously and generously 'imagine' other persons" (2002: 98). This literary imaginative faculty becomes the primary mechanism for a velvet revolutionary establishment of an imaginary international domain in which we participate as "citizens of the world" through storytelling and story-listening that would obviate precisely the sorts of violence historically associated with the founding of a republic, a people. That is, sentimental reading practices would replace fighting in the formation of imagined communities. Stories of suffering thus become primers for the "exercise" of our "citizenship of the world," for the sentimental cultivation of "*our* moral community," and for the training of our sympathetic, moral imaginations (Appiah 2003: 201; Rorty 1993: 75). "By 'sympathy,'" writes Rorty, "I mean the sort of reaction that the Athenians had more of after seeing Aeschylus' *The Persians* than before, the sort that white Americans had more of after reading *Uncle Tom's Cabin* than before, the sort that we have more of after watching TV programmes about the genocide in Bosnia" (1993: 128).

These human rights literacy projects are largely models for peacetime reading, for maintaining the peace and preventing war. In our contemporary idiom, we might say that these are models of preemptory reading, literary doctrines for a sentimental first strike, that do not seem to work so well during wartime, when collective sympathy of the "powerful" for the "powerless" does not seem equally excited by watching programs about the genocide in Darfur, or the daily, normalized sufferings of people in Iraq and the West Bank, as it does by watching a Hollywood film about the genocide in Rwanda ten years after such sympathies might have been actionable. These ethically ambitious models of imaginative identification with the suffering of people unlike us often distract from more common strategies of the narrative manipulation of sentiment employed in films like *Hotel Rwanda*, which asks its audience to identify not with the dead and dying but with the survivors of genocide who themselves, unlike the UN and the rest of the powerful and sympathetic "people like us," responded with compassion for their fellow human beings.

Rorty's and Nussbaum's models of cosmopolitan reading revive the problem of ethics as a problem of imagination that Adam Smith theorized in 1759. "By the imagination," wrote Smith in the opening chapter of *The Theory of Moral Sentiments*,

> we place ourselves in his situation, we conceive ourselves enduring all the same torments, we enter as it were into his body, and become in some measure the same person with him, and thence form some idea of his sensations, and even feel something which, though weaker in degree, is not altogether unlike them. His agonies ... are thus brought home to ourselves, ... adopted and made ... our own. (Smith 2002: 12)

In Smith's description, imaginative identification is not merely a matter of evoking an observer's pity and compassion for the sufferer; it verges on empathy – an imaginative act of self-substitution, a projection of the self into the grammatical position of the subject who suffers. In Nussbaum and Rorty, this model of sentimental identification becomes a form of narrative empathy, "the ability to imagine what it is like to be in [another] person's place" (Nussbaum 1997: 90–1). The relation of the observer (or reader) to the sufferer in these models is metaphorical, or poetic. By contrast, the model of imaginative identification that I explore in Dunant's *A Memory of Solferino* is metonymical, or prosaic: it seeks to reconfigure the relations between the reader-observer and the sufferer as metonymical connections of contiguity between one part of humanity and another.

Humanitarian Interventionist Narrative: A Souvenir from Solferino

17 June 1863: Read the *Souvenir de Solférino* by the Swiss doctor Dunant. These pages carry me away with feeling. ... It is more beautiful, a thousand times more beautiful, than Homer. ... One leaves this book with a curse on war.

> Review in the *Journal* of Edmond and Jules de Goncourt[3]

On 24 June 1859, the Austrian army and the combined forces of France and Sardinia surprised each other at Solferino, in what became the largest and bloodiest battle of the Austro-Sardinian War, the Second War of Italian Independence. In a single day, the vicious fighting left more than 30,000 wounded, many of whom would die slow, horrible, unnecessary deaths due to inadequate provisions and insufficient medical care. The unification of Italy, or the *Risorgimento*, had become a cause célèbre among many European and American intellectuals and artists, and the brutalities inflicted and suffered at Solferino in the name of founding a modern nation-state were already legendary by the time that J. Henry

---

[3]   Cited in Dunant (1939: 7).

Dunant published *Un Souvenir de Solférino* in 1862. If the nation is a
political and sentimental unit in which "we participate through
synecdoche" (as a part to the whole), the rhetorical task of cosmopolitanism and the humanitarian imagination is, as Dunant understood it, to
reconfigure the banal metaphorical analogies between people like and
unlike us (between the self and the other) as metonymical relations of
contiguity that are not based on national belonging (Appiah 2003: 197).

On 24 June, Dunant, a Swiss entrepreneur returning from Algeria in
search of Napoleon III's assistance in rescuing his failing colonial agricultural venture, stumbled into the Battle of Solferino.[4] As the fighting wound
down for the evening, Dunant, some of the other tourists, and the local
population began to provide what comfort they could to the dying soldiers.
Over the next week, Dunant helped to coordinate a relief effort. Three years
later, Dunant self-published 1,600 copies of *Un Souvenir de Solférino*, which
quickly "ploughed a furrow of horror across the sensibilities of many of its
readers" (Dunant 1939: 5). The official response was the convening of two
conferences in Geneva in 1863 and 1864, at which Dunant and some of his
well-placed readers from sixteen European states drafted the first Geneva
Convention that enshrined the humanitarian principles of the newly
founded International Committee of the Red Cross and made it the cus-
todian of the new laws of war.

Dunant's narrative exemplifies the logic of a kind of grammatical
empathy that invites us to project ourselves not into the position of the
sufferer but into the position of the humanitarian, the subject position of
one who already recognizes the human dignity of the wounded and
attempts to relieve their suffering. As opposed to the metaphoric configuration of sympathetic imagination in Smith, Nussbaum, and Rorty,
this affective identification with the humanitarian aid worker is metonymical, constructed through a chain of substitutions that ultimately
links the reader with Dunant. There is a certain formal symmetry to
Dunant's narrative. It begins by describing the general savagery and chaos
of modern warfare, the steadily accumulating masses of the dead, the
unrelieved torments of the dying, and the haphazard, spontaneous efforts
by Dunant and other tourists to relieve some of the suffering; it concludes
with a modest but motley organization of volunteers who work together
to minister to the wounded. Dunant creates an analogy between warfare
and humanitarianism; "what an attraction it would be for noble and
compassionate hearts and for chivalrous spirits, to confront the same

---

[4] See Moorehead (1998: 6–12). On Dunant's implication in French imperialism, see (Pous 1979).

dangers as the warrior ... in a spirit of peace, for a purpose of comfort" (1939: 87). The fighting commences with well-ordered troops that disaggregate and disintegrate in the mayhem of battle. Humanitarian relief, by contrast, emerges from "dispersed" and isolated individual efforts that progressively achieve a kind of chaotic coherence with the assistance of the local women of Lombardy, returning the wounded men to something like their original regimented state as they lie in columns of improvised convalescent beds (47). The martial analogy and the narrative symmetry are, however, imperfect and incomplete: the regiments of "chivalrous spirits" never materialize in sufficient, organized numbers to keep step with and offset the military regiments. This narrative incompletion underscores the fact that the final term in the humanitarian chiasmus is missing; "What was needed," Dunant concludes, "was not only weak and ignorant women, but, with them and beside them, kindly experienced men, capable, firm, already organized, and in sufficient numbers to get to work at once in an orderly fashion" (89–90).

Dunant seeks to imprint the inglorious image of the disfigured, suffering soldier on the collective European social and moral conscience to marshal humanitarian sentiment in favor of the creation of "permanent societies of volunteers which in time of war would render succor to the wounded without distinction of nationality" (7). Thus, he appeals to a transcendental, or more precisely a transnational, sense of common humanity – "*tutti fratelli*," as the famous refrain is sung by the compassionate "girls of Castiglione" (54). Such cosmopolitan fellow feeling matches the indifference and disregard for nationality that suffering and death themselves displayed on the battlefield. Dunant's ideal relief worker is not only indifferent to nations and nationalism, but, more stunningly perhaps, necessarily indifferent to "scenes of pain and distress": "There is no more grieving at the multiple scenes of this fearful and solemn tragedy. There is indifference as one passes even before the most frightfully disfigured corpses. There is something akin to cold calculation, in the face of horrors yet more ghastly than those here described, and which the pen absolutely declines to set down" (55).[5] Rather than an imaginative identification with the agonies of the other, a certain indifference to difference is the practical humanitarian disposition.

Dunant's humanitarian indifference translates into, and is reinforced by, the form and style of his narrative. Since the first printing of *Un Souvenir de Solférino*, readers have praised its classical elegance and its

---

[5] The trope of unwritable, or unspeakable, horrors seems primarily rhetorical, given the text's graphic nature.

aesthetics of suffering. A review in the pages of the *Journal* of the Goncourt brothers (those avid promoters of French naturalism, whose names would later become synonymous with "the best and most imaginative" prose written in French, through the *Prix Goncourt*) gushed about the book: "It is the sublime touching the depths of one's being. It is more beautiful, a thousand times more beautiful, than Homer, than the *Retreat of the Ten Thousand*, than anything. ... It is the truth about the living, about the mutilated, about those dying by violence in the prime of life, about everything described in rhetoric since the world began" (Dunant 1939: 7). Both formally and thematically, Homer is an appropriate comparison. Like the oral formulaic phrasings of the *Iliad*, or "the poem of force" (as Simone Weil described it in her own humanitarian appeal at the height of World War II), *A Memory of Solferino* deploys a few narrative phrasings for the depiction of human suffering, narrative expressions of force that are repeated with small modifications over the course of the text. Force, writes Weil, "is that x that turns anybody who is subjected to it into a *thing*" (1956: 3). For Weil, the *Iliad* demonstrates "the petrificative quality of force" equally on its objects and on those who wield it, and she urges readers to relearn the epic's humanitarian lessons: "learn that there is no refuge from fate, learn not to admire force, not to hate the enemy, nor to scorn the unfortunate" (27, 37).

In the *Iliad*, force manifests itself alike among the Greeks as among the Trojans: "We are all held in a single honour," says Achilles to Odysseus, "the brave with the weaklings. / A man dies still if he has done nothing, as one who has done much" (Lattimore 1951: IX 319–20). From a literary standpoint, Achilleus is not quite correct; death comes to the lesser and major warriors equally and in the same forms, but the minor figures tend to die in three or four lines, compared to the dozen or more lines needed to take out the major figures. Homer's narrative formulae of the indifference of death operate through repetition and substitution; the following is one statement in a series:

> Idomeneus stabbed Erymas in the mouth with the pitiless
> bronze, so that the brazen spearhead smashed its way clean through
> below the brain in an upward stroke, and the white bones splintered,
> and the teeth were shaken out with the stroke and both eyes filled up
> with blood, and gaping he blew a spray of blood through the nostrils
> and through his mouth, and death in a dark mist closed in about him
>
> (XVI.345–50)

This is a single variation of the five-line death sentences for minor figures in the Trojan war that repeat throughout the epic. The victims and killers change; there are a number of possible weapons, whose entrance and exit points have a dozen or so possible locations, but in the end the life force escapes the body as death closes around the warrior and he becomes a thing, a corpse. The rhetorical effect of these serial killings is the creation of a kind of egalitarian imaginary of blood-soaked eyes that transcends nationality. Poetically and physically, death in the *Iliad* treats men of like rank alike.

The petrificative effects of Iliadic war are repeated thematically in Dunant's narrative, but his writing also translates the thingifying quality of force into formal and grammatical effects of his narrative formulae; thus, he transforms the military units (the agents and objects of suffering) into pure grammatical units, parts of speech that may carry any number of referents. Dunant's formulaic narrative phrasings are largely indifferent to individual subjective differences between people; whereas Homer maintains a place in his narrative grammar of fighting and dying for the genealogies of some of his actors, Dunant generally abstracts the grammar of death to a level of indifference that excludes such biographical particulars and proper names.

Nevertheless, like the *Iliad*, *A Memory of Solferino* constructs its meaning through two primary rhetorical operations, or tropes: repetition and substitution. Dunant's formulaic phrasings are self-contained units of meaning that are as repetitive and regular as both the regimented troops of soldiers whose sufferings he describes and the well-ordered corps of relief workers whose absence he laments. These formulaic narrative sequences establish a rhythm for the battle and a regularized syntax for the expression of the text's main themes: the beastliness of war, the unnecessary torments of the wounded, the emergence of humanitarian sensibility, and the urgent need for organized relief societies.

To illustrate these narrative patterns, I draw from a passage appearing early in *A Memory of Solferino*. Coming upon the battlefield, Dunant surveys the horrors of war with a panoramic representation of the scene of fighting, in which one of Dunant's narrative formulae repeats in rapid succession (for easier analysis, I have italicized the primary subjects and underscored the key objects of violence):

> *Austrians and Allies* trampling each other under foot, killing <u>one another</u> on <u>piles of bleeding corpses</u>, felling their enemies with their rifle butts, crushing skulls, ripping bellies open with sabre and bayonet. No quarter is given; it is a sheer butchery; a struggle between savage beasts, maddened with blood and fury. ...
>
> A little further on, it is the same picture, only made the more ghastly by the approach of *a squadron of cavalry*, which gallops by, crushing <u>dead and dying</u>

beneath its horses' hoofs. One poor wounded man has his jaw carried away; another his head shattered; a third, who could have been saved, has his chest beaten in . . . .

Here come *the artillery*, following the cavalry, and going at full gallop. *The guns* crash over the <u>dead and wounded</u>, strewn pell-mell on the ground. <u>Brains</u> spurt under the wheels, <u>limbs</u> are broken and torn, <u>bodies mutilated past recognition</u> – the soil is literally puddled with <u>blood</u>, and the plain littered with <u>human remains</u>. (Dunant 1939: 20–1)

This battle scene sets up the inhumanity of war as a problem for humanitarianism, but it also already presages something of the affective disposition required to approach the wounded as the wheels of the artillery do – with complete indifference to nationality. The sense of the beastliness of war, of its dehumanizing force, is expressed not just through the accumulation of grotesque details; it is also transmitted through the repetition of narrative formulae that establishes a generalized grammar of warfare and death. The basic formula of killing and trampling remains the same in each of its iterations, but its subjects and objects change. The soldiers are twice dehumanized – as killers and killed; they become beastly killing machines, but they also become inhuman as they fall victims to death and are "mutilated past recognition."

The full sequence of these death sentences narrates the transformation of Austrians and Allies into human remains; that transformation is effected by the shifting of Austrians and Allies down a grammatical chain from subject to object to indirect object. In other words, the Austrians and Allies, who initially perform the killing and trampling of each other in their capacities as arms of the nation, become the denationalized "dead and dying" objects of killing and trampling, until they are ground into the landscape and become part of "the plain littered with human remains." At the beginning of the passage, Austrians and Allies are equally likely to kill and to die. As these narrative statements of war's inhumanity repeat, the human beings are demoted in grammatical rank to the indirect objects of "piles of bleeding corpses." The killers become the objects of slaughter, which in turn become the indirect objects of the artillery as it indiscriminately crushes the wounded. A similar rhetorical process of dehumanization and objectification (or mechanization) occurs in the subject position of these narrative formulae; the Austrians and Allies are replaced as the agents of killing and trampling by a "squadron of cavalry" – a feral behemoth devoid of human beings and feelings – which is itself relieved in the narrative formula by the artillery and guns – infernal machines that disfigure the bodies and heads of the dead and dying indiscriminately.

The movement down the narrative chain of death emphasizes the metonymical character of the displacement from human to human remains (in the case of the wounded) and from human to mechanical guns (in the case of the agents of force). The rhetorical process of disfigurement (the undoing, or dehumanization, of the subjects of warfare) parallels the physical disfigurement of the dead that transforms them into nothing more than things that remain after war. In the narrative grammar of war, each man is equally susceptible to the indignities of suffering and death, but, according to the indifferent logic of humanitarian substitution, each also has a legitimate claim on the humanitarian's sympathy. In Dunant's narrative, the task of humanitarianism involves both the physical and rhetorical rehabilitation of the wounded; that is, the humanitarian imagination must rehumanize the disfigured masses as objects of sympathy and as possible subjects of well-being before humanitarian relief can be administered.

The narrative sequences that relate war's barbarity are eventually displaced by formulaic sequences that describe the unnecessary suffering of wounded soldiers, the emergence of humanitarian sensibility, and the ameliorative effects of humanitarian assistance. The narrative paradigm of unrelieved suffering gives way to a series of statements that demonstrate the effects of timely and coordinated humanitarian aid, which ignores the prejudicial claims of nationalism and that restores the disfigured masses to both health and individuality – men with distinct genealogies and biographies: "the Austrian Prince [of Isenberg] was discovered among the dead bodies, wounded and unconscious from loss of blood. But he was immediately treated by the French surgeon and was eventually able to go home to his family" (39). Rhetorically, the narrative formula of successful humanitarian intervention serves a more important function than bringing the dying back to life and back to the subject position of statements such as "small detachments of convalescent French soldiers ... [set] off along the Turin road" (82). In these narrative sequences, the agent of humanitarian assistance becomes simply a position in a grammar of relief that may be occupied by anyone who disregards nationality in the face of human suffering. Over the course of the series of humanitarian statements, Dunant is replaced as the subject of benevolence first by groups of tourists, then by the anonymous women of Castiglione, and later by philanthropists who answer the call for assistance.

There is, however, a transitional formula between suffering and relief that narrates the emergence on the scene of the humanitarian subject who attends the wounded. These sequences that narrate the awakening of the humanitarian imagination depict a figure that wends its way through the piles of dying soldiers, delicately stepping among the bodies, perhaps doing little good but taking pains to do no harm; the humanity and dignity of the wounded are impressed upon the mind of the observer and acknowledged in some relatively minor but significant way. These recognition scenes are introduced in sequences that relate partisan and professional acts of compassion: "The canteen women moved about the field under enemy fire like the soldiers. . . . lifting their heads and giving them drink as they cried piteously for water" (28).

As a "mere tourist with no part whatever in this great conflict," Dunant presents himself as an accidental paragon of humanitarian disinterestedness and indifference, whose only distinction is the "rare privilege" to have "witness[ed] the moving scenes" in person (17). In a sense, accidental tourism is the existential condition that makes it possible for Dunant (and some of the other cosmopolitan tourist volunteers) to move indifferently among the wounded; indeed, the kind of empathy that *A Memory of Solferino* solicits may require no more than a mere tourist's attention and affection. Reflecting self-consciously on the story grammar of humanitarian awakening, Dunant describes the winding path of his journeys among the wounded in terms of a disturbing dilemma of indifference:

> you can never do more than help those who are just before you . . . . When you start to go somewhere, it is hours before you get there, for you are stopped by one begging for help, then by another, held up at every step by the crowd of poor wretches who press before and about you. Then you find yourself asking: "Why go to the right, when there are all these men on the left who will die without a word of kindness or comfort, without so much as a glass of water to quench their burning thirst?" (55)

Humanitarian indifference dictates the random, but careful, path of the aid worker through the masses of wounded men, and the narrative suggests that anyone who exhibits similar pity and compassion for the sufferings of others will discover a similar route. Thus, "[t]he women of Castiglione, seeing that I made no distinction between nationalities, followed my example," weaving "from one man to another with jars and canteens full of pure water to quench their thirst and moisten their wounds" (54, 49).

The substitutions that occur in the subject position of this narrative sequence of humanitarian recognition replace the isolated efforts of individuals with improvised groups of women and tourists working in chaotic concert, but the series is incomplete, due to the lack of a critical mass of trained relief workers to counterbalance the piles of dying soldiers. The final replacements that are formally anticipated by the sequence are marked as an absence that is both physical and rhetorical, brought home to the reader in a series of apostrophic questions that conclude the narrative: "in an age when we hear so much of progress and civilization, is it not a matter of urgency, since unhappily we cannot always avoid wars, to press forward in a human and truly civilized spirit the attempt to prevent, or at least to alleviate, the horrors of war?" (94). Dunant's questions assume that we will *pity* the sufferer, but the narrative invites us to *empathize* with the humanitarian, with one who, indifferent to nationality, seeks to relieve the torments of the *défigurés*.

The Third Actor in the Drama of Suffering

A simple tourist, entirely stranger to and disinterested in the mighty struggle, [M. Dunant] .... did not quit the theatre at the fall of the curtain .... He remained on the spot with a heroism far greater than that of the fiercest combatant, tending and consoling, to the utmost of his strength, the disabled actors in the bloody tragedy.

Charles Dickens, "The Travelling Amateur"[6]

Theatrical metaphors are commonly deployed to euphemize warfare, as if, because war is supposed to be prosecuted in the service of peace, the fighting is merely a diversion from the pacific norm, a spectacle staged for the (eventual) benefit of the noncombatants, an audience of civilians. Dunant's narrative plots the story of the Battle of Solferino as a drama in which the theater of military operations is transformed into a theater of medical operations – still a theater "of fighting" and suffering, but of fighting for life and humane suffering: of lifegiving amputations and blood-lettings, consolatory letter writing, and "reading to wounded men" (Dunant 1939: 13, 82). In a sense, *A Memory of Solferino* turns the *Iliad* into a prologue for the "age of the 'French doctors,'" an era when the humanitarian volunteer, "half-amateur and half-expert," appeared on the international stage as both an actor and a narrator in the drama of human suffering (Brauman 1993: 153). Charles Dickens emphasized precisely this technical intervention in the conventional war story in reviews of Dunant's book, praising Dunant for having quit the relative safety of his seat in the audience and having mounted the stage to assist the "disabled actors in the bloody tragedy."

In the *Poetics*, Aristotle credits Sophocles with having introduced a third actor to the Athenian tragic stage; with the innovation of the "dramatic triangle," Greek tragedy is said to have achieved its most perfect, powerful, and complex form (Knox 1972: 106). The introduction of a third speaking

---

[6] Reprinted in Bennett (2005: 212).

actor not only heightens the drama's pathos by giving the audience the image of a surrogate witness to the tragic events, it also triangulates the lines of affective force between audience and actors. In other words, the third actor is typically both a participant in the apparent tragedy and a screen for the projection of the audience's pity and compassion. Dunant's narrative innovation functions similarly, completing the dramatic triangle of savage-victim-savior, the "three-dimensional compound metaphor" that sustains narratives of humanitarian intervention (Mutua 2002: 10). Dunant's third actor not only heightens the tragedy of war, it introduces the figure of the humanitarian into the intersubjective, two-dimensional drama of imaginative identification scripted by Adam Smith and resuscitated by Rorty and Nussbaum. This humanitarian figure is an intermediary between ourselves and the ones who suffer, acting as a conduit for our emotional investments in the scene of suffering and establishing "both distance and a link between the spectator and the victim," as Rony Brauman writes of the rhetorical strategies employed by *Médecins Sans Frontières* for turning "an upheaval into an international event" (Brauman 1993: 150). If we are to project ourselves into the humanitarian scenario of *A Memory of Solferino*, it is not in the place of the dead and dying – those mutilated masses of disfigured humanity that are not, on the surface of things, very much like us, the rich, safe, powerful people. Rather, the narrative invites us to imagine ourselves in the place of the humanitarian subject who is already the best of "our kind of [philanthropic] people."

The triangulation of humanitarian sentiment begs the question of first causes, or first affects, since it sidesteps the problem "of picturing other persons in their full weight and solidity" by supplying a surrogate on which to anchor our feelings of goodwill towards the wounded (Scarry 2002: 98). However, the affective structure of the humanitarian triangle implicitly recognizes the philosophical and practical limits of our generous imaginings, our historically feeble capacity to imagine ourselves in the place of the suffering other. Dunant's narrative suggests that we may delude ourselves quixotically, or congratulate ourselves prematurely, when we imagine ourselves as "righters of wrongs" ("*desfacedores de agravios*," as Cervantes has it) who have entered into relations of imaginative identification with others who are suffering. The act of imagination that *A Memory of Solferino* solicits is more modest, and perhaps more realistic than those advocated by Rorty and Nussbaum. Part of what is modified by the introduction of a third actor to the humanitarian scenario is the metaphorical feat of imaginative identification with the sufferer. It transforms and reroutes that pathetic force into a metonymical relation between the reader and the humanitarian figure who is an exemplary extension of our better angels.[7]

The other imagined through the humanitarian dramatic triangle is not the absolute other: it is precisely the reader's peers, which suggests that humanitarian sentiment may be an effect of the reader imagining that people like him or her are (or should) be moved by tales of suffering. In other words, the sense of ethical obligation perhaps develops not in response to another's tragedy but as a sense of responsibility to the moral integrity of one's own class of humanity. This is, at least in part, the affective relationship that the figure of the aid worker seems to activate in humanitarian narratives. Indeed, the imaginative feat that *A Memory of Solferino* ultimately asks of its readers is that we begin to imagine ourselves as the kind of people who, unlike the cavalry and artillery, would take pains at least to avoid deliberately stepping on the heads of the dead and dying if, like Dunant and the other tourists, we were to find ourselves unexpectedly traveling through a battlefield. Perhaps this triangulated structure of transnational empathy is not as morally (or intellectually) satisfying as imagining ourselves in an adoptive relation with the agonies of another, but, as Dunant himself wrote about the modesty of his proposal for equipping ambulances with shock absorbers, such sentimental indifference "is in itself something from a humanitarian standpoint" (Dunant 1939: 90).

Tutti Fratelli: Of Horses and Humanitarianism

Such an appeal is made to ladies as well as to men . . . . It is an appeal which is addressed equally to General and Corporal; to the philanthropist and to the writer who, in the quiet of his study, can give his talent to publications relating to a question which concerns all the human race.

J. Henry Dunant, *A Memory of Solferino* (1939: 92–3)

At the end of *A Memory of Solferino*, Dunant breaks the narrative frame to ask a version of the question that underpins this essay about what we are reading for: "But why have I told of all these scenes of pain and distress, and perhaps aroused painful emotions in my readers? Why have I lingered with seeming complacency over lamentable pictures, tracing their details with what may appear desperate fidelity?" (1985). Instead of responding to

---

[7] Different genres of humanitarian interventionist narratives tend to focus on different corners of the humanitarian triangle. For instance, commodity films like *Darwin's Nightmare* attempt to forge metonymic links between the viewer and the "savage" violator of rights by implicating the viewer-consumer in the chain of production and consumption.

the question directly, Dunant chooses to "answer it by another," which, like the rhetorical questions posed by H. G. Wells almost eighty years later, readers are invited not so much to answer for themselves as to join Dunant in asking: "Would it not be possible, in time of peace and quiet, to form relief societies for the purpose of having care given to the wounded in wartime?" (86). Dunant's appeal to all "lofty souls" whose hearts are "stirred by the sufferings of fellow-men" might seem to reinscribe Rorty's bifurcation of the globe into the powerful and the powerless, the safe and the insecure. However, Dunant's distinction is temporal rather than geographical or cultural. Thus, although he addresses most directly "the different branches of the great European family" who suffered (synecdochally) the heaviest losses in this "European catastrophe," he claims that his narrative petition poses "a question which concerns all the human race ... since no man can say with certainty that he is forever safe from the possibility of war" (86, 78, 92–3).

Dunant's vision of a world of suffering and security is not static; it is a world of changing imbalances in fortune and misfortune. If, as Rorty, Nussbaum, and Appiah suggest, international relations and a cosmopolitan sensibility are as much matters of literature as of law, Dunant's narrative insists that the boundaries across which the humanitarian imagination must work are constantly shifting. This dynamic vision contrasts markedly with Rorty's moral Mercator projection map, which divides and distorts the world with its strict longitudinal and latitudinal lines of suffering and safety: "Outside the circle of post-Enlightenment European culture, the circle of relatively safe and secure people who have been manipulating each others' sentiments for two hundred years," Rorty sweepingly asserts, "most people are simply unable to understand why membership in a biological species is supposed to suffice for membership in a moral community. ... They are offended by the suggestion that they treat people whom they do not think of as human *as if* they were human" (Rorty 1993: 75; emphasis mine). In other words, they are offended at Rorty's metaphorical imaginative exercise. For Rorty, the primary difference between "people like us" and "most people" is that, because of "our" literature and liberal education, "we" have a well-developed humanitarian sensibility.

The edification conceived in Rorty's, and to a lesser degree Nussbaum's, model of sentimental education is the cultivation of a *noblesse oblige* of the powerful (rights holders) toward the powerless (those who cannot enact their human rights) that ultimately reconfirms the liberal reader as the primary and privileged subject of human rights and the benefactor of humanitarianism. These unequal divisions of the world into the rich and powerful, who have security and sympathetic understanding on their side, and the poor and powerless, who are in need of both security and sympathy, have a tendency to recenter the traditional subjects of history as the subjects of sentimentality and goodwill. However, this divisive world map of suffering and sympathy contains the seeds of its own undoing and undercuts the patronizing sense of moral superiority and cosmopolitan largesse that it seems to encourage on the part of the rich, safe, and powerful readers.

Both Rorty and Nussbaum imagine a world in which the privileged portion has cultivated capacities for sentimental identification with the despised and oppressed; a larger portion of the world (the unsympathetic sufferers) contains endless stocks of sad and sentimental stories, the raw materials for the refinement of the humanitarian imagination. In this vision of symbiotic international relations based on sympathy, suffering, and stories, the rich, safe, powerful peoples have unused refinement capacities for sympathy that may be supplied by the narrative resources of the suffering who lack sympathy. Rereading Rorty's map this way reverses the terms of moral (or sentimental) superiority that he attributes to post-Enlightenment Europe, and it suggests that when we look for generous imagining on the part of the reader, we may look in the wrong place – or at least we overlook the inaugural act of generous narrative imagining. Indeed, the teller of sad and sentimental stories (the wounded soldier who cries for water or the philanthropic writer who makes an extended narrative from such cries) already generously imagines the reader as his or her kind of people, as the kind of people who can be moved by sad and sentimental stories to extend humanitarian sympathy and empathy to the suffering. The narrator imagines a reader or listener who will respond to both the injustice of the appellant's suffering and his or her shared humanity.

The act of storytelling, particularly of stories of suffering, is a deeply generous act that extends to the reader or listener an "invitation to respond in imagination to narratively constructed situations" (Appiah 2000: 213). Indeed, what tourists (whether reading or real) learn, if they are attentive, is that they are generally generously imagined by the locals – imagined even to be generous. Before we readers extend to the narrators of sad and sentimental stories "membership in *our* moral community" (as Rorty supposes), they have already extended to us membership in *theirs* (Rorty 1993: 75). Narrators who deliver their testimonies of suffering make an appeal not on the basis of some metaphysical leap of faith or in the empathetic mode of metaphorical imaginative identification; rather, the narration is a metonymical claim of belonging to a common community, of membership in the universal class of humanity from which their suffering has effectively excluded them.

... and the Horse?

In my analysis of Dunant's narrative, I have strategically sidestepped the first instance of the narrative formula of humanitarian recognition, the earliest appearance of a cosmopolitan sensibility that disregards nationality on the battlefield. Immediately after the panoramic scene of war's inhumanity, a "run-away horse galloped by, dragging the bleeding body of his rider." Dunant pauses in the narrative of accumulating masses of bodies to make this startling comment: "The horses, more merciful than the men on their backs, kept trying to pick their way so as to avoid stepping on the victims of this furious, passionate battle" (Dunant 1939: 28). At the beginning of the chain of metonymic substitutions that links Dunant to the Lombard women to the missing corps of relief workers and ultimately to the reader is a horse that gingerly picks its way through the bodies of the dead and dying. That is, the entire narrative pattern of the awakening of humanitarian sentiment is initiated with this account of equine indifference. In a scene where living men have become beastly and the dead and dying have been disfigured beyond recognition, a horse is the first creature to model humanitarian behavior that takes no account of the nationality of the dead and wounded – the first creature to perform a humanitarian reading of the battlefield. This tiny act of humanitarianism sidesteps the metaphysical question of imaginative identification with the other even as the horse steps around the bodies of men. *Un Souvenir de Solférino* invites us to begin our sentimental education by responding to the narrative invitation to learn to read the dignity and humanity of others with the indifference of a horse.

REFERENCES

Appiah, K. A. (2000). "Cosmopolitan Reading." In V. Dharwadker, ed., *Cosmopolitan Geographies: New Locations in Literature and Culture*. New York: Routledge, pp. 197–227.

Appiah, K. A. (2003). "Citizens of the World." In M. J. Gibney, ed., *Globalizing Rights: The Oxford Amnesty Lectures 1999*. Oxford: Oxford University Press, pp. 189–232.

Barker, R., and R. Escarpit, eds. (1973). *The Book of Hunger*. Paris: UNESCO.

Bennett, A. (2005). *The Geneva Convention: The Hidden Origins of the Red Cross*. Gloucestershire: Sutton.

Brauman, R. (1993). "When Suffering Makes a Good Story." In F. Jean and Médecins Sans Frontières, eds., *Life, Death, and Aid: The Médecins Sans Frontières Report on World Crisis Intervention*. London: Routledge, pp. 149–58.

Cohen, S. (2001). *States of Denial: Knowing about Atrocities and Suffering*. Cambridge: Blackwell.

Douzinas, C. (2007). "The Many Faces of Humanitarianism." *Parrhesia*, no. 2, pp. 1–28.

Dunant, J. H. (1862/1939). *A Memory of Solferino.* Washington, DC: American National Red Cross.

Herman, E. S., and D. Peterson (2002). "Morality's Avenging Angels: The New Humanitarian Crusaders." In D. Chandler, ed., *Rethinking Human Rights: Critical Approaches to International Politics.* New York: Palgrave Macmillan, pp. 196–216.

Lattimore, R. (1951). *The Iliad of Homer.* Chicago: University of Chicago Press.

Kennedy, D. (2004). *The Dark Sides of Virtue: Reassessing International Humanitarianism.* Princeton: Princeton University Press.

Knox, B. M. W. (1972). "Aeschylus and the Third Actor." *American Journal of Philology*, vol. 93, no. 1, pp. 104–24.

Marx, K., and F. Engels (1975). *Manifesto of the Communist Party.* Peking: Foreign Languages Press.

Moorehead, C. (1998). *Dunant's Dream: War, Switzerland and the History of the Red Cross.* London: HarperCollins.

Mutua, M. (2002). *Human Rights: A Political and Cultural Critique.* Philadelphia: University of Pennsylvania Press.

Nussbaum, M. C. (1997). *Cultivating Humanity: A Classical Defense of Reform in Liberal Education.* Cambridge, MA: Harvard University Press.

Pous, J. (1979). *Henry Dunant, l'Algérien: Ou, Le Mirage Colonial.* Geneva: Grounauer.

Rieff, D. (2002). *A Bed for the Night: Humanitarianism in Crisis.* New York: Simon & Schuster.

Rorty, R. (1993). "Human Rights, Rationality, and Sentimentality." In S. Shute and S. Hurley, eds., *On Human Rights: The Oxford Amnesty Lectures 1993.* New York: Basic Books, pp. 111–34.

Scarry, E. (2002). "The Difficulty of Imagining Other People." In M. C. Nussbaum and J. Cohen, eds, *For Love of Country?* Boston: Beacon, pp. 98–110.

Slaughter, J. R. (2007). *Human Rights, Inc.: The World Novel, Narrative Form, and International Law.* New York: Fordham University Press.

Smith, A. (2002). *The Theory of Moral Sentiments.* Cambridge: Cambridge University Press.

UNESCO (1947). *Fundamental Education: Common Ground for All Peoples: Report of a Special Committee to the Preparatory Commission of the United Nations Educational, Scientific and Cultural Organization, Paris 1946.* New York: Macmillan.

Valéry, P. (1993). "A League of Minds – International Institute of Intellectual Cooperation." *UNESCO Courier*, September.

Vattimo, G. (2001). "Library, Liberty." In E. Portella and R. Argullol, eds., *The Book: A World Transformed.* Paris: UNESCO, pp. 67–72.

Weil, S. (1956). *The Iliad, or The Poem of Force.* Wallingford, PA: Pendle Hill.

Wells, H. G. (1940). *The Rights of Man; or, What Are We Fighting For?* Harmondsworth: Penguin.

4. Global Media and the Myths of Humanitarian Relief: The Case of the 2004 Tsunami

RONY BRAUMAN

The tsunami of December 26, 2004, was among the deadliest natural disasters of the past hundred years. In minutes, it completely devastated thousands of square kilometers, destroying several cities in its wake. The exact death toll will never be known, but the most reliable estimates put it at 230,000, mainly in Indonesia (170,000) and Sri Lanka (30,000). The tsunami also caused considerable damage and loss of life in Thailand and India, as well as to a lesser degree, Myanmar and the Maldives.

The disaster occurred during the Christmas holidays. What first made it real to people in the Global North were the videos shot by Western tourists who were caught up in the turmoil in their holiday resorts – above all in Thailand and Sri Lanka, which are famous holiday destinations with modern communications infrastructure that allowed continued contact with the rest of the world. In reality, though, it was the comparatively more isolated island of Sumatra that was hardest hit.

It is impossible to assess just how much this "tourist effect" and the fact that the disaster occurred over Christmas, when charitable giving is at its height, contributed to the subsequent outpouring of solidarity. To point this out is not to disparage it: no one can feel all the suffering in the world with equal force. What is undeniable, however, is that the images of whole landscapes, of people, swallowed up by the sea, which were broadcast incessantly by every television channel in January 2005, created an unprecedented degree of worldwide identification with the victims, who were represented as innocents who had not deserved their fate – the opposite of what happens in the media coverage of manmade disasters such as civil wars. In terms of emotional resonance, the coverage of the tsunami used much of the same emotional language, and engendered some of the same emotional response as did the images of the terrorist attacks of September 11, 2001.

However humanly understandable the worldwide response to the tsunami might have been, many commentators would subsequently emphasize the difference in media coverage and public response between the tsunami and the earthquake that struck Kashmir just a few months later. This contrast was generally presented as an injustice in that there was no similar outpouring of solidarity for the 75,000 dead and tens of thousands seriously injured in Pakistan. But again, this is hardly surprising. To put the matter starkly, there was never much chance that the massive outpouring of solidarity in response to the tsunami could be repeated within such a short span of time. And, however unpalatable, it is simply a fact that the victims of the earthquake were not perceived as socially proximate to Westerners as the victims of the tsunami had been, at least those largely Western victims on whom media attention focused during the first two weeks.

Mass solidarity is not based on rational reasoning alone. This is why international aid organizations, both private and intergovernmental, are so essential if aid is to be delivered with even a bare minimum of competence and lucidity. The essential point is that these organizations do not quantify their response according to the extent to which a particular crisis has struck an emotional chord with the general public in the Global North (from which private, governmental, and intergovernmental funding overwhelmingly comes), but rather according to real needs – although this is a more complex criterion than it might appear to be at first glance. The earthquake in Pakistan illustrates this point: in stark contrast to the coverage of the tsunami, the media coverage treated it strictly as a news item. Yet this did not prevent the international humanitarian organizations from responding in a way that meant that all the necessary steps that could have been taken were taken to provide the needed relief.

But the tsunami was, from the first, a special case, and the scale of the emotional response to it was as outsized as the disaster itself. The worldwide mobilization of humanitarian relief, in which, participating alongside the UN disaster relief agencies, were central and local governments, NGOs, and also the media, business, mass merchandizers, and schools, was and remains unprecedented. It was reflected, most tangibly, in the collection of a record $5.7 billion in donations by national Red Cross organizations and NGOs and the provision of $7.3 billion in bilateral aid by national governments (in France, €300 million was collected, more than one-third by the Red Cross alone). This funding bonanza was accompanied by (and largely made possible thanks to) the arrival of thousands of relief workers on the scene – some 5,000 for the island of Sumatra alone.

What was to be done with all this money and energy? A week after the tsunami, Médecins Sans Frontières announced they would not accept any further donations for this disaster. The noisy protests caused by MSF's decision shed some light on the constraints and limitations aid operations have to face, not just during the tsunami but in virtually every relief operation. The firestorm of controversy that ensued also illuminated the depth of myths and misinterpretations that surround relief work during natural disasters.

The most widespread misinterpretation is that natural disasters produce the same type of consequences as armed conflicts. They do not. Three major points are to be emphasized, from a relief point of view: First, armed conflicts cause three to five times more wounded than they do deaths, whereas natural disasters lead to more deaths than injuries, most of which are light, requiring relatively simple care; second, wars often affect entire regions for years, destroying health facilities and causing a high proportion of medical personnel to flee, thus creating a medical vacuum, whereas natural disasters strike a clearly defined territory for a very short time, leaving the majority of the country's infrastructure intact; third, protracted violence leads to the uprooting of large groups of the population, to malnutrition, and the weakening of immune systems, which in turn contributes to the outbreak of epidemics, thus engendering the need for an extensive provision of medical care in a context where the health system is partly paralysed. In contrast, natural disasters do not cause lasting displacements of populations, nor do they create large-scale immunological vulnerabilities in the affected groups. In fairness, no one ever claimed, in the wake of the tsunami, that the countries had been stricken by a war, but the way NGOs and UN relief officers described the consequences suggests strongly that they had a war pattern in mind. And what was, when all was said and done, a humanitarian "category mistake" meant that these misunderstandings about the immediate requirements after the tsunami led to a considerable waste of resources.

Specifically, the first such error, already familiar within the relief world since it had been committed time and time again in similar situations, was the epidemics alert. This immediately became a priority of the aid response. Senior officials of the World Health Organization (WHO) and the UN's Office for Coordination of Humanitarian Action (OCHA) predicted that the death toll would double owing to the vast numbers of corpses and the epidemics to which they would supposedly give rise. It was therefore urgent to bury the bodies in mass graves, to set up a system for prevention and detection of infectious diseases, and to undertake mass immunization campaigns. All these efforts and resources were wasted, for, whatever the public – including physicians – may believe or have been led to believe, historically *no* epidemics have ever been reported in such circumstances. The reasons for this are easy to understand, and, moreover, have been well known since Pasteur's time.

According to Dr. Claude de Ville de Goyet (2000), an epidemiologist who specializes in natural disasters and was a former relief manager for the Pan American Health Organization, "the bodies of victims from earthquakes or other natural disasters do not present a public health risk of cholera, typhoid fever or other plagues mentioned by misinformed medical doctors. In fact, the few occasional carriers of those communicable diseases who were unfortunate victims of the disaster are a far lesser threat to the public than they were while alive." Dr. de Ville de Goyet added that the hasty burial of corpses into anonymous mass graves constitutes a further ordeal for the survivors, because it deprives them of the possibility of honoring their dead. Owing to the lack of death certificates, it often also entails endless legal and financial problems.

According to Dr. Ville de Goyet, another fundamental mistake concerns treating medical assistance to the injured as a priority. International surgical teams trying to make themselves useful is a common sight after natural disasters. But unlike in a war situation, where there is little doubt that foreign medical teams are indeed useful in supporting the remaining local medical personnel, in natural disasters health facilities, along with the rest of the social system, are intact except in the area affected by the catastrophe. As a result the utility of these international medical teams is anything but self-evident. In Sri Lanka, for example, the tsunami swept over a coastal strip 100 to 300 meters wide, depending on the contours of the coast. But everywhere past the tsunami's high-water mark, the country was functioning normally. This explains why a thousand local Sri Lankan doctors and nurses were able immediately to rush to the scene to replace their killed or injured colleagues and to relieve the hard-pressed medical teams that had been present all along. Not being obstructed by language problems or difficulties in adapting to the environment, these medical personnel were operational immediately to cope with the substantial flow of patients arriving in hospitals.

While in natural disasters injuries are fewer in number and less serious than in armed conflicts, there are still many injured people to treat and the work of healthcare providers is of great value. But although medical teams are almost invariably overwhelmed by the demands placed on them in the immediate aftermath of a disaster, and temporary external support may be needed at this juncture, international medical teams can rarely be operational on such short notice. This is why by arriving in great numbers and at the wrong time, foreign medical workers often are more of a burden than a boon.

It would seem, however, that this situation is changing. After the earthquake that hit Kashmir in November 2005, killing 75,000 people and injuring nearly 40,000, the massive and sustained presence of medical and surgical personnel proved essential in supplementing and broadening local healthcare provision. This was because the local health system could not cope with such massive numbers of serious surgical cases. On a smaller scale, the May 2006 earthquake in Java (Indonesia), which, according to the initial estimates, killed 6,000 people, left thousands of injured (though scarcely the tens of thousands reported in the immediate aftermath of the disaster) requiring surgical treatment. The usual international actors (i.e. the Northern industrialised countries) immediately sent field hospitals and personnel, but so did states such as Singapore, Qatar, and China. In both these disasters, it is likely that the high number of injured was due to the proliferation of shoddily built and uninspected buildings, clustered in densely urbanised areas. In addition, because so many of the people living in recently established urban centers had no memory of past disasters, few had fully taken in the need for housing adapted to withstand seismic shocks.

In the majority of cases, the need for the deployment of armies of foreign relief workers is anything but as self-evident as it is generally presumed to be. Indeed, a closer look at the comments of Western journalists and foreign relief workers reveals one preconceived notion after another – each one no more valid than its predecessor – to justify these massive deployments of international relief workers. A common thread is the argument that populations who are victims of natural disasters are in a state of collective apathy, which prevents them from taking any action to help themselves. The popularity of the both medically and sociologically questionable concept of "post-traumatic stress disorder" has considerably strengthened this belief, which once again is borrowed directly from the concept of war-inflicted damage. Images of acute despair broadcast over and over on television are real, but focus on individual cases of grief. They do not reflect the collective reality, which is anything but stunned into inaction. To the contrary: what is noteworthy in almost all natural disasters is how quickly the victims of the disaster organize themselves, whether this takes the form of establishing reception facilities for the victims, or distributing food, or clearing debris, searching for the missing, and so on. Isolated cases of shock and antisocial behaviour, such as looting or indifference, do occur, but, overwhelmingly, the most frequent response is one of spontaneous solidarity, cooperation and mutual assistance. Obviously, such effective reactions do not always occur, nor, even when they do, does this mean that external aid is unnecessary. But to ignore the resistance of affected populations all but inevitably leads to an overestimation of the need for emergency relief and to hastily organized, unsuitable, and badly thought-out responses that are more likely to be "pre-fabricated" than to be flexible responses to specific conditions on the ground.

Reconstruction is another area that has too often given rise to many questionable claims, assumptions, and practices on the part of both nongovernmental and governmental aid organizations. For whatever they may claim, humanitarian organizations are almost never in a position to rebuild what a disaster has destroyed. Rebuilding and repairing homes does not just require money, but also a wide variety of skills and, even more importantly, the active cooperation of the government authorities in the affected countries and regions. The reality is that NGOs and UN agencies can do no more than *help* provide temporary solutions. And while it is true that large numbers of victims may urgently need food, tents, and drinking water – something humanitarian organizations can arrange better and faster than most governments – reconstruction is a wholly different, longer, and more complex undertaking. It involves access to real estate registers, debates over urban planning, the settlement of land-related disputes, a process of rebuilding that takes into account future risks, not to mention local economic and political issues and priorities. Beyond the people directly affected, these decisions concern, first and foremost, local and national authorities. And those who will do the actual rebuilding are almost invariably local or foreign contractors, and include civil engineering firms, skilled artisans, architects, and the inhabitants themselves, many of whom built their own homes to begin with, but precisely not aid agencies, which have at best a marginal role to play.

Financing is the only aspect of reconstruction where international aid is useful, and here some progress has been made. A plan, long discussed in the aid community, is finally beginning to be implemented on the ground: funds are distributed directly through bank cards that give affected families "drawing rights" on accounts furnished by humanitarian organizations. Despite numerous security problems and continued controversy over the best criteria for designating the actual beneficiaries, this is undoubtedly the most satisfactory form of financial aid in such situations. It meets an obvious and urgent need while avoiding costly and inefficient tutelage of local populations by foreign organizations. It deserves to be more widely used.

There is nothing new about either misrepresentation or misunderstanding in natural disasters. Nonetheless, the extent to which the post-tsunami situation was misrepresented and misunderstood is surprising. The likeliest explanation of this is that the beliefs underlying the misunderstanding had long been entrenched both in the relief world and with the general public. These beliefs were what informed the description of the disaster and what the response to it needed to be by relief organizations and journalists, many of whom enjoyed a certain credibility owing to the perception of their superior knowledge and experience. The only way to fully understand the reasons for these errors of judgment would be to conduct a targeted inquiry among the people working for these institutions. Not having carried out such an inquiry, I will simply set forth a few hypotheses.

The first concerns the metonymic power of images. Images were both the main vehicles of information and the basic trap, because what people saw on their television screens was taken as an image of reality, rather than as only a part of the reality. This confusion between the whole and its parts was then further accentuated by the exceptional scale of the disaster. But this was certainly not the only factor. Another was the emotional frenzy engendered by the amateur videos disseminated over the Internet and rebroadcast incessantly on television. The consequences of this psychological bombardment was reinforced by (and itself reinforced) popular identification with the victims. In such an atmosphere, any attempt to tone down the discourse or view the situation in perspective was perceived as heartlessness, while sensationalism and excess were seen as manifestations of compassion.

It is worth noting that the print media and the electronic media covered the tsunami and its aftermath very differently. The latter emphasized immediate emotion, while the former presented a more removed, and, at least comparatively, far more thoughtful analysis. Indeed, rarely has the divergence between the two forms of journalism been more apparent, in terms of both content and impact. Carried away by the flood of compassion, relief agencies responded reflexively rather than thoughtfully; mobilizing goodwill and transforming emotion into donations became ends in themselves, and the question of how the funds raised would be used was regarded in practice as meaningless.

But although a profound fear of contradicting the conventionally accepted opinion in the media and the general public was probably a major factor in aid organizations' loss of their grip on reality, it is not sufficient to account for the public positions these groups took. That these organizations too often failed to distinguish between their own interests and their social mission, and their disregard for the lessons learned from the experience of previous natural disasters were major factors as well.

By the interests of organizations, I mean the tendency of any institution to seek to increase its resources and expand the scope of its activity. A disaster on the scale of the tsunami, affecting many aspects of the lives of individuals and societies, could only reinforce this tendency to the point where any call for prudence expressed in relief organizations' positions was likely to go unheeded. I use the word "prudence" here in the sense of the Greek *phronesis*, or practical wisdom. Prudence is not the opposite of boldness; rather, it is what resists *hubris*. It is particularly relevant because the Western experience in modern times is marked by a sense of almightiness, and that it is all the easier to feel and share this sentiment when it is nourished by the conviction of doing good by providing an emergency response to suffering and deprivation. In focusing entirely on this categorical moral imperative of "the emergency," NGOs brought into, or at best were unable to resist, the climate of hysteria that surrounded the tsunami from the outset.

In an atmosphere of hubris, it is easier to understand why the lessons learned from previous natural disasters were largely ignored, since these lessons suggested precisely that emergency relief efforts should be limited, and that there was really only so much that humanitarians could sensibly expect to accomplish. It must be noted, however, that such errors of judgment as to relief needs, particularly the fear of epidemics, are observed whenever a natural disaster occurs, probably because – even for physicians – the fear of corpses supersedes more rational considerations.

The vicious circle constituted by these convictions – the belief that there were enormous basic needs to be met and imminent deadly perils to avert, not to mention the belief that willpower and money can work miracles – seems to have operated with great force, with each of these beliefs powerfully reinforcing the other. The few NGOs that resisted the emotional whirlwind were not in a position to stop it, as their public statements were inaudible in the prevailing pandemonium. As for the journalists, although some print journalists offered far more skeptical and nuanced analyses of the situation, it was difficult for them to cast doubt on assertions that were regarded as "common knowledge" and that, moreover, were ratified by those institutions that claimed and were assumed to be the authority, particularly the WHO.

Given that local emergency services begin operations immediately, the first and by far the most urgent priority for international aid institutions is not rapid deployment at all, but rather an assessment of what is lacking. Having analyzed the needs, the second priority is to meet them in as coordinated a way as possible. Whatever the pressure from public opinion – admittedly enormous in the case of the tsunami – and from a journalistic world whose default position is to constantly demand that we show that we are doing something, relief organizations should always put the need for prudent assessments first. Tents, food, water tanks and purification systems, communications equipment, equipment for clearing away debris, medical supplies and drugs, surgical assistance and means of transport (helicopters and boats, in some cases) are the main elements of emergency relief. But they must be adjusted to match the circumstances. In other words, every relief effort has to take into account local needs, indeed has to give them pride of place, and these needs will vary from one case to another. The *actual* capacities of the many organizations involved need to be factored in as well, and this may well be the most difficult element to assess.

Again, we must not fall prey to hubris. We must accept the fact that the coordination of aid takes time and that only the authorities of the countries concerned, perhaps with the help of the United Nations, are in a position to combine and coordinate the flow of aid on the spot. But we also must be sufficiently realistic to recognize that such coordination cannot be established immediately. In the absence of such prudence, a real danger exists that international disaster relief organizations may be irremediably discredited if they do not reexamine their mission and if they do not seriously question the misleading mental patterns that too often determine their action in precisely those times when it may be most needed.

REFERENCES

De Ville de Goyet, C. (2000). "Stop Propagating Disaster Myths." *Lancet*, vol. 356, August 26.

Favier, R., and A. -M. Granet-Abisset, eds. (2000). *Histoire et mémoire des risques naturels*. Grenoble, MSF-Alpes.

Floret, N., J. -F. Viel, F. Mauny, B. Hoen, and R. Piarroux (2006). "Negligible Risks for Infectious Diseases after Geophysical Disasters." *Emerging Infectious Diseases*, April, vol 12, no. 4, available at www.cdc.gov/eid.

Najman, W. (2005). *Economie de la survie des populations sri-lankaises du district de Batticaloa après le tsunami de décembre 2004*, available at www.msf.fr/site/bibli.

Rechtman, R. (2005). "Du traumatisme à la victime, Une construction psychiatrique de l'intolérable." In P. Bourdelais and D. Fassin, eds., *Les constructions de l'intolérable, Etudes d'anthropologie et d'histoire sur les frontières de l'espace moral.* Paris: La Découverte.

5. Hard Struggles of Doubt: Abolitionists and the Problem of Slave Redemption

MARGARET M. R. KELLOW

Over the past twenty years, a bitter truth has gradually become apparent. Slavery, an evil that most assume had been obliterated by the end of the nineteenth century, still flourishes in many parts of the world. Likewise the slave trade, the abolition of which has long been celebrated as one of the first great triumphs of humanitarianism, now appears resurgent in dozens of locales around the world. Activists and modern media have given faces and voices to contemporary victims of slavery and this has compelled all of us to reflect on how best to respond to this suffering. Like our forebears of 150 and 200 years ago, we struggle to find ways to eradicate this evil. However, if we are more nearly unanimous than our predecessors were in our determination to end modern slavery, the debates about how this should be done have a very familiar ring to anyone acquainted with antislavery activism in the nineteenth century.

One issue that has highlighted these similarities is slave redemption. As reports of large scale enslavements in the Horn of Africa began to emerge in the 1990s, Christian groups, most notably Christian Solidarity International (CSI) began to fundraise to redeem those who had been enslaved. Piteous tales of Christian Dinka tribespeople from southern Sudan, captured and sold into slavery in the Muslim north of that country, evoked a considerable outpouring of money and effort from evangelical Christian churches and community organizations. Inspired by gospel maxims and moved by accounts of men murdered, women raped and children forcibly converted to Islam, representatives of CSI travelled to Sudan and handed over large sums of money to liberate the enslaved and reunite them with their families in the south.[1]

---

[1] See for example the account of Lucian Niemeyer (2000).

118

As the project grew in scope, however, it began to attract severe criticism. Protest came from those opposed to paying captors to release those whom they had unjustly deprived of their liberty. Others argued that money paid to liberate slaves actually encouraged the practice of slave raiding by making it much more lucrative. CSI's willingness to pay, critics pointed out, actually drove up the price of slaves. Though well-intentioned, the actions of CSI and similar organizations appear to have been counter-productive because they put more people at risk of enslavement. By 1999, UNICEF denounced slave redemption as "absolutely intolerable." In 2002, Human Rights Watch similarly condemned these efforts. Even groups of Sudanese Christians concluded that "With all the good intentions in slave redemption, it does not end slavery" (Human Rights Watch 2002).

The result of these denunciations has been an acrimonious debate. Advocates of slave redemption insist that they cannot remain indifferent in the face of human suffering and that relieving some misery is better than doing nothing. CSI and other similar organizations insist that they are ending slavery – one slave at a time. Others, such as journalist Richard Miniter, have argued that slave redemption programs create "perverse incentives" that increase the trade in slaves. He quotes one observer who noted that "we've made slavery more profitable than narcotics" (Miniter 1999).

Subsequently a fragile peace in Sudan may have halted the trade in slaves there, but evidence of modern slavery proliferates. Each instance raises the question and inevitably the debate over slave redemption. Confronted with the reality of sex slavery in South-East Asia, *New York Times* journalist Nicholas D. Kristof opted to purchase and liberate two young women enslaved in a Cambodian brothel only to find one of them returned to slavery a year later.[2] Economists Dean S. Karlan and Alan B. Kreuger have also concluded that slave redemption actually stimulates the trade (2007). Yet when we are confronted with the plight of individual child slaves in South Asia or the faces of Eastern European women enslaved as sex trade workers, the insistence that attention must be focused solely on systemic and international solutions can sound uncomfortably close to a rationalization for complacency and inaction.[3] A survey of nineteenth-century American antislavery reveals that many, if not all of the issues that inform contemporary debate surrounding slave redemption troubled abolitionists as well.

[2] See *New York Times* journalist Nicholas D. Kristof's (2004 January 21, 24, 28, 31; 2005 January 19, 22) series of articles on his rescue of two young women enslaved in a Cambodian brothel.

[3] On trafficking of women see Victor Malarek (2003). On child slavery see Antislavery International (2007).

As long as slavery persisted in the USA, Americans wrestled with the probity of purchasing the freedom of those held in bondage. The transaction seemed simple enough – money paid to a master ended any claim to the person previously held in bondage. By virtue of the transaction, the slave became free. From the early colonial period until the Civil War, untold thousands of enslaved African Americans liberated themselves or were liberated by payments to their masters. As early as the 1640s in Northampton County on Virginia's eastern shore, Francis Payne bargained with his mistress, Jane Eltonhead, to purchase freedom. It took Payne thirteen years to raise the 3,800 pounds of tobacco his mistress required "for the freedom of himself, his wife and children."[4] By these and similar means, usually one body at a time, a small number of African Americans liberated themselves to form the nucleus of the free black population of the American colonies.

By the time of the American Revolution, difficulty in reconciling slavery with the ideals of liberty and equality that Americans espoused began to challenge the institution of slavery and with it the validity of a master's claim to compensation for the loss of those individuals he purported to own. At the same time, however, in a nation founded on private property, public discussion on how slavery might be ended repeatedly raised the possibility of compensation to masters, especially in the light of the crucial role that the sanctity of property rights had played in the revolution. Writing in 1774 to promote an end to slavery and with an eye to American struggles with the British, Connecticut minister Levi Hart took for granted that "no authority on earth can deprive [masters] of their slaves without indemnifying them for their loss" (Hopkins & Saillant 2002: 116).[5] The question of compensating masters for the value of slaves who had either absconded or been captured by the enemy during the War of Independence arose in the context of the peace negotiations in Paris in 1783 and remained a thorny issue until the 1820s. Similarly, debates on the Constitution underscored the enormous investment that slavery represented to Southerners, thus early proposals to end slavery often contained suggestions that African Americans might be emancipated by using the proceeds of the sale of western lands to compensate slaveowners. In Pennsylvania, freedpeople proposed a tax on their own community to raise the money to compensate masters for the

---

[4] As quoted by T. H. Breen and Steven Innes (1980: 75).
[5] On the challenge posed by the American Revolution to slavery as an institution, see David Brion Davis (2006:141–56), and Eva Sheppard Wolf (2006:1–16).

manumission of those still in bondage. Compensation, proponents argued, might win reform the support of at least some slaveowners. These hopes were disappointed and these early proposals came to nothing as the deep South rejected the idea out of hand, political leaders in the upper South were conflicted, and white Americans more generally were unwilling to forgo the revenue that accrued from the sale of public lands.[6]

In the late eighteenth century, religious concerns about slavery built on the political doubts that arose during the Revolutionary era.[7] This questioning of slavery was often paired with the possibility of compensation for slave-owners in what proponents understood as a need to do justice to masters and slaves alike. Manumission Societies formed in the border states to undertake slave redemption as part of a program to end slavery. Quakers in particular sought to balance the interest of slave and master. Thus Friends bought and freed slaves in order to live up to their longstanding testimony against slavery. By 1830, for example, North Carolina Quakers had spent nearly $13,000 to ransom slaves. By these means, more than 600 slaves were freed. However, a significant number of the slaves freed by these means were elderly or invalids, so the Quakers found they had to become guardians for these freed people. More importantly, as racial and economic rationales for the persistence of slavery strengthened in the nineteenth century, Southern Quakers with their commitment to manumission became a dissident minority in an environment in which slavery became increasingly difficult to question. Ultimately, the efforts of these societies freed very few slaves and did little to undermine slavery as an institution.[8]

In 1817, the American Colonization Society (ACS) was founded, in part so as to end slavery gradually. By compensating slaveholders who emancipated their slaves and transporting free blacks to Liberia, colonizationists argued that the problem of American slavery could be resolved. The ACS claimed that slavery had been established by law and upheld by the state, thus the state had an obligation to compensate those who had legitimately acquired and held slaves. In the context of emerging liberal capitalism in this period, legislation and judicial opinion repeatedly

---

[6] See Ira Berlin (1998: 232), Joseph J. Ellis (2002:104–8), Henry Wiencek (2003), and Betty L. Fladeland (1976).

[7] On challenges to slavery arising out of religion, see Andrew Levy (2005: 65–135), Davis (2006: 250–5), and Anne C. Loveland (1966).

[8] On Quaker efforts in North Carolina see Eric Burin (2005, 36–7), Katherine Dungy (2002), and Stephen B. Weeks (1896: 224–9).

affirmed the right of individuals to secure possession of their property.[9]
As one ACS supporter put it:

> When public opinion, or the law, has sanctioned the investiture of property in
> any particular way, then it cannot turn round and destroy that system of
> things, without indemnifying those whom it has encouraged so to invest their
> property. It is a fundamental principle of law, running through all our
> constitutions, that no legislature can so legislate as to destroy the tenure of
> property acquired and held under existing laws without providing for the
> security of such property. (*Liberator* 1834)

"The true question is not between the master and the slave," this writer
observed, "but between the master and the nation who conferred this right
on him."

Negotiations regarding enslaved African Americans who either escaped to
or had been captured by the British in the War of Independence and later in
the War of 1812 also kept the question of compensation alive. The Treaty of
Paris in 1783 forbade the removal of American "property," and this principle was reaffirmed in Jay's Treaty in 1796 and the Treaty of Ghent in 1814.
However, when that "property" consisted of slaves who had fled to the
British, restitution was not possible and American slave-owners demanded
compensation. The issue continued to plague diplomatic relations between
the two countries and therefore remained in the public eye throughout the
early national period. In 1827–1828, following arbitration by the Russian
Tsar, a commission directed Britain to compensate American slave-owners
for their lost "property" and oversaw the payment of these reparations.[10]

Perhaps in the wake of these payments, after 1830 public discussion over
the merits of paying masters to free their slaves became more heated. The
debate emerged from the reaction against gradual plans for emancipation
such as those of the ACS. During the 1820s, African Americans such as
Samuel Cornish and David Walker, angered by the thinly disguised racism
of the colonizationists, denounced ACS plans to deport free blacks to
Liberia. "America is more our country, than it is the whites," proclaimed
David Walker's *Appeal* in 1829, " – we have enriched it with our blood and
tears. The greatest riches in all America have arisen from our blood and
tears: – and will they drive us from our property and homes, which we have

---

[9] Eric Burin argues that the motives of the ACS founders ranged from those who hoped to
end slavery by removing all African Americans from the USA to those who hoped to
strengthen slavery by removing free blacks (2005: 34–56). See also Penelope Campbell
(1971), Douglas R. Egerton (1985), and Christopher Clark (1996).
[10] See Walter B. Hill Jr. (2000).

earned with our blood?" (1829: 73). In claiming full citizenship for black Americans these and other black activists rejected understandings of slavery as a regrettable legacy of the past, by means of which slaveholders had acquired a legitimate interest. Instead, slavery constituted a moral issue. African American abolitionists argued that slaveholding was inherently unjust, and the putative "owners" of enslaved African Americans had no right to compensation. As Frederick Douglass would later insist, "that which is a man's right [i.e., freedom], there is no law of nature to compel him to buy." (Douglass 1849).

Persuaded in large measure by the arguments of Cornish, Walker, and other black abolitionists, white northerners who opposed slavery distanced themselves from colonizationist proposals involving compensation and from any other proposition that in any way legitimated the property rights of slaveholders.[11] As William Lloyd Garrison's Boston newspaper the *Liberator* began arguing in 1831, if the Declaration of Independence meant anything, enslaved men and women should be free. Those who deprived them of freedom were tyrants. Garrison framed the question in the language of morality. The slave-owner was a thief unjustly in possession of the person of the enslaved and one did not bribe a sinner to cease his transgression. In the view of one reader of Garrison's *Liberator*, proposals for compensation were "nothing more than a requisition to obtain money for delivering up property which ... the felon audaciously purloined" (Paul 1833). Moreover, Garrison insisted that to do so would be to participate in the sin: "[I]t is wrong," he wrote in an editorial in the *Liberator* in June of 1832, "and consequently sinful, to give money, or any other pretended equivalent, for 'the bodies and souls of men,' under any pretence whatever" (Garrison 1832b). Garrison's comment suggests that among the many aspects of compensation that troubled him, was the perception that when an abolitionist purchased an enslaved person's freedom, that abolitionist became, however briefly, a slave-owner. A month later, Garrison reiterated "[it] is the duty of the owners of slaves to liberate their victims immediately – they deserve and should receive no remuneration for giving up stolen property" (1832a).[12] In vitriolic editorials, pamphlets and speeches, Garrisonian abolitionists denounced compensation and began to call for immediate abolition. Meeting in Philadelphia in 1833, Garrison and his followers founded the American Antislavery Society (AASS) and drafted a Declaration of Sentiments that proclaimed:

---

[11] On the crucial influence of black abolitionists in the coming of immediatism in the USA, see Richard S. Newman (2002: 96–106), Patrick Rael (2002: 181–2), and Davis (2006: 258–9).
[12] See Davis (2006: 252–3).

> We maintain, that no compensation should be given to planters emancipating their slaves, because it would be a surrender of the great fundamental principle, that man cannot hold property in man; because slavery is a crime, and therefore [the slave] is not an article to be sold; because the holders of slaves are not the just proprietors of what they claim – freeing the slaves is not depriving them [i.e., planters] of property, but restoring it to the right owner – it is not wronging the master, but righting the slave, restoring him to himself .... (1833)

The resolve of the new association was absolute and unequivocal.

Despite this strengthening conviction, circumstances compelled American abolitionists to reconsider the issue of compensation immediately. In the same year that the AASS was founded, the British government legislated the abolition of slavery in its possessions by enacting a program of compensated emancipation. In the British West Indies, slaves were to serve an apprenticeship of five years and then be freed. Their masters would receive twenty million pounds in compensation from the British government.[13] Eager to differentiate themselves from their erstwhile colonial masters, American abolitionists criticized compensation ever more fiercely. Garrison, travelling in England at the time the bill was before Parliament, reported to the *Liberator* in August 1833 that compensation was "money bestowed where no loss can be proved, but [was instead] an abandonment of the high ground of justice." Comments such as this suggest that American abolitionists envisioned a better, purer form of emancipation in which slaveholders would repent and would require no inducements to let their slaves go free.

Despite the firm position of the AASS, the issue repeatedly came to the fore, most notably in 1847, when English antislavery activists raised money to purchase the freedom of Frederick Douglass, then lecturing in Britain. Douglass had escaped slavery several years previously, so the gesture was largely symbolic, but it provoked strong condemnation in many American abolitionist circles. "Seven hundred and fifty dollars have been sacrificed to promote slavery – in clear recognition either of the right of the slaveholder, or the weakness, moral and physical, of the friends of liberty," thundered the Boston *Chronotype* (Wright 1847). Critics cited the AASS denunciation of compensation and pointed out that Douglass needed no "free papers" to make him a free man. Pennsylvania Quaker Lindley Coates made the case against ransoming fugitive slaves most forcefully. He argued that if he paid money to free a slave,

---

[13] On British Emancipation see Adam Hochschild (2006: 299–354).

I would be increasing the traffic in, and enlarging the market for men, women and children, however I might remonstrate with my tongue against the practice; for I would be giving the slaveholder a stimulus to have such commodities for sale. The slaveholder or slave breeder don't care, and need not care whether his market is at the South or at the North, whether the planters at the South or the abolitionists at the North, are the purchasers of his slaves, seeing as his object is to make money out of them. (Coates 1847)

Coates went on to say that the antislavery intent of the practice was immaterial. He believed that it was "wrong to buy a slave at all, because, in so doing, we encourage the seller to fill the place of the one sold with another victim, ... which more than anything else, urges him on to yet further deeds of outrage and wrong towards his fellow-men" (1847). The net effect, Coates concluded, would be to provide an impetus for additional slaves because "as a general rule, it holds good that if a market is created for any kind of goods, it will be supplied." Another commentator put the case even more forcefully, revealing the extent to which prevailing economic principles shaped abolitionist responses.

"Buy slaves and set them free." Yes; lop the branches and strengthen the root; make the destruction of the system more difficult by practising upon it; create a demand for the slave breeder to supply; compromise with crime; raise the market price, when you ought to stop the market; put a philanthropic mark upon the slave trade; spend money enough in buying one man to free fifty gratis and convert a thousand. (Chapman 1855: 3)[14]

Slave redemption, these abolitionists argued, was utterly incompatible with the logic of antislavery.

White abolitionists raised these concerns again when the deepening sectional crisis gave rise to renewed interest in a national scheme for compensated emancipation in the late 1850s. The National Compensated Emancipation Society, founded in 1857, was the brainchild of Elihu Burritt, a committed pacifist with a long career in various reform causes. Arguing that the economy of the South could not sustain the disaster of uncompensated emancipation and that since the North was complicit in slavery, the North should help to pay for its extinction, Burritt proposed that slavery could be ended by using the proceeds from the sale of public lands to compensate slave-owners.[15] Abolitionists saw the question in a different light. Maria Weston Chapman scoffed at the proposal that Americans

[14] See Chapman (1855: 3–4). See also Karlan and Krueger (2007) for a contemporary analysis that reaches similar conclusions.
[15] See Peter Tolis (1968: 235–61).

should "raise two thousand millions of dollars and beg the slaveholders to take it, (not as compensation, but as a token of good will)." In Chapman's view this amounted to trying "to keep out the sea with a mop, when you ought to build a dyke." Americans would do far better to avoid "a disgraceful mistake in the economy of well doing; spending in salving a sore finger what would buy the elixir vitae; preferring the less, which *ex*cludes the greater, to the greater, which *in*cludes the less" (1855: 3–4).

Black Americans continued to denounce compensation and any other manner of recognizing the property right of a master. With the majority of their white colleagues in the antislavery movement, black abolitionists agreed that paying to free a slave legitimated the master's claim to ownership, so they were outspoken in their condemnation of such bargains. Every slave who escaped from bondage denied the legitimacy of his or her master's financial interest in his or her person. Despite the controversy over his own ransom, Frederick Douglass repudiated compensation emphatically. "[E]very act of purchase enhances the market value of human chattels; and makes the monsters cling to their *property* with a more tenacious grasp," Douglass wrote in 1849.

> I would simply advise every man, woman and child, whether black, white, or yellow, that so long as they are guiltless of crime, they have a right to freedom. It is theirs. The idea of making them pay for what is their own by the inalienable gift of their Creator, is most absurd, preposterous, and Heaven insulting.[16]

Similarly, although in slavery he had worked hard to raise enough money to free himself, once he had escaped from bondage, William Wells Brown scorned a former master's offer to sell his freedom to Boston abolitionists. "I cannot accept of Mr. Price's offer to become a purchaser of my body and soul" he insisted. "God made me as free as he did Enoch Price, and Mr. Price shall never receive a dollar from me or my friends with my consent" (Brown 1849: ix). Henry Bibb, a former fugitive, argued in his Canadian newspaper that the practice of paying for escaped slaves was worse than counterproductive, hinting that the practice actually put free blacks in the North at risk: "A great mistake has been made here in the north, by purchasing the freedom of fugitive slaves . . . it has only served to stimulate the hunt for fugitives . . . " (Bibb 1851). Bibb went on to suggest that rather than ransoming fugitive slaves, they should be permitted to return to the South where they could instruct their peers about life in the

---

[16] Frederick Douglass (1849). See also John Stauffer (2007: 213–22).

free states and thus disrupt the system of slaveholding from within. Defiantly, black abolitionists rejected the idea that their bodies were commodities to be bought and sold.

The great paradox, however, was that although white and black anti-slavery activists were virtually unanimous in their opposition to the principle of compensation or to buying the freedom of fugitive slaves, almost everyone in the abolitionist community was involved in redeeming slaves in one way or another. Black churches routinely canvassed their members to ransom the relatives of members of their congregations.[17] Former slaves published narratives of their lives for this express purpose. White and black antislavery newspapers carried notices attesting to the honesty of various African Americans attempting to raise money to free themselves or their family members. White abolitionists who belonged to antislavery organizations that explicitly denounced compensation contributed money to help buy individual blacks out of slavery. Henry Ward Beecher staged slave "auctions" in his Brooklyn church to raise money to purchase freedom for a number of young slave women.[18] Even Garrison himself contributed to the "ransom" of Douglass, arguing that the particular circumstances of the case were such that compassion and prudence had to take precedence over principle. "To save a fellow-being," he wrote in March of 1847, "it is no crime sometimes to comply with even unjust demands" (Garrison 1847b).

Within the black community, the inconsistency created few problems. Family reunification overrode other concerns. Even outspoken activists who refused to be redeemed themselves worked hard to raise the funds to free members of their own families.[19] Ties of affection and kinship outweighed other considerations as black men and women went to heroic lengths to free relatives and reunite their families. Edmond Kelley's efforts to free his family provide a good example of the process.

Kelley was born a slave in Maury County, Tennessee in 1817. After becoming converted to the Baptist faith in 1838, he married Paralee Walker the following year. He soon felt a call to the ministry and was licensed to preach by the Columbia Baptist association in 1842. A few years later word reached him that he was about to be sold. The local Baptist association attempted unsuccessfully to purchase his freedom. Kelley then tried to work out an arrangement with his mistress, agreeing to pay her $10 a

---

[17] See, for example, Roy E. Finkenbine (1993: 180–1).

[18] See Wayne Shaw (2000) and Richard Wightman Fox (2007).

[19] For the efforts of freedpeople to purchase family members see Berlin (1998: 235, 331). Berlin draws attention to the frequency with which "self-purchase" actually represented a group effort. See also Wolf (2006: 66–9) and Larry Koger (2006).

month. Before he could complete the purchase, his mistress, fearing that she would soon become bankrupt, urged Kelley to leave Tennessee and presumably to continue paying her. Kelley took her advice and went first to New York and eventually to New Bedford, Massachusetts, where he was called to be pastor of the Second Baptist church there in September of 1848. Once in New England, Kelley felt no obligation to continue paying for his own freedom, but he desperately wanted to be reunited with his wife and four children.

So in February 1850, Kelley entered negotiations with James Walker, owner of his wife and children. Walker claimed he was extremely reluctant to part with his slaves. Paralee Walker was apparently the daughter of Walker's old nurse and he argued that his own ties of affection and his conviction that Kelley could not properly provide for his family precluded setting them free. However for $2800 Walker was prepared to rethink his sentiments and convictions. In response, Kelley enlisted the aid of friends and parishioners to help raise the money. The Boston Baptist association attempted to persuade Walker to lower his price, but the slave master refused, hinting that if Kelley did not come up with the money promptly, he would retract the offer. Kelley resigned his pulpit so as to work full time on raising the money. Finally, by dint of his own efforts and by canvassing numerous congregations in southern Massachusetts, Kelley managed to raise the money. Yet this did not end his difficulties. As a fugitive, he could not return to Tennessee to get his family. He had to hire an agent to conduct the transaction and transport Paralee Walker and her four children to New Bedford. Once they arrived there in May of 1851, James Walker consented to their emancipation (Kelley 1851). Kelley's experience demonstrates that even when no one raised ideological issues, slave redemption could be a difficult proposition.

As almost every free black family had relatives still in bondage, thousands of African American families went through comparable experiences. Kelley was fortunate in that he was literate and had friends and acquaintances to help him reunite with his family. Other fugitives, without friends or money, found it almost impossible to maintain ties with family members in slavery. For fugitives, especially following the Fugitive Slave Act of 1850, communicating with a former master in hopes of arranging the purchase of a relative meant revealing their location and thus risking recapture. Returning to the South to recover family members involved even more dangers. Even if legally emancipated, freedpeople had few levers to persuade former masters to relinquish slave kinsmen. The scant occupational opportunities open to African Americans meant that the accumulation of the necessary funds to free family members required exceptional efforts. If one was finally able to save enough money, legal problems and the difficulties of transporting money over long distances presented further obstacles. Since a slave could not purchase another slave according to state laws, agents had to be employed and agents were not always trustworthy. Nor were there any guarantees that a master would live up to his promise, and little recourse if he failed to do so. Yet despite all these obstacles, black families painstakingly struggled to redeem their loved ones.

For those still enslaved and hoping to purchase their liberty, the desire for freedom forced hard choices at almost every turn. Typically, one family member managed to free him or herself and then worked to purchase those still enslaved. Yet self-purchase was particularly fraught with difficulties as whatever a slave earned or owned belonged to his or her master according to law. Arrangements could be struck, but a master might renege as Moses Grandy learned to his sorrow. Grandy paid his purchase price three times over before finally achieving his freedom (Grandy 1843). Dimmock Charlton worked for years in Savannah to free himself only to be swindled repeatedly by a series of masters.[20] Frederick Douglass described self-hire as "a step towards freedom," but it was a small step on a very long road.[21] Slaves hired out to other masters might accumulate funds to free themselves or family members, but they frequently encountered animosity from white laborers who resented the competition.[22] Lunsford Lane worked diligently for years to free himself and his family, but he too found that local white communities resented slaves that were seen to be too successful (Lane 1842). In addition, laws requiring manumitted blacks to leave southern states meant that the pursuit of freedom often entailed years of separation. The same laws could require free blacks to become the owners of their own family members.[23] Even the decision about who should seek freedom first was fraught with difficulties. Arguably it made more sense for a man to purchase his freedom first because he could earn more money and then free the rest of his family. Against that, if a black woman remained behind in slavery, any children she might have would be born slaves and thus would also have to be ransomed, adding to the sum needed to

---

[20] See Mary L. Cox and Susan H. Cox (1859: 5–7).
[21] As quoted in Jonathan D. Martin (2004: 175).
[22] See Martin (2004: 161, 163–9).
[23] See Ira Berlin (1974: 273). The argument that most black slave owning involved the purchase of family members has been challenged of late. See especially Koger (2006: 52–74).

purchase freedom. In addition, if an enslaved woman's husband left the neighborhood, she might be forced into another relationship. Either way, the pursuit of freedom could lead to years of separation and uncertainty.[24]

Despite their explicit objections to paying slaveholders to emancipate their slaves, white abolitionists found their hearts touched by stories such as that of Edmond Kelley's family. Ties of family and kin were sacred in the culture of antebellum America and families separated by the machinations of cruel and greedy men were stock themes of nineteenth-century sentimental fiction. The figure of the lost child or the faithful spouse inevitably invoked a moral and emotional response. Thus even while denouncing the idea of compensation for slave-owners, white abolitionists acknowledged that almost every one of their number contributed to these appeals.[25]

White congregations gave generously to collections to ransom particular slaves (Shaw 2000). The religious imperative "to set the captives free" arose from the deepest strains in Christian theology.[26] When abolitionist papers exposed as frauds specific African Americans who sought money purportedly to rescue family members, they implied that most were genuine, and thus implicitly endorsed the practice. Garrison, in defending his support for the ransoming of Frederick Douglass asserted that every one of those who had signed the AASS's 1833 Declaration condemning compensation "had again and again, and have subsequently, contributed toward ransoming some father or mother, husband or wife, parent or child from slavery without ever dreaming that they were trampling upon moral principle in so doing" (1847b). In a letter to an English friend, Garrison went further, saying that he had never

> entertained for a moment, that it is wrong to ransom one held in cruel captivity; though I have always maintained, in the case of the slave, that the demand of the slaveholder for compensation was an unjust one. But I see no discrepancy in saying that a certain demand is unjust, and yet being willing to submit to it, in order to save a brother man, if this is clearly made to be the only alternative left to me. (1847a)

At some point, Garrison seemed to be arguing, the need to rescue overcame repugnance toward compensation. When the enslaved individual had a recognizable face, or was in some way known to white abolitionists,

---

[24] See, for example, Wolf (2006: 67, 74–5, 138–47), Berlin (1974: 334), Lebsock (1984: 96), and Wood (1995: 123–5).
[25] See, for example, Garrison (1847b).
[26] Luke 4:18. See also Flora Keshgegian's study of American responses to the Armenian genocide in Chapter 6 in this volume.

they were much more likely to involve themselves in the projected redemption.

Garrison's ambivalence was not unique. Beyond sentiment, white abolitionists had compelling reasons for supporting the efforts of African Americans to purchase their own freedom and that of their families. Disinterested generosity on the part of white abolitionists differentiated them in their own minds from the crass exploitation they attributed to slave-owners. As white abolitionists struggled not only against slavery but also against the racist attitudes of their contemporaries, the freedmen or women who went to heroic lengths to free members of their families powerfully contradicted Southern assertions that family ties mattered little to slaves. Similarly, racist attitudes regarding the sexual mores of African Americans could be rebutted by references to black men and women who laboured long and hard to free their spouses and who demonstrated fidelity that lasted over years of separation. The slave who freed himself and his family by virtue of his own efforts also contradicted the images of indolence and dependency that many northerners attached to freedpeople. The image of black men toiling resolutely for their own freedom offered a nonthreatening image of black manhood that allayed white fears of racial violence. It also accorded well with the ideal of the self-made man espoused by many white aboli-tionists. Though they deplored the notion of compensation in principle, the logic of the antislavery argument itself compelled white antislavery activists to encourage and to contribute to the efforts of the enslaved to emancipate themselves in this peaceful way. In turn, such former slaves became powerful advertisements for abolitionist arguments about African American character and the essential justice of emancipation.[27]

White abolitionists were even more willing to contribute money to redeem a slave when the slave in question was female, and especially if the woman was young and light-skinned. In their campaign to build public support for abolition, antislavery writers frequently linked slave owning with the sexual exploitation of enslaved women. Lurid comparisons between southern plantations and "oriental" harems constituted a powerful tool to mobilize antislavery public opinion.[28] Eager to extract the maximum impact from these images (and for the most part oblivious to the racist implications of their strategy), antislavery writers emphasized that light-skinned or mulatto women were most at risk of sexual exploitation and therefore most in need of rescue. Fictional accounts such as Lydia Maria Child's

[27] See Keshgegian's "the good victim."
[28] See, for example, Kellow (2007).

"The Quadroons" (1842) or slave narratives such as that of Louisa Picquet described the vulnerability and abuse of such women in terms that appealed directly to nineteenth-century ideals of feminine purity.

Published in 1861, Picquet's narrative was explicitly intended to generate funds to redeem her mother. It begins with a description of Picquet as "a little above the medium height, easy and graceful in her manners, of fair complexion and rosy cheeks, with dark eyes, a flowing head of hair with no perceptible inclination to curl, and every appearance, at first view, of an accomplished white lady," and continues with attestations of her church membership and exemplary character (Picquet & Mattison 1861: 5). However, the substance of the narrative consists of Picquet's efforts to resist the advances of various owners. The account concludes with appeals to assist her in her efforts to ransom her mother. Picquet's narrative invoked the twin values of filial piety and female purity, thus questions of the probity of slave redemption could be put aside as white abolitionists confronted the spectacle of endangered white female virtue.

A more extreme example of this dynamic can be seen in the series of slave "auctions" staged by Henry Ward Beecher, in his fashionable Plymouth Church in Brooklyn, to raise money to ransom a number of enslaved women. Beecher was already a flamboyant figure when he began bringing beautiful young slavewomen before his congregation in order to raise money for their redemption in 1856. As these young women, all of whom were light-skinned and some almost white, stood before the congregation, Beecher would exhort his audience to deliver them from moral as well as physical danger. In one instance, Beecher introduced a particularly beautiful young woman, and an observer recalled that Beecher indicated that the girl was "to be sold by her own father" who was white, "to go South – for what purpose you can imagine when you see her." At Beecher's instruction, the girl "dressed from head to foot in virginal white," loosened her hair which "fell in shining waves to the floor." As she stood silently before the congregation, the plate was passed and congregants heaped money, "jewellery, diamonds, watches and chains" in the offering to secure her freedom. By playing on the sexual, racial and emotional sensitivities of his audiences, Beecher raised thousands of dollars to rescue these young women from bondage without any self-doubt about whether or not it was appropriate to do so.[29]

Gender considerations also underscored black ambivalence about paying for freedom. William Wells Brown asserted his free manhood

[29] As quoted in Shaw (2000: 338). See also Fox (2007).

when he rejected his former master's offer to sell him his liberty. Flight made a clear statement about black men's attitudes to their masters' claims to ownership. However, there were good reasons why some chose to pay for their freedom rather than flee. In some instances, black men appear to have negotiated their freedom with their masters in an attempt to compel their masters to recognize them as equals. Repeatedly cheated out of his freedom, Moses Grandy chose to stay and fight rather than to flee. Two consecutive masters accepted the $600 he had raised to purchase his freedom and then sold him to someone else. A third attempted to renege on his written commitment to free Grandy. Grandy confronted this master publicly and shamed him into fulfilling his bargain. Grandy's actions demonstrated that he saw himself as his master's equal and was determined to force his master to treat him accordingly (Grandy 1843). Cases like Grandy's also demonstrate that slaves bought their freedom in order to put a formal and definitive end to their masters' control over them. The legal process of emancipation constituted public recognition that the individual was no longer a slave. Freedom papers represented concrete and irrevocable evidence that the master had surrendered his control over the enslaved individual. Moreover freedom papers offered some protection from patrols and, after the Fugitive Law Act of 1850, from kidnappers who might try to sell African Americans back into slavery. Self-emancipation also spoke to the African American commitment to what Patrick Rael has called "black elevation" (2002: 183–8).[30] For many former slaves the witnessed, public acknowledgement of their changed status was well worth the price they paid for it.

Responses to the question of the redemption of enslaved African Americans varied over time and according to political situations. Initially, the aftermath of independence set some Americans to thinking about the conflict between slavery and the values of the American Revolution, and also to searching for practical ways to reconcile the property rights of the slave-owner and the natural rights of the enslaved, so as to end slavery. In that context, solutions that involved compensation to slaveholders who manumitted their slaves seemed reasonable. However, with the emergence of immediate abolitionism this idea – never truly feasible, became politically unacceptable. As the founding documents of the AASS and the furor over Douglass's purchase make clear, by the 1830s and 1840s the formal position of most American abolitionists on the question of compensation to slaveholders had

[30] See also Judith Kelleher Schafer (2003: 45–58).

become a fairly categorical rejection. Slaveholding was denounced as a crime and antislavery activists rejected any suggestion that the "criminals" should receive compensation. In the language of evangelical righteousness, abolitionists argued vociferously that it was wrong to bribe a sinner to cease his sinning.

Yet as the debate over Douglass's ransom demonstrated, loud though their protests might be, abolitionists were neither unanimous nor consistent in their objections to slave redemption. Throughout the period individual African Americans and many black families went to heroic lengths to raise money to free themselves and to rescue their loved ones from bondage. Moreover, whether they formally condoned or denounced compensation, black and white antislavery activists engaged in the redemption of enslaved African Americans. Although they knew very well that there were good reasons not to do it, when the slave in question was a known individual, or when the slave's situation resonated with prevailing cultural norms, black and white abolitionists set their principles to one side and, over two generations, ransomed thousands of slaves out of bondage. As Elizur Wright, Jr. acknowledged when he criticized Garrison's support for the ransom of Frederick Douglass:

> When a self-emancipated man has come soliciting money to ransom his wife and children still in bondage, we have had a hard struggle of doubt, whether it was right to give him assistance or not, but a feeling of humanity for the individual victims to be ransomed has overcome the sense of the wrong thereby done to the mass of the enslaved. (Wright 1847)[31]

When brought face to face with the real suffering engendered by slavery, few abolitionists found they could place righteousness before compassion. As in so many instances, the ideological purity of human rights claims coexisted uneasily with humanitarian compassion. Confronted with this dilemma, most nineteenth-century abolitionists appear to have opted consciously for humanitarianism over human rights.

That said, in the light of the growing consensus that contemporary slave redemption is for the most part counterproductive, it is appropriate to ask what the long-term impact of slave redemption in the nineteenth century may have been. African Americans who purchased themselves and their families certainly figured prominently in antislavery discourse. In many ways these self-emancipated blacks embodied abolitionist arguments and activists recognized and exploited their propaganda value. But did

---

[31] As quoted in *Liberator*, 8 January 1847.

emancipation by these means actually weaken the institution of slavery? Slaveholders, as Eric Burin (2005) and Eva Sheppard Wolf (2006) and many others have demonstrated, often used the promise of manumission to extort compliance and submission from their bondspeople. Winthrop Jordan once described free blacks as "leaks in a system which logically should have been watertight" (Jordan 1968: 108). Although slave-owners regretted these "leaks," one wonders if slave redemption or self-purchase may have acted as a kind of safety valve, permitting just enough "upward mobility" to channel and contain anger and frustration within the slave community. What would have been the outcome if American slavery had truly been a closed system?

The fact that well-intentioned efforts can sometimes have unintended consequences is one of several continuities in the debate surrounding slave redemption. Frustration with the perceived failure of governments to act effectively is also a constant. Recently, diplomatic initiatives appear to have had some impact and, at the time of writing, in the Sudan at least, slave raiding may have subsided somewhat. UN conventions and other international initiatives have targeted sex trafficking and child labor, although in no case can the results be categorized as dramatic. In each instance, modern antislavery activists readily identify with their abolitionist predecessors and their campaigns utilize many of the same strategies. In the nineteenth century and in the present, appeals to the emotions and to shared values were and are used to create narratives of suffering humanity in the hope of stimulating a sympathetic response. Antislavery literature in both eras evokes family ties, innocence, childhood, and endangered virtue. Religious sentiment is tapped in discourses that often juxtapose the Christian piety of the victims with un-Christian or Islamic oppression. Gender conventions too are mobilized in attempts to make bystanders regard the victimized as persons like themselves and therefore worthy of rescue.

As other contributions to this volume demonstrate, humanitarian crises often present conflicting imperatives. Flora Keshgegian's study of American responses to the Armenian genocide helps us to understand the ways in which the suffering of particular victims can be constructed to forge a bond of sympathy with those who possess the means to relieve their distress. Michael Marrus' chapter in this volume on the diplomatic context that obstructed responses to Nazi anti-Semitism prior to World War II reveals how fatigue, prejudice, and expediency can attenuate that sympathetic bond and erode the will to act. However, like slavery, the tension between the impulse to relieve suffering and rational analysis of the pragmatic consequences of those actions is not new. A survey of nineteenth-century American antislavery reveals that many, if not all of the issues that inform contemporary debate surrounding slave redemption troubled abolitionists as well. For more than two centuries, the question of slave redemption has presented those who oppose slavery with very hard struggles of doubt.

REFERENCES

American Anti-slavery Society (1833). "Declaration of Sentiments." Retrieved from http://usa.usembassy.de/etexts/democrac/18.htm, April 30, 2008.

Antislavery International (2007). *Child Labor*. Retrieved from http://www.antislavery.org/homepage/antislavery/childlabour.htm,. April 30, 2008.

Berlin, I. (1974). *Slaves Without Masters: The Free Negro in the Antebellum South*. New York: Vintage Books.

———. (1998). *Many Thousands Gone: The First Two Centuries of Slavery in North America*. Cambridge, MA: Harvard University Press.

Bibb, H. (1851). "Editorial." *Voice of the Fugitive*, November 5, Sandwich: Canada West.

Breen, T. H., and S. Innes (1980). *"Myne Owne Ground": Race and Freedom on Virginia's Eastern Shore, 1640–1676*. New York: Oxford University Press.

Brown, W. W. (1849). *Narrative of William W. Brown, an American Slave*. London: C. Gilpin. Retrieved from http://docsouth.unc.edu/neh/brown47/menu.html, April 30, 2008.

Burin, E. (2005). *Slavery and the Peculiar Solution: A History of the American Colonization Society*. Gainesville: University of Florida Press.

Campbell, P. (1971). *Maryland in Africa: The Maryland State Colonization Society, 1831–1857*. Urbana: University of Illinois Press.

Chapman, M. W. (1855). *"How Can I Help to Abolish Slavery?" or Counsels to the Newly Converted* (Antislavery Tract, no. 14). New York: American Antislavery Society. Retrieved from http://antislavery.eserver.org/tracts/chapmancounsels/chapmancounsels.html, April 30, 2008.

Child, L. M. (1842). "The Quadroons." Retrieved from http://www.facstaff.bucknell.edu/gcarr/19cUSWW/LB/Q.html, April 30, 2008.

Clark, C. (1996). "The Consequences of the Market Revolution in the American North." In M. Stokes and S. Conway, eds., *The Market Revolution in America: Social, Political and Religious Expressions, 1800–1880*, Charlottesville, VA: University of Virginia Press, pp. 23–42.

Coates, L. (1847). "To the Editor." *Liberator*, February 19.

Cox, M. L., and S. H. Cox, eds. (1859). *Narrative of Dimmock Charlton, A British Subject ... Retained Forty-Five Years in Bondage*. Philadelphia. Retrieved from Http://docsouth.unc.edu/neh/cox/cox.html, April 30, 2008.

Davis, D. B. (2006). *Inhuman Bondage: The Rise and Fall of Slavery in the New World*. New York: Oxford University Press.

Douglass, F. (1849). "Buying a Mother's Freedom." *North Star*, July 13.

Dungy, K. (2002). "A Friend In Deed: Quakers and Manumission in Perquimans County, North Carolina, 1775–1800." *Southern Friend*, vol. 24, no.1, pp. 3–36.

Egerton, D. R. (1985). "'Its Origin Is Not A Little Curious': A New Look at the American Colonization Society." *Journal of the Early Republic,* vol. 5, no. 4, pp. 463–80.

Ellis, J. J. (2002). *Founding Brothers: The Revolutionary Generation.* New York: Vintage Books.

Finkenbine, R. E. (1993). "Boston's Black Churches: Institutional Centres of the Antislavery Movement." In D. M. Jacobs, ed., *Courage and Conscience: Black and White Abolitionists in Boston.* Bloomington, IN: Indiana University Press.

Fladeland, B. L. (1976). "Compensated Emancipation: A Rejected Alternative." *Journal of Southern History,* no. 42, May, pp. 169–89.

Fox, R. W. (2007). "Performing Emancipation." In S. Mintz and J. Stauffer, eds., *The Problem of Evil: Slavery and the Ambiguities of American Reform.* Amherst: University of Massachusetts Press, pp. 298–311.

Garrison, W. L. (1832a). "Editorial." *Liberator,* July 14.

———. (1832b). "To the Editor." *Liberator,* June 16.

———. (1833). "Editorial." *Liberator,* August 31.

———. (1847a). Letter to Elizabeth Pease. April 1. Retrieved from http://www.yale.edu/glc/archive/1122.htm, April 30, 2008.

———. (1847b). "The Ransom of Douglass." *Liberator,* March 5.

Grandy, M. (1843). *Narrative of the Life of Moses Grandy . . .* London: Gilpin. Retrieved from http://www.docsouth.unc.edu/fpn/grandy/menu.html, *April 30, 2008.*

Hill, W. B. Jr. (2000). "Living with the Hydra." *Prologue,* Winter, vol. 32, no. 4. 247–58.

Hochschild, A. (2006). *Bury the Chains: Prophets and Rebels in the Fight to Free an Empire's Slaves.* New York: Houghton Mifflin.

Hopkins, S., and J. Saillant (2002). "'Some Thoughts on the Subject of Freeing the Negro Slaves in the Colony of Connecticut, Humbly Offered to the Consideration of All Friends to Liberty & Justice,' by Levi Hart (1774)." *The New England Quarterly,* vol. 75, no. 1, pp. 107–28.

Human Rights Watch (2002). *Slavery and Slave Redemption in the Sudan.* Retrieved from http://www.hrw.org/backgrounder/africa/sudanupdate.htm, April 30, 2008.

Jordan, W. (1968). *White Over Black: American Attitudes toward the Negro, 1550–1812.* Chapel Hill: University of North Carolina Press.

Karlan, D. S., and A. B. Krueger (2007). "Some Simple Analytics of Slave Redemption." In K. Anthony Appiah and M. Bunzl, eds., *Buying Freedom: The Ethics and Economics of Slave Redemption.* Princeton: Princeton University Press, pp. 9–19.

Kelley, E. (1851). *A Family Redeemed from Bondage.* New Bedford, MA.

Kellow, M. M. R. (2007). "The Oriental Imaginary: Constructions of Female Bondage in Women's Antislavery Discourse." In S. Mintz and J. Stauffer, eds., *The Problem of Evil: Slavery and the Ambiguities of American Reform.* Amherst: University of Massachusetts Press, pp. 183–98.

Koger, L. (2006). "Black Masters: The Misunderstood Slaveowners." *Southern Quarterly,* vol. 43, pp. 52–73.

Kristof, Nicholas D. (2004c). "Girls for Sale." *New York Times,* January 17, p. A15.

———. (2004b). "Bargaining For Freedom." *New York Times,* January 21, p. A27.

———. (2004d). "Going Home, With Hope." *New York Times,* January 24, p. A15.

———. (2004f). "Loss of Innocence." *New York Times,* January 28, p. A25.

————. (2004g). "Stopping the Traffickers." *New York Times*, January 31, p. A17.

————. (2005e). "Leaving the Brothel Behind." *New York Times*, January 19, p. A19.

————. (2005a). "Back to the Brothel." *New York Times*, January 22, p. A15.

Lane, L. (1842). *Narrative of the Life of Lunsford Lane . . . the Redemption by Purchase of Himself and Family from Slavery. . . .* Boston: J. G. Torrey. Retrieved from http://www.docsouth.unc.edu/neh/lanelunsford/menu.html, April 30, 2008.

Lebsock, S. (1984). *The Free Women of Petersburg: Status and Culture in a Southern Town, 1784–1860.* New York: W. W. Norton.

Levy, A. (2005). *The First Emancipator: The Forgotten Story of Robert Carter the Founding Father Who Freed His Slaves.* New York: Random House.

Loveland, A. C. (1966). "Evangelicalism and Immediate Emancipation in American Antislavery Thought." *Journal of Southern History*, no. 32, May pp. 172–88.

Malarek, V. (2003). *The Natashas: Inside the New Global Sex Trade.* Toronto: Viking Canada.

Martin, J. D. (2004). *Divided Mastery: Slave Hiring in the American South.* Cambridge, MA: Harvard University Press.

Miniter, R. (1999). "Sudan: The False Promise of Slave Redemption." *Atlantic Monthly.* July, pp. 63–70.

Newman, R. S. (2002). *The Transformation of American Abolitionism: Fighting Slavery in the Early Republic.* Chapel Hill: University of North Carolina Press.

Niemeyer, L. (2000). *The Sudan Slave Story.* http://www.lnsart.com/Sudan%20Slave%20Story.htm, Retrieved *April 30, 2008.*

Paul. (1833). "To the Editor." *Liberator*, August 31.

Picquet, L., and H Mattison (1861). *Louisa Picquet, the Octoroon, or Inside Views of Southern Domestic Life.* New York. Retrieved from http://www.docsouth.unc.edu/neh/picquet/menu.html April 30, 2008.

Rael, P. (2002). *Black Identity and Black Protest in the Antebellum North.* Chapel Hill: University of North Carolina Press.

Schafer, J. K. (2003). *Becoming Free, Remaining Free: Manumission and Enslavement in New Orleans, 1846–1862.* Baton Rouge: Louisiana State University Press.

Shaw, W. (2000) "The Plymouth Pulpit: Henry Ward Beecher's Auction Block." *American Transcendental Quarterly*, vol. 14, December, pp. 335–43.

Stauffer, J. (2007). "Frederick Douglass and the Politics of Slave Redemptions." In K. Anthony Appiah and M. Bunzl, eds., *Buying Freedom: The Ethics and Economics of Slave Redemption.* Princeton, Princeton University Press, pp. 213–22.

Tolis, P. (1968). *Elihu Burritt: Crusader for Brotherhood.* Hamden, CT: Archon Books.

Unknown. (1834). "To the Editor." *Liberator*, July 12.

Walker, D. (1830). *Appeal . . . to the Coloured Citizens of the World.* Boston: David Walker. Retrieved from Http://docsouth.unc.edu/nc/walker/walker.html, April 30, 2008.

Weeks, S. B. (1896). *Southern Quakers and Slavery: A study in Institutional History.* Baltimore: Johns Hopkins University Press.

Wiencek, H. (2003). *An Imperfect God: George Washington, His Slaves and the Creation of America.* New York: Farrar, Straus and Giroux.

Wolf, E. S. (2006). *Race and Slavery in the New Nation: Emancipation in Virginia from the Revolution to Nat Turner's Rebellion.* Baton Rouge: Louisiana State University Press.

Wood, B. (1995). *Women's Work, Men's Work: The Informal Slave Economies of Lowcountry Georgia.* Athens, GA: University of Georgia Press.

Wright, E. (1847). "Frederick Douglass." *Boston Chronotype, as quoted in Liberator,* 8 January 1847.

6. "Starving Armenians": The Politics and Ideology of Humanitarian Aid in the First Decades of the Twentieth Century

FLORA A. KESHGEGIAN

As an Armenian American growing up in 1950s and 1960s America, I had repeated encounters with Americans who knew nothing about Armenians or Armenian history, including the genocide of Armenians by the Turkish government during World War I. However, many of these Americans did know the phrase, "starving Armenians." Even though they did not know why the Armenians were starving, they recalled their parents admonishing them, in the name of the starving Armenians, to eat all the food on their plates. Perhaps the parents no longer remembered either, and so had ceased to provide a context for this formulaic reminder to be thankful for the bounty they enjoyed.

A few decades earlier, however, due to a widespread, popular and successful fundraising and propaganda campaign, Americans were familiar with stories of "starving Armenians." For more than fifteen years, Americans provided aid for Armenians and others suffering from starvation, disease and displacement as a result of the genocidal campaign of the Turkish government during World War I and its aftermath. There were indeed many Armenians who were in need of such care and nourishment, especially in the Middle East. However, the images of "starving Armenians" and the narratives that attended those images were produced, disseminated and perpetuated in America (and Europe) by an impressively organized media and promotional campaign, mostly under the auspices of the organization Near East Relief.

The roots of Near East Relief are intertwined with those of American missionary organizations in Turkey and throughout the Middle East. Those American Protestant missionaries witnessed the genocide and the plight of

I am grateful to Barbara Merguerian, Richard Brown, and Richard Wilson for reading and commenting on an earlier version of this paper and for those who offered responses to my presentation at the Humanitarian Narratives of Inflicted Suffering Conference at the University of Connecticut, October 13–15, 2006.

the surviving Armenian refugees and orphans. Their leaders called upon Americans, as a Christian people, to help their fellow Christians. In this chapter, I survey this history of Near East Relief and its humanitarian aid efforts in the early twentieth century. I also offer an interpretation of the narrative motifs it deployed, especially in its media campaigns, and the theology underlying these narrative motifs.

History of Missionary and Humanitarian Efforts

In the early decades of the nineteenth century, American Protestants – mostly Congregationalists and Presbyterians – deployed missionaries to the Ottoman Empire and the Middle East. Driven by a desire to evangelize in "biblical lands," these missionaries aimed to convert the Muslim populations, proselytize Jews, and revive Christian churches. They made few inroads among Muslims, especially since conversion from Islam to Christianity was punishable by death in that empire (Grabill 1971: 7). More and more, the missionaries in Turkey turned their attention to the Armenians. Although Armenians were Christians, the Armenian Church, ancient in form and ritual bound, seemed deficient to these missionaries, who were focused on the biblical word, preaching and individual salvation.[1] The missionaries sought to evangelize and revitalize Armenian Christianity by infusing it with Western Protestant approaches emphasizing personal religion, along with biblical authority and literacy, rather than ancient rites and arcane practices. Their efforts led to the founding of Protestant church communities and the development of indigenous leadership.

Along with their evangelizing efforts, the missionaries established schools, colleges and hospitals, thereby offering important resources to the Armenian population. In this process, they oriented the Armenian people more and more towards the West and its values and norms. As has been true with other missionary endeavors, these influences could be both positive and problematic. For example, the missionaries valued education for women and, correspondingly, helped to enhance women's status and offer roles for women outside the home. However, they also criticized Armenian norms and practices, such as the treatment of women, as backward and inferior. The missionaries' focus on Western individualism also contrasted with the collective ethos and practices of Armenian religion and culture.

---

[1] See Grabill (1971: 8): "... the American Board in 1831 shifted to the spiritual enlightenment of what it called 'the degenerate churches of the East.'"(Quoted from American Board, *Annual Report*, 1831: 21).

In these ways, missionaries engaged in cultural intervention as well as Christian evangelism. They introduced Armenians to Western cultural and social practices, at the same time that they displayed cultural superiority. The missionaries tended to view Armenians and Turks as unenlightened and not fully civilized. As the Armenians responded to the missionaries' presence and influence, as their daughters embraced education and more of their sons began to wear Western clothing, the cultural differences between Armenians and Turks grew. In these ways, the presence and interventions of American missionaries in the cultural balance in the Ottoman Empire contributed to the tensions leading up to genocide, as has been argued, for example, by Joseph L. Grabill in *Protestant Diplomacy and the Near East: Missionary Influence on American Policy, 1810–1927.*[2] Turkey came to regard educated Armenians who looked to the West as rising above their station and even as a threat.

During and after the genocide itself, American Protestant missionaries served as witnesses. They informed their superiors and agencies, and through them the American and European publics, about the plight of the Armenian populations. They sent home letters detailing what they witnessed: people on forced marches, dead bodies left by roadsides, and other horrors.[3]

The missionaries in Turkey also functioned as agents of relief, and of protection and rescue during the genocide itself. Survivor accounts narrate how Armenians sought refuge in missionary compounds or entrusted children to missionary orphanages. Missionaries intervened with local leaders to negotiate for supplies of food and water and sometimes for life itself for the Armenians. Missionary hospitals also offered medical treatment and care. Even though these missionaries were often powerless to stop the deportations and persecutions, they did what they could, often heroically.[4]

During and after the war, relief workers, many with ties to missionary organizations, turned to the task of providing for the needs of the survivors, both adult refugees and massive numbers of children, either left orphaned by the genocide or with parents, themselves barely surviving and unable to supply the children's needs. Missionary leaders in America joined with others, including business and government leaders, to establish humanitarian organizations to support and direct the relief work. The first

---

[2] See Grabill (1971: ch. 2).
[3] See, for example, Barton (1998). This volume contains solicited reports sent to Barton, then head of the American Board of Commissioners for Foreign Missions.
[4] One such missionary was Mary Louise Graffam, in Sivas. See Sahagian (2004) and Harper (2004). See also Moranian (1994) for references to such accounts.

of these, the American Committee for Armenian and Syrian Relief (ACASR), formed in 1915, near the beginning of the war. In 1918, it changed its name to the American Committee for Relief in the Near East (ACRNE) and then again in 1919 to Near East Relief (NER).[5]

Near East Relief was a national organization with government support. In 1919, Congress granted it a charter, which President Woodrow Wilson signed. This charter recognized NER as the official American agency for relief work in the Middle East.[6] Although NER's extensive board membership included a variety of religious and civic leaders, including Jewish and Roman Catholic representation, its chief and most extensive ties were to the Protestant missionary movement. James Barton, longtime secretary of the American Board of Commissioners for Foreign Missions, the primary missionary agency for work in the Middle East, served as head, first of ACASR, then ACRNE, and then NER.

Barton was thus a leading and powerful figure, both in the missionary efforts in the Middle East and in the humanitarian relief efforts during and after World War I. He remained involved with those efforts until his death in 1936. Barton's activism also extended beyond missionary and humanitarian work to the political and diplomatic issues attending the future of the Armenian population and of Turkey. For example, he argued for an American role in the future of Armenia after the war, when Armenia enjoyed a brief period of independence. Later in 1922–23, he attended the Lausanne Conference, which met to decide the future of Turkey and, therefore, of Armenian territory.

With James Barton as its head and Charles V. Vickrey of the Layman's Missionary Alliance as general secretary and paid administrator, Near East Relief and its predecessors recruited and oversaw relief workers and set up and operated hospitals, orphanages, schools, and other institutions to meet the needs of survivors and refugees. For fifteen years, from 1915–1930, these organizations also raised money in America for this humanitarian work halfway around the globe. By the standards of the day, they did so with immense success. Between 1915 and 1918, ACASR raised 11 million

---

[5] Near East Relief continues to exist today, in its present incarnation, as the Near East Foundation. In 1930, the organization changed names and focus. It shifted its emphasis from relief aid and support to provide for ongoing development needs, especially in the Middle East and later in Africa. See website: http://www.neareast.org/main/default.aspx. See also Tejirian (2000) for an overview of its history and transition from relief organization to NGO.

[6] James Barton's *Story of Near East Relief* contains a copy of the charter as an appendix (Barton 1930: 432–4). The charter was granted for twenty-five years, so it expired in 1944, by which time Near East Relief was Near East Foundation.

dollars. Then it established a campaign to raise 30 million dollars. ACRNE and NER continued these efforts. By the end of the 1920s, NER had expended over $116 million for relief work, of which over $91 million was raised and $25 million contributed, mostly in goods and equipment, from the United States government. The donated money, goods and equipment aided over a million refugees, many of whom were Armenian. Among those aided were well over 100,000 orphans, who were educated and cared for until they could be self-sufficient (Grabill 1971: 300–1).[7]

Even though Near East Relief was incorporated as a philanthropic organization, endorsed by the American government, it maintained its ties, both in personnel, allegiance and sensibilities, to the Protestant missionary movement. In the opening chapter of the study report on Near East Relief, published towards the end of its relief work, the authors state: "Here is the heart of the story told by this report. A new policy is called for, one that, if successfully adopted, may exercise a profound influence upon American *missionary* enterprise throughout the world" (Ross, Fry & Sibley 1929: 8, emphasis added). For these authors, humanitarian work and the missionary enterprise were one. This view is echoed by Suzanne Moranian in her study of the missionary movement in the Middle East: "through sophisticated fund-raising techniques, the American Protestants eventually created a multimillion-dollar business of Near-East aid" (2004: 192).

In practice, Near East Relief represented a wedding of missionary and philanthropic interests, perhaps a precursor of today's faith-based organizations. Even though Near East Relief emphasized, in its literature and incorporation, that it was a philanthropic organization and nonsectarian, this claim seemed to exist side by side with Christian language about its mission, and America's, as Christian. The symbol of the Good Samaritan pointed to American virtue as much as Christian behavior. Being Christ-like seemed to be a universal value.

The network of relationships at the center of Near East Relief displayed the overlap among missionary, humanitarian, and political worlds and further reinforced the lack of clear distinction between national and Christian values. For example, a founder, benefactor and trustee of Near East Relief, Cleveland H. Dodge, was a close friend of Woodrow Wilson's. They shared Princeton ties, as did several of the leaders of Near East Relief.

---

[7] See also the study and report, commissioned by Near East Relief (Ross, Fry & Sibley 1929). The report offers detailed surveys of the work of NER in Armenian, Albania, Bulgaria, Greece, Turkey, Iraq, Palestine, and Syria. It also recommends the shift from relief aid to development work.

Dodge also had strong missionary connections. Both his daughter and son were involved in missionary education endeavors in Turkey; he served on the board of Robert College in Turkey. Charles R. Crane, treasurer of ACASR, was a businessman and philanthropist who served on the boards of Robert College and Constantinople Woman's College. He was also close to Wilson and appointed by Wilson, along with Henry Churchill King, a Congregational clergyman, president of Oberlin College and board member of NER in the 1920s, to the King-Crane Commission to investigate the situation in Turkey after the war. Both King and Crane were close to Barton. In addition, Charles V. Vickrey, as general secretary of NER, developed an extensive network of state and local committees that reflected the connections among Protestant, philanthropic and political interests on the regional and local level.[8]

Near East Relief was not just successful, but also immensely popular. Although wealthy philanthropists and businesses donated large sums and the American government contributed significantly, mostly in goods and equipment, Near East Relief and its former incarnations conducted wide-ranging fund-raising drives. Many of these took place in churches, but there were also appeals to the general public, year after year. A significant portion of the funds raised came from such public donations. Such efforts continued for fifteen years, even though published reports attest to the struggle of sustaining those efforts, especially into the later years of the 1920s.[9]

Media Campaigns and Promotional Strategies

These fund-raising efforts used massive media campaigns consisting of newspaper articles, posters, advertisements, public events, and even films. The plight of the Armenians was headline news in major newspapers. Prominent artists designed posters and advertisements. Public figures, such as the child actor Jackie Coogan, leant their support and endorsement.

These campaigns were intended as propaganda. They had clear aims: to elicit sympathy for the Armenians and to raise money. In order to achieve these aims, they deployed particular strategies and portrayals. Armenians were fellow Christians who were suffering because of the brutal and heathen Turks. The Armenian victims were most often represented as women and children, helpless and abandoned. The visual depictions also

---

[8] See Grabill (1971), Moranian (1994), and Balakian (2003) for further examples and discussion of the network of Protestant, philanthropic and political connections among the leaders of Near East Relief.

[9] See Barton (1930), Ross, Fry & Sibley (1929), as well as annual reports presented to Congress.

contained racial and sexual overtones. Armenian skin was lightened to contrast to the darker skinned Turks and to render Armenians as clearly white. Portrayals of Armenian women and young girls were also eroticized, to make them more appealing.

The first film about the genocide and its aftermath, *Ravished Armenia*, produced by Hollywood and released in 1919, illustrates these strategies. *Ravished Armenia* tells the story of one survivor, Aurora Mardiganian, who also played the lead. Aurora is a young girl of 14 at the beginning of the genocide. Although almost everyone else in her family dies, she escapes and survives, but not before she is raped, forced into a harem, tortured and subject to many degradations. Whatever horrors she is forced to endure, she does not renounce Christianity. The film is ostensibly based on Aurora's memoir, narrated to those associated with Near East Relief, who committed it to writing.

Controversy attended this story and film, almost from the beginning. Since Mardiganian did not herself write her story, it is difficult to know how much of the narrative depicted in the text and in film is true in its details. There are no known extant versions of the film, only fragments. Aurora Mardiganian claimed that she was exploited by the filmmakers during the filming, made to work to the point of exhaustion and not paid as promised. In the end, she stopped promoting the film and sued her guardians for money owed to her.[10] Although Mardiganian's experience is not unique in the annals of humanitarian work, there is a certain irony in manipulating and exploiting a refugee in order to raise money to care for other refugees.

Other films, such as *Alice in Hungerland*, *One of These Little Ones*, and *Stand by Them a Little Longer*, followed in the early 1920s. They too portrayed the immense need of the survivors and sought to elicit sympathy and contributions. Print media, such as the journal the *New Near East*, published numerous articles and reports, again with the purpose of raising awareness and funds. Near East Relief issued an annual report to Congress, chronicling and lauding its efforts. Relief workers and their leaders wrote and published accounts of all they were doing and accomplishing. These were used to support continuing fund-raising efforts. For example, Mabel Elliott, a doctor working with American Women's Hospitals, which provided medical personnel for hospitals and orphanages sponsored by Near East Relief, published her memoir, *Beginning Again at Ararat*, about her many years of service in Turkey and then in Soviet Armenia. This memoir

[10] See Slide (1997) and Torchin (2006).

described both the plight of the Armenians and the important and virtuous role of American Christian assistance;

> ... a powerful foreign nation has invaded the country, bringing not hate, but love. Twenty million Americans, who had never seen and never would see Armenia, so felt the spirit of Christ that they did this thing. ... That, to me, is the real meaning of the American work in Armenia. Not the multitudes that were saved from starvation, nor the tens of thousands of little children bathed and clothed and fed, not the unofficial but actual economic administration of an entire country, but the great fact of Christ's spirit working through the machinery of the modern world. (Elliott 1924: 308)

Near East Relief employed multiple other fund-raising strategies as well, some of which changed and developed over the years. Among those are methods still used to raise money, especially in large-scale and popular campaigns.[11] For example, Near East Relief sold books of stamps, like Easter seals. Entitled, "Stamp Out Starvation," one book of stamps cost five dollars and included 90 stamps, which represented "life for a child for one month." Sunday School drives and other campaigns among children, including a milk drive, appealed to American children to help the Armenian orphans who were starving and suffering. In the mid-1920s, Charles Vickrey inaugurated an annual program entitled Golden Rule Sunday, which continued from 1923 to 1929. On Golden Rule Sunday, usually the first Sunday in December, people would gather to eat an "orphan's meal," often in large communal halls, and then contribute what they would have spent on an average dinner meal to a fund for orphan care.[12]

These relief campaigns and media productions created and fixed the image of the "starving Armenian" whom the Christian and benevolent West was called upon to aid and rescue. The Armenians were the victims in need; Christian (Protestant) Americans, those who could care and help them. In these publicity drives and fund-raising programs, numerous references were made to the "biblical lands" inhabited by Armenians and others, such as Syrians and Greeks, that the relief efforts targeted. Americans could thus identify with these starving Armenians as fellow Christians being persecuted by infidels. Because Armenians were suffering Christians, Americans were expected to reply with sympathy and support. Meanwhile, since Armenians were victimized and considered powerless, Americans could feel superior in their caretaking. Armenians were thus

---

[11] See Near East Foundation website: http://www.neareast.org/main/default.aspx.
[12] Golden Rule Sunday was actually international in scope. Vickrey wrote a manual (1926?), both to extol its success and provide instructions for organizing such an event.

both like the benevolent Americans and not like them. At the same time, the Turks were portrayed as the sinister "other." Suzanne E. Moranian's description of the way the press presented the plight of the Armenians and America's response serves as a concise summary of these perspectives:

> The reports and commentaries were gripping. They seized the heart and were high human drama. The plot repeated in the American media for years was a basic one: good versus evil. The press championed the underdog fighting the oppressor, who naturally hated his prey. The Armenians were portrayed as the innocent, martyred Christians whom the barbaric Muslim Turks victimized. Americans identified with the Christian Armenians. The Armenians were considered the advanced race. ... To Americans, the Turks were backward and sadistic. (Moranian 2004: 210)

Theological and Ideological Motifs

Often the theological issues that accompany discussions of missionary work and humanitarian aid fall under the general category of Christianity's relationship to other religions and societies, including the interplay of Christianity and culture. They focus on what the proper role of Christianity is or should be in the world. The Social Gospel movement of the late nineteenth and early twentieth centuries emphasized the contributions that Christianity could make to society and culture. It sought to intervene in the world to bring the social order more in line with the divinely promised Kingdom of God. Christian duty required efforts to make the world better and to aid those in need.

The work of Near East Relief reflected these ideas. Christians were obliged to help those who suffered, especially fellow Christians, and to side with the good in the battle against evil. Good and evil were portrayed as light and dark. Christianity represented enlightenment in all its forms. It hailed the virtues of charity and compassion.

Protestant missionary efforts, however, emphasized not social better-ment so much as individual salvation. Missionaries ventured into far away fields in order to convert souls to Christ and thus to save them. The Protestant missionaries in the Middle East, precursors of the relief workers, shied away from social service and embraced education primarily to enable biblical literacy. The Christ they preached was the savior of souls.

What motivated these missionaries was the drama of redemption: the belief that the way to salvation was through Christ. They understood this salvation as the essence of Christianity: Christ had died for their sins and thus had defeated the forces of evil, including darkness and death. Jesus

Christ was the light and life of the world. Those who embraced and followed Christ stood with the forces of good in the ongoing process of redemption, including the defeat of evil, darkness and death.

This Christian story of redemption, as the missionaries would have generally understood it, follows a particular plotline. It begins with God's good creation, the paradise known as the Garden of Eden. There is no evil in this garden. As long as those who inhabit it act as God intended and instructed them to, they do not suffer and know only life. However, the first human beings succumb to temptation and disobey God. As the Christian story of the Fall indicates, God's good creation is disrupted by the actions of the first human beings and sin and evil are thus introduced into the world. Sin and evil turn creation and humanity away from their God's intended ends and doom them to suffering, death and condemnation.

In order for this story to have a happy ending, in order not to leave humanity condemned, but bring about salvation and fulfill God's original intentions, God sends Jesus, as God's son, fully human and fully divine. Through his death on the cross and subsequent resurrection, so the Christian story goes, Jesus Christ effects redemption. This action of redemption is often termed atonement, a making right of the disruption caused by sin. In much of Christian theology, and especially in the theology in which the Protestant American missionaries were steeped, Jesus died for humanity's sins, in order to save sinful humankind. The cross is the way of salvation. Suffering is transformed through suffering. Death is defeated by death.

Two aspects of this narrative are important to highlight especially as they are transposed into the story of humanitarian aid, as told by Near East Relief: first, the moral dualism inherent in a view of evil as categorically other than God and coming from an "outside source," so to speak; and second, the claim that Jesus' suffering and death effect redemption. When linked together, the implication is that Jesus' death is the way to deal with the presence of evil, or, as I would put it, the dilemma of dualism, in some way.

Christian theology has always employed multiple motifs and metaphors to understand that death, and the "offering" or "sacrifice" that Jesus made through his death for sin. One is a rescue motif. This is generally developed as a three-part drama. Humanity, because of sin, is under the power of evil, perhaps personified as the devil, an instantiation of moral dualism as an opposing power. In order to rescue humanity, God engages with the devil in a battle of good and evil. In some version, God offers Jesus Christ in exchange, as a ransom, to free captive human beings. In this narrative the agent of exchange is God. Therefore, Jesus' role may be rather passive, essentially as ransom or even in some versions of the narrative, as bait. In this telling of the story of redemption, it is necessary that Jesus be an innocent victim. Jesus' innocence is what makes the act of redemption effective. Because Jesus is without sin and so innocent, the devil, evil one, cannot hold on to him or lay legitimate claim to him. In the language of the narrative, the devil has no rights to him. In the end, God acts, in and through the resurrection, to free Jesus, and along with him, to free humanity, from its bondage to evil.

Another common motif in redemption narratives is that Jesus' death is a sacrifice. Although there are many variations on the meaning of the sacrifice and to whom it is offered and why, a shared thread is that the shedding of blood or the giving of self holds redemptive power. Christians who suffer and die can then be viewed as emulating Christ. Whether as martyrs or victims, their suffering is connected with that of Jesus. Suffering can even bring one closer to God through Christ. An appropriate Christian response to Jesus' sacrifice is to give of self, to sacrifice self for others. Self-giving is the way to follow Christ, either to suffer as he did or to show love as he did. Through suffering and self-giving, Christians participate in the way of the cross.[13]

Near East Relief's humanitarian aid campaigns drew upon the narrative of redemption and adapted the motifs of rescue, defeat of evil, redemptive suffering, and Christ-like sacrifice. In so doing, they appealed to the Christian sensibilities of Americans. They portrayed America as the rescuing nation, giving of itself to save others. Armenian refugees were depicted as helpless victims and passive recipients, who would perish without American aid. In this narrative of aid, Turkey and Turks were demonized. They were not Christian, but heathens who were the source of the evil. Armenians were fellow Christians and so like Americans. However, having fallen into the clutches of evil Turkey, they were not like the Americans because they were powerless captives, in need of outside intervention and rescue. In this rendition, Turkey was evil and America good. Armenians were also good by virtue of their innocence. Because Jesus' innocence is the reason the devil could not claim him, the narrative of redemption renders victims considered worthy of care and rescue as innocent.

Armenians were also portrayed as the crucified ones, the sacrificial victims of the terrible Turks. Again, innocence is important: a worthy sacrifice is an innocent one, without blemish. Armenians were not suffering as a

---

[13] There is a vast body of literature, theological and critical, on the meaning of redemption through Jesus Christ's suffering and death. The exposition offered in this essay draws especially on Aulén (1932), Brown and Bohn (1989), Driver (1986), Fiddes (1989), Gorringe (1996). The particular interpretation is this author's.

result of what they did, but what was done to them. They were, therefore, innocent by virtue of their powerlessness. The cross symbolized the undeserved suffering of Armenians. The cover of the *New Near East* magazine, published by Near East Relief in March of 1921, displayed a large cross looming above a group of refugees, mostly women and children, who were clustered around its base. The foreground contained drawings of several refugees, whose eyes looked towards the reader, while another female refugee stood with arms and eyes raised towards the cross. The caption at the bottom of the cover read: "The Way of the Cross in Armenia."[14]

By implication, helping the Armenian victims was akin to seeing the suffering Christ and seeking to alleviate such suffering. Americans were thus asked to sacrifice out of love and mercy, as a way to emulate Jesus and show love for him by giving. Their benevolence added to their goodness; it was a sign of God's favor in relation to them. Their ability to aid in the survival of Armenian refugees also reinforced America's position of power. America played the part of God in the three-part story of rescue.

This redemption drama also plays well emotionally. The contest between good and evil evokes strong feels of identification and righteous action. It can also be used to stir up feelings of guilt for one's own bounty, as well as pity and sympathy for those who suffer. At the same time, it allows for indignation towards and condemnation of those deemed evil. Those who organized the relief efforts and employed the media to get their message across were adept at generating and directing such feelings in order to elicit support and raise funds.

The moral dualism of the redemption drama, however, also functions to reaffirm relations of power. The Americans, playing the role of God in the drama, were both powerful and good. Armenians, victims of the forces of evil, were rendered as powerless. They were the starving ones, who would perish without the generous help of Americans. Humanitarian aid in this mode did not empower recipients. It rescued them and cared for them, but did little to change their social conditions so that they were no longer powerless.

In the logic of the narrative, innocence and powerlessness are connected. Powerlessness, including passivity, is often a condition of innocence, of being a worthy victim. For example, Jesus' redemptive sacrifice is described in terms such as "a lamb being led to slaughter." This logic complicates the

[14] Journal is in archives of the Armenian Library and Museum Association, Watertown, Massachusetts.

situation of those who suffer. If they assert themselves on their behalf, their innocence, and so worthiness, is questioned. If they remain passive, the conditions of their suffering remain unchanged.

Because the narrative of redemption has most often been told from the viewpoint of the rescuer and rarely from that of those who suffer, scant attention has been given to these dynamics. In humanitarian discourse, they have surfaced mainly in debates about aid versus empowerment and about who is deserving of assistance. In addition, unambiguous dividing lines between good and evil work better for promotional campaigns. Everyone wants to be against evil and on the side of the good. However, in reality the victimized rarely experience the world as so morally unambiguous or simplistic. In this way too, their experiences are submerged beneath the way their rescuers tell their stories.

Notwithstanding these problems, Near East Relief – as measured by the amount of money it raised, the endurance of its fundraising campaigns, the effectiveness of its fundraising networks, and the dedication of its relief workers – employed these narrative motifs in ways that were successful for its purposes. In the late 1910s and 1920s, the plight of the Armenian refugees became embedded in American consciousness, so much so that "starving Armenians" became a household term.

At the same time, these motifs fit cultural patterns that were already established, of American – that is, Christian and civilized – superiority and benevolence. They reinforced existing relations of power and accompanying judgments of good and evil in the world. In these ways, they did little to enable the future of Armenia and Armenians amid the complexities of Middle Eastern politics and the power plays of Western allies.

Implications of Near East Relief's Humanitarian Work

As Michael R. Marrus and Margaret M. R. Kellow have argued in their chapters in this volume, politics and ethical dynamics in contexts of oppression and violence are rarely simple or straightforward. Purity and innocence remain particularly elusive. Kellow ably shows how, in practice, even those who most held to the principle that human freedom should not require payment, did precisely what they opposed, that is, they paid to redeem slaves. Marrus navigates the murky waters of shifting political and humanitarian impulses across two centuries to explore the role and meaning of bystander witnesses. Any notion of innocence remains elusive, if not problematic, in these contexts. Humanitarian work that purports such innocence and/or expects purity and innocence of those it seeks to aid will inevitably get trapped by its own rhetoric. This happened in the case of Near East Relief, especially in its fixing of the image of starving Armenians as suffering fellow Christians in popular America consciousness.

The propaganda campaigns used by Near East Relief both enabled its success and stymied it at crucial points, especially as it pursued more political aims and sought to protect its missionary interests in the Middle East. In the years immediately after World War I, the Western powers, along with Turkey and Russia, jockeyed for position and territory. Armenia declared itself an independent republic, but with few resources to help it survive amidst the territorial moves of more powerful countries. President Wilson supported the proposed mandate for Armenia, but politically and physically weakened, he was not able to win congressional approval. The leadership of Near East Relief, including James Barton, worked and lobbied long and hard for the mandate, but proved ineffective in the end as well. The spirit of isolationism, which characterized American politics after the war, proved stronger than appeals to protect and empower a fledgling republic.

Meanwhile Mustafa Kemal Ataturk emerged as a powerful military and political leader in Turkey. As Turkey regained strength, it asserted itself and its claims to territory. At the Lausanne Conference in 1922–1923, Ataturk's demands prevailed. At first, James Barton, an observer at the conference, tried to lobby for the Armenian cause, but when it seemed that the allies would not succeed in stopping Ataturk, he made a pragmatic move. In order to have some role in the emerging Turkey and in order for the missionary schools and other institutions to survive, it seemed prudent to support the Lausanne Treaty. However, because the missionary propaganda about Turkey and the Turks had been so effective, most Americans opposed an alliance with Turkey. Barton remained relatively alone in his support and America did not sign on to the treaty.

Yet, in practice, American economic and geopolitical interests in Turkey continued to influence policy for decades. As America sought alliances with Turkey, the cause of the Armenian minority moved into the shadows, as did American recognition of the genocide. The irony is this: America, the powerful rescuing nation, whose people were the life blood, financially and practically, of the relief efforts after the Armenian genocide, has not formally recognized that genocide. As the relief efforts waned, American awareness of the history of the genocide faded as well, and "starving Armenians" became a floating signifier, devoid of context.

Given the shifting tides of empire in the Middle East and the complex politics at play in the history of American and Turkish relations, those seeking to navigate such waters might well benefit from understanding the impact of Christian narratives and motifs, especially as adopted and adapted to play upon popular sentiment and mobilize popular support. While those narratives provide rhetorical strategies effective for generating humanitarian aid responses, particularly in times of emergency and crisis, they do little to change the dynamics of power that caused the crisis in the first place. Nor do they enable the transition from an emergency response mode to ongoing work for the future, especially the shift from aiding victims to supporting agents of change.

Employing the rhetoric of moral dualism, which depicts the world stage as a battle of good versus evil, remains a popular humanitarian strategy for describing America's presence in the world as champion and rescuer. Armenian American activists continue to draw upon such views as they pressure America to recognize the genocide and, to that end, seek to recall America to its "mission" of being on the side of good in the world. However, the implications of these views for the rescued, that they be powerless, innocent and pure, confound their struggles for life. In the end, history shows that although the humanitarians, philanthropists, and missionaries of Near East Relief provided much aid for the "starving Armenians," they were less successful in offering the sustenance needed for recognition, empowerment and self-determination.

REFERENCES

Aulén, G. (1932). *Christus Victor.* Trans. A. G. Herbert. London: SPCK.

Balakian, P. (2003). *The Burning Tigris: The Armenian Genocide and America's Response.* New York: HarperCollins.

Barton, J. L. (1930). *Story of Near East Relief (1915–1930): An Interpretation.* New York: Macmillan.

———, Comp. (1998). *"Turkish Atrocities": Statements of American Missionaries on the Destruction of Christian Communities in Ottoman Turkey, 1915–1917.* Ann Arbor, MI: Gomidas Institute.

Bloxham, D. (2005). *The Great Game of Genocide: Imperialism, Nationalism, and the Destruction of the Ottoman Armenians.* Oxford: Oxford University Press.

Brown, J. C., and Bohn, C. R. (1989). *Christianity, Patriarchy, and Abuse: A Feminist Critique.* New York: Pilgrim Press.

Driver, J. (1986). *Understanding the Atonement for the Mission of the Church.* Scottdale, PA: Herald Press.

Fiddes, P. (1989). *Past Event and Present Salvation: The Christian Idea of Atonement.* Louisville, KY: Westminster/John Knox Press.

Elliott, M. (1924). *Beginning Again at Ararat.* New York: Fleming H. Revel Company.

Gorringe, T. (1996). *God's Just Vengeance: Crime, Violence and the Rhetoric of Salvation.* Cambridge: Cambridge University Press.

Grabill, J. L. (1971). *Protestant Diplomacy and the Near East: Missionary Influence on American Policy, 1810–1927*. Minneapolis: University of Minnesota Press.

Harper, S. B. (2004). "Mary Louise Graffam: Witness to Genocide." In Jay Winter, ed., *America and the Armenian Genocide of 1915*. Cambridge: Cambridge University Press.

Merguerian, B. J. (2006). "'Missions in Eden': Shaping an Educational and Social Program for the Armenians in Eastern Turkey (1855–1895)." In Helen Murre-van den Berg, ed., *New Faith in Ancient Lands: Western Missions in the Middle East in the Nineteenth and Early Twentieth Centuries*. Leiden, Netherlands: Brill.

Moranian, S. E. (1994). "The American Missionaries and the Armenian Question, 1915–1927." Ph.D. diss. University of Wisconsin.

———. (2004). "The Armenian Genocide and American missionary relief efforts." In Jay Winter, ed., *America and the Armenian Genocide of 1915*. Cambridge: Cambridge University Press.

Ross, F. A., C. L. Fry, and E. Sibley (1929). *The Near East and American Philanthropy*. New York: Columbia University Press.

Sahagian, H. (2004). "Mary Louise Graffam, Ernest C. Partridge, and the Armenians of Sivas." In Richard G. Hovannisian, ed., *Armenian Sebastia/Sivas and Lesser Armenia*. Costa Mesa: Mazda Publishers.

Slide, A., ed. (1997). *Ravished Armenia and the Story of Aurora Mardiganian*. Lanham, MD: Scarecrow Press.

Tejirian, E. H. (2000). "Faith of Our Fathers: Near East Relief and the Near East Foundation – From Mission to NGO." Electronic document, http://www.ciaonet.org/conf/mei01/teel01.html, accessed August 21, 2006.

Torchin, L. (2006). "*Ravished Armenia*: Visual Media, Humanitarian Advocacy, and the Formation of Witnessing Publics." *American Anthropologist*, vol. 108, no. 1, pp. 214–20.

Vickrey, C. V. (1926?) *International Golden Rule Sunday: A Handbook*. New York: George H. Doran Company. (Note: The book contains no date of publication, although it includes a letter of endorsement by President Coolidge, dated 1926.)

7. International Bystanders to the Holocaust and Humanitarian Intervention

MICHAEL R. MARRUS

Is there anything new to say on the subject of bystanders to the Holocaust? Some twenty years ago, summing up the received wisdom on the matter, I wrote that this was largely a history about what *failed* to happen: "Information about the Holocaust was not digested, Jews were not admitted, Jewish communities failed to unite, Allied governments spurned rescue suggestions, and access to Auschwitz was not bombed. It is, essentially, a negative report – the history of inaction, indifference, and insensitivity" (Marrus 1987: 156–7). My main concern at that time was anachronism: "the strong tendency in historical writing on bystanders to the Holocaust to condemn, rather than to explain" – and by implication to condemn on the basis of present-day perceptions and judgments of what *ought* to have happened. On matters of rescue, Yehuda Bauer's (2001) admonition not to exaggerate the possibilities of rescue or escape is instructive, given the hopeless circumstances in which Jews found themselves.[1] As an antidote, I urged fellow historians to heed historical context, to be alert to the sometimes unimaginable and certainly unprecedented conditions that the Holocaust presented. I called for "a painstaking effort to enter into ... the minds and sensibilities" of bystanders, suggesting that, "to a degree, everyone was in the dark." And finally, I called for a "fair hearing" for those who lived through these terrible events, suggesting that we put more effort into comprehension than condemnation (Marrus 1987: 157).

Since then, I believe, historians have made considerable efforts to develop a more nuanced view – particularly on the subject of international bystanders to the Holocaust, by which I mean the reaction of liberal democracies to Nazi anti-Semitism and the implementation of the Final

---

[1] See Yehuda Bauer (2001: ch. 10). In my view, William D. Rubinstein (1997) exaggerates this point in the opposite sense.

Solution. While interpretations differ, of course, writing on this subject is considerably more sophisticated and analytically multidimensional than two decades ago.[2] Still, popular perceptions lag. Much of the general public still believes that "the world did nothing," and that there is not much more to say about the matter. And they adhere to a closely related understanding: that the Holocaust was unique, not only in terms of the character of Jewish victimization, that is, the Nazis' obsessive commitment to murdering an entire people, but also with respect to the abandonment of the victims by the international community. At the sixtieth anniversary of the liberation of Auschwitz, in January 2005, Israeli Prime Minister Ariel Sharon emphasized that "the world did nothing" to stop the killing (Banville 2005). In May 2006, writing in the *Washington Post*, columnist Charles Krauthammer declared that, "in 1938, in the face of the gathering storm – a fanatical, aggressive, openly declared enemy of the West, and most determinedly of the Jews – the world did nothing."

My starting point here is that this abrupt dismissal – "the world did nothing" – is at best a half truth. It obviously ignores the most important response: bringing down the Third Reich. But the dismissal also requires an additional element of context. And with this comes my effort to say something new. I want to propose a largely unconsidered contextual theme for the assessment of liberal bystanders to the Holocaust, one that can deepen our understanding and perhaps relate as well to our present concerns about the terrible fate of some minorities in today's world. My theme has been much discussed in recent years by commentators on international affairs, but their reach has seldom, if at all, extended to the Holocaust.[3] It is what political scientists and others call humanitarian intervention. However articulated and defined, this is the general concept that people have in mind when they talk about how countries failed to react, or should have reacted, to the persecution and massacre of European Jewry. So it is humanitarian intervention that I seek to put into historical perspective. This discussion of international bystanders to the Holocaust will begin with some comments on the history of the concept, before surveying the

---

[2] For an excellent selection of recent work, see David Cesarani and Paul A. Levine, eds. (2002). For a more theologically oriented approach, see Victoria J. Barnett (1999).

[3] One exception is Samantha Power's *"A Problem from Hell": America and the Age of Genocide* (2002), which has some important historical perspectives on the Holocaust, but not humanitarian intervention. Nathan Feinberg, the authority on international law, perhaps overstated the matter when he began an article as follows: "Every student of international law who deals with the history and problems of humanitarian intervention knows how considerable is the part played by intervention on behalf of the Jews" (1974: 59).

undermining of humanitarian intervention in the wake of World War I. Finally, I will comment on the relationship of these ideas and commitments to the Holocaust of European Jewry.

Modern Emergence of Humanitarian Intervention

Particularly since the crises in Somalia, Rwanda, Bosnia, and Kosovo, there has been considerable analysis of humanitarian intervention, or more likely the failure of humanitarian intervention in such catastrophes – but with remarkably little historical grounding to the concept. Hence my question: Might the evolving notion of humanitarian intervention in cases of extreme persecution, massacre, or genocide be relevant to a study of bystanders during the Holocaust?

Throughout the early modern period, extending into the era of democratic revolutions at the end of the eighteenth century, neither law nor custom countenanced interference in another country's mistreatment of its own populations and those over which it extended dominion. With regard to victims in such cases, the doctrine of sovereignty by and large prevailed. To be sure, thinkers going back to Hugo Grotius (1625) and Emerich de Vattel (1758) had speculated on the right of states to act against other states whose cruelty, oppression, and massacres rose to the level of international scandal. However, such notions conflicted not only with emerging understandings of sovereignty, but also with the realities of international power and diplomacy, as well as the incapacity of state actors to agree on what a threshold of scandal might be. By the early twentieth century many commentators seem to have reached a consensus that such a doctrine existed, however imperfectly followed or inadequately defined.[4] How did things move from one set of conditions to the other?

Nineteenth-century writers on the subject peppered their texts with clues as to the origins of this doctrine, with references to such ideas as the "laws of humanity," "the right of humanity," intervention "for humanity," "principles of decency and humanity," and the comportment of "civilized society." Such notions connect with eighteenth-century humanitarian thought and with visions, energized in some circumstances by the French and American Revolutions, of human rights operating in a global perspective.[5]

---

[4] For some historical perspectives on humanitarian intervention, see M. Ganji (1962), and Jean-Pierre L. Fonteyne (1974).

[5] See Paul Gordon Lauren (2003: chs. 1–2). Among the most articulate and determined campaigners were unquestionably the organizers of the antislavery movement. For a recent study, see Adam Hochschild (2005).

During the nineteenth century diplomatic theory considered the cause of the egregiously oppressed as a compelling basis for diplomatic action – even though, to be sure, the actual conduct of affairs rarely cast this motivation in pure relief. "Since 1815," writes historian Carole Fink in her aptly titled book, *Defending the Rights of Others*, "general statements on national rights, religious toleration, and civil equality had become a standard condition in international diplomacy"(2004: 7). Students of international affairs have tracked episodes in the early and mid-nineteenth century in which the Great Powers interfered with the lesser – either as part of the counterrevolutionary objectives of the Concert of Europe or the imposition of European interests in the ramshackle Ottoman Empire.[6] International relations specialist Nicholas Onuf (c. 2000), who has studied these, notes how humanitarian concerns – the "interests of humanity" – were often entangled in the justifications made at the time.[7] Certainly this was the case with the two high-profile affairs in which Great Powers intervened on behalf of beleaguered Jews – the Damascus Affair in 1840 (Frankel 1997), and the Mortara Affair twenty years later (Kertzer 1997). There was, indeed, a tradition of humanitarian intervention on behalf of Jews precisely because of their weakness in geopolitical terms and perhaps also because of sympathy generated on their behalf as a result of their long history of persecution.[8]

However mixed the motives in actual practice, the modern notion that humanitarian considerations might on their own justify intervention in the affairs of another sovereign state, and indeed the use of the term, *l'intervention d'humanité*, first appears as part of the Great Powers' contention with the Ottoman Empire – most often in the claims of those states, especially the tsarist empire, to extend their protection over long-suffering Christian subjects of the sultan. With this came the developing notion,

---

[6] See, for example, Stephen Kloepfer (1985).

[7] See also Martti Koskenniemi (2001).

[8] For an early statement of this point of view, see Edumund Burke's speech to the British House of Commons at the end of the eighteenth century: "Having no fixed settlement in any part of the world, no kingdom nor country in which they have a Government, a community and a system of laws, [the Jews] are thrown upon the benevolence of nations and claim protection and civility from their weakness as well as from their utility. ... From the east to the west, from one end of the world to the other, they are scattered and connected. ... Their abandoned state and their defenseless situation calls most forcibly for the protection of civilized nations. If Dutchmen are injured and attacked, the Dutch have a nation, a Government and armies to redress or revenge their cause. If Britons are injured, Britons have armies and laws, the laws of nations ... to fly to for protection and justice. But the Jews have no such power and no such friend to depend on. Humanity then must become their protector and ally" (quoted in Feinberg 1974: 59).

fully consonant with the era of liberal imperialism, of humanitarian standards that were held to be the common inheritance of "civilized" nations, on behalf of which powerful countries had an obligation to act in the name of "humanity." And so, referring to the oft-cited example of the Greek uprising against the Turks in 1827, the American authority on international law, Henry Wheaton, identified an established right of "interference," in circumstances "where the general interests of humanity are infringed by the excesses of a barbarous and despotic government" (1866: 95).

To be sure, diplomatic rhetoric was one thing and the actual application of force was quite another: the nineteenth century did not so revolutionize diplomatic exchange as to change the historical balance that was quite long on the first and short on the second. Nevertheless, we must recognize that long before the Holocaust, humanitarian rhetoric and to a much lesser degree the actual practice of humanitarian intervention had become a respected European and international legal norm – something that constitutes, through its historical evolution, a neglected background to "standing by" during the Holocaust.

To give a feel for this discourse, I refer for a moment to a spectacular example – the 1876 campaign on behalf of Bulgarian Christians, launched by the veteran British Liberal Party leader and former prime minister, William Ewart Gladstone, in one of the most famous political pamphlets ever: the *Bulgarian Horrors* (1876). Gladstone's stinging message, stamped indelibly by his evangelical Protestant spirituality, and written when he was in opposition to the ruling Tories who were led by his great enemy Benjamin Disraeli, denounced the massacre by Ottoman irregulars of some 15,000 to 20,000 Bulgarian civilians and insurgents, while nearby British naval forces stood aside. British policy, intoned the Liberal tribune, amounted to "moral complicity with the basest and blackest outages upon record within the present century, if not within the memory of man" (8). Promoting intervention, a campaign with calculated political significance in Gladstone's war against his Conservative opponent, the great Liberal warhorse knew he was venturing on thin ice. International law, he understood, might not *require* intervention. Nevertheless, he told his readers in a metaphor wonderfully flattering to British identity, "the great heart of Britain has not ceased to beat" (27). The proper business of British arms in Turkey was humanitarian: the British people should declare that "it is for purposes of humanity alone that we have a fleet in Turkish waters" (28). British naval vessels should "be so distributed as to enable its force to be most promptly and efficiently applied, in case of need, on Turkish soil, in concert with the other Powers, for the defence of innocent lives, and to prevent the repetition of those recent scenes, at which hell itself might almost blush" (30).

Gladstone called upon his countrymen to do even more: "to insist that our Government ... shall apply all its vigor to concur with the other States of Europe in obtaining the extinction of the Turkish executive power in Bulgaria." And then came the great flourish, which in its vitriol and outrage bears comparison to any humanitarian expression uttered during the Nazi Holocaust. Clearing the Turks out of Bulgaria, he said,

> this most blessed deliverance, is the only reparation we can make to the memory of those heaps on heaps of dead; to the violated purity alike of matron, of maiden, and of child; to the civilization which has been affronted and shamed; to the laws of God or, if you like, of Allah; to the moral sense of mankind at large. There is not a criminal in a European gaol, there is not a cannibal in the South Sea Islands, whose indignation would not rise and overboil at the recital of that which has been done, which has too late been examined, but which remains unavenged; which has left behind all the foul and all the fierce passions that produced it, and which may again spring up, in another murderous harvest, from the soil soaked and reeking with blood, and in the air tainted with every imaginable deed of crime and shame. That such things should be done once, is a damning disgrace to the portion of our race which did them; that a door should be left open for their ever-so-barely possible repetition would spread that shame over the whole. (38)[9]

In the end, nothing much happened. Gladstone's contemporaries understood his pamphlet at least in part politically, as many modern readers do not – and on politics there was plenty, in the 1870s, on which to disagree. It took a war with the Russians, which began the next year, to force the Turks out of Bulgaria, and the incident has passed into history more as a clash of political machinations than as a turning point in British foreign policy and a spur to further interventions.[10] My point, however, is to call attention to the way in which, by the 1870s, a robust rhetoric of humanitarian intervention was a familiar part of debate about international affairs.

To be sure, we can hardly take Gladstone's florid appeal as proof of the priority of humanitarian intervention in European norms of the day. Its standing was hardly that. But by the latter part of the nineteenth century Western diplomats were fully conversant with governmental appeals

---

[9] See also, R. T. Shannon (1999), Mark Rathbone (2004), and C. Brad Faught (2006).
[10] See David Harris (1939).

"on behalf of our common humanity," as an American secretary of state put it in 1882 (Stowell 1921: 75).[11]

These justifications of humanitarian intervention drew their character from important developments in the nineteenth century: first, expanded notions of human rights, fortified over the course of the nineteenth century by claims that a faithful adherence to them was one of the attributes of all "civilized people"; second, in the case of Great Britain at least, by an evangelical religious sensibility that first impacted on international affairs with the movement to abolish the slave trade; and third, more practically, revolutionary developments in communications and the developed states' capacity to project power internationally – without which there would be neither knowledge of humanitarian emergencies nor the capacity to do anything about them. Together these three developments helped define an age of liberal imperialism, in which solid, bourgeois governments acted confidently on the world's stage, certain not only of their right to rule, but also of their beneficent objectives in doing so. In his survey of the era, Paul Lauren refers to the few years between the turn of the century and the outbreak of World War I as a remarkable seed-time for human rights as well as for international humanitarian mobilization on their behalf: more than a dozen intergovernmental bodies and over three hundred religious and secular nongovernmental organizations sprang up during this period; global visions of human rights and international responsibility for their promotion, had never been stronger among international actors (Lauren 2003).

Slowly, tentatively, incompletely and insufficiently, but nevertheless perceptively, humanitarian intervention became part of diplomatic parlance before 1914. Arguing the case in 1876, the Belgian jurist, E.R.N. Arntz, defined the necessary conditions for its application:

> When a government, although acting within its rights of sovereignty, violates the rights of humanity, either by measures contrary to the interests of other States, or by an excess of cruelty and injustice, which is a blot on our civilization, the right of intervention may lawfully be exercised, for, however worthy of respect are the rights of state sovereignty and independence there is something yet more worthy of respect, and that is the right of humanity or of human society, which must not be outraged. (Stowell 1921: 53)

---

[11] Secretary of State Frelinghuysen's communication of April 15, 1882, involved humanitarian intervention on behalf of the Jews of Russia and introduced the American argument as follows: "The prejudice of race and creed having in our day given way to the claims of our common humanity, the people of the United States have heard, with great regret, stories of the sufferings of the Jews in Russia."

Looking back from the 1930s, the émigré Russian human rights champion Andrei Mandelstam described the guarantees of religious, political and civic rights imposed on the Sublime Porte in the Treaty of Berlin, in 1878, as "one of the most striking manifestations of humanitarian intervention in favor of the oppressed races of the Ottoman Empire" (1970: 16).[12] Writing in 1900, the American jurist William Lingelbach had noted a new feature of intervention "which is peculiarly a growth of the present century. The moral sentiment of civilized peoples in modern times has been frequently aroused and governments have been forced to intervene in cases where intolerance has become apprehensive and cruel" (1900: 19).

Jurists such as Lingelbach made the case that the authority for humanitarian intervention did not rest upon politics, or rather politics alone, but also on international law. "The theory of intervention on the ground of humanity," wrote Professor Antoine Rougier of the University of Lausanne in 1910, "is properly that which recognizes the right of one state to exercise an international control over the acts of another in regard to its internal sovereignty when contrary to the laws of humanity" (1910: 472).[13] "Intervention for humanity, or humanitarian intervention, as it is more properly called, is also an instance of intervention for the purpose of vindicating the law of nations against outrage," wrote the American authority, Ellery C. Stowell (1921: 51). But what constituted outrage? The eminent English commentator William Edward Hall spelled it out: "Tyrannical conduct of a government towards its subjects, massacres and brutality in a civil war, or religious persecution," were the kinds of things he had in mind. Such acts, he went on, "are so inconsistent with the character of a moral being as to constitute a public scandal, which the body of states, or one or more states, as representative of it, are competent to suppress" (1924: 342).

"A public scandal." Or for that matter, Gladstone's "damning disgrace." To our more hardened generation, these declarations of intolerable public offense, of authority shamed by unthinkable misdeeds, sound quaint and perhaps class-ridden, hopelessly inadequate to conceptualizing reactions to modern-day persecution and oppression, extending sometimes to the commission of genocide. Moreover, for present-day readers the language is deficient in another respect – the distinctly ethnocentric cast of humanitarian intervention. Interveners saw themselves as civilized, Christian, modern, enlightened, and sometimes also, it must be said, white; that was

[12] On Mandelstam's work see Jan Herman Burgers (1992).
[13] Quoted in Stowell (1921: 53).

how they understood their mandate to act – and why they failed to acknowledge their own shortcomings. Unsurprisingly, the violators they identified were on the European periphery – the Ottomans, the Russians, and occasionally the indigenous ruling authorities of formal or informal parts of Western empires in the undeveloped world of Africa and Asia.

It is also far from clear that the theorists understood humanitarian intervention as requiring the exercise of armed force. Stowell spoke of action "to assume the burden of administration of the territory" in question, or, more delicately, "to constrain the unworthy sovereign to mend his ways" (1921: 52–3). Diplomats and international lawyers spoke of the "protection" of populations, and left it at that. Indicating uncharted territory, Stowell cited the famous Martens Clause, now recognized as an "ambiguous and evasive" construct. First introduced as a preamble to the Hague Convention on the Regulations on the Laws and Customs of War on Land in 1899, the Martens Clause suggested a considerable scope for interpreting humanitarian practice: "Until a complete code of the laws of war has been issued," it declared, "the High Contracting Parties deem it expedient to declare that, in cases not included in the Regulations adopted by them, the inhabitants and the belligerents remain under the protection and the rule of the principles of the law of nations, as they result from the usages established among civilized peoples, from the laws of humanity, and the dictates of the public conscience" (52).[14] So we are still a long way, here, from the post–Cold War use of the term. But by 1914 humanitarian intervention, at least in some form or other, had entered the diplomatic discourse of the day.

The Eclipse of Humanitarian Intervention in the Interwar Period

In practically every way one could imagine, the War of 1914–1918 transformed beliefs and practices of how states should interact internationally. World War I subverted commitments to humanitarian intervention in two ways: first, by making all countries deeply wary of any obligation to expend blood and treasure internationally on behalf of the persecuted and oppressed; and second, by focusing postwar attention on the issue of minorities, previously the most common focus for humanitarian intervention and for which an international mechanism, the League of Nations, was introduced to act on behalf of civilized international society for the rectification of wrongs.

---

[14] On "ambiguous and evasive," see Antonio Cassese (2000).

Staggered by the bloodletting of the early part of the war, the Allied powers fighting Imperial Germany and Austria still retained enough of their prewar humanitarian commitments to issue a stern admonition to the Ottoman authorities as information reached them about the beginnings of genocide against the Armenian population of the Ottoman Empire. On May 24, 1915, in an echo of Gladstone's great charge against the Ottomans, they solemnly warned the Turks that they would hold responsible those who were committing "new crimes of Turkey against humanity and civilization" (Dadrian 1995: 216). However, far from opening a new chapter of humanitarian intervention in which the Allies would take some action on behalf of the victims, or at least promote justice for their cause afterwards, this was practically the last moment in which the Armenians enjoyed unreserved support in the West.

After four years during which the contending parties had mercilessly battered each other's claims to civilized standards, statesmen emerged from the war wary of any risk-taking on behalf of international justice, and inclined to leave the cause of particular cases of inhumanity to someone else. Notwithstanding provisions for the trial of the perpetrators of the Armenian genocide in the 1920 Treaty of Sèvres, the Allies bowed to an insurgent Kemalism in Turkey and, as historian Vahakn Dadrian reports, "the urgency of retributive justice gave way to the expediency of political accommodation" (1995: 310–11).[15] In other areas too, the war sapped the military and diplomatic energies that the Great Powers were prepared to commit to humanitarian projects. During the so-called "*kaddish* years" of 1918–1921, prefiguring the Holocaust, the victorious powers stood by passively while hundreds of thousands of Jews were forcibly uprooted, and tens of thousands lost their lives in pogroms and other anti-Jewish violence accompanying civil wars and regional conflicts in East Central Europe (Wróbel 2005).

To be sure, it was widely accepted that something had to be done to stabilize the European continent. To that end, the peacemakers focused on the onerous tasks of realizing national self-determination, the containment of revolution and the harnessing of German power. Everything else was considered a luxury, and so while the postwar period saw a flourishing of humanitarian claims and narratives, including demands for colonial independence, national recognition, the rights of workers, women, and children, these were relegated to the newly established League of Nations or nongovernmental organizations, rather than being championed by the Great Powers themselves.

---

[15] See also Donald Bloxham (2005 ch. 4).

Particularly worrisome, from the standpoint of statesmen committed to the stabilization of the new European order, was the problem of minorities – national, ethnic, religious, or linguistic claimants whose accommodation within the borders drawn in Paris seemed problematic, and whose insistent demands were a discomforting reminder of prewar radical nationalists, especially those whose destabilizing of the Balkans had been so important in the origins of the war in 1914.[16] Because so much was at stake, settling the problems of minorities could not, it was felt, be left to the newly created states themselves, to interested neighbors, or to willing interlocutors.

Instead, the victorious powers promoted the rights of minority groups as "obligations of international concern" – a kind of echo of prewar humanitarian intervention, but without a commitment to act diplomatically or militarily. Rather, Allied negotiators set these as conditions of settlement imposed upon newly defined states in a series of treaties, taking as a model the treaty imposed on Poland, where wary minorities constituted one-third of the total population. Relinquishing what might have been their commitments to humanitarian intervention in the preceding era, the peacemakers looked to the League to speak and act on behalf of them all. And to be sure, the victorious powers were reluctant *themselves* to be bound by such agreements – creating a standing grievance among the "minority states" that festered over the period.

Defining obligations more capacious than had ever been contemplated for the international community as a whole, the minorities treaties obligated signatories "to assure full and complete protection of life and liberty to all inhabitants ... without distinction of birth, nationality, language, race or religion."[17] Extending to educational, communal and other protections the provisions were generous, admirable, and in keeping with

---

[16] It is important to stress that "minorities," as understood in the interwar period, were not quite what we understand as minorities today – usually immigrant groups, or descendants of immigrants, or groups of individuals who have maintained, usually in some particular respect, particular group identities. Rather, in the diplomatic and political parlance of the 1920s and 1930s, these were national, religious or racial collectivities who, as a result of the collapse of three European empires, did not share the attributes of the majority populations whose self-determination Woodrow Wilson and others had so idealistically promoted in the establishment of successor states at the peace settlements of 1919. As such, the Versailles agreements may be said to have created the minorities. As Mark Mazower puts it, "Versailles had given sixty million people a state of their own, but it *turned another twenty-five million into minorities.*" (1998: 42, emphasis mine).

[17] Article 2 of the treaty with Poland, which was a model for the other minorities treaties. See J. Robinson, O. Karbach, M. M. Laserson, et al. (1943: 314).

humanitarian traditions. But note: concern about minorities did not mean solicitude for them. Indeed, as historian Mark Mazower observes, minority spokesmen were often seen as troublemakers who ought to settle down and assimilate – the quid pro quo of a settlement on which everyone counted. "Between the wars," he writes, "minorities were often seen as a fifth column for neighbours' irredentist ambitions, or for Bolshevism, and were regarded as security risks rather than as citizens" (1998: 58–9). And so although the statesmen spent much time in the postwar period on the rights of minorities, their support for them was far from a transcendent humanitarian commitment.[18]

That is why the League and its secretariat did not act as defenders of minorities per se, but rather as referees between them and the countries in which they lived, trying to facilitate settlements and make it easier for states to work out some sort of arrangement with petitioners. Genuine abusers of minorities, long before the Nazis, sometimes got away with severe violations; sometimes, even, they got away with murder.

Where did this leave humanitarian intervention? The answer is that it atrophied, perhaps a good demonstration of the adage that where humanitarian commitments must rely on collective expression, they are no one's responsibility. For most of the interwar period, appeals for international action on behalf of the persecuted and downtrodden looked to an improved League of Nations, rather than to one or a group of Great Powers, acting on behalf of what Gladstone called "the broad and deep interests of humanity" (1876: 13). In retrospect there was too much reliance on the League to apply what Dorothy Jones calls "the bright chain of reason" to the international quest for justice (2002: 15). Neither Britain nor France had the confidence in their capacity to intervene wherever they liked in the service of humanitarian causes. The Great Powers were exhausted and sought a settlement that would enforce itself. The United States did not even give lip service to continued involvement and never did join the League. The Soviets had neither interest nor inclination in working with the capitalist West. And the defeated nations, for their

---

[18] Mazower (1998) captures, I think, the assumptions of the day: "the original intent [of the peacemakers] was not so much minority protection as border protection. The thinking went like this: Peace in the future would depend on the stability and acceptance of the borders newly drawn by the peacemakers across much of Europe. Dissatisfied minorities within those borders had the potential to be, at best, centers of unrest and, at worst, invitations to intervention. Protect the minorities, make their protection a part of fundamental law that could not be changed without permission of the League, and you protect the settlements on which peace will depend" (Jones 1994: 88).

part, had little use for the League except as a sounding board for their revisionist claims.[19]

Effectively, the minorities regime collapsed during the Hitler era: Germany (which was never bound by a minorities treaty except for Upper Silesian territory after 1922) gave notice of withdrawal from the League in November 1933, and the following year the Polish foreign minister, Colonel Józef Beck, renounced Poland's commitments to the treaties until such time as these obligations were made universal. By the second half of the 1930s, the minorities system of the League of Nations was in shambles. States that had signed minorities treaties looked with contempt upon the refusal of those who had not. Germany and Poland were out. All states now focused on the menacing prospect of war, feared by most, plotted by others. With supreme irony, it was Nazi Germany that took on the role of minorities intervener-in-chief, rattling the sabre on behalf of the German inhabitants of the Sudetenland of Czechoslovakia and Germans in the Free City of Danzig. And it was Konrad Henlein, the Nazi leader of the Sudeten German Party, and a future SS *Obergruppenführer*, who, ingloriously, became Europe's most famous and most heeded minorities advocate.

Jews, Bystanders and the Holocaust

Coming now to the era of the Holocaust, let us return to the Jews and the interwar wreckage of humanitarian intervention. In doing so, my concern is to put the shortcomings of international Holocaust bystanders into a somewhat different perspective from the common assumption that "the world did nothing." To be sure, while "the world did nothing" is an unhelpful generalization, whatever the world did certainly has about it an aura of insufficiency – too little was undertaken, for too few, and too late. So long as historians are moved by ethical responsibility they will rightly point out how the "universe of obligation," to use sociologist Helen Fein's term (1979), failed adequately to extend to victims – in this case the victims of the Nazis' genocidal program. But, as I suggest, their challenge is also to understand how and why. Part of the explanation for the conduct of international bystanders during the Holocaust was that liberal governments and societies abandoned, during World War I and the succeeding interwar period, a commitment to humanitarian intervention. They lost their

---

[19] "German lawyers," says Martti Koskenniemi in an admirable summary, "cultivated a predominantly strategic attitude toward the League. Although its functional activities were seen as useful, its collective security and peaceful settlement tasks were understood as a half-serious smoke-screen over Anglo-American imperialism" (2001: 238).

resolve to act internationally in the face of grave acts of injustice – a response that had been slowly evolving over the course of a century or more and that had extended, in some important instances, to the Jews.

Admittedly, this perspective shifts the focus, somewhat, from the specifically Jewish dimensions of the catastrophe. Some additional evidence for this perspective comes from comparison – particularly, as in the work of historian Meredith Hindley (2002), comparing policies towards Jews and non-Jews facing humanitarian crises in closely related circumstances. Hindley's conclusions, examining the reaction of the Western Allies both to the Holocaust and to the prospect of mass starvation in Nazi-occupied Europe, is consistent with this account of the interwar retreat from humanitarian intervention and the prioritizing of other political and strategic objectives. While the two situations she investigates were not precisely parallel, in both cases humanitarian appeals went unanswered: "No amount of public pressure could provoke Allied leaders to change their priorities, leaving little room for addressing the needs of civilians," she writes. "When concessions were made, they were granted to achieve specific political and strategic objectives," Hindley concludes – a calculation made rarely in favor of the Jews, for they had no political or strategic goods to deliver (2002: 97–9).

For all the belligerents, war making not only overwhelmed humanitarian projects, as in World War I, it also shaped the way the war was understood and how leaders presented it to the general public. In his discussion of bystanders to the Holocaust, Raul Hilberg put it this way:

> The Soviet Union gave more publicity to the limited exploits of armed partisans harassing the Germans behind the battle front than to the mass dying of Soviet prisoners of war in German captivity. The Western Allies were moved to lavish more sympathy on the underground Poles who struck out in a vain attempt to free Warsaw in 1944 than on the many young Polish men shot in reprisals or languishing in concentration camps. The currency of World War II was the bullet, shell, and bomb; those who did not have these means were the war's forgotten poor. With weapons one could obtain praise and often additional arms; with plight one could buy neither care nor help. (1992: 249–50)

It is often noted that bystanders had no lack of information about wartime genocide, but rather a deficiency of knowledge – or what I would see as *awareness*.[20] That is why the war's poor were so easily forgotten. This

---

[20] One of the first to point this out was Yehuda Bauer (1968), in his "What did they Know?" Bauer's distinction was between information and *knowledge*; in my own view *awareness* better captures his meaning of the latter term. For a recent examination of this phenomenon, which I believe overstates the case, see Laurel Leff (2005).

failure to move from information to awareness made sense for those for whom humanitarian intervention had become someone else's business. Awareness, a consciously willed understanding, implies action, and it was action that the bystanders explicitly did not want to undertake.[21]

For the Jews, there is a particularly close link between the Holocaust and the collapse of humanitarian intervention after World War I. Jews, as the Jewish historian Salo Baron noted, were "a minority *par excellence*" (1985: 14). For much of the interwar period, Jews appeared on the international stage in their minority guise as the sort of people on behalf of whom humanitarians would sympathize, could properly intervene, and had actually done so on several occasions in the preceding century.[22] Not only were Jews in the minority in every state in which they lived, they had an important place in East Central European societies where the maps were redrawn at the end of the global conflict. Jews therefore played a crucial role virtually whenever intervening on behalf of minorities was discussed at an international level after World War I. A visible presence, they were often to be found leading such discussions, arguing the case for minority rights, lobbying delegations, searching for allies, and challenging governments to live up to their commitments according to the minorities treaties.[23]

Before World War II there was considerable sympathy for persecuted Jewish minorities, and significant condemnation in humanitarian terms of their experience at the hands of the Nazis and their supporters. In the 1933 League of Nations debate on the so-called Bernheim Petition, for example, representatives from every country that spoke upon the case of one persecuted Jew denounced the persecution of the Jewish minority as a violation of German treaty obligations.[24] Western opinion was horrified at *Kristallnacht*, the riotous outbreaks orchestrated by the Nazis against Jews across Germany in November 1938, and Western media continued to be outraged at their persecution and even worse, in wartime. The problem was not sympathy, but policy. When demands were made – either to accept Jewish refugees in the depths of a depression, or to divert energies towards rescue efforts, or to take risks by confronting the Third Reich – bystanding governments were unwilling to

[21] For a discussion of this mechanism, referred to as "a form of denial," see Barnett (1999: 51).
[22] In addition to the books by Jonathan Frankel (1997) and David Kertzer (1997), see also older works by Max J. Kohler (1918), Lucien Wolf (1919), and Cyrus Adler & Aaron M. Margalith (1946).
[23] For a survey, see Fink (2004: chs. 3–11).
[24] See Greg Burgess (2002).

contemplate the humanitarian intervention that an earlier generation of theorists had defined as an obligation of civilized society.

Minorities, we have seen, were often disparaged because of the way that they seemed to be seeking just such intervention – and Jews, Baron's minority *par excellence*, bore a special odium as a result of their association with the treaties and the unpopular obligations they imposed upon the so-called minority states.[25] The objections to minorities, indeed, sound remarkably like the classic inventory of anti-Semitism: minorities had helped subvert the postwar settlement in Europe. Minorities had been a force for destabilization: they refused to assimilate into majority populations; they relentlessly exploited the system to the detriment of their "host" societies; they tried to drag the great powers into serving their interests; they schemed together; they were susceptible to communism and campaigned for a new war. Does this list not sound familiar? And to it may be added another element familiar to chroniclers of anti-Semitism – the manner in which, in different countries, opposition to minorities could extend across the political spectrum, right to left, nostalgic or aggressive nationalists as well as progressive or antiwar liberals.[26]

Anti-Semitism itself, to be sure, has its place in the explanation of what moved, or failed to move, the bystanders. Historians have not been wrong to identify toxic elements of anti-Jewish prejudice in the bureaucracies of Western countries, and to find antipathies to Jews, as Jews, in the prewar and wartime decision making of governments and international agencies. But perhaps at least as strong, in the perspectives of those who rejected Jewish appeals, was the policymakers' general turning away from humanitarian intervention – not just for Jews, but for other persecuted minorities throughout Europe and beyond.

It is not quite true that "the world did nothing" during the Holocaust, although by the standards set by the modern rhetoric of humanitarian intervention, the world did little enough. For the reasons suggested here, the impulse to intervene in extraordinary circumstances of the oppression of minorities, perceptible among the great powers during the

---

[25] For an excellent discussion of the distorted perceptions of Jewish influence on the minorities treaties, arising particularly from the negotiations with Poland, see David Engel (2002).

[26] "Discrimination against minority rights was not primarily the work of reactionaries and conservatives," says Mazower. "On the contrary, in eastern Europe it was above all the work of modernizing liberals who were trying to create a national community through the actions of the state. For them, the state had to show that its power was above 'everyone and everything,' and to override its opponents whether these be the Church, brigands, communists or ethnic minorities" (1998: 59).

nineteenth century, was one of the casualties of World War I, and thus atrophied before arguably its greatest test to that point. Great champions of humanity of the nineteenth century like Gladstone would have been mightily disappointed with their successors in the twentieth.

REFERENCES

Adler, C., and A. M. Margalith (1946). *With Firmness in the Right: American Diplomatic Action Affecting Jews, 1840–1945*. New York: American Jewish Committee.

Banville, S. (2005). "Sharon Remembers Holocaust." *Breaking News English*, January 28. Retrieved from http://www.breakingnewsenglish.com/0501/28.sharonRemembersHolocaust.html, July 18, 2006.

Barnett, V. J. (1999). *Bystanders: Conscience and Complicity during the Holocaust.* New York: Praeger.

Baron, S. (1985). *Ethnic Minority Rights: Some Older and Newer Trends (The Tenth Sacks Lecture delivered on 26th May 1983)*. Oxford: Oxford Centre for Postgraduate Hebrew Studies.

Bauer, Y. (1968). "What Did They Know?" *Midstream*, April, pp. 51–8.

————. (2001). *Rethinking the Holocaust*. New Haven, CT: Yale University Press.

Bloxham, D. (2005). *The Great Game of Genocide: Imperialism, Nationalism, and the Destruction of the Ottoman Armenians*. Oxford: Oxford University Press.

Burgers, J. H. (1992). "The Road to San Francisco: The Revival of the Human Rights Idea in the Twentieth Century." *Human Rights Quarterly*, 14, pp. 450–4.

Burgess, G. (2002). "The Human Rights Dilemma in Anti-Nazi Protest: The Bernheim Petition, Minorities Protection, and the 1933 Sessions of the League of Nations." CERC Working Papers Series, no. 2. Retrieved from, http://www.cerc.unimelb.edu.au/publication/CERCWP022002.pdf, June 28, 2006.

Cassese, A. (2000). "The Martens Clause: Half a Loaf or Simply Pie in the Sky?" *European Journal of International Human Rights*, no. 11, pp. 187–216.

Cesarani, D., and P. A. Levine, eds. (2002). *"Bystanders" to the Holocaust: A Re-evaluation*. London: Frank Cass.

Dadrian, V. N. (1995). *The History of the Armenian Genocide: Ethnic Conflict from the Balkans to Anatolia to the Caucasus*. New York: Berghan Books.

Engel, D. (2002). "Perceptions of Jewish Power – Poland and World Jewry." *Simon Dubnow Institute Yearbook*, I, pp. 17–28.

Faught, C. B. (c. 2006). "An Imperial Iconoclast: William Ewart Gladstone, the Rights of Small States and Beleaguered Peoples, and the Roots of Modern Internationalism," unpublished paper. Retrieved from, http://www.bu.edu/historic/06conf_papers/Faught.pdf, July 19, 2006.

Fein, H. (1979). *Accounting for Genocide: Victims and Survivors of the Holocaust.* New York: Free Press.

Feinberg, N. (1974). "The Recognition of the Jewish People in International Law." In J. N. Moore, ed., *The Arab-Israeli Conflict, vol. I: Readings*. Princeton: Princeton University Press.

Fink, C. (2004). *Defending the Rights of Others: The Great Powers, the Jews, and International Minority Protection, 1878–1938.* Cambridge: Cambridge University Press.

Fonteyne, J. L. (1974). "The Customary International Law Doctrine of Humanitarian Intervention: Its Current Validity under the U.N. Charter." *California Western International Law Journal,* vol. 4, pp. 205–36.

Frankel, J. (1997). *The Damascus Affair: "Ritual Murder," Politics, and the Jews in 1840.* Cambridge: Cambridge University Press.

Ganji, M. (1962), *International Protection of Human Rights.* Geneva: Université de Genève.

Gladstone, W. E. (1876). *Bulgarian Horrors and the Question of the East.* New York/ Montreal: Lovell, Adam Wesson & Col.

Hall, W. E. (1924). *A Treatise on International Law,* 8th edition. Oxford: Clarendon Press.

Harris, D. (1939). *Britain and the Bulgarian Horrors of 1876.* Chicago: University of Chicago Press.

Hilberg, R. (1992). *Perpetrators Victims Bystanders: The Jewish Catastrophe 1933–1945.* New York: HarperCollins.

Hindley, M. (2002) "Constructing Allied Humanitarian Policy." In D. Cesarani and P. A. Levine, eds., *"Bystanders" to the Holocaust.* London: Frank Cass.

Hochschild, A. (2005). *Bury the Chains: Prophets and Rebels in the Fight to Free an Empire's Slaves.* Boston: Houghton Mifflin.

Jones, D. V. (1994). "The League of Nations Experiment in International Protection." *Ethics in International Affairs,* no. 8, p. 88.

———. (2002). *Toward a Just World: The Critical Years in the Search for International Justice.* Chicago: University of Chicago Press.

Kertzer, D. I. (1997). *The Kidnapping of Edgardo Mortara.* New York: Alfred A. Knopf.

Kloepfer, S. (1985). "The Syrian Crisis, 1860–61: A Case Study in Humanitarian Intervention." *Canadian Yearbook of International Law,* 23, 246–60.

Kohler, M. J. (1918). *Jewish Rights at the Congresses of Vienna (1814–1815) and Aix-la-Chapelle (1818).* New York: American Jewish Committee.

Koskenniemi, M. (2001). *The Gentle Civilizer of Nations: The Rise and Fall of International Law 1870–1960.* Cambridge: Cambridge University Press.

Krauthammer, C. (2006). "Never Again?" *Washington Post,* May 5.

Lauren, P. G. (2003). *The Evolution of International Human Rights: Visions Seen,* 2nd edn. Philadelphia: University of Pennsylvania Press.

Leff, L. (2005). *Buried by the Times: The Holocaust and America's Most Important Newspaper.* Cambridge: Cambridge University Press.

Lingelbach, W. E. (1900). "The Doctrine and Practice of Intervention in Europe." *Annals of the American Academy of Political and Social Science,* no. 16.

Mandelstam, A. (1970). *La Société des Nations et les puissances devant le problème arménien,* 2nd edn. Association libanaise des universitaires arméniens.

Marrus, Michael R. (1987). *The Holocaust in History.* Hanover/London: University Press of New England.

Mazower, M. (1998). *Dark Continent: Europe's Twentieth Century.* New York: Random House.

Onuf, N. (c. 2000). "Humanitarian Intervention: The Early Years," unpublished paper. Retrieved from, http://www.socsci.uci.edu/gpacs/research/working_papers/nicholas_onuf_humanitarian_intervention.pdf, July 18, 2006.

Power, S. (2002). "A Problem from Hell": America and the Age of Genocide. New York: Basic Books.

Rathbone, M. (2004). "Gladstone, Disraeli and the Bulgarian Horrors." History Today, December, vol. 50, pp. 3–7.

Rubinstein, William D. (1997). The Myth of Rescue: Why the Democracies Could Not Have Saved More Jews from the Nazis. London: Routledge.

Robinson, J., O. Karbach, M. M. Laserson, N. Robinson, and M. Vichniak (1943). Were the Minorities Treaties a Failure? New York: Institute of Jewish Affairs.

Rougier, A. (1910). "Théorie de l'intervention d'humanité." Revue générale du droit international, no. 17.

Shannon, R. T. (1999). Gladstone, Heroic Minister, 1865–1898. London: Allen Lane.

Stowell, E. C. (1921). Intervention in International Law. Washington, DC: John Byrne & Col.

Wheaton, H. (1866). Elements of International Law, 8th edn. Boston: Little Brown.

Wolf, L. (1919). Notes on the Diplomatic History of the Jewish Question. London: Jewish Historical Society of England.

Wróbel, P. (2005). "The Kaddish Years: Anti-Jewish Violence in East Central Europe, 1918–1921." Simon Dubnow Institute Yearbook, IV, pp. 211–36.

PART II: NARRATIVES AND REDRESS

8. Victims, Relatives, and Citizens in Argentina: Whose Voice Is Legitimate Enough?

ELIZABETH JELIN

Argentina can be considered an emblematic case of the strength and power of testimony and personalized narratives of suffering in the public sphere. In fact, in post-dictatorial Argentina, "truth" came to be equated with testimony of those "directly affected," first and foremost in the voices of blood relatives of the "disappeared" victims of state repression (the mothers and grandmothers, and later the children and siblings of the victims). Survivors of clandestine detention centers, militants, and activists of the early 1970s were not heard until later on – coming to occupy center stage almost thirty years after the military coup of 1976.

The voice of the "directly affected" in denouncing and condemning dictatorship and state terrorism has carried considerable power in defining the human rights agenda of the country. The very notion of "truth" and the legitimacy of voice (or even the "ownership" of the issue) became embedded in personal experience and in biological and genetic bonds.[1] This symbolic and political dominance of "familism," and more recently the identification with the political activism and militancy of the 1970s, leaves relatively little if any room for other and broader societal voices – for example, those based on citizenship or a universal perspective on the human condition – in the public discussion of the meaning of the recent violent past and in the discussion about policies regarding that past. At its

---

[1] In comparison to other countries in the region, the expression "directly affected" (*afectado/a directo/a*) has a surprising strength in Argentina. This expression refers to those who have suffered, "in their own flesh and blood," the repressive actions of the state (disappearance, political imprisonment, torture, and, on a lesser scale, exile) and their closest blood relatives. The expression excludes nonkin criteria (e.g. political militancy, friendship, or even partnership) for suffering and proximity to horror.

I thank my colleagues at the *Núcleo de Estudios sobre Memoria* at IDES in Buenos Aires and Richard Wilson for their comments and suggestions.

extreme, the issue involves a shift from recognition and entitlement to a monopoly of the voices of victims.

The end of dictatorial regimes and state-sponsored political repression involves a multilayered process of transition. It entails the development and implementation of a democratic institutional apparatus. Yet, at the same time, "settling accounts with the past" becomes a significant task, converging with the need to build a different future. The ways to settle accounts with past political violence have been quite varied world-wide. They encompass the full range of policies and initiatives, from state and international institutional responses (tribunals, trials, special commissions, reparations, policies regarding archives, commemoration, and territorial markers) to cultural expressions in the arts, involving multiple societal activities and organizations. It is always the state and societal actors who participate – often expressing dissenting and conflicting perspectives – in defining the political, cultural and social agenda about settling accounts with the past. Yet the state is, ultimately, the final arbiter and legitimizing authority that renders an official or hegemonic narrative and interpretation of the past.

Argentina's is a case where the wide variety of innovations and initiatives regarding ways to deal with the past of political violence and state terrorism has set the path for the international community (Sikkink 2008). Despite the diversity of institutionally sanctioned responses, personal experiences of victims and survivors and kinship-based relationships to victims have become the criteria for the legitimation of voice regarding both state-sponsored and socially promoted political, cultural, and social activities. The establishment of such criteria perhaps negates other more universal and citizenship-based criteria. Furthermore, in periods of political transition, this preeminence may work against the need to build a wide political community of citizens.

To develop these ideas, I will take up first the place of "familism" in the politics of memory in Argentina during the last thirty years, since the military coup of 1976. The historical path followed in the country is not a linear one, as there have been many junctures in which significant shifts of direction took place. In fact, it was during the dictatorship (1976–1983) that the familistic interpretive framework was developed. Afterwards, in the initial stage of the post-dictatorship period, there was a move toward taking up the issues of the recent past in the institutional settings of the new democracy. The trials of the military in 1985 transformed the voices of victims into those of citizens with rights. But this was not a lasting state of affairs. Familial and genetic bonds regained center stage, as expressed in the important struggle of the organization of Grandmothers (*Abuelas de Plaza de Mayo*), carried out with the purpose of restoring the stolen identities of kidnapped children. Thirty years after the military coup, the testimonial voice of political militancy and survival has become the leading one in the political arena, granting further legitimacy to the voices of victims. The successive instances I will present in this chapter help shape the dilemmas that Argentine society faces in the attempt to broaden and deepen equality and citizenship.

The ideas presented in this chapter carry with them a political subtext: the belief that the voice of personal suffering and concurrent humanitarian concerns based on sympathy and compassion for "those others who have suffered" constitute significant and important elements in contemporary politics. However, these elements cannot, in themselves, constitute the solid foundations for human equality and the broadening of feelings and practices of respect in the sense proposed by Sennet (2004). As a consequence, the historical and political challenge faced by democratic forces in Argentina and elsewhere is to open up and invite the wider participation of citizens in the political debate on "settling accounts with the past."

The Family in the Politics of Memory

A military coup occurred in Argentina in March 1976 in the midst of deep political conflict and widespread political violence. The military government implemented a systematic policy of clandestine repression, including massive "disappearances," as the mainstay of its policy to handle political conflict and to wipe out the existing armed political groups. The military dictatorship lasted until December 1983. Repression was harshest during the initial years of the regime.

At the time of the coup, the military forces defined themselves as the saviors of the nation and identified their central task as that of bringing back "peace and order" in place of the chaos and "subversion" that were destroying "natural" Argentine values and institutions.[2] To recapture these values, it was mandatory to protect the nation, the family, and the people

---

[2] The Argentine military coup and military government was not an isolated phenomenon in the region. Brazil had been governed by a military dictatorship since 1964, Uruguay and Chile had their military coups in 1973, Paraguay had dictator-president Stroessner for thirty-five years of its history (1954–1989), and Bolivia also experienced dictatorship and military coups in the same period. In the late 1960s and early 1970s, the revolutionary left resorted to armed struggle in several of these countries. It was also a time of a heightened Cold War and of the prevalence of the Doctrine of National Security.

from the dangers of "subversion." Familism and family were at the center of military discourse. They were to lead a "Process of National Reorganization," calling upon "fathers, mothers and healthy children of the country" to "take care of your homes. Keep your security. Do not accept generously the ideas implanted in the young minds by international subversive experts ... The security and peace of the people are to be built inside homes and schools."[3]

The reference to the traditional family was paramount in justifying the military coup. First, it defined society as an organism constituted by cells, or natural families. In this way, it grounded social organization and social structure in a biological order, naturalizing its vision of family roles and values. There was only one way, the "natural" way, in which Argentine society could be organized. Thus, the military developed a massive campaign to strengthen family unity. Family ties were defined as "indissoluble" and the rights of parents over their children were seen as "inalienable." Because the metaphor of the family was used for the nation as a whole, the father-state had inalienable rights over the moral and physical fate of its children-citizens. The image of the nation as the "Grand Argentine Family" implied that only the "good" children-citizens were truly Argentine. Official discourse represented citizens as immature children in need of a strong father.

In such discourse, paternal authority was paramount. Sons and daughters were expected to follow the moral duties of obedience; there was no room for citizens with rights, for human beings with personal autonomy. In a "natural" rather than social or cultural world, the danger of evil and illness is always seen as external, coming from the outside – an extraneous body that invades and infects. To reestablish the natural equilibrium, a surgical intervention becomes necessary, so as to extract and destroy the infected social tissues. The military regime thus became the protective father taking upon himself the arduous responsibility of cleaning and protecting his family, helped by other surrogate or "minor" parents, in charge of controlling and disciplining rebellious adolescents. State-sponsored television advertisements urged parents to reproduce ad infinitum the military's policing and control by asking: "Do you know where your child is?"

The image of the family as the "basic cell" of the nation implied that parents had to protect the family cell from outside influence because a virus or infection that invades a single cell spreads through the whole body. Children and youth represented the weak boundaries of the national family body, and through contact with the outside, they could bring the

---

[3] *La Nación*, June 19, 1976, quoted by Filc (1997: 35).

infection into the social body. The only way to defend the nation was therefore to confront the enemy at the point of entry: the link between the young and their families. At this point, if the father-state was to protect the nation, it had to look inside the family. The distinction between public life and private family disappeared. The dictatorship bestowed parents with the ultimate responsibility to prevent their children from becoming subversives. When parents of disappeared people approached the government to question the fate of their children, they met accusations of not having exerted adequate parental authority: "If young people became 'subversives' it was because of deficiencies in their upbringing."

The defense of the traditional patriarchal family was a clear and explicit policy of the government. Yet, at the same time, the military implemented a systematic policy of clandestine repression that directly affected thousands of families. Part of the military junta's counterinsurgency policy included massive kidnappings of people from their own homes (people who were then tortured and disappeared) as a means of extinguishing armed political groups (Calveiro 1998). Young children were also kidnapped with their parents, and pregnant young women were kept alive until giving birth. With changed identities, the newborn babies were then appropriated by military personnel and others linked to their ranks. Estimates of disappearances vary, with figures of up to 30,000; estimates of surviving kidnapped children with false identities reach 500 (and by 2007, about ninety cases had been solved).

In 1976, relatives of detained and disappeared persons organized themselves as *Familiares de Detenidos y Desaparecidos por Razones Políticas* (Relatives of the Detained and Disappeared for Political Reasons). April 1977 marked the initial meetings of what later became the emblem of the human rights movement, the *Madres de Plaza de Mayo* (Mothers of Plaza de Mayo). In November of that same year, the *Asociación de Abuelas de Plaza de Mayo* (Association of Grandmothers of Plaza de Mayo) was created.

Why would the denunciations and demands of the emerging human rights movement be couched in kinship terms? In the political context of dictatorial repression and censorship, political organizations and labor unions were suspended, and there was no room for public expression of dissent as fear and terror were the basic tools of the exercise of power. Under these conditions, the denunciation and protest of relatives was, in fact, the only one that could be voiced. After all, it was a mother searching for her child, and the image of motherhood was a part of the "naturalization" of the family bond.

The paradox in the Argentine military regime of 1976–1983 was that the language and the image of the family were the central metaphor of the military government but also the central image of the discourse and practices of the most visible part of the human rights movement.[4] What they were denouncing were crimes against the family, projecting at the same time an image of the "good child" and of "normal" family life. The paradigmatic image is that of the "mother," symbolized by the *Madres de Plaza de Mayo* with their diaper-like headscarves, the mother who leaves her "natural" private realm of family life to cross the threshold into the public sphere in search for her kidnapped – disappeared – child. In parallel with the figure of Antigone in Greek tragedy, the Mother challenges the powerful, expressing family principles associated with caring and protecting.[5] Relatives, mothers and grandmothers in the 1970s, *H.I.J.O.S.* (Children [of the Disappeared] for Identity and Justice Against Forgetting and Silence) twenty years later, and *Herman@s*[6] (Siblings) afterwards are the organizations that keep active demands for truth, justice and memory. What is significant here is that they entered the public sphere not as metaphors or symbolic images of family ties, but grounded in literal kin relations.

Despite their contrasting and conflicting orientations, both sides talked about families. For one side, the family was patriarchal control and authority, couched in terms of protection against threats and evil. For the other, the private, personalized, and emotionally charged family ties

[4] In fact, the denunciation of political repression in Argentina was not the exclusive terrain of kinship-based organizations. What is known as the "human rights movement" was quite heterogeneous from its inception – even before the military coup. It included progressive and humanist politicians, intellectuals, clergy, and other religious-based activists, grouped in several organizations (*Asamblea Permanente de Derechos Humanos, Liga Argentina de los Derechos del Hombre, Servicio de Paz y Justicia,* and later on *Movimiento Ecuménico de Derechos Humanos,* and *Centro de Estudios Legales y Sociales,* among others). For an analysis of the development of the human rights movement in Argentina, see Jelin (1995) and Jelin (2005).

[5] The immediate question to this presence of women in the public space is, "why mothers?", and "where were the fathers?" The prevalent interpretation of this public presence of mothers – which to some extent has become a mythical narrative – points to the fact that fathers had to continue working to maintain the family, but, more importantly, that mothers were more "protected" because of the importance of motherhood, culturally defined as "sacred." As the tragic reality showed a few months after the first round of the *Madres,* maternal status was no protective shield: in December 1977 several mothers disappeared, becoming visible victims of the regime. Furthermore, not all of them were housewives, as the popular image crystallized.

[6] Non-gendered spelling in Spanish is increasingly using the sign "@" as the combined feminine and masculine "a" and "o". This organization's name is following this spelling. Thus the official name is "*Herman@s.*"

justified and motivated public action, with the purpose of subverting the image of the "bad family" that the military wanted to convey about the families of the victims. The disappeared and the imprisoned were presented by their relatives as exemplary children, good students, and members of families living in harmony; in sum, as ideal or "normal." Family loss acted to push private ties and feelings into the public sphere, rupturing the boundaries between private life and the public realm.

This public emergence of family ties in political life had further implications. It entailed a reconceptualization of the relationship between private and public life. The private family link to the victim became the basic justification and legitimacy for public action. For the justice system, it was actually the only one. Only relatives were and are still considered to have the legal grounds to pursue personalized and individualized demands for information, for justice and for reparation. This public and political familism had political and cultural impacts. The mothers may have shared their maternity, by stating that all the disappeared are children of all mothers. Yet the interpretation of motherhood was a literal one: only actual mothers of disappeared persons could participate as "mothers." There was no symbolic extension of motherhood or kinship to others. This literal understanding of family – based on blood (or genetic) ties – creates a distance in public mobilization between those who are the "actual" carriers of suffering, and therefore of "truth," and those motivated by political, humanitarian, or citizen-based reasons. The latter came to be seen as not equally transparent or legitimate. Therefore, in the public sphere of debate and denunciation, participation became stratified according to the public exposure of family ties with the victims.

From Victimhood to the Rule of Law: Truth and Justice in Argentine Transition

The emphasis on familism, however, conveys only part of the story. The end of the military regime and the installment of the constitutional regime in December 1983 entailed the search for institutional responses to the past dictatorial regime's violations. "Settling accounts with the past" became a vital component for establishing the legitimate rule of law. The next steps were to change the story from the conveyance of the suffering of victims and their relatives to the open recognition of the state's crimes and the condemnation and punishment of the perpetrators. In the process, victims – who had been stripped of their rights and even of their human condition – were to turn into recognized citizens.

At the time of transition, the confrontation between the demands of the human rights movement and the new government was intense. The movement demanded civilian courts and a parliamentary commission to investigate state repression, searching for some sort of legitimate punishment that would also serve to reaffirm the basic ethical values of democracy. Instead of a parliamentary commission, the government decided that the investigation was to be conducted by an independent commission of "notables," the CONADEP (*Comisión Nacional sobre la Desaparición de Personas*). The CONADEP was designed to receive testimony from relatives of the disappeared and from survivors of the clandestine camps. The Commission set up special offices in several Argentine cities in order to collect evidence. Exiles returned from abroad to testify, and evidence was also taken in embassies abroad. Police and military facilities, as well as clandestine detention centers and cemeteries, were inspected. Based on the experience and accumulated data of the human rights organisations that had independently constructed a databank on individual cases of abuses and violations, the Commission collected crucial evidence that would be used a year later in the trials of the members of the military Junta.[7]

The Commission's actions produced strategic information about repressive techniques and methods, and the Argentine public began to learn what had happened. The atrocious violations, up to then unimaginable to many, became real. The Commission became the site of the formal acknowledgment of the "truth" and so powerfully symbolized the indictment of the military dictatorship and the legitimization of the victims' claims.

The Commission gathered 50,000 pages of evidence and presented its report to the president in September 1984. A special program based on the report, with testimonies of survivors and relatives, was aired on national television. The official report, including an annex listing the names of almost 9,000 disappeared, was published in a book called *Nunca Más* (Never Again) in November 1984. The book soon became a bestseller, and is still being reprinted and distributed widely.[8]

The title of the CONADEP report provides a clue to the cultural climate of the country at the moment, as well as to the meanings attached to remembrance. The idea that the experience should not be repeated – *Nunca Más* – became associated with documenting the "truth," with collecting a full record of the atrocities the country experienced. In order not to repeat, then,

---

[7] The policies of transition are discussed in detail in Acuña and Smulovitz (1995).
[8] A full account of the workings of the CONADEP and the impact of the report is found in Crenzel (2008).

one has to keep memory alive: "Remember! So as not to repeat!" (*Recordar para no repetir*) emerged as the message and the cultural imperative.

CONADEP was a way to discover what had happened, to discover and acknowledge the *truth*. After that was accomplished, it was the time for *justice*. The trial of the ex-commanders of the military juntas was a moment of maximum impact – both nationally and internationally – of the struggle for human rights in Argentina. The nine junta members who ruled Argentina from 1976 to 1982 were brought to trial in the Federal Court of Appeals of Buenos Aires in 1985.[9] The trial was a test of whether the rule of law could impose itself over the rule of force. It applied a juridical procedure, with all the rituals and formalities that put the judiciary at the center of the institutional scene: victims became "witnesses," perpetrators became the "accused," and political actors had to remain "observers" of the action of judges who presented themselves as "neutral" authorities, defining the situation according to preestablished and legitimate rules.

From a juridical vantage point the task was almost impossible, not least because the justice system had to use existing penal legislation designed to try common homicide to try crimes more akin to genocide. It also had to try persons who had not themselves committed murders, who had not given the orders to commit specific acts of violation of rights of specific persons, but who had organised and ordered massive kidnappings, torture and the killings of (for them) unknown or anonymous individuals. The junta members might not have killed any single person; they might not have given the order to kill individual victims, and yet they were held responsible for crimes that they had organised. The strategy of the prosecution was to present evidence (there were more than 800 witnesses) that there was a systematic plan, carried out in all parts of the country following the same method of illegal detentions, torture and disappearances. Despite the difficulties, after five months of moving testimonies of persons who had to overcome fears of revenge and the reluctance to reveal shameful and humiliating personal experiences in public, five of the nine commanders were found guilty.[10]

---

[9] The civilian Court of Appeals took over jurisdiction from military tribunals when the latter decided that there was not enough evidence to proceed with military trials. This civilian appeal mechanism was part of the reformed Military Code law adopted by Congress soon after the democratic government took office (Acuña and Smulovitz 1995).

[10] General Jorge Rafael Videla and Admiral Emilio Massera were given life sentences; General Viola was given seventeen years in prison; Admiral Lambruschini was given eight years and Brigadier Agosti was sentenced to three years and nine months. The members of the junta that governed between 1979 and 1982 were acquitted because the Court found the evidence against them inconclusive.

The construction of juridical proof was based on the testimony of the victims, since military records were unavailable. This implied the juridical recognition of their voices and their right to speak. In the context of this institutional setting, the harm they had suffered had to be presented according to the legal rules of acceptable evidence. Allowing testimony as proof followed the logic that what cannot be visibly shown (the act of aggression) had to be told, but under precise and controlled conditions, so that what was denounced could be verified. In fact, what usually is acceptable as juridical proof is physical, bodily injury. Feelings and victims' narratives of suffering could not be measured or included; during testimony, they had to be suspended from consideration by the court. When emotion overtook the witnesses, the judges halted testimony until "calm and sanity" returned. This intermittent pattern had a very special effect: the covert message was that, in its full details, in its entirety, the experience could not be told, much less could it be heard.

Victim or witness testimony in court was still a personal narrative about past experiences, but the juridical process broke testimony down into its various components: the requirement of personal identification, the pledge to tell the truth, the description of the circumstances, and the specific relationship with the case. The discourse of the witness had to be detached from experience and transformed into the kind of evidence that was legally recognizable. If disappearance was an experience where there was no law and no rule, where the victim ceased to exist as a subject of rights, the experience of the testimony in court (of the victims themselves and of those who had been searching for them) was an insistence on recognition. As one witness, who was himself a victim of disappearance and then incarceration, expressed, the trial "eliminated the spectral nature of the testimonies that were moving around in society. It presented the victims as *human beings*, giving them equal standing with the rest of humanity" (Norberto Liwski, interview, 1990).

Thus, the pendulum was shifting from a personal, concrete, and historically situated narrative to the more impersonal, even universal, claim of human rights. The historical moment of the trial implied the triumph of the rule of law, transformation of the victim into a subject of rights and the embodiment of a newly found democratic regime. Equal citizenship rights were established and reaffirmed. Suffering and the need of redress were not abolished by this act. The specificity of the personal and the familial was to reemerge in various ways later on, perhaps more forcefully.

In CONADEP's registry of testimonies and, in a much more dramatic way, in the trial hearings later on, something important was happening. Disappearances, torture, and clandestine detention implied the suspension of social and political bonds.[11] The relationship between victim and perpetrator was a direct one; there was no social or political normative frame to govern it. The notion of victimhood implied here does not refer specifically to the degree of harm or suffering experienced, but rather to the radical condition of having been deprived of voice, and of the means to reveal that which has been experienced (Lyotard 1988). The voice of the victim did not belong to the recognized real world, insofar as there were no means to verify it in the context of arbitrary terror and total power. It was as if it had never existed. Thus, victims were driven to silence or to a place of disbelief. In contrast, the position of the rightful subject is one in which the opposing sides of a conflict have access to a higher authority, a tribunal that can judge the truth of what is claimed, according to the rules and procedures that demonstrate proof. In this way, the appeal to law implied a radical shift in the position of the opponents, because both became recognized as sides in a conflict.

The appeal to law was a way in which victims could transform themselves into adversaries. When this happened, the position of the victim faded (in juridical terms) and allowed the emergence of a "subject of rights." His or her voice had now a testimonial value and could be recognized and heard by the judges and by society. The intervention of a third party, the law, represented in the figure of the tribunal, recognized both sides as adversaries in a conflict that had to be decided through legal procedures.

The facts about political repression, which for many on both sides of the conflict had been interpreted within a paradigm of "war" (often including the adjective "dirty"), were now judged within a legal framework of "violations of human rights." Yet the growing consciousness about the rule of law and its juridical embodiment in the human rights paradigm involves a paradox: the belief in a universal subject of rights implies an abstract subject. The law reinstates the human condition to victims, yet it does so by removing them from their concrete historical and political context. Thus, the rules of law and justice have the effect of blurring and inhibiting the claims of particular political and moral views. In that sense, two of the effects of the installation of a juridical paradigm prompted by the trials of the military were the concealment of substantive political identities and the silences of ideological and political aspects of the confrontation.

---

[11] The interpretation offered in this and the following paragraphs follows González Bombal (1995).

The outcome of the trial, in December 1985, had many more implications than the verdict condemning the top members of the military regime. The trial proved the systemic nature of repression by the military government and implied the collection of a body of information that could become evidence in new indictments of others responsible for repression. Rather than providing a closure to the demand of "settling accounts with the past," as President Alfonsín had hoped, the verdict of the court actually opened the door for further indictments and trials.[12]

Political tension escalated significantly, and the executive, under mounting pressure from the military, tried to prevent further indictments through the *Ley de Punto Final* (the Law of Full Stop), which placed a sixty-day limit on new criminal indictments in December of 1986. Soon after, the government embarked upon other extreme measures to obstruct any future prosecutions. The *Ley de Obediencia Debida* (Due Obedience Law) in mid-1987 was the final answer for those cases that had not yet reached a verdict. It was, in effect, an amnesty for most members of the armed forces. The only excepted offences were rape, theft, and falsification of civil status (i.e., irregular adoptions). A few years later, in 1989 and 1990, President Menem used his presidential prerogative to pardon the members of the military junta who were in jail, as well as lower-ranking military officials and certain civilians (prosecuted for their participation in armed guerrilla groups) facing prosecution or already convicted and serving jail sentences.

The process did not stop there, however. President Menem sought to turn the institutions of the state away from pursuing further accountability and to roll back the progress that had been achieved thus far, thus moving state institutions away from the path of establishing the "rule of law" and recognizing the lawful rights of the victims. When the state abandoned the path of institution building, the project of pursuing redress returned to the arena of social actors, especially victims and their relatives. The Mothers of Plaza de Mayo did not stop their actions. Neither did the *Abuelas*, who were concerned with cases of illegal adoption. Furthermore, during the 1980s, and with much greater force during the 1990s, international and diplomatic pressures were very active. French and Italian courts investigated the responsibilities of the Argentine military in the disappearance of French and Italian citizens; other European countries followed suit. These investigations led to the 1990 sentencing of former Captain Astiz to

---

[12] For an analysis of the effects of the verdict, especially its "Point 30" on further mandatory indictments, see Acuña and Smulovitz (1995).

life imprisonment by the French courts. Astiz, an infamous perpetrator responsible for the disappearances of two French nuns, could not be convicted in Argentina because of the indemnity legislation. In the late 1990s, Spanish courts took up the issue of human rights violations in the Southern Cone, drawing upon Spain's legislation on "crimes against humanity," leading to the detention of Chilean General Augusto Pinochet in London in 1998.[13]

The Search of the *Abuelas*: DNA Testing and Recovered Identities

As already indicated, the Argentine history of political repression is in many ways unique: the military kidnapping and "disappearing" of thousands of people; children kidnapped with their parents; young pregnant women being abducted, and their children born in captivity. At times, abducted children were returned to their relatives, often their grandparents, but not always. This led to a double search on the part of the relatives of the kidnapped: searching for the disappeared young adults and at the same time searching for the children. The *Abuelas de Plaza de Mayo* began their organization when, in late 1977, several women – who repeatedly met each other in their unending visits to police stations, governmental offices, churches, and other organizations – realized that they shared their ordeal of searching for their missing children and their kidnapped grandchildren. At the same time, there were rumors indicating that after being kidnapped, pregnant women were kept alive until they gave birth in clandestine detention centers. Then, their newborn babies were taken away from them, and the women entered the ranks of the disappeared.

This led to the realization that children had become "war trophies," appropriated and illegally "adopted" by the kidnappers themselves, or given away to others – mostly people related to the repressive apparatus. When it became clear that not all abducted children were killed, and that many were living with changed identities, the Grandmothers displayed their action in various different directions: on the one hand, they were searching for hints about where the children could be; on the other, they began to search for international support to develop the technical tools

---

[13] Argentine courts have been very active again since the late 1990s, when the members of the military juntas were indicted for the kidnapping of children and the "Truth trials" began. Later on, the Supreme Court declared the unconstitutionality of the impunity laws, which was followed by new trials. A brief account of juridical developments in Argentina since the historical trial of 1985 is found in Jelin (2006). Regarding the processes that led to the Spanish courts' actions, see Anguita (2001).

for the hoped-for moment when an abducted child could recover his or her identity. For that they depended on the international scientific community, which had made advances in blood testing and DNA identification techniques. Because the biological parents had disappeared, innovations were necessary to identify the children through second- or third-degree kinship connections with grandparents, uncles, and aunts. Immediately following the transition to the constitutional government in 1983, initial moves were made to establish a genetic bank, where relatives of disappeared children could deposit their genetic material for eventual future tests. In 1992, the Argentine government established the National Committee of the Right to Identity (CONADI), creating the National Genetic Bank. As of 2007, ninety cases of kidnapped children had been solved.

Thirty years after the military coup, the abducted children and those born in captivity are now young adults in their late twenties and thirties. The information and publicity campaigns of the *Abuelas* are geared towards young people: "If you are between *this and that* age, and have doubts about your identity, contact the *Abuelas*." Each individual case is full of tension, full of emotion, full of ethical and moral dilemmas.[14]

Identity restitution is a complex legal, psychological, scientific, and social intervention. The justice system is, in the end, the instance in charge of solving the conflicts and tensions involved. There are at least two parts to each case: the crime of kidnapping and changing identity committed by the military (or others), and the "true" personal identity of the kidnapped child or young adult. Involved are also the claims of the family of the disappeared and their right to truth, and the demand of society as a whole in maintaining the public interest in truth and justice. In a controversial case in 2003, the Supreme Court ruled that a young woman, the kidnapped daughter of disappeared parents, had the right *not* to submit herself to DNA testing to determine her biological identity. The young woman justified her stance as a means to prevent possible damage to her "father's" defense. She declared that she would submit to the test by her own free will when the case against her "father" was finished. The societal reaction – voiced by relatives of the disappeared and by the human rights movement – was, as expected, critical of the Supreme Court decision. The identity of the young woman was established in 2008, using other means to carry out the test (underwear, tweezers and a toothbrush). In fact, by April 2008 three cases had been

---

[14] Full information and specific stories are found in www.abuelas.org.ar.

solved using these noninvasive techniques, since the children refused to have their blood test done.[15]

The social and cultural impact of these and similar cases of conflict and restitution of identity is quite significant, although difficult to gauge at the present time. There is widespread societal support for the *Abuelas* and for the restitution of the identity of children of the disappeared. The Genetic Bank and DNA testing are seen as the proper means to proceed. Such views rely upon the belief that the final test of truth lies in DNA testing, in genetics, in biology, and in blood. Undoubtedly, these have been major developments and the Argentine public largely welcomes them.

Yet, in this issue lies a paradox. The reliance on biological proof comes at a time when there are also major developments in assisted reproductive techniques, which stress blood (or genetic) belonging, while parenthood and family are cultural and social ties. How will society and law systems deal with the tensions between these two normative principles? Certainly Argentine society – and perhaps even world society – faces the need to address the ethical issues in the application of reproductive technologies, norms regarding adoption, and the right of children to know their lineage or filiations (introduced in the International Convention on the Rights of the Child), and advances in medicine that stress genetic dispositions, among others. Given the cultural and political significance of the processes of recuperation of stolen identities that have occurred in the last thirty years, the case of Argentina may be crucial to determine how the links between biology and culture in the family are interpreted and transformed in light of global developments in genetic research.

Survivors and Relatives in Public Commemoration

Struggles for meaning of past suffering and repression express themselves in rituals and commemorations. Who are the protagonists of such rituals? Which voices are to be heard? Which meanings are conveyed?

March 24th is the date of the military coup of 1976. Since then, the "24th" has become an important date, one that evokes different meanings for various actors. It has never ceased to be commemorated, although it has been the focus of highly antagonistic discourses. During the dictatorship,

---

[15] Also, there are cases that go in the opposite direction. As the young kidnapped children grow and become young adults, they are the ones who may initiate the search. In a recent case, a young man found out while surfing the Internet that he was the son of a disappeared person and that his "father" was a perpetrator.

the public scene of commemoration was totally occupied by the military in power. Every year, they organized a ceremony inside their barracks with no civilian participation. The only point of contact of the military with civil society was a "Message to the Argentine People," praising their own service to the country, explaining that they were forced to occupy the state to save the nation from chaos, lack of governance, and a terrorist threat. Repression was too intense to even imagine the possibility of publicly expressing opposition. There were no alternative public voices inside the country, only private suffering and silent resistance (Lorenz 2002). Abroad, however, a space for political dissent did flourish: campaigns to denounce repression in Argentina and solidarity with the victims led usually to rallies and meetings on the 24th.

As the most outspoken antagonists to the military interpretation of the events of the 24th, human rights organizations have occupied the public space of commemoration since 1984. Every year, silhouettes, murals, and theater performances have accompanied the marches and the white scarves of the *Madres*. Books, documentary films, special television programs, and a variety of exhibits have presented and represented the voices of the violence and suffering of victims and their relatives.

March 24, 2004, was a particularly special commemoration. For our present purposes, two features were crucial: the leading role of survivors, with a strong presence and legitimacy in the media, and the active role of President Néstor Kirchner, not in his role of president (which would have been a true novelty given the absence of the presidential voice in previous commemorations), but in his identity as a *compañero*,[16] a "survivor" of the political militancy of the 1970s.

The recently installed President Néstor Kirchner and the Mayor of the city of Buenos Aires, Aníbal Ibarra, were about to sign a document regarding the ESMA *(Escuela Superior de Mecánica de la Armada)*, by which this ominous site, where up to 5,000 people were clandestinely detained and then disappeared, was to be converted into an official site of memory. During the previous days, survivors of the ESMA (there are fewer than 200 people who survived their ordeal at that clandestine detention center) were at the forefront of the public view; their voices were continuously heard on radio and television, and newspapers carried their stories. They were also shown guiding public figures (including the president and his senator-wife) through the paths of their Calvary behind the monumental walls and

---

[16] "*Compañero*" (literally, partner or companion) is a key term in Argentina, one that indicates a shared belonging to the Peronist movement.

gardens of the naval academy, located in a choice neighborhood in the city of Buenos Aires.

Although the voices of survivors had been heard before – they were key witnesses during the trials of the ex-commanders of the military juntas in 1985, and they had given testimony many times since then – their position in society was not a comfortable one, and their voices were not easily accepted. There was always an aura of suspicion about their very survival. The question "why you?" had always been present in the minds of many. From the earliest declarations of survivors (in the late 1970s and early 1980s, usually in exile in Europe) it was known that the naval authorities used the detainees' abilities to their own ends. Inside the clandestine detention camp at the ESMA, the navy had organized an "elite" of detained people (including professionals, journalists, and key leaders of the armed guerrilla group *Montoneros*), known as the "staff" and the "mini-staff," and involved them in several activities according to their political abilities – such as writing reports, translating foreign-language texts, and preparing archives of news clippings.[17] A bizarre cultural mechanism then took hold of part of Argentine society; the way many people had earlier tried to make sense of detentions and disappearances (thinking that there must have been some reason, "*por algo será*") was now transferred to survival (there must be some reason for having survived, "*por algo será*").

In fact, after the moment of legitimacy and public acceptance during the 1985 trials, a sense of suspicion and distrust started to affect the reception of the voices of survivors. The restricted credibility of their voices involved a clear recognition of their suffering and the acceptance of their description of the conditions of detention camps as "true." Suspicion regarding their own "privileged" conditions was more a suspicion about the silences in their testimony (implying collaboration? betrayal?) than about their voices. As Calveiro (1998) shows, however, to imagine that detainees had any chance of participating in the decision about their fate is an illusion; power was in the hands of the perpetrators, and nothing victims could say or do could affect their fate. Power was total and arbitrary. Yet images of distrust, disbelief, betrayal, and treason appear time and again in reports of the period (including fiction), especially the recurrent image of the woman who betrays her militant cause and saves herself through her sexual services or love affairs with perpetrators (Longoni 2004).

The event which took place on March 24th, 2004, is emblematic in this context. As mentioned, survivors of the detention camp occupied the

---

[17] The perverse system of clandestine detention is described in Calveiro (1998), herself a survivor.

center stage of the public space. As the reappropriation of the site neared, they were the ones to explore the place and mark the itineraries of detention, the locales of torture and confinement, tracking the noise and smell, touch and body movements involved, since in most cases, there was little opportunity to see during detention, being always blindfolded. Their testimony was the backdrop for the public ceremony to come.

The ceremony itself involved several stages with different protagonists, including human rights organizations (especially *Familiares*, *Madres*, and *HIJOS*), President Kirchner and Mayor Ibarra signing formal papers for the creation of the museum. For the first time, thousands of people entered the buildings and followed the paths of repression and torture. The event culminated in speeches from the stage and acts of commemoration. I want to focus on the latter commemorative acts because of their significance for this study.

The speakers were the Mayor, two young people who were born in the ESMA (one as a spokesperson for the organization of *HIJOS*, the other the son of disappeared parents who was raised under a false identity and had only recently recovered his identity), and President Kirchner. There was also the reading of a poem written during detention at ESMA by a woman who was subsequently disappeared, and emblematic popular singers and songs. Each and every gesture was linked with the ESMA site. Each and every speaker laid claim to a personal connection with the site: the poem chosen by the President had been written by someone whom he described as a friend and political companion; the Major talked about one of his schoolmates who was detained and disappeared at ESMA; the young people who spoke were children born in captivity inside the walls of that place.[18]

The President's speech merits special attention. It began: "Dear Grandmothers, Mothers, Children: when I was looking at the [raised] hands while singing the anthem, I saw the arms of my *compañeros* [or "comrades"], of the generation that believed, and keeps believing through those of us who stayed alive, that this country can be changed."[19]

---

[18] The full text of the speeches of María Isabel Prigioni Greco and of Juan Cabandié Alfonsín, both in their twenties, born at ESMA and with mothers who then disappeared – the former raised by her relatives, the latter kidnapped and raised with false identity until two months before the event – as well as the full text of President Kirchner's speech can be found in http://www.pagina12.com.ar/flash/24marzo/index.php. This page includes the voice and images of the full ceremony.

[19] *Queridos Abuelas, Madres, Hijos: cuando recién veía las manos, cuando cantaban el himno, veía los brazos de mis compañeros, de la generación que creyó y que sigue creyendo en los que quedamos que este país se puede cambiar ...*

The addressees of the speech kept reappearing: "Grandmothers, Mothers, Children of the detained-disappeared, those *compañeros* and *compañeras* who are not here, yet I know that you are present in each hand raised here and in so many other places in Argentina ... "[20]

The reference to the President's own societal and political position was clear: "I do not come here in the name of a political party, I come as a *compañero* and also as the President of the Argentine Nation and of all Argentines."[21]

And finally:

> For that reason, brothers and sisters, *compañeros* and *compañeras* who are present here even when you are not here any more, Mothers, Grandmothers, Children: thank you for the model of struggle ... We want to have justice, we want a strong recuperation of memory, so that in this Argentina we can again remember, recuperate, and take as guidance those who are able to give everything they have for their values and ideals – a generation in Argentina that was able to do so, that left a path, their lives, their mothers, that left their grandmothers and their children. Today they are present in your (raised) hands.[22]

In his speech, the President identified himself as a member of a special generational political group, stressing his belonging to the generation of militants who struggled for a better society and disappeared, with repeated references to his *compañeros* and *compañeras* and to his identity as a *compañero*. Furthermore, his message was directed to a specific audience: the relatives – mothers, grandmothers, and children – of the disappeared. And these relatives, as the last sentence of Kirchner's speech makes clear, were there to testify for the absent ones. There were almost no references to the rest of the people or to society as a whole, beyond the victims, relatives and *compañeros*.

There were only two references to his role as president of the country in his speech. In one of them, he said, " ... not as a *compañero* and

---

[20] *Por eso Abuelas, Madres, hijos de detenidos desaparecidos, compañeros y compañeras que no están pero sé que están en cada mano que se levanta aquí y en tantos lugares de la Argentina ...*

[21] *Yo no vengo en nombre de ningún partido, vengo como compañero y también como Presidente de la Nación Argentina y de todos los argentinos.*

[22] *Por eso, hermanas y hermanos presentes, compañeras y compañeros que están presentes por más que no estén aquí, Madres, Abuelas, chicos: gracias por el ejemplo de lucha. Queremos que haya justicia, queremos que realmente haya una recuperación fortísima de la memoria y que en esta Argentina se vuelvan a recordar, recuperar y tomar como ejemplo a aquellos que son capaces de dar todo por los valores que tienen y una generación en la Argentina que fue capaz de hacer eso, que ha dejado un ejemplo, que ha dejado un sendero, su vida, sus madres, que ha dejado sus abuelas y que ha dejado sus hijos. Hoy están presentes en las manos de ustedes.*

brother of so many *compañeros* and brothers who shared those times, but as the President of the Argentine Nation, I come to ask forgiveness in the name of the Nation-State, for the shame of having silenced (*callado*) so many atrocities during twenty years of democracy."[23] In the other, he said, "I do not come here in the name of a political party, I come as a *compañero* and also as the President of the Argentine Nation and of all Argentines." Here, his presidential role was secondary to his identity as a *compañero*. At the same time, he used the expression in a way that did not seem to recognize the specific Peronist political identity implied in the use of the term.

What does all this mean? Why pay attention to this event and this speech? Its main significance, from my point of view, rests in the emphasis on particularistic ties or bonds to specific groups (in this case, political militants and activists of the 1970s belonging to the Peronist left, although the word *Montoneros* was not uttered during the ceremony by the speakers). Although there were other victims (among them the revolutionary left, mostly repressed by the army rather than the navy) of political repression, and repressed occurred all over the country (not only at ESMA), the ceremony was couched in this particularistic language, expressing once again the centrality of familism and of personal involvement.

Once Again, Victims and Relatives. And Citizens?

Could the "settling of accounts" in Argentina have happened in a different way? Is there room in Argentina for a more universalistic approach to the redress of violations of human rights? Why did the historical process following the transition lead to this familialistic and victim-centered approach rather than to a perspective that could foster a wider form of citizenship and participation based on the principles of civic commitment and equality? Is the legitimacy of the personal testimonial voice a hindrance for such a process? Obviously, it does not have to be. Yet the primacy of the voices of family loss during and immediately after

[23] ... *ya no como compañero y hermano de tantos compañeros y hermanos que compartimos aquel tiempo, sino como Presidente de la Nación Argentina, vengo a pedir perdón de parte del Estado nacional por la vergüenza de haber callado durante 20 años de democracia por tantas atrocidades.* This sentence aroused much criticism because in it he disregarded all that was done by previous governments, especially by President Alfonsín in the 1980s. President Kirchner had to back up a couple of days after the ceremony, recognizing his mistake.

dictatorship, and the insistence on the direct personal experience of repression and on past political militancy in more recent times seem to define a political scenario where the notions of "directly affected" and "citizen" are opposed to each other, granting preeminence to the former.

Where does familism come from? What does it imply in political terms? As a set of values and beliefs, its roots can be traced throughout the cultural and political history of the country. In Argentina and in other Latin American countries, the Catholic Church has been a powerful political and cultural actor since colonial times. Its basic standpoint implies the primacy of the "natural" family as the "basic cell" of society and a strong cultural tradition of "*Marianismo*," the cultural primacy of motherhood embodied in the figure of the Virgin Mary. This set of beliefs has guided state policies and programs regarding family life and has profoundly shaped the connection between the family and the public sphere.[24] Additionally, during the later part of the nineteenth and the first half of the twentieth centuries, European immigrants to Argentina (predominantly from Italy and Spain) brought with them expectations of progress and upward mobility, not in the form of an individualistic idea of the "self-made man" but rather based on intergenerational family terms.[25] Immigrants were not isolated individuals looking for progress; they were part of a wide kin and community network where links of solidarity, reciprocity, and mutual responsibility were the rule. The same pattern persisted in later migratory flows from other Latin American countries. Thus, the ethics of family life has a strong historical ancestry.

In broader terms, familism implies a particularistic and personalized basis for interpersonal and political solidarity. How are networks of solidarity constituted? To whom does one offer solidarity? What kind of relationship is implied? Basically, this relationship is not a faceless abstract relationship: there must be a personal bond that ties both sides to one another. It may be the patriarchal hierarchical family and kinship network or, going beyond blood ties and extending familism into public political life, the vertical links of personalized patronage (a pattern that became

---

[24] For a history of maternalism in political life in Argentina, see Nari (2004). For a comparative analysis of family and gender policies under dictatorship in Argentina, Chile, and Brazil, see Htun (2003).

[25] The cultural expectation was that children could attain higher levels of education, and through this, a significant process of intergenerational upward mobility could take place. The emblem of this view is *M'hijo el doctor* ("My son, the doctor"), the title of a very popular theater play of the early twentieth century (the author is Florencio Sánchez).

politically salient in the way charismatic leadership has operated in Argentina through Peronism).

In such a context, the construction of a culture of universal citizenship has not been easy or totally successful. The contrast between ideas related to "formal" democracy and formal justice on the one hand, and "social" justice and distribution of political favors on the other has been a constant feature of political culture in the country (Jelin 1996). Impersonal institutional principles of lawfulness and rights were not easily established. Whatever had been accomplished up until the 1970s, however, was then destroyed during the period of dictatorship, which involved the eradication of rights of citizenship and an absolute and arbitrary power of the perpetrators. Victims were not part of the human community; they were outsiders and outcasts to be smashed. With the bonds of the political community destroyed, the only bonds that remained were the primordial bonds of kinship.

The transition from military dictatorship and the reestablishment of legitimate state authority, especially through the scenario created by the 1985 trial, restored the victims' political and civic subjectivity. This was, in a sense, the performative event of reinstatement of citizenship and the rule of law. It was a foundational moment, one that later led to further developments in the relationship between the citizenry and the law (Jelin, et al. 1996).

Yet historical processes are seldom linear. The trial of the military in Argentina was followed by a retreat and the withdrawal of a state commitment to settle accounts with the violent past. Given societal activism on issues related to the past, and the magnitude and organizational capacity of the community of the "directly affected," the public space was rapidly occupied again by their voices, with all the power of personal suffering and the legitimacy of testimony. More recently, when the state was ready again to occupy the stage, the cultural and political climate was such that the voices being heard (including that of the President) were couched in family and survivor's logic or frame, not in a broad understanding of the full political community of the country.

No one doubts the pain of the victims, nor the victims' right to recover the truth of what took place under repressive regimes. Nor is there any question of the leading role that "direct victims" and their relatives had (in Argentina and elsewhere) as the initial voices of denunciation of repression and the demand for truth and justice. The issue is a different one, and, in fact, it is a double issue. On the one hand, who is the "us" who enjoys the legitimacy to engage in remembering? Allow me to introduce an insight from Guaraní, an indigenous language spoken on a daily basis by the Paraguayan population. In Guaraní, there are two words to express the idea of "us." The first, *ore*, marks the boundary separating the speaker and his or her community and the "other," the one who listens and observes, who clearly is excluded from the "us." The second word, *ñande*, is an inclusive "us" that invites the interlocutor to be part of the community. The tensions between the two notions, and the misunderstandings and ambiguities that are involved, are always present. They can become culturally and politically significant at certain critical junctures. Thus, the questions about the cultural climate in present-day Argentina become: Is the "us" that can remember the recent past an exclusive "us," in which participation is restricted to those who "lived through" the events? Is there room to broaden that "us," whereby legitimate mechanisms of incorporation of others might begin to function? Is it an *ore* or a *ñande*?

On the other hand, to what extent do memory and justice regarding the past serve to broaden the horizon of experiences and expectations? Are they restricted to the specific event being remembered? A relevant differentiation is that between "literal" and "exemplary" memories, to use Todorov's (1998: 30) words. In the first case, what is preserved is unique; it is not transferable, it does not lead anywhere beyond itself. All the labors of memory are situated in direct contiguity to the past. The searches and efforts to recall will serve to identify all the people who were involved in the initial suffering, to reveal each detail of what happened, to try to understand the specific circumstances of the events, and to deepen and immerse oneself in them. Literal memory is incommensurable, and the transferability to other experiences is impossible. It "makes the past event something insuperable, and ultimately makes the present subject to the past" (Todorov 1998: 31). Action is explained and justified as a "duty to remember," and there is a moral mandate to be constantly vigilant against all forms of forgetting and erasure.

"Exemplary" memories are the opposite. These are memories where, without denying the singularity of the experience, it can be translated or turned into more generalized demands. Working through analogy and generalization, the recollection turns into an example that leads to the possibility of learning something from it, and the past develops into a guide for action in the present and in the future (Todorov 1998). This position involves a dual task. First, it is necessary to overcome the pain caused by remembrance and successfully contain it so that it does not invade life completely. Second, and here we move from the private and personal level to the public realm, it is necessary to learn from it, drawing the lessons that would make the past the guide for action in the present and the future. In that, the greatest responsibility is in the hands of democratic states. And, at this point, memory comes into play in another context, that of justice and institutions. When the possibility of generalization and universalization is introduced, memory and justice converge, in opposition to intentional oblivion (Yerushalmi 1989).

The question of the authority of memory and "truth" can take on an even more disquieting dimension. The danger lies in anchoring the legitimacy of expression of "truth" in an essentialized conception of biology and the body (a mirror image of biological racism). Personal suffering (especially when it was experienced directly in "your own body" or by blood-linked relatives) can become the basic determinant of legitimacy and truth. Paradoxically, if legitimacy for expressing memory of a painful past is socially assigned to those who suffered repression on their own bodies or those of their kin, this symbolic authority can easily (consciously or unconsciously) slip into a monopolistic claim on the meaning and content of memory and truth.[26] The recognized "us" is thus exclusive and nontransferable. Taken to the extreme, this situation can lead to the obstruction of the mechanisms for broadening societal involvement with memory, by not opening up the symbolic space for a reinterpretation and resignification of the meaning of the conveyed experiences. Hence, the historical challenge lies in the process of construction of a more democratic, inclusive, and civic engagement with the past.

REFERENCES

Acuña, C. H., and C. Smulovitz (1995). "Militares en la transición argentina: del gobierno a la subordinación constitucional." In C. H. Acuña, I. González Bombal, E. Jelin, et al., e. *Juicio, castigos y memoria: Derechos humanos y justicia en la política argentina*. Buenos Aires: Nueva Visión.

Anguita, E. (2001). *Sano juicio: Baltasar Garzón, algunos sobrevivientes y la lucha contra la impunidad en Latinoamérica*. Buenos Aires: Sudamericana.

Calveiro, P. (1998). *Poder y desaparición. Los campos de concentración en Argentina*. Buenos Aires: Colihue.

---

[26] Symbols of personal suffering tend to be embodied in women – the mothers and grandmothers in the case of Argentina – while the institutional mechanisms seem to belong more often to the world of men. The significance of this gender dimension, and the difficulties of breaking gender stereotypes with respect to the resources of power demand much more analytical attention.

Crenzel, E. (2008). *La historia política del NUNCA MÁS. La memoria de los desaparecidos en Argentina.* Buenos Aires: Siglo XXI Editores.

Filc, J. (1997). *Entre el parentesco y la política. Familia y dictadura, 1976–1983.* Buenos Aires: Biblos.

González Bombal, M. I. (1995). "'Nunca Más.' El juicio más allá de los estrados." In C. H. Acuña, I. González Bombal, E. Jelin, et al., *Juicio, castigos y memoria: Derechos humanos y justicia en la política argentina.* Buenos Aires: Nueva Visión.

Htun, M. (2003). *Sex and the State. Abortion, Divorce and the Family under Latin American Dictatorships and Democracies.* Cambridge: Cambridge University Press.

Jelin, E. (1995). "La política de la memoria: El movimiento de derechos humanos y la construcción democrática en la Argentina." In C. H. Acuña, I. González Bombal, E. Jelin, et al., *Juicio, castigos y memoria: Derechos humanos y justicia en la política argentina.* Buenos Aires: Nueva Visión.

———. (1996). "La matriz cultural argentina, el peronismo y la cotidianidad." In E. Jelin, L. Gingold, S. G. Kaufman, et al. *Vida cotidiana y control institucional en los años noventa.* Buenos Aires: Nuevo Hacer.

——— (2005). "Los derechos humanos entre el estado y la sociedad." In J. Suriano, ed., *Nueva Historia Argentina,* vol. 10. Buenos Aires: Editorial Sudamericana.

——— (2006). "La justicia después del juicio: Legados y desafíos en la Argentina postdictatorial." *Tribuna Americana,* no. 6, Spring.

Jelin, E., L. Gingold, S. G. Kaufman, M. Lieras, S. Rabich and L. Rubinich. (1996). *Vida cotidiana y control institucional en los años noventa.* Buenos Aires: Nuevo Hacer.

Longoni, A. (2004). "Traiciones. La figura del traidor (y la traidora) en los relatos acerca de los sobrevivientes de la represión." In E. Jelin and A. Longoni, eds., *Escrituras, imágenes, escenarios ante la represión.* Madrid/Buenos Aires: Siglo XXI de España Editores/Siglo XXI de Argentina Editores.

Lorenz, F. (2002). "¿De quién es el 24 de marzo? Las luchas por la memoria del golpe de 1976." In E. Jelin, ed., *Las conmemoraciones: las disputas en las fechas "in-felices."* Madrid/Buenos Aires: Siglo XXI de España Editores/Siglo XXI de Argentina Editores.

Lyotard, J. F. (1988). *La diferencia.* Madrid: Gedisa.

Nari, M. (2004). *Políticas de maternidad y maternalismo político. Buenos Aires, 1890–1940.* Buenos Aires: Biblos.

Sennet, R. (2004). *Respect in a World of Inequality.* New York/London: Norton.

Sikkink, K. (2008). "From Pariah State to Global Protagonist: Argentina and the Struggle for International Human Rights." *Latin American Politics and Society,* vol. 50, no. 1. Spring.

Todorov, T. (1998). *Les abus de la mémoire.* Paris: Arléa.

Yerushalmi, Y. H. (1989). *Zakhor. Jewish History and Jewish Memory.* Washington: University of Washington Press.

9. Children, Suffering, and the Humanitarian Appeal

LAURA SUSKI

Neil Postman's widely read *The Disappearance of Childhood* (1982) called upon Americans to engage in the "noble service" of protecting children from American media culture. Positioning the construction of childhood as perhaps one of the most "humane" inventions of the Renaissance, Postman sees the merging of adulthood and childhood as a social disaster: "One might go so far as to claim that to the extent that there has been any growth in empathy and sensibility – in simple humaneness – in Western civilization, it has followed the path of the growth of childhood" (64). For Postman, our relationship to children and to childhood is an important opportunity to develop humane behaviour. Examining the state of affairs in his home country of South Africa, Njabulo Ndebele is also led to reflect on what he sees as a loss of childhood. He asks whether a society without children can have a "concept of innocence." The loss of innocence, he suggests, creates "a world of instant adults with no sense of having lost something," and "if there is no sense of loss, there can be no sense of paradise to be regained" (1995: 331). For him, a politics of childhood requires a recovery of childhood in an effort to restore a metaphor of hope and the restoration of freedom and "the range of human values that should go with it" (332).

Clearly the association between innocence, vulnerability, and childhood demands further consideration. I want to examine this relationship through the exploration of a second link: the link between the humanitarian impulse and children. Children sit at the center of many appeals and programs deemed "humanitarian." We can take up the concerns of thinkers like Ndebele and Postman by asking whether our relationship to childhood invites a humanitarian sentiment, and thus, whether humanitarianism *requires* a concept of childhood innocence to legitimate it. To build this analysis, I will draw on interdisciplinary scholarship around

202

the analysis of children, international development, and international humanitarianism. To close the exploration, I will look briefly at the contemporary humanitarian appeals used by World Vision Canada. Christian international relief agencies like World Vision have funded their development work largely through programs that ask sponsors to adopt children from the Global South financially and emotionally. The success of these campaigns suggests that the programs work to form some kind of ethical attachment between the sponsor and an otherwise "distant" child. Some critics suggest that such appeals replicate a parent-child ethical relationship that is problematic and dangerous for global ethical relationships. In turn, we must inquire as to whether a humanitarianism that privileges children denies a more thorough humanitarianism, one that joins equally empowered "distant strangers" in a collective project of social justice.

The Global Child and the Global Childhood

By suggesting that children were autonomous beings, Rousseau ushered in childhood as both a site of inquiry and as a unique state of human development. Our contemporary concern with childhood follows the philosophical line of inquiry set out by Rousseau: we have, as Stephen Heath phrases it, maintained the "projection" of childhood as a "special state of being" (1997: 18). Childhood becomes even more highly valorized in the West – and arguably "discovered" – during the economic shift to industrialization. The now standard historical reading notes that the emotional and psychological value of children increases precisely when they become economically useless to society (Ariès 1962).

Despite the fact that the modern notion of childhood positions children as unique and "special" members of society, they still do not occupy status positions in society and are in many ways absent in the key institutions of power in Western society. This begs the question that Gillian Avery and Kimberly Reynolds raise in their edited collection on childhood death as to why the emotions around the death of children are so powerful and why children continue to be society's "most poignant victims" (2000: 6). Part of the answer as to why the suffering of children is compelling and problematic seems to lie with the fact that children are so firmly grounded in the future. The pain surrounding the death of children is heightened by a loss of hope about the larger future of society.[1]

---

[1] See, for example. Hawes (1991) and James & Prout (1997).

The lament about childhood suffering in modernity is also connected to the notion of childhood innocence. There is, of course, a long historical tension in the reading of children as innocent. Rousseau argued that children were closer to a state of natural goodness. In traditional Christian thought, children have been positioned as inheriting original sin, and therefore, sinful in nature. This belief has often led to less humane treatment of children and harsh efforts to educate children. In the case of Roman Catholic missionaries in early New France, for example, children were viewed as most in need of salvation. As Clarissa Atkinson (2001) explains, there was a deep cultural gulf between Jesuit and Huron definitions of childhood education and human nature. The Jesuits saw the Huron's approach to the treatment of children as lacking discipline and as "spoiling" children. This fuelled the assumption that Huron children should be separated from their parents and families if proper instruction and conversion were to take place. While contemporary Christian theologians continue to explore alternate perspectives on sin and children,[2] there is now a general (secular) acceptance that childhood is a period of innocence. As childhood is cast as a period of play, exploration, and innocence, childhood can be idealized as a space outside the demands of adult life.

While the innocence of childhood is founded upon the assumption that adulthood is a site of "pollution" (Ariès 1962), and that adults themselves, and adult life, are dangers to children, not all children are innocent. The contemporary approach to childhood is both "nurturing and constraining" and also carries with it an image of an "unsocialized" or "antisocial" child whose darker nature requires social control (Boyden 1997). Street children, and children who do "un-child-like" things, such as murder, have often been conceptualized in this way. The growing concern with terrorism also triggers a panic around the potential actions of alienated and disaffected youth in major urban centers. The "un-child-like child" carries with him or her the "end of childhood" and this is deeply troubling to the adult witness. So set are the boundaries of contemporary childhood that we name children who labor "un-child-like." Child soldiers are interesting and critical examples of children who cannot be fully contained by the label of child. They blur the line between innocence and guilt and urge us to question whether the definition of child must be suspended in times of conflict. While the stories that make it to the Western media often focus on children who are abducted into violence and soldiering, some recent research has

---

[2] See Bunge (2001).

emphasized the agency of child soldiers and asks the "painful" question of whether there are times that "children might choose to fight, and perhaps to die" (Rosenbloom 2007: 111).

Propelled in part by a current public lament about the loss of childhood in the West, the suffering of children of the Global South[3] has become an important site for the struggle for the global preservation of childhood. Children of the so-called Third World deviate from the modern notion of childhood when they work, when they suffer from severe hunger and malnourishment, and when they face illness or death. The mainstream development project that emerged in the post–World War II period is founded on the assumption that such deviations can be "fixed" or "ameliorated" (Stephens 1995: 17). When the International Year of the Child was launched in 1979, images of suffering children began to build a concept of "the world's children" that, according to James and Prout, "threw the very idea of childhood into stark relief," and united all children while "revealing the vast differences" between the realities of children's lives in the Global South and the idealized concept of modern childhood (1997: 1).

It is well documented that children are among the "poorest of the poor." The emphasis on the plight of children in the Global South rejuvenates a colonial campaign that suggests that Western institutions and organizations are better able to provide for the needs of children than are their own parents (Pupavac 2001). The mainstream development project dovetails neatly with ideas about childhood development. When poverty is viewed as an individual failure or shortcoming, it can be corrected. Intervention in the lives of "poor children" is done to increase their progress and maximise their potential, and in this way, turn them into individuals who can trigger both personal and national development (Penn 2005).

The imposition of the modern notion of childhood has not been universally positive for children of the South. Robert Serpell (1996) notes that the pressure put on Zambian youth to embrace the school as a site of development progress traps the youth into a set of unattainable aspirations and contributes to them losing sight of their own families' "indigenous ethnohistories," according to which they might perceive themselves as more successful. Brazilian children living in extreme poverty also feel the pressures of a hegemonic symbol system of Western childhood, which,

---

[3] I use this imperfect term to denote the "developing" world. In using the term, I emphasize some of the similar ways in which children of the Global South are viewed, but I am also aware that by using such a shorthand term I contribute to such a tendency and deemphasize the diversity of the Global South.

according to Campos and Gomes (1996), hides the differences in objective living conditions. The World Bank, in its promotion of Early Childhood Development programs modelled on the USA, "uses the configuration of the innocent individual child" both to avoid the harm being done to children by neoliberal economic policies and simultaneously to position children in a "technological" and "redemptionist" discourse that argues that the lives of young children can be bettered by the "right" kind of stimulation (Penn 2002: 129–30). In the case of children's labor, more culturally specific scripts can produce accounts that are far less condemning of the work of children. Elsbethe Robson's work on "hidden child care workers" in Zimbabwe explores children who work as care providers of ailing family members. She concludes that for many children working is an opportunity to contribute to the family, and not simply "pitiful," and that "more children-centred radical approaches to research and policy making are required" (2004: 243).

In sum, the promulgation of childhood as a period of innocence in much of mainstream development practice and discourse often serves to position children of the South as deprived versions of children of the North and distracts us from seeing the social and economic divisions that prevent some children from being considered "priceless." The imposition of culturally specific Northern notions of child rearing, family life, and early education not only neglect alternate visions of childhood, but also fail to address the complexities that children face when economic pressures take them far from the "ideal" and "normal" childhood (Penn 2005).

The ratification of the United Nations Conventions of the Rights of the Child in 1989 is also read by some critics as the institutionalization of a universal concept of modern Western childhood. Critics of the international rights regime argue that it errs too heavily on protection of the middle class, Western conception of childhood.[4] Its insistence on the need for external advocacy on behalf of children also works to maintain a paternalistic relationship between the North and the South.[5] While contemporary childhood studies have embraced a model of a more empowered child, which positions children as active participants in their own socialization (James and Prout 1997), the conception of the "empowered child" proves difficult for the negotiation of children's rights. It confronts the tension between "protection

---

[4] Others suggest that rights regimes may function better if they account for childhood as a growth period towards responsibility, and therefore employ a concept of "incremental entitlement to rights." See, for example, Leonard (2004).

[5] See for example, Pupavac (2001) and Boyden (1997).

and participation rights" (Woodhead 1997: 80), and between the conception of children as having both "needs" and "rights." So too, suggest critics like Stuart Aitken (2001), do conceptions of the rights of children rely heavily on how adult/child and public/private boundaries are drawn. Shifts in the liberal principles of reason and autonomy have often worked to render the "otherness and peculiarity" of children as "safe and manageable for programmatic research and instrumental notions of justice" (119). He argues for a model of justice that sees the boundaries between adulthood and childhood as more permeable and contested.

The Global South remains a comparatively more comfortable space for confronting the suffering of children.[6] While the "global child" has emerged as a category, children suffering from famine, for example, can be contained and distanced by their deviation from the modern childhood experience. Still, this deviation can be profoundly shocking. When we encounter an image of a child suffering from hunger with the obvious physical signs of illness and impending death, the image functions to express an ultimately destabilizing rupture with the modern child. For the international witness, this suffering child is both child and non-child. His or her vulnerability is characteristically childlike but the open proximity to death is fundamentally "un-child-like." Our reactions to the starving child have as much to do with the particularities of the individual child as they have to do with our relationship to childhood more generally. The problem for a more radical international humanitarianism is that these two moral narratives are often in deep conflict.

Silence and Suffering

As the "poorest of the poor," children function in the discourse of development as testaments to international suffering. As deviants from modern childhood, their fundamental narrative role is to plead for the restoration of their childhoods. This kind of narrative does not fundamentally require a voice and, as many development campaigns have discovered, is often better communicated visually, through tears or vacant looks. When children do speak, their voices often tell us more about the adults' concerns about childhood than about the children themselves (Willinsky 2004).

---

[6] Witness a recent controversy that emerged surrounding US-based photographer Jill Greenberg's exhibition "End Times," which is a collection of crying children whose outbursts were triggered by Greenberg when she suddenly took away a lollipop that had been given to them. Some critics labeled this action "child abuse." See http://arts.guardian.co.uk/news/story/0,,1830213,00.html.

The shift towards a more empowered child parallels a shift in development discourse towards models of participatory research and projects. M. F. C. Bourdillon cites a UK Save the Children Zimbabwean project aimed at improving the health and hygiene of children by improving access to clean, safe water. The failure to recognize children as actors in the development process and as key users and collectors of water for the household led to the failure of the project for children: new water sources were too far for children to access, associated more with adult gathering spaces, and utilized pumping methods that were often too hard for children to use. Bourdillon concluded that while there are limits to children's agency and knowledge, children cannot be assumed to be incompetent and the local knowledge of poor children, in particular, should be consulted and validated (2004). As another example, Marilyn Leonard (2004) found that children in the UK had different views on their right to work and many argued against the adult desire to ban children's work, suggesting that the traditional approach to protect children is somewhat outmoded. While noting that children are not often the best judges of what is good for them, Leonard suggests that their views should still be consulted during the policymaking process. Clearly then, poor children and working children have something to say about the desire of others to protect them. If we support a language of power and of resistance for children, then we remove one of the barriers to the "transformation of children from within" (Kitzinger 1997: 183), and, in turn, lessen the need for children to be protected.

Beyond the general inclusion of children's voices in development policy and planning, the more pressing analysis is the analysis of how suffering itself can be voiced. The narration of international suffering has been affected by a legal language of human rights that emphasizes the importance of speaking about pain and participating in the public discussion of truth.[7] However, because children's suffering is presumed to be easily interpreted by external witnesses, images of suffering children are often viewed as equivalent to voices in their ability to convey the denial of innocence, freedom, and play that children experience in suffering. Even the shift towards more positive imagery in development, and away from the archetypal suffering bodies that emerged most predominantly with the media coverage of the 1984–85 Ethiopian famine, represents the notion that such images capture some kind of truth about suffering or its elimination (Lidchi 1999). If development agencies picture a smiling child, the

[7] See Sandvik, Chapter 10, and Jelin, Chapter 8, in this volume.

intent is to communicate efficiently the success of the development project in achieving happiness.

Leslie Butt questions whether the presence of "suffering strangers," either visually or through voice, can incite any kind of social action to justice, and instead, their function is to sustain the "illusion" of a global "human rights culture" (2002: 3). Like other critics of universal, rationally based ideas of rights, Butt's comments reveal a deep suspicion of the ability of a rights regime to represent the interests of those in the so-called developing world. However, she is also extremely critical of the necessity to deliver moral claims in Richard Rorty's narrative, "sad story" form. The push for the inclusion of voice in recent development scholarship presents voice in limited, universalizing ways that reproduce a moral code that "allows for sustained dependency between one group and another" (17).

The position of the humanitarian giver as privileged in relation to the sufferer invites a reading of suffering as a kind of "spectacle" that is *witnessed* by the humanitarian. In its most excessive form, the visual spectacle of humanitarianism could be described as a kind of "pornography of pain" where the viewing of human suffering is both a scene of desire and revulsion (Halttunnen 1995). Some see the visual component of humanitarianism as useful, particularly in the era of mass-mediated images where cases of human suffering could be delivered to the living rooms of the privileged, and in effect, introduce new forms of caring at a distance (Silk 1998). Still others speak of a "compassion fatigue" that emerges when images of suffering become too numerous in the media. Again, situating the debate in the analysis of innocence, Ndebele has dire warnings regarding images of suffering children. If too ghastly an image of the suffering of children begins to dominate a society, he argues, that would indicate "there were few horrors left in society" and "if such a point is ever reached, it would surely demand the most far-reaching efforts for a society to rediscover its conscience" (1995: 322).

Global Humanitarianism

Humanitarianism demands its position in the realm of morality through being an act that is "other-regarding," and similarly, seems to lose this intrinsically moral position if the act of "other-regarding" serves the pursuit of self-interest (Badhwar 1993). Its "other-regarding" nature situates it more squarely in the sociological, rather than the economic, because the economic subject is assumed always to act in self-interest (Wolfe 1998). In these dichotomous terms, our relationship as humanitarians to children is somewhat complicated. Childhood, as we are well aware, is seen as a site of sentimental loss about our own lives (Pupavac 2001). When adults help children, we are in negotiation with our own childhood, and the line between self and other is blurred, as is the distinction between altruism and self-interest.

If the intuitive connections between humanitarianism and "good," altruistic intentions do not provide a reliable or solid definition for the term humanitarianism, we might build one by mapping its unique character as a social and political impulse. I argue that part of this uniqueness lies in its character as an emotion-based impulse, and, also, in the way that it is an *active* response: a humanitarian intends to alleviate the suffering of others. In this regard, I join thinkers like Thomas Laqueur (1989) and Thomas Haskell (1985a; 1985b). As Laqueur concludes in his analysis of humanitarian narratives, the extension of compassion to others requires both "habits of feeling" and "theories of causation" and it is these two foundational ideas that form the basis of humanitarian narratives (1989: 204).

While humanitarianism is a rare entry in dictionaries of politics or sociology, when it does appear, the humanitarian impulse is described as an "emotional dedication" to reform (Dunner 1964). The emotional base of humanitarianism could be described as sympathy, empathy, compassion, or perhaps even guilt. Theorists of emotion and morality are quick to point out that each of these emotions has different ethical implications. While for Adam Smith (1853/1984) sympathy offered the possibility for a moral spectator to imagine himself in the position of suffering others, contemporary commentators have interrogated how sympathy often leads to pity,[8] rather than the more modern – and somewhat more acceptable version of "real" identification with suffering – empathy (Garber 2004).

The emotional pull of humanitarian appeals is always dependent upon the worthiness of those suffering, and constructions of the morality of sufferers shift in different historical and social contexts. For example, the cultural concern with sexuality in the West partially contributes to the relatively recent selection of female genital "cutting" of young women as an international human rights issue. More generally, the contemporary political emphasis on gender equality supports the new focus of development organizations like UNICEF on increased access to education, health, and basic human rights for the "girl child." Humanitarianism may be driven by claims to a universal humanism, but historically it has been selectively applied, often according to how humanitarian "clients" are

---

[8]	See, for example, Boltanski (1999) and Butt (2002).

themselves constructed. In her exploration of transnational efforts to protect civilians in war zones, R. Charli Carpenter notes that human rights discourses rely heavily on gendered essentialisms. "Women and children" are used as the proxy for "citizens," and, as a result, the protection of males of draft age is undermined (2005). The presumed innocence and vulnerability of contemporary children has saved them from the excesses of the selective patterns of humanitarianism. Nonetheless, the lives of some children are not deemed sacred nor are they sentimentalized, and their suffering can go relatively unnoticed to international eyes. African children are presented as archetypal famine victims, whereas children of the Gaza Strip, who also suffer from severe food shortages, are not.

Compassion gained momentum in the seventeenth and eighteenth centuries when humanitarian feelings were positioned as "natural" (Fiering 1976), but the spread of the practice of humanitarianism requires changes to the understanding of personal agency. In reference to the emergence of humanitarian narratives in the realist novels of the eighteenth century, and in medical writing, such as autopsies and clinical reports, Laqueur highlights that the new and key element of this body of writing was the way in which it detailed human suffering and laid out lines of "causality" between readers and those suffering. The narratives presented a moral imperative, although often selectively applied, for social action: "Someone or something did something that caused pain, suffering or death and that could, under certain circumstances, have been avoided or mitigated" (1989: 178). The advent of the welfare state and the spread of modern democracy no doubt served to buttress the notion that human suffering not only could, but should, be eliminated (Sznaider 1998). The contemporary suffering of children is often deemed "needless" and this heightens a sense of agency on the part of humanitarian actors. The fact that children are seen as "vulnerable" also works to validate the agency of adults as protectors of children.

As a practice, humanitarianism cannot be entirely separated from governmentality and the modern development of more nuanced forms of social control. The construction of childhood itself can be cast with ideological motivations such that the socialization of children involves an ideological interpellation into the relations of power and violence (see Zornado 2001). As Elizabeth Jelin (Chapter 8 in this volume) shows in her discussion of post-dictatorial Argentina, the patriarchal parental relationship, and the discourse of family more generally, can be seized upon by military states to enact authority and control over its citizens. The spread of global capital and culture also contributes to the increasing commodification of children's lives (Stephens 1995), and to the cultural expansion of contemporary images of ideal childhood (Boyden 1997). Public forms of compassion can work to legislate appropriate social and political action and define certain behaviors as "cruel" (Sznaider 1998). Thus, humanitarianism can be read as a Foucauldian discourse of discipline. However, the analytical key to uncovering the liberatory potential of more modern humanitarian narratives is to pay attention to the terms by which humanitarianism will be enacted, terms that often serve the interests of the humanitarian, *and* to the way in which such terms reveal their own inadequacy as a discourse of universal humanism. Put differently, humanitarianism can be liberating when it uncovers the conflicts of individual identification in the name of universal interest. When we are moved by the suffering of children, we must also ask why we are not similarly moved by the suffering of adults.

This faith in the possibilities of human agency to alleviate suffering, coupled with its emotional resonances, is ultimately a source of deep ambivalence for modern humanitarianism. Modern humanitarians must confront the failures of universal humanism whenever they are drawn to alleviate suffering. This entails what has been labelled a kind of "moral embarrassment" (Ellison 1999; Halttunnen 1995; Jaffe 2000), and what Natan Sznaider has highlighted as the "inconsistency" of the two images of a liberal society: one seeking such social reforms as equality, and the other haunted by individualism and public indifference (1998: 119). This ambivalence is heightened in the case of children, where their suffering again functions as an overt reminder of neglect and the failures of modern progress to eliminate a kind of suffering that is deemed the most horrific, and yet the most remediable. More radically, the ambivalence is grounded in acting from a position of privilege where we become aware of our own implication in the structures that determine the need for humanitarian action. Given this feeling of conflict, we may then be drawn to sites of social action, such as a humanitarianism of childhood, where this ambivalence can be tempered or managed.

The Example of Child Sponsorship: "It's the Kind of Life We Could Never Imagine for Our Own Children"

As a fundraising tactic for international development, few methods rival the success of child sponsorship. Child sponsorship has long been a funding mainstay for large NGOs like Save the Children, Plan International, and World Vision and is a growing phenomenon (Smillie 1994). Child sponsorship programs are utilized by many religious-based development organizations including Muslim, Catholic, and Protestant organizations, as well as secular organizations. Despite their growing popularity, there is very little published research on child sponsorship programs, both in terms of their developmental impact and their impact on sponsors themselves.[9] There are two kinds of sponsorship programs: those that focus on the individual child as recipient; and those that use funds to support development programs where the child lives to benefit all children in the community (Brehm & Gale 2000). World Vision Canada fits into the latter category. Through World Vision Canada, Canadians sponsor 400,000 children worldwide, and, by connection, their communities.

Most successful NGOs use highly emotive tactics rather than appeals to "intelligent development education" to attract supporters (Smillie 1994: 179), and as Canada's largest NGO, World Vision's appeals are no exception. The television appeals of World Vision in Canada follow a fairly standard format.[10] Canadian celebrities, such as television personality Alex Trebek, narrate the profiles of a number of children. The appeals show both children who need sponsors and the success stories of children who have been sponsored. The needing child is pictured, often dark and shadowed and alone. He or she is never smiling, although World Vision tends to avoid images of children crying or in severe pain. Most of the crying is in fact done by sponsors when they describe the sponsorship experience, or when they are shown watching videotape of their sponsored child, or by the television hosts visiting the children in their home communities. When the appeals track the progress of a child who is sponsored, the "end child" is smiling or even laughing or giggling, and is shown involved in "happier" activities, such as attending school. Some children are orphans. More recent World Vision campaigns have highlighted the plight of AIDs orphans in parts of southern Africa. However, not all sponsored children are orphans. Still, parents or any other community members do not figure prominently in the initial appeal. When parents appear, as in the case of the profile of a young Cambodian girl or a single father in Mozambique, they too are presented as victims who are unable to parent their own children. Through a translator, a Cambodian mother confesses that it was "her fault" that she was not more discerning and careful when her daughter was sold

---

[9] This absence is certainly revealing, but it is an exploration I will have to leave for another conversation. There are several possible reasons for this but one key may be that such programs are considered to be primarily fundraising tactics rather than sustainable development programs.

[10] I examined appeals that aired on Canadian television from 2004 to 2007.

into prostitution by a neighbor. To draw would-be sponsors into the sponsorship relationship, the appeals must be sure to present children as purely children; in effect, they are presented as the ideal children waiting for ideal childhoods. They are shown as vulnerable and always grateful for any kind of support offered, be it a letter or agricultural training. In the case of a Protestant-based organization like World Vision, the presentation of children as "good victims" also allows would-be donors to take on the role of the benevolent giver in the narrative of Christian redemption.[11]

Like all organizations that employ child sponsorship programs, World Vision facilitates communication between a sponsor and a sponsored child. Resembling an official adoption, sponsors receive a photograph of their child. Sponsors send and receive letters and are sent annual progress reports. The television appeals include many comments from sponsors on the value of this kind of communication. One sponsor comments on how she "rushes to open letters" and another comments on how these letters gave him a "sense of connection" that he did not expect. World Vision sponsors are discouraged from sending large gifts and instead encouraged to send token gifts or cards. The television appeals also explain that sponsors have some choice in the process. They can choose the gender, age, and home country of their sponsored child. Sponsors are also encouraged to visit their sponsored child, although this is an offer that few can take up.

Part of the success of the campaigns is certainly founded on the sponsor's sense that they are really making a difference in the lives of particular children. They describe a "great feeling of satisfaction" and affirm that they know that their gift is "making an impact." Television appeals in Canada repeat the phrase "change a life, change your own," which is the current operating agenda of the organization. This is quite different from other Christian-based organizations, for example Canadian Save the Children's call to "become an everyday hero," or Christian Children's Fund's "you have the power to change a child's life," or indeed, Compassion Canada's "releasing children from poverty in Jesus' name." World Vision positions child sponsorship as a reciprocal relationship.

The appeals suggest the possibility of real bonding and connection, and sponsors are quoted describing their relationship to their sponsored child as being "like a family." One appeal explains how a child "looks sad" in his picture because both of his parents have died. It is then suggested that although the child is living with relatives, the support of a sponsor would "mean so much," and in this way suggests that the sponsorship relationship could be

---

[11] See Keshgegian, Chapter 6 in this volume.

more meaningful than the relationship with his relatives. The appeals position the sponsorship process as an emotional exchange, not a purely economic one. Alex Trebek asks Canadians to let unsponsored children know "that someone in Canada loves and believes in them." A Christian plea is also made to would-be sponsors to help children be "all that God wants them to be."

There is nothing radically cosmopolitan about the ethical relationship between sponsor and sponsored child. World Vision appeals frame the commitment to help sponsored children in the language of family. When sponsoring a child, sponsors are simply extending the comfortable and safe moral spaces of family in a form that allows ethical attachment to an otherwise distant child. The appeals repeat that it is impossible to change the world but very possible to change the lives of individual children. This highly individualized moral relationship consciously diverts a sponsor away from reforming the structural economic and political causes of poverty. Yet, the success of such appeals speaks to the way in which children are able to motivate a variety of Canadians to act on their behalf. While not purely cosmopolitan, sponsorship enacts a global connection. It is not merely a fundraising tactic but an exercise in global morality. The comments of some sponsors suggest a complexity in this morality. For example, one sponsor explains that through child sponsorship she wanted her kids to know that "these are real people who are suffering." One couple holding an obviously newborn baby and watching a tape of their sponsored child states that they hope the sponsorship will make their birth child know "how lucky she is."

One of the few academic treatments of World Vision's child sponsorship programs is found in a chapter of Erica Bornstein's useful analysis of Protestant NGOs in Zimbabwe, entitled *The Spirit of Development* (2005). Bornstein verifies some of the suspected problems of child sponsorship including its tendencies to dislodge the authority of parents, create jealousies within communities, create a sense of loss after the period of sponsorship has ended, and fracture local practices and understandings of giving. While sponsors willingly chose to enter a "global, Christian humanitarian community," sponsored children often felt tensions at the local level as a result of the sponsorship process. Yet, she also found evidence of the "unifying and expansive potential of humanitarianism" in the words of a sponsored child who claimed that the sponsorship process "felt nice" because "I am feeling like I am becoming part of their family" (94). In addition to analyzing the importance of a Protestant theology to World Vision's sponsorship program, Bornstein's conclusions focus on the tensions between the local and the global: sponsorship had a truly transformative potential to form relationships that transcended distance, but they also had "the potential to create localized experiences of lack that stood in the face of benevolent attempts to bridge distance" (94).

One of the key lessons of the examination of child sponsorship is that the picture of sponsored children is narrowed not only by the absence of the voices of children, but also by the absence of parents and other community members. The World Vision sponsorship process draws sponsored children into the families of sponsors, but the notion of a transnational family is mostly connected to donors. We need to hear more about how the families and communities of sponsored children understand the sponsorship process. A shift to an empowered, voiced child would be illuminating, but it would be incomplete without a more polyphonic, multi-actor narrative of sponsorship. While organizations like World Vision insist that the sponsorship relationship is reciprocal, the narrative power remains in the hands of the sponsor. As one appeal states: "You can rewrite the story of a needy child's life."

Child sponsorship is a striking example of the complexity of a global morality based on helping individual children. It is, again to quote Bornstein, "not easy to accept nor easy to dismiss" (95). Regardless of some of its problematic outcomes, many children do benefit from the sponsorship process, and many sponsors are indeed "transformed" by it. The ability to build a lasting ethical attention that extends beyond a pure financial exchange speaks to the ability of childhood to trigger a conversation of universal humanity and a commitment to action.

Conclusions

It is difficult for modern Westerners not to be moved by the suffering of children, and both their connection to the future and their present vulnerability make the alleviation of their suffering necessary, possible, and hopeful. To critics of humanitarianism, the apparent affinity between humanitarianism and children produces the worst kind of humanitarianism: one that envisions humanitarians as sentimental, misguided idealists, and that treats the receivers of humanitarian attention as pitiful, dehumanized victims to be "fixed" or "saved." Too close an affinity, these same critics may suggest, makes all receivers of humanitarian intervention childlike, again rehearsing a discourse of colonialism that enacts a parent-child relationship at the international level.

But the merging of a child-based humanitarianism and a pity-based humanitarianism is too hasty. The affinity between humanitarianism and children demands attention not only for its perils but for its promises. Children are difficult objects for social justice precisely because they require that we address untraditional and difficult terrains of political thought. Children are connected more with the realm of "nature" and to the intimate, private realm of the family. They stand outside both the market and politics (Stephens 1995). Our apprehension with children-centered narratives of social justice is also due in part to our unease with the role of emotion as a moral guide. Humanitarians operate outside explicit political engagement because the principles of neutrality and impartiality that mark the movement of international humanitarian actors as nonpolitical also serve to emphasize the position of humanitarians as compassionate actors (Campbell 1998). If, however, the principles of neutrality and impartiality are the only measurements of the (a)political nature of humanitarianism, we are certainly employing a limited view of the political. Like the dichotomy between altruism and self-interest, the supposed neutrality of humanitarian action denies the complexity and "imperfection" of the humanitarian subject, who is never wholly neutral.

An emotion can be labelled political when it incites an *active* response to suffering. Take, for example, Joan Tronto's argument for caring as a process. In her discussion of the phases of caring, she draws a distinction between "caring about" and "caring for" (1998: 16–17). "Caring about" simply signals an attentiveness to the need for caring, while "caring for" is the stage where responsibility for the care of others is taken more seriously. In the tradition of a feminist ethics of care, we can envision an ethical model that focuses on the concrete situations of moral relations, takes into account the role of emotion in moral judgment, and assumes that we are embedded in and obligated to social relationships (Clement 1996). This is not a call to replicate a mothering relationship in all global moral encounters nor to embrace an "ideal image of childhood as the focus of structured adult protection and compassionate nurturing" (Stephens 1997: 25). Instead, it is a call to assess our emotional engagement with children and childhood with greater precision and rigor.

Lauren Berlant notes that compassion is inherently tied to its withholding: "When we are taught, from the time we are taught anything, to measure the scale of pain and attachment, to feel *appropriately* compassionate, we are being trained in stinginess, in not caring, in not knowing what we know about the claim on us to act, as Nietzsche would say scathingly, all too human" (2004: 10). At a bare minimum, then, the albeit imperfect discourse of a humanitarianism of childhood invites a less "stingy" compassion. Because we feel implicated in the lives of distant children, we are able to reflect more on the act of caring, rather than the question of who we should care about.

Does childhood contribute to the validation of the humanitarian as protector of the innocent? Does childhood, in the words of Ndebele, become a key space for locating the "metaphors of hope" that fuel the humanitarian sentiment? In relation to children and childhood, humanitarianism is faced with two political tasks: how to act in the name of the specific needs of culturally, socially, economically situated children; and how to act in the name of hope for a future that childhood has come to represent. As I have suggested, these two ethical agendas are often in conflict. The desire to defend childhood is often fought at the expense of the needs and wants of children of the Global South.

One might infer, then, that the best way to deal with these conflicted agendas is to separate them; to aim our humanitarian hopes and dreams in some place other than the realm of childhood. Vanessa Pupavac, for example, argues that the child has come to epitomize the contemporary ethical subject. Children are seen as at risk, including at risk of the effects of parenting, and the child international rights regime has been negatively marked by the current popularity of this therapeutic culture. She concludes that the culture of children's rights moves within the colonial and missionary template of victim-abuser, and that this rights regime "effectively denies the moral, emotional, and political capacity of adults and children alike" (2001: 109). However, childhood is a complex space for which we do not yet have an adequate ethical language (Lombardo 1997). Indeed, humanitarianism cannot be meaningfully understood without addressing its relationship to childhood as a space where the tensions between dependency and empowerment are managed and mismanaged. When we intervene in the lives of children we do so not only because our dominant position as adults allows us such an intervention, but also because we believe that the suffering of children is a troubling testament to the present and the future. When we confront the loss of childhood in the Global South, we are confronting not only notions of innocence, but, as Sharon Stephens suggests, "of nature, individual freedom, social values of enduring love and care ... and the possibility of non-commodified social domains outside the realm of market and market-driven politics" (1997: 9–10). When we confront the attitudes around the death of children, we are better able to uncover what our culture "wants for and wants from those invested with the responsibility for its future" (Avery & Reynolds 2000: 10). All of these intellectual reflections are of critical concern to a discourse of humanitarianism.

The "humane" task, then, is not to idealize childhood as a space of innocence and to engage in a project largely aimed at its global export. A universalized notion of childhood innocence can work to discipline children of the South and to draw a dangerous distinction between "their" children and "our" children. Rather, the task is to deepen the narrative of childhood suffering and the moral response it inspires. This requires attention to the experience and voices of children. As Sandvik (Chapter 10) reminds us, the voices of those who suffer are often generated to produce certain forms of victim identities and to establish "credible" suffering. This may be particularly true of child sponsorship appeals used to attract donor attention. Obviously, we will have to look beyond such narratives to find children whose testimonials of pain and suffering are far less palatable and "pure." A deepened narrative of childhood also requires attention to the voices and experiences of families and adults in the Global South. In exporting a global notion of innocent childhood, we have turned our attention to the important plight of children worldwide, but we have also, sometimes inadvertently, extracted children from the social, political, and emotional context of their lives.

Humanitarianism is deeply implicated in a political venture that is anguished by the failures of modern global projects of redistributive justice. It is drawn to the experience of children as an example of these failures. As the case of child sponsorship illustrates, to act on behalf of children does not automatically make us more humane, but it can engage us in a global ethical project that attempts an "abstract emotional configuring of one's place in the world" (Bornstein 2005: 94). This may have more transformative implications for humanitarians themselves, but it does reclaim a hope for a moral relationship between the South and North. Humanitarian actors move closer to a politics of structural transformation when "lost" childhoods represent not merely an opportunity to restore these childhoods, but an opportunity to support the reclamation of children's lives on terms different than their own. A notion of innocence need not be entirely discarded from the language of humanitarianism. A concept of innocence can be invaluable if it communicates a profound rupture in an individual life and the ethical attention that this rupture demands of us.

REFERENCES

Aitken, S. (2001). "Global Crises of Childhood: Rights, Justice and the Unchildlike Child." *Area*. vol. 33, no. 2, pp. 119–27.
Ariès, P. (1962). *Centuries of Childhood: A Social History of Family Life*. Trans. Robert Baldick. New York: Vintage Books.
Atkinson, C. R. (2001). "'Wonderful Affection' : Seventeenth-century Missionaries to New France on Children and Childhood." In C. Bunge, ed., *The Child in Christian Thought*. Grand Rapids/Michigan/Cambridge: William B. Eerdmans Publishing Company, pp. 227–46.

Avery, G., and K. Reynolds, eds. (2000). *Representations of Childhood Death.* New York/London: St. Martin's Press/MacMillan Press.

Badhwar, N. K. (1993). "Altruism Versus Self-interest: Sometimes a False Dichotomy." *Social Philosophy & Policy,* vol. 10, no.1, pp. 90–117.

Berlant, L., ed. (2004). *Compassion: The Culture and Politics of an Emotion.* New York/London: Routledge.

Boltanski, L. (1999). *Distant Suffering – Morality, Media and Politics.* Trans. Graham Burchell. Cambridge: Cambridge University Press.

Bornstein, E. (2005). *The Spirit of Development: Protestant NGOS, Morality, and Economics in Zimbabwe.* Stanford: Stanford University Press.

Bourdillon, M. F. C. (2004). "Children in Development." *Progress in Development Studies,* vol. 4, no.2, pp. 99–113.

Boyden, J. (1997). "Childhood and the Policy Makers: A Comparative Perspective on the Globalization of Childhood." In A. James and A. Prout, eds., *Constructing and Reconstructing Childhood: Contemporary Issues in the Sociological Study of Childhood,* 2nd edn. London/Philadelphia: Routledge, pp. 190–229.

Brehm, V., and J. Gale. (2000). "Child Sponsorship: A Funding Tool for Sustainable Development?" *Informed: NGO Funding and Policy Bulletin,* no.3, November, pp. 2–7.

Bunge, C., ed. (2001). *The Child in Christian Thought.* Grand Rapids/Michigan/Cambridge: William B. Eerdmans.

Butt, L. (2002). "The Suffering Stranger: Medical Anthropology and International Morality." *Medical Anthropology,* vol. 21, pp. 1–24.

Campbell, D. (1998). "Why Fight: Humanitarianism, Principles and Post-Structuralism." *Millennium: Journal of International Studies,* vol. 27, no. 3, pp. 497–521.

Campos, M. M., and J. V. Gomes (1996). "Brazilian Children: Images, Conceptions, Projects." In C. P. Hwang, M. Lamb, and I. Sigel, eds., *Images of Childhood.* Mahwah, NJ: Lawrence Erlbaum Associates, pp. 143–66.

Carpenter, R. C. (2005). "'Women, Children and Other Vulnerable Groups': Gender, Strategic Frames and the Protection of Civilians as a Transnational Issue." *International Studies Quarterly,* vol. 29, pp. 294–334.

Clement, G. (1996). *Care, Autonomy, and Justice: Feminism and the Ethic of Care.* Boulder: Westview Press.

Corsaro, W. A. (1997). *The Sociology of Childhood.* Thousand Oaks, CA: Pine Forge Press.

Dunner, J. (1964). *Dictionary of Political Science.* London: Vision Press.

Ellison, J. (1999). *Cato's Tears and the Making of Anglo-American Emotion.* Chicago: University of Chicago Press.

Fiering, N. S. (1976). "Irresistible Compassion: An Aspect of Eighteenth-century Sympathy and Humanitarianism." *Journal of the History of Ideas,* vol. 37, no. 2, pp. 195–218.

Garber, M. (2004). "Compassion." In L. Berlant, ed., *Compassion: The Culture and Politics of an Emotion.* New York/London: Routledge, pp. 15–28.

Halttunen, K. (1995). "Humanitarianism and the Pornography of Pain in Anglo-American Culture." *American Historical Review,* vol. 100, April, pp. 303–34.

Haskell, T. (1985a). "Capitalism and the Origins of the Humanitarian Sensibility, Part 1." *The American Historical Review,* vol. 90, no. 2, pp. 339–61.

————. (1985b). "Capitalism and the Origins of the Humanitarian Sensibility, Part 2." *The American Historical Review*, vol. 90, no. 3, pp. 547–66.

Jaffe, A. (2000). *Scenes of Sympathy: Identity and Representation in Victorian Fiction.* Ithaca: Cornell University Press.

James, A., and A. Prout, eds. (1997). *Constructing and Reconstructing Childhood: Contemporary Issues in the Sociological Study of Childhood*, 2nd edn. London/ Philadelphia: Routledge.

Hawes, J. M. (1991). *The Children's Rights Movement: A History of Advocacy and Protection.* New York: Twayne Publishers.

Heath, S. (1997). "Childhood Times." *Critical Quarterly*, vol. 39, no. 3, pp. 16–27.

Kitzinger, J. (1997). "Who Are You Kidding? Children, Power, and the Struggle Against Sexual Abuse." In A. James and A. Prout, eds., *Constructing and Reconstructing Childhood: Contemporary Issues in the Sociological Study of Childhood*, 2nd edn. London/Philadelphia: Routledge, pp. 165–89.

Laqueur, T. (1989). "Bodies, Details, and the Humanitarian Narrative." In Lynn Hunt, ed., *The New Cultural History*. Berkeley: University of California Press, pp. 176–204.

Leonard, M. (2004). "Children's Views on Children's Right to Work: Reflections from Belfast." *Childhood*, vol. 11, no. 1, pp. 45–61.

Lidchi, H. (1999). "Finding the Right Image: British Development NGOs and the Regulation of Imagery." In T. Skelton and T. Allen, eds., *Culture and Global Change.* London: Routledge, pp. 87–101.

Lombardo, P. (1997). "Introduction: The End of Childhood?" *Critical Quarterly*, vol. 39, no. 3, pp. 1–7.

Ndebele, N. (1995). "Recovering Childhood: Children in South African National Reconstruction." In S. Stephens, ed., *Children and the Politics of Culture.* Princeton: Princeton University Press, pp. 321–33.

Penn, H. (2002). "The World Bank's View of Early Childhood." *Childhood*, vol. 9, no. 1, pp. 118–32.

————. (2005). *Unequal Childhoods: Young Children's Lives in Poor Countries.* London/New York: Routledge.

Postman, N. (1982). *The Disappearance of Childhood.* New York: Delacorte Press.

Pupavac, V. (2001). "Misanthropy Without Borders: The International Children's Rights Regime." *Disasters*, vol. 25, no.1, pp. 95–112.

Robson, E. (2004). "Hidden Child Workers: Young Carers in Zimbabwe." *Antipodes*, vol. 36, no. 2, pp. 221–48.

Rosenbloom, S. R. (2007). "Review Essay: Transgressive Questions about Child Soldiers." *Qualitative Sociology*, vol. 30, pp. 109–11.

Serpell, R. (1996). "Cultural Models of Childhood in Indigenous Socialization and Formal Schooling in Zambia." In C. P. Hwang, M. Lamb, and I. Sigel, eds., *Images of Childhood.* Mahwah, NJ: Lawrence Erlbaum Associates, pp. 129–42.

Silk, J. (1998). "Caring at a Distance." *Ethics, Place and Environment*, vol. 1, no. 2, pp. 165–82.

Smillie, I. (1994). "Changing Partners: Northern NGOs, Northern Governments." *Voluntas*, vol. 5, no. 2, pp. 155–92.

Smith, A. (1853/1984). *The Theory of Moral Sentiments.* Indianapolis: Liberty Fund.

Stephens, S., ed. (1995). *Children and the Politics of Culture*. Princeton: Princeton University Press.

Sznaider, N. (1998). "A Sociology of Compassion: A Study in the Sociology of Morals." *Cultural Values*, vol. 2, no. 1, pp. 117–39.

Tronto, J. (1998). "An Ethic of Care." *Generations*, vol. 22, no. 3, pp. 15–20.

Willinsky, J. (2004). "Childhood's Ends." In H. Goelman, S. K. Marshall, and S. Ross, eds., *Multiple Lenses, Multiple Images: Perspectives on the Child Across Time, Space and Disciplines*. Toronto: University of Toronto Press.

Wolfe, A. (1998). "What is Altruism?" In W. W. Powell and E. S. Clemens, eds., *Private Action and the Public Good*. New Haven: Yale University Press, pp. 36–46.

Woodhead, M. (1997). "Psychology and the Cultural Construction of Children's Needs." In A. James and A. Prout, eds., *Constructing and Reconstructing Childhood: Contemporary Issues in the Sociological Study of Childhood*, 2nd edn. London/Philadelphia: Routledge, pp. 63–84.

Zornado, J. (2001). *Inventing the Child: Culture, Ideology and the Story of Childhood*. New York: Garland Publishing.

10. The Physicality of Legal Consciousness: Suffering and the Production of Credibility in Refugee Resettlement

KRISTIN BERGTORA SANDVIK

Introduction

Increasingly, global governance happens through a new humanitarianism that involves the strategic legal alignment of vulnerable populations with categories of rights violations. Annually, UNHCR (the United Nation High Commissioner for Refugees) resettles thousands of refugees from wartorn, poverty-stricken countries in the Global South to wealthy countries in the North. The pursuit of resettlement occupies a dominant position in the encounter between UNHCR's legal protection officers and refugee populations. While the UNHCR Resettlement Handbook and the legal officers postulate "the perfect victim" as the ideal resettlement candidate, resettlement requires substantial individual entrepreneurship. Based on my experience as a caseworker for UNHCR (2004), and data from fieldwork among urban refugees (2005) in Kampala, Uganda, this chapter traces the complex strategies through which refugees and humanitarians together translate experiences of physical and psychological injury into legal scripts.

Reflecting the outdated 1997 UNHCR policy on African urban refugees, and based on an agreement between UNHCR and the Ugandan government, refugees are expected to live as farmers in rural settlements. Officially, there is no sizeable refugee population in Kampala, but tens of thousands of refugees live there permanently or part time. Because of their inability or unwillingness to "go to the camp" and difficult living conditions in the city, urban refugees see leaving Uganda as the only realistic

My research was made possible by research grants from Harvard Law School, the University of Oslo and the Norwegian Research Council. I am grateful to the conference organizers, Jane Fair Bestor, Anne Hellum, Martha Minow, Sally Falk Moore, Susan Silbey, and Lucie White for comments and support.

means of social improvement. Despite often challenging circumstances in their new home countries, resettled refugees frequently glorify their new lives as Australian factory workers, American minimum wage earners, Canadian small-town dwellers, or Norwegian welfare recipients to their relatives or friends who remain displaced. The presence of perpetually affluent expatriate workers in Kampala reconfirms fantasies of an "easy" life in the West. The desire to migrate fostered by these stories creates an enormous pressure on the resettlement process (Horst 2006a, 2006b).

As Brown and Wilson note in the Introduction, a substantial anthropological literature has focused on the silencing of victims of torture and violence and the difficulty in rendering human misery theoretically meaningful. Trying to overcome this impasse, newer scholarship has attempted to render suffering intelligible, often by exploring how the narration of pain and victimization through human rights language contributes to the "remaking" of the world. A more politicized stream of socio-legal studies, which aims to locate suffering as a public and political issue, has been criticized for commodifying suffering and for instrumentalizing the pain of sexual, racial or ethnic "others" (Ticktin 1999). In recent years, concerns about agency and victimization rhetoric in international human rights discourse have emerged as important issues (Kapur 2002), and the idea of testimonials about violence and abuse as empowering has been tempered by recent scholarship showing the incapacitating aspects of this activity (Segall 2002; Colvin 2004).

My aim is to examine how the legal recognition of particular forms of suffering functions discursively in the global moral economy of which humanitarianism has become such a central component. The tensions exhibited in the creation of resettlement narratives should lead us to question our perceptions of purity and credibility embedded in the humanitarian subject, and consequently the role given to suffering in international law.

Testimonies about abuse, exploitation and violence have come to constitute a particular cosmopolitan practice and take place on a proliferation of international and transnational stages. The first International Tribunal on Crimes Against Women, in Brussels, Belgium, in 1976, was an early example of organization of testimonies for therapeutic purposes (Russell 1977). From the late 1980s onwards, victims in such varied locations as Argentina, South Africa, and Morocco have given testimonies to truth commissions and participated in truth and reconciliation hearings. Some of these processes of reconciliation have involved formalized apologies or monetary compensation (see Slyomovics, Chapter 12 in this volume).

Other processes, such as the South African Truth and Reconciliation Commission, aimed to achieve a more abstract form of restorative justice (Wilson 2001). Building on the lessons from Nuremberg, a broad reactivation of international criminal law is currently taking place. To allocate individual responsibility for atrocities, the international community summons victims to testify in front of the International Criminal Court and the tribunals for the former Yugoslavia, Rwanda, and Sierra Leone. Perhaps the most prevalent and popularized source of narratives of suffering are the highly mediated eyewitness accounts produced by advocacy groups such as Human Rights Watch and Amnesty International (see Dudai, Chapter 11 in this volume).

In contrast to these examples, the narratives of suffering produced in the encounter between humanitarians and refugees are not part of any therapeutic, reconciliatory, monetary, punitive, or informational framework. While the content of the narrative may be very similar to the stories rendered through these other formats, access to third-country resettlement is in essence a question of administrative discretion about whether to grant admission to the First World. Legal bureaucrats, not judges, therapists, political leaders, human rights researchers or journalists, are in charge of determining the adequate threshold of suffering.

While often poorly understood, these types of legal mechanisms also function as potent vehicles for social change and individual and collective mobility. These legal institutions are not undone if we talk about them differently; as noted by Ron Dudai, postmodernism, anthropology, and oral history can criticize and reinterpret, but only go so far in challenging dominant practices. They do not erase either what Kirsten Hastrup calls the "hardness of facts" (1993: 727) or the reality of power differences between humanitarians and their clients. We cannot critique away thresholds for admissibility or burdens of proof. Yet it is obvious that we need to scrutinize these processes of administrative humanitarian interventionism, and the technologies of control that the machineries for human rights protection provide for legal bureaucrats. I propose that as a strategy for global justice, the legal recognition of particular taxonomies of pain in the resettlement procedure generates regimented and instrumentalized accounts of human rights violations. We need to understand how the efforts to conform to official requirements and informal bureaucratic norms both unfasten and entrench the experience of suffering.

I consider here the process of constructing narratives of rape, torture, and physical insecurity geared towards fulfilling the legal criteria set out under the resettlement procedure. I look at how these narratives intersect with the discretionary assessment of credibility embedded within this process. I examine these strategies to investigate how my informants' understanding of the resettlement requirements shape their lives, and, more specifically, what it means to construct an officially approved past through the use of legal conventions and discourses. It is possible to explore the convoluted relationship between legal interpretation and narrative by gauging the way the actors make distinctions between "true" narratives and manufactured stories, and how they mediate and negotiate ideas about personhood, credibility, and chronology.

Background

According to the 2004 edition of the UNHCR Resettlement Handbook, resettlement involves the selection and transfer of refugees from a state in which they have initially sought protection to a third state that has agreed to admit them with permanent residence status. Resettlement is primarily a solution for refugees with "legal and physical protection needs," meaning that their fundamental human rights are at risk in the country of refuge. However, the handbook also describes seven other categories, embodying various aspects of post–Cold War humanitarianism. These include survivors of violence and torture, refugees with acute medical needs, women at risk, refugees without local integration prospects, children and adolescents who are unaccompanied, elderly refugees whose families are already in the West, and the reunification of separated families. The legal basis for resettlement is the tripartite agreements between host states, receiving countries, and UNHCR. The largest resettlement countries are the United States of America, Australia, and Canada, followed by the Scandinavian countries, the Netherlands, and New Zealand.

Resettlement must be understood in the context of global migration movements. Civil unrest, environmental problems, and lack of economic opportunity have spurred millions of people across Sub-Saharan Africa to seek a better life, with dramatic and often tragic consequences for individuals and communities. UNHCR emphasizes that resettlement should not be used as a substitute for the right to seek and enjoy asylum in the developed countries, and that policymakers should not put the asylum and resettlement mechanisms to work against each other. In 2005, the number of resettled refugees was a mere 80,800, which accounts for less than 0.5 percent of the total refugee population. However, with borders closed, and massive displaced populations contained in countries in the Global South, resettlement is becoming one of the few avenues for legal migration to the North.

According to UNHCR, Uganda is home to some 270,000 refugees, produced by the many political conflicts that have plagued this part of Africa. While the vast majority come from Sudan, thousands of refugees from Burundi, the Democratic Republic of Congo, Eritrea, Ethiopia, Rwanda, and Somalia have also sought protection in the country. An increasing number of individuals get resettled from Uganda annually. For 2006, the number was projected at 2500, up from 1500 the year before and 35 in 1997 (UNHCR 2006; RLP 2002). While resettlement remains a scarce resource available to less than one percent of the refugees, obtaining resettlement is no longer a statistical impossibility.

Officially, refugees cannot "apply" for resettlement. Implementing NGO partners or UNHCR staff identify suitable candidates during screening to determine their refugee status. In the course of the resettlement interview, bureaucrats mold the IC's (shorthand for "individual case's") experience onto the various requirements of the selected resettlement category, and subject the IC's rendition of biographical data, history prior to flight, and his or her predicament in Kampala to thorough credibility assessments. For every "successful" resettlement candidate, hundreds are considered ineligible. Some who come forward are deemed to be economic migrants looking for a better future, or to be people suspected of having committed war crimes. Others fulfill the criteria set out in the resettlement procedure, but they are rejected for procedural, purely subjective, or haphazard bureaucratic reasons, including the failure to generate credible performances of suffering. If unsuccessful, the refugee usually receives a standardized letter of rejection, which makes it impossible to determine the precise reason for the rejection. This leaves the individual in question, and his or her associates, bewildered about the specific rejection and about the process of resettlement screening generally.

Producing Resettlement Identities

While resettlement remains a scarce resource, both the UNHCR and the refugee population are interested in obtaining the highest possible number of resettled persons.[1] While UNHCR's rules and guidelines direct the resettlement process, they do not fully determine it. The gap between the guidelines set forth in various UNHCR documents and practice in the field has been subjected to considerable academic

---

[1] According to NGOs, resettlement quotas remain unfilled, year after year. NGO Statement (2003).

criticism.[2] Less attention has been directed at what actually happens at this site, and *how* actors move to exploit the flexibility this gap affords.[3] I suggest that we can best understand everyday transactions as taking place in the shadow of law. The actors involved do not perceive legal procedure as the only, or even the predominant *normative* framework within which negotiations over narrative and credibility are taking place. The institutional inability to follow bureaucratic procedures may be costly for refugees, because it deprives them of procedural guarantees. Nonetheless, these shortcomings have also expanded the room for refugee agency, initiative, and creativity (Kibreab 2004).

For refugees, the encounter with UNHCR staff is high drama with enormous implications. Refugees make intense efforts to play up to humanitarian categories, legal or otherwise. For prospective candidates it is vital that the humanitarians perceive them as in possession of "authentic" fear or suffering, on the basis of a convincing story. The representation of the subject as it operates in international law significantly affects the performance of victimhood. The idea is that the planning and performance of a "credible narrative" is intrinsic to a successful resettlement candidacy *without necessarily corresponding to, or differing from, the factual veracity of the presented narrative.* At the same time, the relationship between the level of rights consciousness possessed by individual refugees and the achievement of credibility is multifaceted and fraught with pitfalls.

Establishment of Credibility

Both refugees and humanitarian agencies are hard at work constructing "credible" resettlement stories. For the agencies, the preoccupation is with formats. When humanitarian organizations publicize accounts of suffering, personalized images of the pain and distress experienced by their clients are intrinsic to their effectiveness as a mode of communication with a global audience. Carefully calculating the response of their audience, UN agencies and NGOs spend considerable resources framing their messages about urgent human need in a suitable manner. For example, Peter Redfield notes that *Médicins Sans Frontières* prizes "immediacy of contact and direct quotations seeking to maintain some semblance of specificity of voice amid a wash of routinized images" (2006: 13).

---

[2]   See Wilde (1998), Verdirame (1999), Barnett (2001), Loescher (2001), Barutciski (2002), and Kagan 2006.

[3]   Although Malkki (1995), Hyndman (2000), and Horst (2006c) have started to fill this gap.

Foregrounding the legal and bureaucratic structure creates an idea of fair and ordered access and distribution of resettlement. For UNHCR, a well-managed resettlement program is essential to maintaining the appearance of competence and integrity traditionally associated with the organization. According to the Resettlement Handbook, "A rational and transparent approach will, furthermore, strengthen the credibility of UNHCR in general and widen the confidence of refugees, resettlement countries and other partners, which in turn should help to ensure that resettlement can be done efficiently and effectively" (UNHCR 2004: IV/3). Playing up the image of a carefully determined *legal* credibility as the benchmark for the selection process demonstrates that the organization is living up to its humanitarian mandate.

In its Note on Burden and Standard of Proof in Refugee Claims, UNHCR states that "Credibility is established where the applicant has presented a claim which is coherent and plausible, not contradicting generally known facts, and therefore is, on balance, capable of being believed" (Kagan 2003: 381). In Western legal culture, spontaneity and immediacy in the communication of suffering are indications of genuineness. In the encounter between humanitarian and refugees, these features translate into a demand for authenticity. Nevertheless, such performances are rarely unplanned events. The competent management of speech and technology and the generation of artifacts figure prominently in the tactics refugees use to obtain legal assistance or to gain access to administrative legal processes such as resettlement. These tactics are also crucial in establishing a level of credibility *during* resettlement interviews.

Credibility assessments play a key role in both refugee status determination (RSD) and resettlement, albeit with differing emphases. While the RSD procedure is an adjudicatory process, resettlement is an administrative process governed by bureaucratic discretion. The available evidence concerning credibility assessments in RSD points to a haphazard state of affairs, where assessments dependent on personal judgment, perceptions, and disposition appear to have been the norm. These decisions are difficult to review and are likely to be inconsistent from one decision maker to another (Kagan 2003; Noll 2005).

Over the past decade, UNHCR has attempted to give credibility assessment a more objective and legalistic basis. Michael Kagan explains: "Objective credibility assessments apply standard criteria and require adjudicators to conduct a more structured inquiry. Because objective assessments tend to involve more specific and concrete explanations for decisions, they are easier for appellate tribunals to review" (2003: 5).[4] In line with a more open approach, the Resettlement Handbook suggests that the interview should be a collaboration between interviewer and interviewee. UNHCR advises that notions "of *time*, of *truth* and *falsehood* can also vary from culture to culture and give rise to misunderstandings that put the asylum-seekers' credibility in doubt." Despite this display of crosscultural awareness, the Handbook firmly fixes the anatomy of truth: "As an essential part of the decision-making process you must assess the applicant's story and credibility in connection with the principles and criteria for determination of refugee status. This requires that the applicant's story be carefully documented and cross-checked" (UNHCR 2004: Annex b).

Due to the absence of any form of appeals process, and the tendency for policy guidelines produced in Geneva to remain on the shelf in branch offices, it appears that subjective credibility determinations may continue to be the norm, rather than the exception. This situation leaves room for the personal likes or dislikes of UNHCR staff and NGO workers, and the practices of bureaucratic self-preservation to continue to permeate the resettlement process relatively unchallenged (Verdirame & Harrell-Bond 2005).

Coaching and Information Technology

Understanding the resettlement encounter as governed by what Erving Goffman called "interaction rituals" allows for an understanding of how identities are produced, and how marginalized individuals such as refugees need to behave according to stereotypes in order to avoid incurring social costs. According to Goffman, social actors have the ability to choose stage and props, as well as the costume to be worn in front of a specific audience. Their main goal is to maintain coherence, and adjust to the different settings (Goffman 1958). The "setting" is the visual representations of refugeeness circulated by humanitarian organizations (Malkki 1996). These global images permeate conceptions of how narratives of suffering should be constituted. As a result, they determine the benchmarks for legal credibility in valid accounts of rape, torture, and physical insecurity. But to conform to such global representations of hardship requires specific forms of "local" knowledge. The particular feature of this knowledge for resettlement purposes is its transnational character.

---

[4] This quote appears in a draft of Kagan (2003), but not in the final publication. The draft is available at http://isites.harvard.edu/fs/docs/icb.topic84147.files/Class_6_Eye_of_Beholder.doc.

The creators of resettlement narratives frequently rely on direct guidance from "successful applicants" already resettled, or rumours about successful entrepreneurs. It is usually relatives who wish to reunite with family or clan members, and who are not eligible under reunification schemes, who give this advice. In addition, as observed by D. A. Martin and Cindy Horst in Kenya, professional brokers offer their customers empty "family member" slots and coaching in stock stories (Martin 2005; Horst 2006c). Due to the rapid spread of internet use and cell phone ownership among the urban refugee population in Uganda, communication and the monitoring of resettlement narratives have become extremely efficient (Mutabaasi 2005).

In tandem with the humanitarian emphasis on testimonies, the reliance on "syndicated" testimonies has increased drastically. Refugees create "syndicated" narratives with the use of authoritative global media, such as human rights reports, or through human rights talk and discussions of gendered, racialized or sexual identities. UNHCR perceives this strategic use of "coaching" and "rehearsal" as cheating. This creates a larger problem of authenticity. The idea of "fake" stories displacing the "authentic" stories that float around somewhere "out there" has implications for generalized perceptions of trustworthiness and sincerity among UNHCR staff. It also means that refugees may choose to dispense with "true narratives" and personal stories in favour of "commodified narratives," since they are perceived as having a higher chance of success. The result, however, is that storylines that were once persuasive are now perceived as polluted and not credible. The routine character of stories arouses suspicion and frequently results in the failure to establish credibility, despite the actual suffering underlying the choice of communication strategy.

Performing Resettlement Identities

The expansion of legal protection to include formerly "private" issues such as gender-based violence, forms of medical trauma, and "local integration problems" arising from attributes such as homosexuality or accusations of witchcraft has been closely connected to the emergence of the new humanitarianism (Rieff 2002). In order to correspond to the evolving representations of the humanitarian subject as a human rights bearer, the construction of resettlement identities relies heavily on sufficient command of the human rights discourse. Meg McLagan proposes that the widespread embrace of human rights discourse by disenfranchised peoples after the fall of communism reflects its emergence as a dominant organizing moral narrative. This development is unsurprising given the expansiveness and flexibility of human rights in bringing new problems to light for public deliberation (McLagan 2005).

A key element in the performance of credibility is to maintain the immediacy of pain in the narrative. While suffering can productively be communicated as a human rights violation, the requirement for immediacy suggests that presenting oneself as a victim inflicted with tangible forms of physical or psychological trauma, as opposed to the more abstract persona of a rights bearer, may be preferable. Demanding one's rights leads to the perception that one has an "entitlement" attitude. This communicates a lack of any urgent vulnerability. Thus, to succeed in communicating the required immediacy one must display an appropriately deferential demeanor.

Goffman refers to demeanor as that element of the individual's ceremonial behaviour, typically conveyed through deportment, dress, and bearing, which serves to express to those in the individual's immediate presence that he or she is a person of certain desirable or undesirable qualities. Demeanor involves attributes derived from the interpretations of others made during social intercourse (Goffman 1967). Failing to observe and achieve these prerequisites may lead to a label of "cheating." The inability to establish the authenticity of one's claims leads to a general contamination of one's identity. Failure can also result from insufficient concealment of the staged self-presentation, for example, as with any overt or "revealed" use of technology for coaching and rehearsal purposes. Given the premium put on UNHCR's ability to elicit "true narratives," in the organizations' exchanges with donors and resettlement countries, strategies to ensure the detection of "cheating" assume particular prominence, and much is done on both the policy and program level to ensure the visibility of these control mechanisms.

Human Rights Defenders and Rights Talk

The refugees most often considered to have "physical protection problems" are human rights defenders who are persecuted because of their promotion of civil or political rights. Often, these activities lead to threats, harassment, insecurity, arbitrary detention, and extrajudicial executions. The international community has deemed it a priority to protect and shelter these individuals and their families.[5] Human rights defenders in Africa's Great

---

[5] There is a UN Special Representative of the Secretary-General on the Situation of Human Rights Defenders (Ms. Hina Jilani) who is mandated by the Commission on Human Rights resolution 2000/61 on Human Rights Defenders. *See also* http://www.humanrightsfirst.org/defenders/hr_defenders.asp.

Lakes region often operate under conditions of extreme danger, and many have to flee because of threats directed against *anyone* involved in human rights activities.[6] While those who are, or claim to be, human rights defenders frequently have succeeded in obtaining resettlement, the negotiations surrounding this category are becoming increasingly complicated.

The ability to give a credible performance as a human rights defender has emerged as an important strategy for pursuing resettlement. According to a coordinator for one prominent advocacy group, "friends or relatives of people who have been categorized as human rights defenders are using the same scheme."[7] Goffman observes that in interactions, the parties may simultaneously be audience and performers. In the case of resettlement, the refugees strive to foster impressions that reflect well upon themselves and by various means encourage bureaucrats, civil servants, and NGO workers to accept their preferred definition (Goffman 1967). Their efforts entail striking an appropriate balance between Western conceptions of the human rights defender as a liberal, heroic agent, and more submerged notions of what constitute appropriate displays of Third World victim subjectivity, both in speech and demeanor. While attempts to establish a common liberal humanity often pay off, using human rights language in any way that would indicate a self-understanding as a human rights subject could backfire, if the attempt to achieve rapport is seen as an opportunistic claim.[8]

Attempts at strategic use of human rights discourse beyond the human rights defender category is a common, but hazardous enterprise. Goffman points out the fundamental importance of having an agreed upon definition of the situation in a given interaction, in order to give the interaction coherency (1958). For UNHCR, it is important that the refugees understand that resettlement is not a right to be applied for. On the other hand, this becomes an issue of contention for refugees with some legal literacy, who look at the criteria and judge that they fulfill them. During an interview, I asked Thomas, a former UNHCR officer, how he considered personal histories that drew on rights language. He replied, "I have a checklist, which is the procedures of UNHCR," but "in order to put labels, the story itself, with a credible language of suffering was enough." In fact, the people who would most often use rights language belonged to a particular group of individual

---

[6] See Amnesty International (2005a, 2005b).

[7] NGO Office, Kololo, June 26, 2005. Interview on file with author.

[8] The benefits and dangers of establishing rapport are nothing new in refugee management: Knudsen has similarly noted that, in the 1980s, English literacy and religious affiliations among Ugandan refugees in Sudan were perceived as a means through which refugees could establish a particular bond with aid personnel, and thus cheat (Knudsen 1995).

cases whom he did not find very convincing, and he saw it as an expression of an entitlement attitude. Refugees who actively use rights language and conspicuously identify as "human rights defenders" may be conceived as less credible, because of their inadequate command of legal terms. Thomas noted that when someone is using rights language in very general terms, but it is clear they do not really understand that language, or when refugees have problems relating their "human rights work" to their reasons for flight, UNHCR staff members tend to get suspicious.[9]

Women at Risk

During recent decades, the focus on the extent and gravity of gender-based violence in situations of unrest and displacement has led to the recognition of refugee women as a particularly vulnerable group. The resettlement category "Women-at-Risk" (AWR) has evolved gradually from the 1980s, when, because of political lobbying, the protection of women refugees became a topic for UNHCR (Kneebone 2005). "Women-at-Risk" is designed to provide a remedy for women who are single heads of families or who are accompanied by an adult male who is unable to support them, and thus they assume the role of the head of the family. They may suffer from a wide range of problems, including expulsion, refoulement and other security threats, sexual harassment, violence, abuse, torture and exploitation.

Many female refugees have survived terrible ordeals in their country of origin. They continue to be at high risk of sexual violence in Kampala. These women are perceived to have basic but impossible needs. A rape counselor explained with a sigh that the real personal needs the refugees have are money and accommodation:

> they come with so high expectations of the centre ... they expect more than counselling ... they say they don't have transport to come back for the next session, so usually you end up dispensing some of your own gas ... they never come back for a session ... you bump into them on the street, Kampala being a small city, and you ask, what happened? Lately, the numbers have gone down ... when they know there is nothing to be gained; the word went around, that there is nothing there ... sometimes you wonder if you are really helping people ... they are hungry ... they have been raped, seen their husbands and children be butchered ... children and husbands have seen the mother be raped, mother and daughter raped by the same person ... they are very bitter about it.[10]

---

[9] At Thomas' home, Kololo, June 15, 2005. Interview on file with author.

[10] Hope after Rape office, July 25, 005. Inteview on file with author.

As with other sex crimes, the issue of proof as well as cultural taboos surrounding rape silence many victims. The bias against "hearing" still exists, as Thomas, the former UNHCR staffer suggested: "You have certain expectations as to what a person should look like when telling the story. For example, some people manage a smile when they tell their story. The decision is somewhat made based on appearance" (Interview with Thomas 2005).

Traditionally, "the refugee" was understood to be male, unless otherwise stated. Making gender and its social expressions visible, refugee researchers noted a profound difference between the way men and women conceived of "refugeeness" and exile. Despite feminist critiques of the dangers of essentialism and victim rhetoric, the prevailing orthodoxy often put forward by humanitarian relief agencies and women's organizations is a view of refugee women as perpetually "at risk" (Kneebone 2005). Whatever the politics of representation, I observed that while men are expected to be proactive in the public sphere, absence and silence characterize the normative expectations as well as much of the factual relationship between refugee women and formal law. For women, the opportunity to access government agencies, UNHCR, or various service providers is reduced by care obligations, transport problems, and by the security risk embedded in encounters with male officials.

Women's level of legal literacy and knowledge of institutions is often low compared to that of refugee men. According to legal officers, service providers and refugees alike, in the great majority of cases, men speak on behalf of the family, and the narratives of male refugees typically mirror the patriarchal society around them.[11] The recurrent disappearance of women's stories into that of the husbands is a concern for both protection officers and legal advocates, as they believe it affects their ability to assess legal needs accurately, and resettlement needs in particular. A general observation is that while refugee women, to a larger extent than men, include the problems of family members in their narratives about everyday struggles, they appear much less likely to make a *connection* between their personalized suffering and the law than are male refugees.

Whereas male refugees try – and often fail – to conform to legal language, sometimes it appears that women's unfamiliarity with the resettlement criteria results in a failure to attempt to stage a proper performance. William, a legal aid advocate, offered this description of the behaviour of a female client, who had been referred by a relative to "apply" for resettlement:

[11] Similarly, the Refugee Consortium of Kenya reports that 75% of their clients are male.

> She had just been crying and crying for ten minutes before answering every question. I referred her to [ ] to counselling, but that is a month and a half ago, and she has not come back. I was using an interpreter, and at some point I was leaving the room, she said to the interpreter "what are these questions for, I only came for resettlement."[12]

Despite low levels of legal literacy, "Women-at-Risk" has become a resettlement identity for which female refugees spend time and resources to construct evidence of their experience. The women's rights discourse emphasizes the importance of acknowledging and believing that widespread sexual abuse is taking place in situations of displacement. In practice, while frequently remaining ignored, claims about sexual violence have also become a source for doubt and misgivings. Service providers and legal protection officers alike are confounded as to how to deal with the perceived "commoditization" of sexual and gender-based violence as the basis for resettlement. Thomas saw the situations where female refugees used their "womanness" to obtain sympathy and, as a consequence, resettlement as related to the attempts to hijack the human rights defender category. Yet the matter was difficult. He detailed how he had met women, and men, who were victims of sexual violence and other forms of atrocities. He had felt rather hopeless in dealing with it: "because you have to be careful, UNHCR takes these things very seriously ... but then the shock effect wears off, you become used to stories, they become trivialized ... the problem could also be with me, not wanting to believe" (Interview with Thomas 2005).

In his discussion of the survivor skills of Sierra Leonean refugee women, Mats Utas explores the ways in which self-representations of victimhood and empowerment alike represent different "agency tactics" available to women in war zones. Utas describes how, during a consultancy focusing on Sierra Leonean refugee women in northern Liberia, he was taken by surprise when "every single woman interviewed immediately and without hesitation declared that she had been raped during the Sierra Leonean Civil War" (Utas 2005: 409). Utas gradually came to realize that presenting themselves as victims was a means by which women effectively established themselves as "legitimate recipients" of humanitarian aid.

The process of constructing narrative becomes a very costly one in particular instances. While many refugee women have experienced terrible violence, subsequent acts of trying to "perform" the resettlement identity can have serious consequences for the individual, illustrating

---

[12] Refugee Law Project, July 15, 2005. Interview on file with author.

the gap between legal literacy and legal consciousness. Similarly, as noted by Caroline Moorehead, "The tragedy comes when the real story, the true story, is stronger than the made-up one and would guarantee refugee status while the false one does not" (2005: 3). The making up of "fantastic stories" of mass rapes, or gory details of "imagined" acts, when the "real story" of commonplace acts of aggression would have been enough, is a tragic example of the fissure between the legal consciousness of refugees and the interpretive practices and experiential horizons of bureaucrats.

Artifacts as Tactics

Discursive identities must be painstakingly studied and rehearsed, but the main work is the assemblage of an appropriate self. Liisa Malkki noted that the visual representation of the refugee condition appears to have become a singularly translatable and mobile mode of knowledge about refugees, constituting a "vigorous, transnational largely philanthropic traffic in images and visual signs of refugeeness" (1996: 386). The tactical production of artifacts constitutes preparatory work that has to be carried out in *advance* of the resettlement encounter. The extensive documentation of self is a complementary strategy to the building of the "resettlement" identity.

Refugees often carry around a personal archive, consisting of copies of their refugee identity card, letters from the government or the police, and letters requesting assistance from UNHCR and NGOs. Most commonly, the refugees seek out the LC1, who is the lowest public official in the decentralized Ugandan government system, the police or the special branch for documentation of security threats and/or violence. The human rights coordinator described how refugees sometimes presented him with obviously false documents detailing accounts of mistreatment due to human rights activism: "'What is this," I asked, "you guys! Where did you get this?' ... 'we bought it from the police' they would answer" (Interview with Thomas 2005). Related, but different forms of documentation are the visible scars of torture many refugees display. Some refugees have been clients at a rehabilitation center for torture victims, and have obtained certificates stating that they are victims of torture. To complicate matters, staff at the center reported that frequently neither victims nor perpetrators really understood which practice constituted torture. Many refugees came with expectations of socioeconomic assistance for housing, food or school fees, or seeking general medical attention.

On a number of occasions, I heard about refugees who had become seriously injured after having paid someone to "cut them with pangas" in order to simulate attacks by "agents" or "rebels." "AE", a longtime refugee from the horn of Africa, described how "people would pay someone to beat them up or cut them with a panga, so they could go to the police and get a report that they had a security problem, then the UNHCR could be called to the hospital, and there you were, with a security problem."[13] As noted by Miriam Ticktin in her discussion of asylum seekers who allegedly infect themselves with HIV in order to get asylum in France, these stories are hard to verify or quantify (2006). However, it may at least be suggested that trying to pass off old injuries or scars that are the outcome of intentionally inflicted torture is a fairly common practice. The various counseling providers I interviewed stated that the majority of refugees who approached them primarily wanted them to write letters of documentation for rape or torture.

Documentation of security problems is considered necessary by all parties in order to succeed. The stages of "the game" are so familiar to everyone that officials routinely dismiss as forged the "proof" the refugees may be able to produce. A refugee woman described her encounter with a UNHCR official, whom she met with to share documents concerning atrocities in the Democratic Republic of the Congo: "When I met with the legal officer, he accused me of having bought the documents in Kampala. It hurt me so much ... I was so shocked! I think he understood how I felt ... he took the documents, and has not returned them ... I thought he was helping me, but now I am only thinking that he is trying to complicate my life."[14] At the same time, these documents are instrumental for communication between UNHCR and the resettlement countries if the case is accepted.[15]

The mistrust towards refugees' stories as well as the ambiguous position of "documentation" is a source of great frustration among the refugees as well as legal protection staff. Because the refugees invest significant resources in the encounter with UNHCR, many are angry about the a priori rebuttals, which seem to be embedded in administrative procedures. Nevertheless, as the stakes remain enormously high for both sides, the performances continue. UNHCR still has resettlement quotas to fill and

---

[13] Indian Restaurant, Old Kampala, June 22, 2005. Interview on file with author.

[14] Refugee Law Project, July 15, 2005. Interview on file with author.

[15] This resembles the observations made by Fassin and D'Halluin in their analysis of French immigration control (2005).

must be seen to engage in proper doctrinal interpretation. Meanwhile, the refugees are willing to do just about anything as long as there is a slight prospect of leapfrogging into a new and better existence.

Recognition and Regimentation

I have tried to show the many ways in which narratives constructed from miscellaneous sources are necessary to secure protection against further anguish and insecurity, though they are at the same time potentially detrimental to these attempts. The aim has been to highlight the tension between the refugee experience and the legal idea of "truth," not to question the authenticity of refugee suffering. Agency, innovation, and tactical communication indicate a rights-bearing and empowered self, yet the active appropriation of suffering functions in ambiguous ways. Displays of skillful personal testimonies may be counterproductive when they collide with ideas about demeanor or authenticity in refugee and human rights law, or when they directly challenge organizational ideologies or the ideas and understandings of the individual protection officers. The seeming "trivialization" of past experiences embedded in future-oriented efforts to capitalize on social identity incorporates a complicated view of suffering, where the self slips in and out of sight.

As Wilson and Brown have suggested, it is necessary to be cautious about our ability to separate the "true and authentic" from the manufactured in these types of narratives. Making sense of how we make distinctions between what is factual and what is false is fundamental to the work of understanding the underlying connotations of purity embedded in narratives of suffering in international law. I have argued that human rights protection of marginalised groups rests both on a reductive view of suffering as being individual and immediate, and on a presumption that a universal truth about suffering is available when channelled through appropriately formulated legal categories. I also want to make the point that these types of bureaucratic narratives of suffering are instrumental to the broader project of consolidating liberal ideas about human rights as the reigning standard for notions of common forms of humanity. Law generally tends to assume itself capable of solving normative quandaries. But the very explicitness with which the idea of truth as being pure and available through requests for testimonies has been codified, and the implicit idea that this bureaucratic truth in fact says something more general about the human condition – these are rather unique to the human rights/humanitarian configuration.

In the resettlement procedure, the human rights narrative is organized around a set of hierarchical roles, where those that Makau Mutua calls "saviours" subjectively determine the degree to which those labelled "victims" are deserving, based on the quality of their suffering (Mutua 2001). The legal effort deployed to secure fair access to human rights protection has contributed to a shift in the content of the performance, but not necessarily to better access to the "truth about suffering." While the process of juridical acknowledgment of the subaltern as fully capacitated for injury has moved towards formal completion, we do not yet fully understand the tensions embedded in the properties of this reconfigured humanitarian subject. For example, as noted by E. Baines, Utas, and Horst, female refugee leaders and entrepreneurs are astutely political; they are not passively "at risk." Their activities are simultaneously a source of danger and power; and they include both to construe the personal narrative that best furthers their goals (Baines 2004; Utas 2005; Horst 2006c).

The history of resettlement points to progressively expanding categories of recognized suffering, which have been developed as a result of transnational human rights activism on behalf of subaltern groups. Two paradoxical aspects of this slice of social action are worth contemplating. The familiar problem of emancipatory law reform that segments into rigid structures of legal domination surfaces here. Hastrup expresses concern that human rights discourse refers to no actual experience: rights-based conceptions of justice may distort our understandings of suffering and pare down social and moral narratives, into a "censorious rights-based regime of truth" (Hastrup 2003). I agree to some extent. When resettlement categories are constructed around universal truths about material conditions and the premises of human interaction, this may in itself lead to less "truth" actually being available. Yet, even if the language of human rights has come to stand in for what Hastrup terms a semantically empty category, this imagery is for the time being the best we have to work with.

The second aspect pertains to the understanding of the resettlement interview as a collaborative, testimonial practice. Michael Jackson proposes that refugees struggle with a sense that language cannot do justice to their experience. In addition, the suspicion and indifference of administrations in both camps and countries of asylum reinforces the tragic sense of not only having lost one's autonomy and homeland, but of having one's life story doubted or dismissed as a form of deceit. As a result of this disbelief, he suggests, "storytelling may cease to mediate between private and public spheres and go underground – the disempowered seeking refuge in magical thinking to retrieve some sense of control and comprehensibility in their lives … "(Jackson 2002: 92, 95). I argue that the storytelling imagined by Jackson, and the survival tactics involved in resettlement narratives are two different projects: While legal protection officers may feel differently about this, for the refugee clients resettlement interviews *are not* similar to truth commissions, nor are they more than superficially endowed with the therapeutic value of self-narration so cherished in Western culture.

The stories refugees tell humanitarians are largely instrumental. They are told to conform to explicit and implicit expectations of suffering. Thus, the tragedy does not lie in *not* getting one's so-called personal story recognized on an intersubjective level, but in failing to reap any advantages from one's investment in truth performance. The conclusion is not that "refugees lie," but that it is necessary to learn more about how the law choreographs suffering and empathy. If human rights-regimented law demands the counter-positioning of agency and credibility, thereby barring existential struggle, we should at least retain a keen awareness of it. The enormity of what is at stake is real.

REFERENCES

Amnesty International (2005a). *The Democratic Republic of Congo, North-Kivu: Civilians Pay the Price for Political and Military Rivalry.* AI Index AFR 62/013/ 2005. Available at http://web.amnesty.org/library/index/engafr620132005, last visited 7 June 2007.

————. (2005b). *Rwanda: Human Rights Organisation Forced To Close Down.* AI Index: AFR 47/001/2005. Available at http://web.amnesty.org/library/Index/ ENGAFR470012005?open&of=ENG-RWA, last visited 7 June 2007.

Akuei, S. R. (2004). *Remittances as Unforeseen Burdens: Considering Displacement, Family and Resettlement Contexts in Refugee Livelihood and Well-being: Is There Anything States or Organisations Can Do?* UNHCR's Evaluation and Policy Analysis Unit (EPAU) background documents. Available at http://www.unhcr. org/research/RESEARCH/40b1ea8a4.pdf, last visited 7 June 2007.

Baines, E. K. (2004). *Vulnerable Bodies: Gender, the UN, and the Global Refugee Crisis.* Aldershot, Hants, England/Burlington, VT: Ashgate.

Barnett, M. (2001). "Humanitarianism with a Sovereign Face: UNHCR in the Global Undertow." *International Migration Review*, vol. 35, no.1, pp. 244–76.

Barutciski, M. (2002). "A Critical View of UNHCRs Mandate Dilemmas." *Journal of Refugee Law*, vol. 14, no. 2, pp. 365–81.

Chanoff, S. (2002). "After Three Years: Somali Bantus Prepare to Come to America." *Refugee Reports*, November, pp. 1, 3–4. In D. A. Martin, *A New Era for U.S. Refugee Resettlement.* University of Virginia Law School Public Law and Legal Theory Working Paper Series, no. 27, p. 10, (2005).

Colvin, C. J. (2004). "Ambivalent Narrations: Pursuing the Political through Traumatic Storytelling.." *PoLAR*, vol. 27, no.1, pp. 72–89.

Fassin, F., and E. D'Halluin (2005). "The Truth from the Body: Medical Certificates as Ultimate Evidence for Asylum Seekers." *American Anthropologist*, vol. 107, no. 4, pp. 597–608.

Goffman, E. (1958). *The Presentation of Self in Everyday Life*. Edinburgh: Social Sciences Research Centre.

———. (1967). *Interaction Ritual: Essays on Face-to-Face Behavior*. New York: Pantheon Books.

Hastrup, K. (1993). "Hunger and the Hardness of Facts." *Man, New Series*, vol. 28, n. 4, pp. 727–39.

———. (2003). "Suffering and Human Rights: Anthropological Reflections." *Anthropological Theory*, vol. 3, no. 3, pp. 309–23.

Horst, H. (2006a). "Buufis amongst Somalis in Dadaab: The Transnational and Historical Logics behind Resettlement Dreams." *Journal of Refugee Studies*, vol. 19, no. 2, pp. 143–57.

———. (2006b). *Connected Lives: Somalis in Minneapolis, Family Responsibilities and the Migration Dreams of Relatives*. UNHCR New Issues in Refugee Research, Research paper no. 124. Available at http://www.unhcr.org/cgibin/texis/vtx/research/opendoc.pdf?tbl=RESEARCH&id=44b7b6912, last visited 7 June 2007.

———. (2006c) *Transnational Nomads: How Somalis Cope with Refugee Life in the Dadaab Camps of Kenya*. New York: Berghahn Books.

Hyndman, J. (2000). *Managing Displacement, Refugees and the Politics of Humanitarianism*. Minneapolis/London: University of Minnesota Press.

Jackson, M. (2002). *The Politics of Storytelling: Violence, Transgression and Intersubjectivity*. Copenhagen: Museum Tusculanum Press, University of Copenhagen.

Kagan, M. (2003). "Is Truth in the Eye of the Beholder? Objective Credibility Assessment in Refugee Status Determination." *Georgetown Immigration Law Journal*, vol. 17, no. 3, pp. 367–416.

———. (2006). "Frontier Justice: Legal Aid and UNHCR Refugee Status Determination in Egypt." *Journal of Refugee Studies*, vol. 19, no.1, pp. 45–68.

Kapur, R. (2002). "The Tragedy of Victimization Rhetoric: Resurrecting the 'Native' Subject in International/Post-Colonial Feminist Legal Politics." *Harvard Human Rights Journal*, vol. 15, pp. 1–38.

Kibreab, R. (2004). "Pulling the Wool over the Eyes of the Strangers: Refugee Deceit and Trickery in Institutionalized Settings." *Journal of Refugee Studies*, vol. 17, no. 1, pp. 1–26.

Kneebone, S. (2005). "Women within the Refugee Construct: Exclusionary Inclusion in Policy and Practice, the Australian Experience." *International Journal of Refugee Law*, vol. 17, no. 7, pp. 7–42.

Knudsen, J. C. (1995). "When Trust Is on Trial." In E. V. Daniel and J. C. Knudsen, eds., *Mistrusting Refugees*. Berkley: University of California Press, pp. 13–35.

Loescher, G. (2001). *The UNHCR and World Politics: A Perilous Path*. Oxford/New York: Oxford University Press.

Malkki, L. (1995). *Purity in Exile, Violence, Memory, and National Cosmology among Hutu Refugees in Tanzania*. Chicago: University of Chicago Press.

———. (1996). "Speechless Emissaries: Refugees, Humanitarianism and Dehistoricization." *Cultural Anthropology*, vol. 11, no. 3, pp. 377–404.

Martin, D. A. (2005). "The United States Refugee Admissions Program: Reforms for a New Era of Refugee Resettlement." The Migration Policy Institute.

McLagan, M. (2005). "Circuits of Suffering." *PoLAR: Political and Legal Anthropology Review,* vol. 28, no. 2, pp. 223–39.

Moorehead, C. (2005). "Necessary Lies." *Eurozine,* available at http://www. eurozine.com/articles/2004–05-03-moorehead-en.html. Last visited 7 June 2007.

Mutabaasi, E. (2005). "Celebrating the Mobile Phone that Has Eased Communication." *Daily Monitor,* October 28.

Mutua, M. (2001). "Savages, Victims and Saviours: The Metaphor of Human Rights." *HVIJL,* vol. 42, pp. 201–45.

NGO Statement (2003). "Part 8: The NGO Perspective Global Consultations on International Protection Third Track, Theme 3: The Search for Protection-Based Solutions: NGO Statement on Resettlement (22–24 May 2002)." *Refugee Survey Quarterly,* vol. 22, nos. 2 and 3, pp. 432–41.

Noll, G. (2005). "Introduction." In G. Noll, ed., *Proof, Evidentiary Assessment and Credibility in Asylum Procedures.* Martinus Nijhoff Publishers.

RCK Legal Clinic Statistics, available at http://www.rckkenya.org/facts-statistics. html. Last visited 7 June 2007.

Redfield, P. (2006). "A Less Modest Witness – Collective agency and Motivated Truth in a Medical Humanitarian Movement." *American Ethnologist,* vol. 33, no. 1, pp. 3–26.

(RLP) Refugee Law Project (2002). *Refugees in the City: Status Determination, Resettlement, and the Changing Nature of Forced Migration in Uganda.* Working Paper no. 6, available at http://www.refugeelawproject.org/resources/papers/ workingpapers/RLP.WP06.pdf, Last visited 7 June 2007.

Rieff, D. (2002). *A Bed for the Night: Humanitarianism in Crisis.* New York: Simon & Schuster.

Russell, D. E. H. (1977). "Report on the International Tribunal on Crimes against Women." *Frontiers: A Journal of Women Studies,* vol. 2, no. 1, pp. 1–6.

Segall, K. W. (2002). "Postcolonial Performatives of Victimization." *Public Culture,* vol. 14, no. 3, pp. 617–19.

Ticktin, M. (1999). "Selling Suffering in the Courtroom and Marketplace: An Analysis of the Autobiography of Kiranjit Ahluwalia." *PoLAR: Political and Legal Anthropology Review,* vol. 22, no. 1, pp. 24–41.

———. (2006). "Where Ethics and Politics Meet: The Violence of Humanitarianism in France." *American Ethnologist,* vol. 33, no. 1, pp. 33–49.

UNHCR (2004). *UNHCR Resettlement Handbook.* Available at http://www.unhcr. org/protect/3d4545984.html, last visited 7 June 2007.

———. (2006). "Global Appeal, Uganda." Available at http://www.unhcr.org/publ/ PUBL/4371d1ab0.pdf, last visited 7 June 2007.

Utas, M. (2005). "Victimcy, Girlfriending, Soldiering: Tactical Agency in a Young Woman's Social Navigation of the Liberian War Zone." *Anthropological Quarterly,* vol. 78, no. 2, pp. 403–30.

Verdirame, G. (1999). "Human Rights and Refugees: The Case of Kenya." *Journal of Refugee Studies,* vol. 12, no. 1, pp. 54–77.

Verdirame, G., and B. Harrell-Bond (2005). *Rights in Exile: Janus-Faced Humanitarianism.* New York/Oxford: Berghahn Books.

Wilde, R. (1998). "Quis Custodiet Ipsos Custodes? Why and How UNHCR Governance of 'Development' Refugee Camps Should Be Subject to International Human Rights Law." *Yale Human Rights and. Development Law Journal,* vol. 1, no. 5, pp. 107–31.

Wilson, R. A. (2001). *The Politics of Truth and Reconciliation in South Africa: Legitimizing the Post-Apartheid State.* Cambridge: Cambridge University Press.

11. "Can You Describe This?" Human Rights Reports and What They Tell Us About the Human Rights Movement

RON DUDAI

In the prologue to her poem "Requiem," the Russian poet Anna Akhmatova wrote:

> In the awful days of the Yezhov terror I passed seventeen months in the outer waiting line of the prison visitors in Leningrad. Once, somebody 'identified' me there. Then a woman, standing behind me in the line, waked up from the torpor, typical for us all there, and asked me, whispering into my ear (all spoke only in a whisper there):

> "And can you describe this?"
> And I answered:
> "Yes, I can."

> Then the weak similarity of a smile glided over that, what had once been her face.

This short paragraph from Akhmatova is like the dense short parables of the Jewish Talmud: we can spend a whole year analyzing and interpreting its themes and potential meanings. I will utilize this quote to highlight some points that provide the background themes for this chapter. A first noteworthy point is that the woman asks "can you *describe* this," not "can you *help* me." The poet is not expected to provide direct assistance (the woman does not ask "can you help release my husband") but to provide a description. There are times when, for various reasons, what is sought after is a description.

This leads us to another major point: why does the woman, who is present in the scene, there and then, seek someone else to describe "this," rather than doing it herself? One possible answer is based on the moment of

---

I would like to thank Paul Gready, Sarah Marcus, Claire Moon, and Richard Wilson for thoughtful comments on an earlier draft and, more broadly, I am indebted to Stan Cohen.

recognition, when the woman spots Akhmatova with her status as a famous poet. From this point of view, what the woman seeks is someone whose description would have a higher status: it would be read by many, reach an audience, be perceived as credible. The meaning of her question can be read as "do you have the *authority* to describe this."

A second, and not mutually exclusive, interpretation is that the woman feels she lacks the capacity to produce an eloquent representation of the scene, which will affect the readers and therefore she calls for a "professional." Her question can be read as "are you *able* to describe it?" by which I mean, do you have the technical ability, do you have access to a meaningful discourse that would make sense of the scene of terror and mobilize readers?

This double meaning is a feature of all valuable witnessing: those who describe must have both the technical ability to write in a way that creates a new superior understanding of the facts and influences the readers, as well as the status and authority to ensure that an audience will read them in the first place and accept their version as valid. Often there can be a potential tension between these two ambitions. I want to look at one particular genre of describing suffering – the modern human rights report – and I will argue that while this format succeeds in establishing an authoritative voice, this can come with the price of limiting its actual effects on the readers.

Framework of Discussion

While the analysis of descriptions of suffering is usually focused on works of fiction, media accounts, or historical studies, my focus here is on the work of human rights organizations and the way they document, report, frame, and describe abuses. I have approached the issue of human rights reports through an interest in the work of human rights organizations, building on studies whose aim is to understand the choices and dilemmas of these organizations (e.g. Cohen 1991a; Hopgood 2006), rather than, for example, on the lineage of studies which deal with theoretical questions of representations (e.g. LaCapra 2001) – which would have probably entailed a different take on the motive of "can you describe this" than the one pursued here.

The objects of this study are what Bell and Keenan define as "'core mandate' human rights NGOs": those that deal with "the promotion and protection of human rights, as defined internationally" (2004: 336), and whose characteristic modes of working are "monitoring" human rights violations. Often they are also referred to as "watchdog" human rights organizations

(Cohen 1991b). Human Rights Watch and Amnesty International are the typical international examples: B'Tselem, an Israeli NGO, is an example of a local organization which has adopted this mode.[1]

The production of human rights reports constitutes a major part of the work of such organizations, and these reports have generated an "extraordinary volume of information" over the last thirty years (Cohen 1996). As Orentlicher observes, "While NGOs undertake a range of activities to promote their concerns, perhaps none has been more influential than their efforts to document and publicize human rights violations" (1990: 84).

The assumption here is that, in order to fully appraise the strengths and limitations of the human rights movement's response to atrocities and suffering, we need to look not only at the abstract legal and normative principles associated with it but also at the concrete tools it uses. The human rights report – its language, parameters, the type of materials that are included in it, and the discourses excluded from it – can tell us about the assumptions, ambitions, and state of mind of the human rights movement. By focusing on this narrow product and treating it as a genre, we can expose the advantages and shortcomings of human rights organizations in contributing to political change.

While I aim to offer generalized insight, the main case study will be the Israeli-Palestinian conflict.[2] This conflict "occupies a special niche in the story of human rights" (Rosenblum 2002: 313) and is among the most visible and analyzed of contemporary conflicts. In addition, "the history of human rights in Israel/Palestine is a local manifestation of [a] global trend" (Hajjar 2001: 21), and human rights work on this place, by both local and international NGOs, is symptomatic of human rights work in general. Finally, it is a suitable case study because the level of abuses is coupled with a lack of censorship in Israel, where "human rights organizations can do the sort of documentation impossible in societies where gross human rights violations take place under a regime of total state control" (Cohen 1991b).

From 2000 to 2002, I was a researcher at a leading Israeli human rights NGO, tasked with writing human rights reports. These three years saw unprecedented levels of abuses by the Israeli government against

---

[1] See Felner (2003) for background on B'Tselem.
[2] For human rights reports on Israel/Palestine see the website of B'Teslem at http://www. btselem.org/English/Publications/Index.asp, Human Rights Watch at http://www.hrw. org/doc/?t=mideast_pub&c=isrlpa, and Amnesty International at http://web.amnesty. org/library/eng-isr/reports.

Palestinians from the Occupied Territories, as well as atrocities by Palestinian groups. These were busy and demanding times for Israelis engaged in human rights work, hardly conducive for metaquestions, and, at the time, I was not planning in any concrete way to write an academic piece analyzing human rights reports. Nevertheless, as this chapter is widely influenced by my experiences then, I can somewhat awkwardly refer to this methodology as retrospective participant observation. In addition to this and to analyzing reports and consulting various secondary sources, I also held interviews with several Israeli human rights researchers.

While doing important and often selfless work, human rights NGOs are frequently a target of vicious critique from governments and nonstate actors. One feels a bit wary, from the temporary safety of academia, to add more critique. My approach is invariably sympathetic to human rights as an ideal and to NGOs as important vessels carrying this ideal forward. However, while conscious that critique from academia is often met by resentment from human rights practitioners, I agree with Kennedy (2006) that the academic study of human rights should move from "cheerleading from the bench" to more serious engagement with the human rights experience. I will at least aspire to follow what Rosenblum described as "ambivalent advocates" of human rights activism: "committed to action, but alert to multiple consequences ... sympathetic to the plight of people trying to do good, while at the same time more critical of those who do it without reflecting on the possible negative consequences" (2002: 305). To the degree that my argument criticizes decisions and choices by NGOs, it should be seen as a painful self-critique.

The Genre of Human Rights Reports: Characteristics

In his work on the British antislavery movement of the late eighteenth century, Hochschild often refers to this movement as a prototype of the modern human rights movement and points out practices that can be seen as antecedents of modern human rights campaigning. One of these is the 1791 publication of Thomas Clarkson's *Abstract on the Evidence*, which, Hochschild argues, "reads more like a report by a modern human rights organization than the moralizing tracts against slavery that had preceded it" (2005: 197). For Hochschild this point is a one-page casual aside, but I will use it as intuitively and, by the contrast with "the moralizing tracts," it serves as an excellent starting point for the characterization of the modern human rights report, and what sets it apart from other ways of describing suffering and violence.

Hochschild finds the difference from the tradition of earlier political pamphlets in an important choice: "Clarkson and his comrades somehow sensed they could better evoke sympathy if they stood back and let the facts speak for themselves" (2005: 198). Letting the facts speak for themselves is indeed a main feature of the contemporary human rights report (Wilson 1997: 143, Hopgood 2006: 123). Clarkson made sure the facts were seen as credible, supporting the arguments with "statistics, documents and sworn testimony ... damning quotations from ... laws and newspapers" (Hochschild 2005: 198). The eighteenth century antislavery advocates aimed to present an elaborated and realistic picture, relying on the premise of "detail as a sign of truth" (Laqueur, Chapter 1 in this volume). The same premise is evident in the contemporary human rights report. It is empirical and emphasizes methodology and credibility of facts: "Perhaps no asset is more important to a human rights NGO than the credibility of its fact-finding" (Orentlicher 1990: 85).

A second feature, instrumental in allowing the facts to speak for them-selves, is the tone of the writing. Hochschild described the antislavery document as written in "a crisp and businesslike way" (2005: 198). This could just as well refer to modern human rights reports, where "the aversion to using emotive phrases" (Hopgood 2006: 74) is an important trait. Many of my interviewees have highlighted an informal ban on using adverbs and adjectives.

Another main aspect Hochschild describes is what the *Abstract* did not contain: unlike its predecessors it had no references to the Bible and had excluded all theological arguments. Being theology free is a main trademark of human rights reports, and in their "radical acts of exclusion" (Wilson 1997: 145) human rights reports also exclude historical, moral, or political frameworks. A merciless Occam's razor is used on anything which cannot be presented as true beyond doubt.

Yet where we leave Clarkson behind and reach the final and necessary component of modern human rights reports is in another feature (unavailable to Clarkson and his comrades at the time): the reliance on international human rights law. Without the use of international law, "human rights" is a purely rhetorical device, and a "lack of substantive engagement in the human rights or humanitarian law framework removes a necessary anchor on policy and practice" (McEvoy 2003: 331). Reliance on the framework of international law (and an exclusive reliance on it) is a condition to be included in this genre.

These are, then, the characteristics of the genre of human rights reporting: letting credible facts speak for themselves; a non-emotional tone; and exclusion of all interpretive frameworks apart from international human rights law. An Amnesty International researcher summarized his organization's reporting ethos (shared by many other organizations): "objective information ... it was careful, it was accurate, it was not grinding political axes ... a voice of cool, calm, documentation" (quoted in Hopgood 2006: 14).

The Rationale

What is it about the genre of human rights reporting that appeals so much? Why would both local and international organizations adopt this particular combination of features when addressing the Israeli-Palestinian violence? At the core, it is the organizations' need to legitimize themselves as authoritative and credible commentators and to distinguish their mode of "describing" from the others.

The "competition" for a human rights framework – political arguments, religious dictates, historically grounded analyses – always hovers around, especially in a case such as the Israeli-Palestinian conflict. Human rights activists "depend for their legitimacy upon their reputation as providers of objective expertise" (Price 2003: 589). The mode of the human rights report is meant to meet these challenges. The "objective expertise" status is achieved first by collecting and presenting facts using a specialized methodology of fact-finding, making the facts look reliable, and then by applying the specialized discourse of international law, with its aura of objectivity, creating an authoritative interpretation of the facts. The report's format is both an indication of the processes of professionalization human rights activists have been going through and an attempt to convey such a professional mode.

Both the fact-finding (statistics, eyewitnesses' accounts, "damning quotations" from state officials) and the legal analysis (references to a specific instrument of international law and its authoritative interpretations) are sourced in the reports' footnotes, and I have elsewhere argued that perhaps the symptomatic expression of the human rights report format is the extensive use of footnotes (Dudai 2006). Grafton's insights in his analysis of the use of footnotes in academic historical works are especially relevant here: "they identify the work in question as the creation of a professional" (Grafton 1997: 3); "they give legitimacy ... footnotes confer authority on a writer" (7–8). The "professional" mode of description in the reports (with the use of footnotes as an emblematic feature) creates an authoritative voice for the reports, reinforced by the non-emotive tone.

Orentlicher has pointed out the crucial importance of human rights NGOs "surviving scrutiny" (1990: 92). Such concerns are general to human rights work everywhere, but perhaps particularly so in the intense space of the Israeli-Palestinian conflict (Montell 2004). The imperative of surviving scrutiny (by both governments and the public) indeed shapes the way in which the reports are produced. Even if not viewed in these terms by many of the researchers themselves, I think that the important principle affecting the report's style and language is "scientific refutability," in its Popperian sense. That is, the reports present findings and interpretations in a rational and easy to communicate way; the sources of both findings and interpretations are presented in a transparent way, open to critique, and self-confident that any rational reader will accept them as valid. Claims that abuses are taking place are never general: they refer to specific incidents (e.g. two children were killed, 20 houses were demolished), whose authenticity is carefully sourced. The meaning of these events is not created, as often elsewhere, using moral or religious self-justifying claims, but through the employment of the objective, universal framework of international law. As Freeman argues, human rights law has "a kind of objectivity that moral and political discourses are thought to lack;" it "enables campaigners to appeal to established law rather than to contentious moral and political principles" (2006:49). In emotional, political-national conflicts, international law can "offer a set of standards that are formally independent of the parties to the conflict, offering a host of inter-national and comparative reference points in relation to which the debate can be shaped"(Campbell, Ni-Aolain & Harvey 2002: 326).

To give one illustration, reports that deal with Israeli policies, such as administrative detentions of Palestinians or the construction of the Wall in the West Bank, which are justified by the Israeli government for their effectiveness in preventing terrorist attacks against Israeli civilians, will be analyzed only according to human rights standards. Common "dinner-table" arguments against these policies might also point out that in fact they cannot prevent suicide bombings, and, indeed, because they damage the economy and enhance frustration and humiliation among the Pales-tinians, they may be counterproductive. Yet human rights reports mostly eschew such speculative arguments and are restricted to documenting these policies and submitting them to legal analysis.

With all that, the human rights report successfully establishes its authority to speak. Its rational, objective, non-emotive voice is distin-guished from subjective or nationalist polemics. Its self-confident presen-tation of facts and its interpretation using the universal framework of international law create a unique type of description.

Forensics, Codes, and Stories

Another way of elucidating the reports' format is through examining alternatives, and by locating human rights reports within several typologies of "descriptions," the limitations of the format will become apparent. The first typology comes from one of the most important human rights documents of our time: the *Final Report of the South African Truth and Reconciliation Commission* (TRC 1998). One of the report's premises was that we can distinguish several types of descriptions of truth. The TRC's influential typology defined four types of truths: factual or forensic truth; personal narrative truth; social truth; and healing truth (TRC 1998: vol. 1, ch. 5). The language and ambition of the NGO report fits squarely, and almost exclusively, into the first category, that of "factual or forensic truth," which the TRC defined as "the familiar legal or scientific notion of bringing to light factual, corroborated evidence, of obtaining accurate information through reliable (impartial, objective) procedures."

Another relevant framework was introduced by Collins (2004) and Huggins (2000), who contrast two styles of collecting and organizing records of abuses: "stockpiling" on the one hand; and "storytelling" on the other. Stockpiling is based on the collection of facts, the piling up of statistical information; storytelling is based on recording personal and subjective experiences. Of these, human rights reporting clearly employs a "stockpiling" technique.

A third kind of typology comes not from the human rights world but from the eminent sociologist Charles Tilly's recent attempt to make sense of accounts in general (2006). Tilly suggests that the accounts people or organizations give of events can be divided into four groups: "conventions," "stories," "codes," and "technical accounts." This division is based on two factors: popular or specialized accounts, and formulas versus cause-effect accounts. Thus, conventions are popular formulas that do not involve cause-effect elements; stories are a popular mode of explanatory narrative; codes are specialized formulas; and technical accounts are specialized modes of cause-effect narrative. Of these, human rights reports most closely resemble codes. They are a specialized mode (Tilly's examples for codes include legal codes, religious prescriptions, and systems of honors) and one that does not engage in causal reasoning. As Tilly describes, codes may overflow with reasons, "but these reasons describe how what happened conforms to the code at hand rather than what actually caused the outcome" (2006: 17); this description fits human rights reports as well.

The definitions of styles suggested here – forensic, stockpiling, and codes – share the contrast to narratives and stories. And indeed "the classic Amnesty style," a style which is shared by other organizations, "is designed not to tell a story but to try to do the opposite" (Hopgood 2006: 205). The choice of human rights NGOs to adopt this style is grounded in necessity, in their need to present objective and non-emotive descriptions. It allows the presentation of reliable facts in a credible manner. It successfully establishes the organizations' authority as "objective experts," and makes their findings communicable to audiences around the world and to bodies such as courts or UN committees.

But adopting a mode of forensic stockpiling codes rather than narratives and stories has also more complex implications. For Huggins (2000), "stockpiling" reduces the victims to the status of homogenized cases. Wilson similarly observes that human rights reports create a "universal decontextualized individual" (1997: 148). Huggins also argues that stockpiling renders victims powerless by their statistical visibility as victims only. She adds that the stockpiling style – statistical facts on atrocities – can make subordinate non-victims feel impotent in their horror at cruelty against others.

Collins also contends that the stockpiling techniques of human rights reports result in a perception of "passive victimization" (2004: 45). He demonstrates this by showing how human rights reports on Israel/Palestine have emphasized children as victims of violations (often stretching the definition of "child" to include as many victims as possible). Thus "active participants in the intifada" are "reduced to the status of passive, innocent 'children,'" whereas many of these children view themselves as "self-motivated activists" (45). Similarly, Collins contends, the experience of imprisonment was for many Palestinians a rite of passage conferring social legitimacy and political prestige, and an experience that is associated with dynamic resistance, personal growth, and education. Yet stockpiling style cannot capture this, and portrays the prisoners as purely passive victims (125).

While pointing to the relative advantages of oral history or anthropology, Collins and Wilson do an important service by highlighting the shortcomings of human rights reports, but they do not convincingly demonstrate why these should replace, rather than complement, the human rights report. The ambition of the genre is to report facts in order to promote change; it is not its ambition to contribute to richer collective memory, nor necessarily to empower victims, at least not as an end in itself. Reports by human rights NGOs aim to gain the attention of an "other" – whether the perpetrator government or society, or a third-party government or public. Mobilizing the oppressed community is not typically their role. Should human rights reports portray prisoners not as victims but as "dynamic resisters?" Should they treat children not as victims but as violent activists? I think that recording these complex experiences should indeed be the role of oral historians or anthropologists, but, for human rights organizations, trying to raise awareness of a third-party, that would be an imprudent tactic – if we accept that the ultimate ambition is to halt violent confrontations and imprisonment, not to merely record its – dynamic or fixed – experience.

Yet perhaps the important shortcoming of the rejection of storytelling in favor of forensic, "stockpiling" codes, is that it may limit a report's potential to generate the readers' empathy toward the victims. Human rights organizations are guided by a "hope that by provoking the emotional responses of compassion and empathy, people would become involved with the fight against human rights abuses" (Seu 2003: 183). Yet the stockpiling format may be ill-suited to the creation of an emotional response and identification with the victims, if "instead of narratives ... what the reader gets is a pared down and frozen stream of action" (Wilson 1997: 145). The legal language, for all its advantages, may be less successful in engendering compassion.

One way in which elements of personal narratives do in fact enter the human rights report is the use of first-person testimonies, from both eyewitnesses and direct victims. This is one of the hallmarks of the genre, and few reports are being published without such testimonies. Here is a typical illustration, from a B'Tselem report on harassment of Palestinian villagers from the Southern Hebron area:

> Around 2pm three soldiers came up to me on foot ... one of the soldiers tied my hands and covered my eyes. They put me in the van and told me not to move ... I felt as if they had put me in a room. One of them grabbed my head and slammed it into the wall three times ... a few hours later they put me back into the vehicle. I saw in a watch that it was midnight.

The use of such testimonies allows the creation of a richer scene, beyond the statistics and legal rules. The victims are identified by name, as well as other personal details such as age, gender, and occupation, and they locate the event that the authors describe as a "human rights violation" within a broader personal narrative. With this, the testimonies can help generate empathy.

Nevertheless, this could be only a partial answer. There is often a dissonance between the victims' subjective voices and the rational tone of the reports' authors. The authoritative interpretation of the events, and the meaning attached to them are provided by the authors. Political or religious pronouncements by witnesses will be erased. The meaning of their testimonies is provided by the legal interpretation of the authors. Even if the witness is able or willing to construct his or her story in legal terms, this will also not reach the report – this interpretation will be done by the authors' cold and objective voice. Although not always clear to all readers, the testimonies are produced through answers to the specialized questions of human rights researchers. These are not free narratives, but responses to questions the organization's fieldworker is asking, guided by the organization's needs and working style. The testimonies are then often edited, using a more relaxed Occam's razor, but still one that will not allow everything.

Thus, the insertion of personal testimonies does not alter the overall forensic and stockpiling mode of the reports. They are there to support the organization's factual and legal claims, not the other way around, and while their visibility in the reports varies, they are always marginal to the claims made by the authors themselves. The readers will see glimpses of first-person stories, but these will be edited and fragmented, subordinated to the overall style and mode.

The forensic, "stockpiling," style adopted by human rights reports establishes their authority to speak. We can all tell stories and be emotive. But only professional experts can produce a forensic report, and the potential readers would recognize this style and locate it above all the ordinary storytellers. Or, to use Tilly's terms, conventions can be produced by anyone, but the creation and application of codes necessitate the professional and the resulting report is perceived by an audience as more authoritative. Yet what is won in gaining authority may be lost in the impact on the readers: forensic style may have higher credibility but will generate less empathy.

Let me illustrate this by using a randomly picked example, from a study co-authored by Amnesty International and Human Rights Watch on incarcerated children in the USA. The topic of imprisoned children is acutely emotive, one that could create instinctive empathy among most readers. Yet here is how the press release starts:

> There are at least 2,225 child offenders serving life without parole (LWOP) sentences in U.S. prisons for crimes committed before they were age 18, Human Rights Watch and Amnesty International said in a new joint report published today. While many of the child offenders are now adults, 16 percent were between 13 and 15 years old at the time they committed their crimes. An

estimated 59 percent were sentenced to life without parole for their first-ever criminal conviction.[3]

All the advantages and problems are here: the authoritative claim ("Amnesty International said"), the technical jargon ("LWOP"), and the stockpiling of statistics ("16 percent were between 13 and 15"). This is identified as the work of a professional; these people know what they are talking about, any reader would feel. But does it generate empathy? Personal stories might follow, but those who will continue to read after this cold introduction will digest these stories already under the heading of acronyms, statistics, and percentages. To be sure, over-emotive descriptions have their own drawbacks. Often, the use of emotional language can conceal unsubstantiated claims, exaggerations, and manipulations, as some of the advocacy publications in the wake of the 2004 tsunami demonstrated (Brauman, Chapter 4 in this volume). Yet if Richard Rorty is right that the way to mobilize people to act for the human rights of strangers is by telling "sad and sentimental stories" (1993), then the forensic style of human rights reports might be severely limited in its capacity to achieve this goal.

The Exclusion of Political Contexts

Another potentially negative ramification of the stockpiling and forensic codes format is the exclusion of context. Indeed, a common criticism of human rights reporting is centered on the lack of broader context in these reports. Wilson, for example, writing on the conflict in Guatemala, warned that by the decontextualisation in human rights reports they "depoliticize human rights violations by drawing attention away from structural processes of class or ethnic power" (1997: 148).

In the Israeli-Palestinian setting, the problem of "depoliticizing" lies in the fact that due to their nonpolitical stance, human rights reports do not address the issue of Israeli occupation of the West Bank and Gaza as such, but rather look at the human rights violations that take place during the occupation. The risk that is created by referring to the symptoms (specific policies and incidents that violate human rights) rather than to the structural problem (a military occupation of foreign people) is that it distorts the relation between the political situation (lack of peace agreement) and its results (abuses). It allows, theoretically, for a possibility of occupation without specific human rights violations – a notion that has

[3]   At http://news.amnesty.org/index/ENGAMR511602005.

actually been at the center of the Israeli psyche, embodied by the phrase "enlightened occupation" (Gorenberg 2006).

The reports are silent regarding a crucial question: are the abuses inevitable in a political situation of occupation? If we accept that in Israel "the conditions that allow abuses are endemic rather than incidental" (Cohen 1991b), is there any point in fighting against isolated cases of abuses at checkpoints or the destruction of property, without progress in political-diplomatic course? The format of the reports seems to suggest an affirmative answer. Israeli human rights NGOs believe they "should remain neutral on overt political questions, taking no positions on the causes or solutions to the conflict and keeping institutional distance from the broader political 'left' camp" (Felner 2003: 23). Yet, an argument can be made that it might be a better use of energy to fight a political struggle for peace, for a structural change, rather than against specific violations, which in any case would continue as long as the political situation remains static. This echoes the general critique of Kennedy that "human rights occupies the field of emancipatory possibility" (2002).

Moreover, by conceptualizing the situation exclusively through the lens of human rights violations and neglecting structural issues, the reports distort the responsibility of the Israeli society as a whole. By focusing on direct abuses by the army, police, and security services, the reports eschew the role of broader segments of society, which benefit from and sustain the occupation (Haas 2006). Mamdani has criticized the South African TRC, arguing that, by dealing only with gross human rights violations, it has distorted the broader reality of the Apartheid era and left unaddressed the role of those who have sustained the system (2000). By looking only at the small group of direct perpetrators of acts such as torture, the TRC left uncovered the role of the many others who were passive supporters or beneficiaries of the regime. While Mamdani's analysis was directed at how the TRC has conceptualized the past, it seems equally relevant to the way human rights reports conceptualize the present in Israel/Palestine. The reports distort a total system of domination by looking only at the particularly brutal manifestations of it. This, even if indirectly, curtails their potential effects on readers, who can see themselves as not responsible for the situation.

The distortion of personal responsibility is enhanced by the fact that the reports do not include recommendations for the readers. They do present recommendations for the governments or armed groups covered by the reports: usually terse statements that call upon the government to cease the reported policy and sometimes also to punish the perpetrators and compensate the victims. Yet, the reports do not tell the ordinary readers what they can do; they refrain from recommending that the readers take actions such as voting for certain political parties, or refusing to serve in the army, or going on strike, refusing to pay taxes, organizing demonstrations for a nonviolent overthrow of the regime, and so on. At least partly, this can be seen as a result of the state-centered focus of the human rights framework, which looks at the duties of governments rather than of individuals.[4]

Thus, through their content and conclusions, human rights reports do not present an explicit causal chain between the readers' actions and inactions and the creation of – and the potential to change – the reported abuses. Without such a causal chain, the reports' potential to mobilize their readers to act is limited.

"Division of Labor" and Other Counter-arguments

Several arguments that counter these charges were suggested by my interviewees. One argument is that it would be inaccurate to suggest that human rights reports are useless in agitating for structural political issues, as accumulated over time they demonstrate, even if implicitly, the impossibility of an "enlightened occupation," and thus contribute to the political struggle as well. In addition, there is the appeal for the possibility of narrow, yet concrete and immediate, help: if one person is saved from abuse tomorrow it might be better than a political peace agreement ten years from now.

A more structural argument points out that the irrelevance of political context is exactly the major strength of human rights analysis. It does not matter who started the intifada, which side is to blame for the collapse of the Camp David peace talks, if suicide bombings are the tool of the weak or the tool of the jihadist, and so on. Even in times of war there are minimum rules, no matter which is the "right" side. This avoidance of context is the guiding principle of the human rights framework and what makes it effective when all other questions are contested. The role of human rights NGOs is to carve a space for human rights in highly politicized environments; causes and solutions to complex political questions should be left to academics and policy makers. Thus, the argument goes, if human rights researchers start to address these they "risk losing the comparative

---

[4] Compare this with publications of the environmental movement which, alongside recommendations to governments, contain recommendations to individuals: to fly less, recycle, and so on, thus highlighting individual responsibilities in addition to governmental duties.

advantage of focused scope, and are easily drowned out in the cacophony of political pundits" (Felner 2003: 4). The most common phrasing of this argument is through the idea of a "division of labor": human rights organizations address narrow policies and abuses, others fight for the structural issues. There is no contradiction, and in order to report with credibility human rights NGOs must indeed refrain from addressing political issues.

The idea of a division of labor is also mentioned in response to the omission of direct recommendation for the readers. According to this response, human rights NGOs do not operate in a vacuum; political parties and organizations are always active as well. Whoever reads human rights reports is exposed also to other kinds of advocacy and messages. Thus, the argument goes, there is a division of duties: the human rights reports should retain their crystal-clear voice by presenting only facts without direct calls for actions; the readers can get their ideas for such actions from other actors.

These observations are important and valid but, I think, not sufficient to resolve the discussion. The issue of politics in human rights work is not an either/or choice, but one that is on a spectrum, with various options (see Gready 2003). Cohen, for instance, showed how the South African human rights movement was much more political than the Israeli, without losing its claim to speak on behalf of "human rights" (1991a). It is not clear, for example, if making broader pronouncements would necessarily undermine the comparative advantage of Israeli human rights NGOs and to what extent their "self-imposed moratorium on addressing political issues" (Felner 2003: 27) is ultimately justified.[5]

Moreover, the assumption that readers would get their facts from human rights reports and then seek recommendation for action from other sources may be too optimistic. Cohen, using controlled psychological experiments, showed that information on human rights violations often does not lead to action even when the accuracy and characterization of the reported abuses is not contested by the readers (it should be noted that Cohen used shorter appeals, rather than full reports).[6] Due to claims of "desensitization," "compassion fatigue," and "information overload," people often "shut-out" in response to such information. Cohen reports on results from

---

[5]   On a more practical level, for the division of labor argument to be fully valid, one must assume that limitless resources are available to support both human rights and political groups, and that all actors are performing their respective tasks effectively. Where this is not the case, as in Israel, the argument loses at least some of its strength.

[6]   See also Seu (2003).

focus groups of students who were asked to read appeals by Amnesty International that dealt with abuses such as disappearances or torture. He describes a spiral process where "there is a peculiar sense in which the *more* you acknowledge all this distressing information, the more responsible and 'bad' you feel for not doing anything, so the *less* you feel motivated to absorb more information" (2001: 216, emphasis in the original). If these findings apply to human rights reports as well, it seems likely that the omission of concrete calls for action may result in a disempowering message that can potentially exacerbate this spiral process, leaving readers unmotivated to seek direct recommendations elsewhere.

Before concluding, one important qualification is due. The shortcomings of the human rights report format presented here are mainly in the context of its potential effects on the general public, the "ordinary reader." Yet the same format, for all its shortcomings, may be essential in its uses vis-à-vis official bodies. Wilson wrote that the "category of 'human rights violation' does not exist independently of its representation in human rights reports" (1997: 134). This may be true if one follows a narrow theoretical analysis of representations but, in fact, the category of human rights violations exists elsewhere as well: in the court that orders a halt to the building of the wall; in the committee of inquiry that grants compensation to victims; in the international criminal tribunal that charges perpetrators; in the UN committee that calls for release of prisoners; in the immigration tribunal that finds an asylum request credible. Human rights reports, with their authoritativeness and credibility, are used in all these cases. These possibilities of redress, as Cohen wrote, "depend on mode of knowledge that must use the language of facts and universal human rights standards" (1991). This mode, for all its other limitations, exists in the current format of human rights reports.

A final question remains then: is the gain in credibility worth the price of the various shortcomings?

Conclusions

I would like to leave this question open: a "final verdict" on the genre of human rights reports is beyond the ambition of this chapter, as are decisive answers to the dilemmas presented here. My main conclusion is the need to encourage introspective self-critique among those who produce human rights reports. Human rights researchers confront tremendous challenges in their attempts at accurate fact-finding and legal analysis; they are socialized into the common mode of NGO work and often also acquire a certain self-righteousness. With all this, they rarely pause to reflect on the nature of their genre.[7] Moreover, after devoting enormous resources to the production of reports, human rights organizations are often almost willingly ignorant regarding the impact of these reports once they are published; their effects "remain unknown and unmonitored" (Cohen 1996: 517). There is a dire need, then, to promote self-examination of the methods and engagement with the questions raised here. In the end the conclusion might be that the report format is an imperfect yet essential tool; but even if so, a sense of humility and an honest acknowledgment of the genre's limitations could only benefit the human rights movement.

It should be pointed out that some of the dilemmas I have presented above may be less stark in reality. Not all readers need an emotive tone to solicit their empathy; not all of them require direct recommendations to be mobilized for action. Indeed, perhaps the most constructive way forward is to gain more empirical insights on the way the reports are read and received – a move from analysis of the production of these texts to an analysis of their reception. We need better quantification and identification of who actually reads human rights reports, and a better understanding of how they are read. How many people read reports by Amnesty or B'Tselem? Who are they, where do they live, where do they work? How do they read the reports – cover to cover, or just some sections, and, if so, which sections? How do they interpret the meaning and message of the reports? What do they do, if at all, when finished reading? I hope, in future research, to start addressing some of these empirical questions. Such insights could provide a premise to a process of fine-tuning and modifying the format.

One potential source of inspiration in this process could be reports by truth commissions, which have become a second important genre of human rights documentation, often breaking new grounds in comparison with NGO reports, by using more flowing prose or by providing thicker descriptions of the political background. For example, the report of the Argentinean truth commission, titled *Nunca Más* (Never Again), was written mainly by a novelist (Ernesto Sabato) and has become a bestseller,

---

[7] In the interviews for this discussion, I asked several human rights practitioners what they think is the role of the personal testimonies inserted in reports. Some replied that it is the emotional effects on the readers that are sought and that the testimonies are redundant regarding the factual side; others argued the complete opposite. Some of these people have worked in the same organization for years and did not seem to have ever discussed this question with their colleagues. Wherever the merit lies, this is but one illustration of the lack of organizational self-reflection.

reaching a much wider audience than any human rights report can hope for (Hayner 2002: 33–34). The Guatemalan truth commission has produced a rich and sophisticated historical analysis of the contexts and causes of human rights violations there (Hayner 2002: 45–9). And the South African TRC, has demonstrated a range of modes to describe human rights violations, using both forensic and narrative styles.[8] All these "deviations" from the familiar NGO report format did not, it seems, undermine the authority and credibility of these reports,[9] and with all the important critique leveled at truth commissions, they can at least illustrate the potential of experimenting with new formats. In sum, a process of reexamining the genre of human rights reports would be a demanding task for human rights organizations, yet essential if they are to face better their contemporary challenges.

A Final Thought: "To Describe . . . and Not to Add . . ."

The thrust of my discussion, in line with most scholars and NGOs, was to analyze human rights reporting as a tool. Cohen, for example, writes that "the report is usually seen as a means to an end . . . part of a wider strategy to prevent violations" (1996: 516). Similarly, Keenan assumes that a "fundamental axiom of the human rights movement" is that "the act of witness is not simply an ethical gesture but an active intervention" (2004: 446). Human Rights Watch emphasizes that reporting is not done for its own sake: "Documenting abuses is inherently a preventive strategy."[10]

Yet, there might also be another way to view the human rights report. Cohen suggests that while the instrumental perception of the report is the more common, "reporting also may become an end in itself: the belief that even without results there is an absolute duty to convey the truth, to bear witness" (1996: 516). There is an instinctive appeal for such a formulation, to the view, reminiscent of Quaker notions, that "bearing witness" has intrinsic value. Reporting facts thus can be seen as "valuable in itself," acquiring almost a metaphysical aura; yes, simply an ethical gesture. I find this view convincing but, as with all "intrinsic value" claims, it is impossible to justify it by any external criteria. I see the smile of the woman from Akhmatova's poem as endorsing this view: the intuitive solace of recording

---

[8] Although the TRC has been criticized for its overreliance on statistics and positivist techniques; see Wilson (2001).

[9] Although it should be noted that, in being officially sanctioned bodies, truth commissions may have an inherent advantage over NGOs in their assumed authoritativeness.

[10] At http://www.hrw.org/about/faq/#3.

and reporting facts of suffering, in "a crisp and businesslike way," while adding nothing to the facts themselves.

I began this piece by quoting an East European poet and will conclude by a quote from another, the Polish Nobel Laureate Wislawa Szymborska, a quote that captures the sentiment I was trying to convey in the previous paragraph. In her poem "A Photograph from September 11," Szymborska writes about the people jumping to their death from the Twin Towers. Her poem ends like this:

There are only two things I can do for these people now:
To describe their last flight
And not to add a final sentence

REFERENCES

Bell, C., and J. Keenan (2004). "Human Rights Nongovernmental Organizations and the Problems of Transition." *Human Rights Quarterly,* vol. 26, no. 2, pp. 330–74.

Campbell, C., F. Ni-Aolain, and Colin Harvey (2002). "The Frontiers of Legal Analysis: Reframing the Transition in Northern Ireland." *Modern Law Review,* vol. 66, no. 3, pp. 317–45.

Cohen, S. (1991a). *The Human Rights Movement in Israel and South Africa: Some Paradoxical Comparisons.* Jerusalem: The Truman Institute for Advancement of Peace.

———. (1991b). "Talking about Torture in Israel." *Tikkun,* 6, pp. 23–30, 89–90.

———. (1996). "Government Responses to Human Rights Reports: Claims, Denials, and Counterclaims." *Human Rights Quarterly,* vol. 18, no. 3, pp. 516–43.

———. (2001). *States of Denial: Knowing about Atrocities and Suffering.* Cambridge: Polity.

Collins, J. (2004). *Occupied by Memory: The Intifada Generation and the Palestinian State of Emergency.* New York: New York University Press.

Dudai, R. (2006). "Advocacy with Footnotes: The Human Rights Report as a Literary Genre." *Human Rights Quarterly,* vol. 28, no. 3, pp. 783–95.

Felner, E. (2003). "Human Rights Leaders in Conflict Zones: A Case Study of the Politics of Moral Entrepreneurs." Working paper, Carr Center for Human Rights, Harvard.

Freeman, M. (2006). "Putting the Law in its Place." In B. Cali and S. Meckled-Garcia Saladin, eds., *The Legalization of Human Rights: Multidisciplinary Approaches.* London: Routledge, pp. 49–64.

Gorenberg, G. (2006). *Accidental Empire: Israel and the Birth of Settlements.* New York: Holt.

Gready, P. (2003). "The Politics of Human Rights." *Third World Quarterly,* vol. 24, no. 4, pp. 745–57.

Grafton, A. (1997). *The Footnote: A Curious History.* Harvard: Harvard University Press.

Hajjar, L. (2001). "Human Rights in Israel/Palestine: The History and Politics of a Movement." *Journal of Palestine Studies,* vol. 30, no. 4, pp. 21–38.

Hass, A. (2006). "Can You Really Not See?" *Ha'aretz*, August 30.

Hayner, P. (2002). *Unspeakable Truths: Facing the Challenge of Truth Commissions.* New York: Routledge.

Hopgood, S. (2006). *Keepers of the Flame: Understanding Amnesty International.* Ithaca: Cornell University Press.

Hochschild, A. (2005). *Bury the Chains: The British Struggle To Abolish Slavery.* London: Macmillan.

Huggins, M. (2000). "Reconstructing Atrocity: How Torturers, Murderers and Researchers Deconstruct Labels and Manage Secrecy." *Human Rights Review*, vol. 1, no. 4, pp. 50–70.

Keenan, T. (2004). "Mobilizing Shame." *South Atlantic Quarterly*, vol. 103, nos. 2/3, pp. 435–49.

Kennedy, D. (2002). "The International Human Rights Movement: Part of the Problem?" *Harvard Human Rights Journal*, 15, pp. 101–25.

———. (2006). "Two Sides of the Coin: Human Rights Pragmatism and Idolatry." Paper presented in the London School of Economics.

LaCapra, D. (2001). *Writing History, Writing Trauma.* Baltimore: Johns Hopkins University Press.

Mamdani, M. (2000). "When Does Reconciliation Turn into a Denial of Justice? The Truth According to the TRC." In I. Amadiume and A. An-Ma'in, eds., *The Politics of Memory*, Pretoria: HSRC.

McEvoy, K. (2003). "Beyond the Metaphor." *Theoretical Criminology*, vol. 7, no. 3, pp. 319–46.

Montell, J. (2004). "The Search for Truth: Human Rights Documentation in the War of Representation." *Humanitarian Exchange*, 28, pp. 13–15.

Orentlicher, D. (1990). "Bearing Witness: The Art and Science of Human Rights Fact-Finding." *Harvard Human Rights Journal*, 3, pp. 83–135.

Price, R. (2003). "Transnational Civil Society and Advocacy in World Politics." *World Politics*, vol. 55, no. 4, pp. 579–606.

Rorty, R. (1993). "Human Rights, Rationality and Sentimentality." In S. Shute, ed., *On Human Rights: The Oxford Amnesty Lectures*, pp. 111–34. New York: Basic Books.

Rosenblum, P. (2002). "Teaching Human Rights: Ambivalent Activism, Multiple Discourses, and Lingering Dilemmas." *Harvard Human Rights Journal*, vol 15, pp. 301–15.

Seu, B. (2003). "Your Stomach Makes You Feel That You Don't Want to Know Anything about It: Desensitization, Defense Mechanisms and Rhetoric in Response to Human Rights Abuses." *Journal of Human Rights*, vol. 2, no. 2, pp. 183–96.

Tilly, C. (2006). *Why?* Princeton: Princeton University Press.

Truth and Reconciliation Commission (1998). *Final Report of the South African Truth and Reconciliation Commission.*

Wilson, R. (1997). "Representing Human Rights Violations: Social Contexts and Subjectivities." In R. Wilson, ed., *Human Rights, Culture and Context: Anthropological Perspectives.* London: Pluto Press, pp. 134–60.

———. (2001). *The Politics of Truth and Reconciliation in South Africa.* Cambridge: Cambridge University Press.

12. Financial Reparations, Blood Money, and Human Rights Witness Testimony: Morocco and Algeria

SUSAN SLYOMOVICS

Necessary to post–World War II reparation processes was some form of publicly establishing the truths of victims' and survivors' experiences. Based on international human rights norms ushered in after Germany's defeat, financial reparative remedies came to rely heavily on reporting procedures. When human rights violations are presented primarily in material terms to obtain financial indemnification, then acknowledging and filing an indemnity claim becomes one way for victims to testify, tell their story, and be recognized. What are the effects of money as a primary form of reparation to survivors of torture, disappearance, and illegal imprisonment? The pursuit – or refusal – of financial reparation is part of a growing field of research and literature in human rights legal studies. A large body of scholarly work has emerged under the rubric of "witness studies" to underscore French historian Annette Wievorka's characterization of the late twentieth century as *"l' ère du témoin,"* the era of the witness – the century that has accorded the victim of political violence a cultural salience and representative characteristics to such a degree that an individual may stand for the collective experience and become a voice in the public realm (Wievorka 1998; Douglass & Vogler 2003; Torpey 2006: 18). The initial chosen avenues of reparation by both the Algerian and Moroccan governments, unique to the Arab world, are indemnity commissions granting financial awards. Reparations achieved through these quasi-independent, state-mandated bodies have also resulted in Moroccan and Algerian citizens mobilizing in order to frame facts and tell different stories about past histories of opposition and human rights violations.

A variety of transnational and governmental, quasi-governmental, and nongovernmental institutions have emerged to listen to, process, quantify, and issue reports based upon witness testimony in order to compensate for the lack of international enforcement or implementation. Reparations protocols have become one measure of the speed at which different human rights legal regimes contact and influence each other. Despite the transnational contexts in which national laws have been changed by various agents of globalization, interjurisdictional interactions, transnational human rights groups, truth commissions, legal reform NGOs, and an army of experts on transitional justice, the implementation of human rights reparations occurs largely in the national context (for better or worse). Consequently, compliance with globalized international standards of redress that involves witness testimony is subject to national variations. A focus on national efforts by Morocco and Algeria highlights the vagaries of state-mandated commissions targeting financial remedies to their own citizens *within* their respective countries, even though the concept of reparations emerged as a way to make peace *between* states while acknowledging and "repairing" the injuries caused by war.

Historically, reparations cases involved remedies for damages associated with genocide, slave labor, human subject experimentation, and the seizure of lands and property without due process or compensation. The 1948 adoption of the Universal Declaration on Human Rights and the subsequent expansion of international and national human rights law have meant that in recent years reparations have been negotiated to repair breaches for violations committed in the name of colonial expansion, economic development, and national security. In April 2005, the UN adopted guidelines defining remedy in its varied forms as restitution, compensation or indemnity, rehabilitation, and satisfaction and guarantees of nonrepetition:[1]

---

[1] United Nations, Basic Principles and Guidelines on the Right to a Remedy and Reparation for Victims of Violations of International Human Rights and Humanitarian Law, E/CN.4/2005/L.48. Compensation refers to economic payment for any assessable damage resulting from violations of human rights and humanitarian law. This includes physical and mental harm, and the related material and moral damages. Rehabilitation includes legal, medical, psychological, and social services and care. Satisfaction includes almost every other form of reparation, including measures that halt continuing violations, verification of facts and full and public disclosure of the truth in rights-protective ways, the search for the missing, the identification of bodies, and assistance in recovery, identification, and reburial in culturally appropriate ways. Satisfaction also includes official declarations or judicial decisions that restore the dignity, reputation, and legal rights of the victim and persons connected with the victim, public apology and acceptance of responsibility, judicial sanctions against responsible parties, and commemorations of and tributes to the victims. Guarantees of nonrepetition include measures that contribute to prevention; ensure effective control over the military and security forces; ensure that proceedings occur with due process, fairness and impartiality; strengthen the independent judiciary; protect human rights defenders; prompt the observance of codes of conduct and ethical norms, including international standards, by public servants; promote mechanisms for preventing and monitoring social conflicts and their resolution; and review and reform laws contributing to or allowing the gross violation of international human rights laws.

Restitution aims to reestablish to the extent possible the situation that existed before the violation took place; compensation relates to any economically assessable damage resulting from the violations; rehabilitation includes legal, medical, psychological and other care; while satisfaction and guarantees of non-repetition relate to measures to acknowledge the violations and prevent their recurrence in the future. (Hayner 2002: 171)

With the recent establishment of the Moroccan and Algerian commissions, internationally minded human rights activists perceive globalization as a good thing: the common concerns of humankind supersede the sovereign rights of states. If ideas and protocols about reparation for human rights atrocities circulate transnationally across borders while their implementation is on the national level, then the heart and soul of any enterprise involving reparation payments rest with the individual recipient.

Morocco and Algeria: Case Histories and Variations

Acknowledgment of international protocols and definitions by sovereign states is partly exemplified by Algeria and Morocco, countries whose reparation projects favor financial compensation (to attempt to assess harm as a *consequence* of the violation) over restitution (to return the victim to the financial conditions *prior* to violation). In Morocco, since independence from France in 1956, so many tens of thousands of Moroccan dissidents have been imprisoned that specific decades are known to Moroccans as "black years" and "years of lead," when political opponents of the monarchy, many of them leftists, Sahrawis (Saharan nationalists), Amazigh/Berber activists, feminists, and Islamists, were often "disappeared," tortured, or killed while in state custody. Since the 1990s, current Moroccan projects to reorganize judicial, court, and police systems have gone hand in hand with a national response to create governmental organs intended to address histories of human rights violations that have been propelled by processes of indemnification and reparation.[2]

As early as 1990, King Hassan II of Morocco established the Advisory Council on Human Rights (ACHR; in Arabic, *al-Majlis al-Istishari li-Huquq al-Insan*), avowedly modeled on a similar 1984 French institution (CCDH, *Conseil consultative des droits humains*), to begin the rehabilitation of his regime's reputation for repression (Waltz 1999;

---

[2] These two commissions focus on the post-independent years from 1956–1999. For historical background see Slyomovics (2001, 2003, 2005b, and 2005c).

Slyomovics 2005c).[3] While initial criticisms of the ACHR were vocal concerning both its workings and composition (non-independent and staffed with well-paid royal appointees and cronies), it is the case that since the 1990s, ACHR members have been involved in perhaps three, even four, overlapping programs of pecuniary reparation to compensate Moroccan victims of human rights violation (Benayoub 2004). The most recent is the 2004–2005 Moroccan Justice and Reconciliation Commission (*Instance Equité et Réconciliation*, IER in French; and in Arabic, *Lajnat al-Insaf wa-al-Musalaha*), whose analysis of past indemnification programs and recommendations for extensive future reparation protocols are taken up in volume 3 of the final six-volume December 2005 report. Victims of torture and disappearance since Morocco's independence from France, through the reigns of three monarchs from 1956 to 1999, have produced over 22,000 human rights violation claims sent to the Rabat commission headquarters, with thousands of additional reparation requests arriving after the February 2004 deadline. According to the final report, over 9,000 victims were granted financial indemnities while another 1,500 claimants, who had benefited from the earlier 1999 Indemnity Commission, received supplementary funds.[4] Thus, two of the latest Moroccan commissions were formed by royal decree: the 1999 Indemnity Commission, created by King Hassan II, and the 2004–2005 Justice and Reconciliation Commission (henceforth referred to by its French initials, IER), created by his son and heir, King Muhammad VI. Both commissions have concluded with real and extensive financial indemnification.

In Algeria, the National Consultative Commission to Promote the Protection of Human Rights (*Commission nationale consultative de la promotion et de la protection des droits de l'homme*, CNCPPDH), a body similar to the Moroccan and French ones, and headed by Mustapha Farouk Ksentini, reported 6,146 persons forcibly disappeared by the state since 1992. Algerian President Abdelaziz Bouteflika's voter-approved 2005 "Charter for Peace and National Reconciliation" consists of government apologies and pecuniary reparation to victims of Islamist violence as part of Algeria's post-conflict politics of reconciliation (Human Rights Watch 2005). In addition,

---

[3] The Advisory Committee on Human Rights (ACHR) is also translated in some English works as the Consultative Council on Human Rights (CCHR). Morocco's final text is found in dahir no. 1–00-350 of 10 April 2001, published in *Bulletin Officiel* no. 4926 of 16 August 2001. In the speech to celebrate the establishment of the ACHR, Hassan II claimed the Moroccan ACHR was a copy of the French, point for point (Essaid 1994: 409–48).

[4] See online report at www.ier.ma and reparation section at: http://www.ier.ma/_rapport_fr_article.php?id_article=1432.

Algeria allocates 10,000 dinars (US$1,000) per month for life to each victim (or to rightful heirs of victims, such as a surviving spouse and children), whose numbers are estimated between 150,000 and 200,000 people – a monthly global payment of approximately 2 billion dinars.

In contrast to remedies promoted by the regimes' victims, both Morocco and Algeria granted immunity to perpetrators. The current status of such national amnesties in international law is not clear, especially outside the borders of the granting country. Inspired by the "Pinochet precedent," a legal tactic to pursue tyrants through foreign courts (Clapham 2001), Mohammed El Battiui, a student activist who was arrested and tortured in the 1983 Oujda University riots protesting huge price increases in basic foods, filed a case against the man deemed responsible for and symbolic of the Moroccan regime's human rights abuses, former Minister of the Interior Driss Basri, fired by the new king on 9 November 1999. After his removal from a position he had held since 1979, Basri, now stripped of his immunity and residing in Paris, was accused by El Battiui, a Belgian resident, of "crimes against humanity" on 16 November 1999 at the Tribunal of First Instance in Brussels. El Battiui's file includes descriptions of incommunicado detention as well as innocent family members held hostage in jail and subjected to weeks of torture[5] (Slyomovics 2005c: 23). Should Basri set foot on Belgian soil, Moroccan amnesties would be tested, and their justifications scrutinized in a public forum.

Were blanket amnesties based on Moroccan government-imposed amnesia, as critics complain? Or, as proclaimed by both Algeria and Morocco, were they instituted in the name of national reconciliation? Responses to these questions play an important role for potential claimants as they decide whether to file and hence legitimate the Moroccan and Algerian commissions. This is strikingly true for Algeria where government amnesties went beyond the norms proposed for transitional governments. In Algeria, on 27 February 2006, the law implementing provisions of the National Charter was passed to grant immunity to perpetrators – both to members of armed groups opposing the regime with claims of acting in the name of Islam and their enemy opposite, "the defense and security forces of the Republic." More dangerous for Algerian human rights activists, their opposition to impunity was criminalized by the Algerian state's creation of a new imprisonable offence: attributing any responsibility to those who

---

[5] I thank Mohammed El Battiui for sending me photocopies of his deposition. In 2003, in response to international political pressure, notably by the USA, Belgium introduced modifications restricting its "law on universal competence" to Belgian citizens, which El Battiui is. El Battiui informs me that absent is "one condition: Driss Basri must be on Belgian soil to be judged": email correspondence, 10 March 2004. Basri died in Paris on August 27, 2007.

organized violations of the law or covered up or justified the atrocities committed during the fifteen years from 1992 to 2006. According to Article 46, anyone accusing an alleged perpetrator faces three to five years in prison plus fines from a quarter to a half million dinars for a declaration, denunciation, or activity that "instrumentalizes the national tragedy, harms Algerian . . . . state institutions . . . or tarnishes the image of Algeria internationally" (Algerian Ministry of Foreign Affairs 2006). Meanwhile the alleged perpetrator (the very object of a victim's accusation or denunciation) goes free. As a countervailing dynamic to perpetrators unpunished, especially in the absence of public and publicized hearings of witness testimonies (in Algeria, unlike Morocco), the victim's stories gain credibility once transmitted through informal, oppositional, nonlegal forms of circulation such as protest marches, memoirs, speeches, internet listservs, and so on.

The German Model?

As I followed, from 1999 on, the Moroccan and Algerian combination of paying indemnities to victims and at the same time absolving the guilty, my focus was redirected to the case of postwar Germany for comparative scholarly reasons. Chancellor Konrad Adenauer, who launched the postwar German reparations effort (*Wiedergutmachung*, literally "making good again"), also began his government in 1949 by dismantling Allied de-Nazification programs for Nazi-era crimes. Amnesty programs were created for those guilty of serious crimes and restitution laws reintegrated hundreds of thousands of Nazi party members into their former jobs (Frei 2002: xi–xv). Unlike South Africa or postwar Germany, Morocco and Algeria have not changed regimes. Yet with or without a clear political break, countries are forced to live with a greater or lesser number of known perpetrators in the government apparatus. Both Morocco and Algeria do so to a greater extent, at the same time as they attempt to transform themselves from the inside and still retain control, a process that is reflected in their approaches to human rights, the silencing of witnesses, and the counter-discourses of victim testimonies.

Other than degrees of perpetrator guilt versus exoneration, additional parallels between postwar Germany and the decolonized, post-independent North African states are concerned with witness testimony and reparation, each possessing radically different features and functions within human rights and truth commissions. How are the truths of witness testimony implicated in the outcome of reparation? According to the much-debated formulation by one of Chile's truth commissioners, Jose Zalaquett, "the truth is in itself both reparation and prevention," and "revealing is healing" (Quoted in Weschler 1990: 243–5). Consequently, Zalaquett counsels against the court and trial process, because if a survivor of torture, for example, speaks the truth, alleged perpetrators of torture always dispute the story of the survivor. With regard to the process of reparation, Zalaquett concludes that the relationship between truth and justice is somewhat separated. Truth is awarded compensation but does not assign blame (Zalaquett 1995). Zalaquett's model depends on the eloquence of the speaking survivor, who is healed by his or her act of narration and heard by a sympathetic institution that rewards the act of storytelling.

In contrast to Zalaquett, other psychological models maintain that the process of applying for reparations, the interview itself no less than any construction or imposition of a narrative, is traumatic and may protract victimization. For witnesses in the South African Truth and Reconciliation Commission, two contradictory claims were made: that reliving pain and sharing feelings could facilitate recovery, or it could result in its horrific opposite, retraumatizing in the form of flashbacks, hysteria, and depression (Caruth 1996). Furthermore, as I have noted elsewhere, Moroccans, whether female or male, rarely testified about rape (Slyomovics 2005a). For many witnesses who spoke on behalf of the dead and missing, and even those who could speak on their own behalf about stories of torture and disappearance, the haunting phrase thrown in disgust at many reparations processes is "blood money."

Reparations and "Blood Money"

Reparations (the plural form is routinely used) now mean one thing – money (Torpey 2006: 47). While many victims choose not to speak, and even those who do speak do not speak with one voice, they do pronounce a strikingly consistent reaction to money. Irrespective of an individual's decision to claim or reject reparation funds, most describe participation in monetary remedies as the calculating, materialist, instrumental monetization of their sufferings. Money received through reparations is therefore "morally earmarked," following sociologist Viviana Zelizer's descriptor for the social life of money: "In everyday existence, people understand that money is not really *fungible*, that despite the anonymity of dollar bills, not all dollars are equal or interchangeable" (Zelizer 1997: 5). In many historic and legal cases, financial reparations have been morally earmarked as "dirty," as sullied money, and labeled in diverse crosscultural settings as "blood money."

Many Jews from Israel's community of Holocaust survivors, estimated at a third of the immediate post–World War II population, refused negotiations with West Germany. Joseph Sprinzak, then Speaker of Israel's Knesset, maintained that Israel should not accept "blood money" from Germany, reflecting the initial revulsion of Israel and the Diaspora community.[6] Some fifty years after Germany's postwar indemnities, recipient responses pronounce the same epithet; "blood money" has reappeared in widely disparate cases based on financial reparations, whether the atrocity indemnified is ethnic cleansing, genocide, or a state's ideological war against its own citizens.

Anthropological theories describe a progressive evolutionary model from "blood money" to reparations, according to which feuding communities without compensation mechanisms evolve into advanced societies with blood money payments that exclude the retaliatory eye for an eye. A final stage of sociocultural sophistication is posited when, for example, a suprajuridical body is established, such as the tribal assembly, to adjudicate damages and specify "blood money" in cases of death, rape, and violent disputes (Cherry 1890; Girard 1977; Otterbein & Otterbein 1965: 1470–80; Posner 1981). Thus, for victims to refuse financial compensation precisely because it is "blood money" is to remain mired in the primitive stages of perpetual feuding, revenge, bitterness and savagery. Nonetheless, many refuse.

Beginning in 1999, when Morocco instituted the first of its two commissions, there were victims of the regime's torture and incommunicado disappearance from 1956 to 1999 who ignored their right to file claims in order to denounce publicly as "blood money" (in French, *prix du sang*, and in Arabic, *diyah*) any protocol of payments to victims that was linked to amnesty for perpetrators. Still other Moroccans whom I interviewed chose to tell their stories of victimization, while stipulating a symbolic compensation of one dirham, or approximately US10 cents. Noureddine Belakbyer, a researcher at the 2004 Truth Commission (IER) and like many of its employees a former political prisoner, informed me that he chose not to file for reparations because he is already gainfully employed as a teacher on leave and paid to work for the 2004 Moroccan IER. He estimated that some 400 political prisoners refused to file claims with any commission (interview, Rabat, 20 June 2005).

[6] See discussion in Sznaider (2000); also Joseph B. Schectman, "Case Against Negotiations with Germany," quoted in Tomer Kleinman (2002).

Another group of Moroccans, having refused the first 1999 commission because it awarded money solely for torture and disappearance at their own government's hands, were willing to file for the subsequent 2004 IER awards because of the promise to go beyond mere financial indemnities to encompass collective reparations. Victims pointed to community projects for the Amazigh/Berber-speaking regions, which had paid dearly for their uprisings against the monarchy in 1973. The 1999 commission employed the Arabic term *ta'wid*, or "indemnities," a translation of the French *dédommagements*, derived from contract law, part of the legal vocabulary for economic disputes involving reimbursement and arbitration of damages, all of which are regulated by Morocco's codes governing obligations and contracts, and are procedures that closely conform to French-inherited contract laws.

Fatna El Bouih, a Moroccan leftist dissident and political prisoner, experienced radically different reactions to Morocco's two historical reparations commissions of 1999 and 2004. She was forcibly disappeared for three years from 1977 to 1980, finally earning the right to a trial as a result of the prolonged hunger strike of her incarcerated women's group. When El Bouih was faced with the decision to file for reparations for the 1999 Indemnity Commission, she refused. Her reason, she informed me in interviews in late 1999, was "blood money." When the 2004 Moroccan IER had replaced the formulation *ta'wid* with another Arabic term, *jabr al-adrar*, translated as "reparation" and explicitly defined as restitution, apology, medical and psychological therapies, social and community rehabilitation, El Bouih chose to file for the more just and expansive terms of *jabr al-adrar*. Other collective reparative remedies recommended by the IER were government apologies and the conversion of Casablanca's infamous secret detention and torture center, Derb Moulay Cherif, into a memorial museum.

Not only the terms of reparations – for whom, what purpose, and which monetary calculations recognize the crimes of torture, disappearance, and imprisonment – but also the institutional benefactor of money compelled El Bouih to actively distinguish between an apparently corrupted 1999 Indemnity Commission process and the victim-centered 2004 IER. Reparative values, therefore, are also attached to the *source* of money. That there is a morality to funding sources and that the standards of this morality are set by the recipient seems to hold true even for litigants involved in American personal injury cases, far removed from the domain of human rights atrocities. Legal scholar Tom Baker has analyzed the experiences of claims against American insurance companies versus claims against actual individuals encountered face-to-face in the courtroom. He concludes that claimants interpret blood money as a good thing because of its resemblance to the biblical *lex talionis* ("an eye for an eye ... a life for a life"). Cases involving physical injury in particular call forth the law of retribution in which the perpetrator pays directly, unable to hide behind impersonal institutions, companies or states.

> Real money from real people – money paid directly by defendants out of their own pocket. As their term reflects, blood money hurts defendants in a way that money paid on behalf of a defendant by a liability insurance company cannot. For that reason, blood money is an entirely different currency than what lawyers refer to as "insurance money." (Baker 2001)

Baker asks us to imagine impersonal sources of money as "cold, hard, and flat," while money directly and painfully issuing from the perpetrator is "hot, soft and highly textured" (Baker 2001: 276). Baker concludes for personal injury cases that "the key assumption is that people who have harmed others have to feel some financial pain" and financial pain may act as a deterrent against future harm (Baker 2002).

Even in those cases where blame cannot be directly assigned to an individual or even a state, morality and money are linked. Sociologist Viviana Zelizer cites the early history of resistance, especially by women, to the business of insuring their husband's life, seen as deriving profit from the demise of a spouse:

> Some women say that life insurance seems to them too much like benefiting by the husband's death. Others feel that if a good man were to die, and the proceeds of a policy should be paid to them, it would seem like accepting "blood money," and others say they would not enter any such sordid calculation of his future expectation of life. (Zelizer 1979: 46)

Financial indemnification programs confront an implacable unease: managing death and disease as an economic event offends. Cash awards to the living on behalf of the dead are so deeply enmeshed with the repugnant notion of blood money that all those associated with claims processes, even outsiders such as lawyers and administrators, are morally implicated as if by contagion. Kenneth Feinberg, the American lawyer charged by the Bush administration as the "Special Master" to dispense the September 11 Victim Compensation Fund of 2001, decided to forgo lawyer's fees for his work "to avoid additional criticism ... that some families would accuse [him] of earning 'blood money' on the backs of the injured" (Feinberg 2005: 26). Feinberg's inadvertent metaphors – which compared the narration of suffering to a business deal, or worse, portrayed victims as rationally strategizing games – were loathsome; they challenged the recipients' belief that these were special sacred funds, at one and the same time "marked" and "earmarked" money. The slightest allusion to monetary metaphors, Feinberg concluded, jeopardized the US government's desired outcome of a single mass settlement in lieu of the feared thousands of individual suits:

> I committed a couple of genuine faux pas during early town meetings. On one occasion when trying to stress the uniqueness of the 9/11 fund, I remarked, "This program is not business as usual." Eyes got wide in the audience, and some families exchanged glances. Then a stricken husband got to his feet and angrily retorted, "This is not a *business* you're talking about, Mr. Feinberg. You're talking about my *wife*." Another time, I was urging a group of Staten Islanders to participate in the fund rather than mount lawsuits, a path I was convinced would lead nowhere. To emphasize my conviction, I told the families, "This is the only game in town." As soon as the words escaped my lips, I caught a glimpse of my lieutenant, Camille Biros, wincing in the front row of the audience. With a sinking feeling I realized what I'd said. The room practically erupted in anger. One outraged wife spoke for the group. "To you, this may be a game," she spat, "But not to us." Heads nodded around the room. What could I do? I apologized profusely and inwardly vowed to never, ever use that kind of language again. I never did. (Feinberg 2005: 54–5)

Hierarchies of Victimhood: Disappearance

While the 9/11 Fund is considered primarily pecuniary, because of the ways it mimics insurance estimates of the financial equivalence for loss and death, it also shares with other reparations programs what Feinberg termed a "scale of victimhood measured in dollars." Hierarchies based on the economic success of individuals (e.g. the wealthy stockbrokers in the World Trade Center towers) not only served to diminish the lives of victims awarded less (e.g. the firefighters sent to rescue), but also meant that high-income earners were equated with higher value, since estimations were based on future earnings as opposed to actions and deeds (Feinberg 2005: 184).

As elaborated by Morocco's 1999 Indemnity Commission, the hierarchy of victimhood scaled the highest compensation to the narration of suffering based on forcible and prolonged disappearance. Lower compensations were granted to recognized, known, and internationally supported political detainees incarcerated in official Moroccan prisons and with rights to family visits, letters, and the pursuit of an education. The highest financial indemnities went to twenty-eight survivors of Morocco's most notorious secret prison, Tazmamart (since razed), a former French-built military barracks in a remote region of southern Morocco. Tazmamart is the extreme case of state terror, the example against which all other Moroccan disappearances are measured. In 1973, fifty-eight men involved in two failed coups in 1971 and 1972 against King Hassan II were kidnapped from Kenitra Central Prison where they were serving sentences after a closed military tribunal. They were forcibly disappeared until 1991. Eventually, during those eighteen years, a trickle of reports and books helped bring international attention to the story of Tazmamart, although the individual accounts of disappeared prisoners awaited their 1991 release.[7] Beginning in 1995, Tazmamart survivors were granted monthly pensions of 5,000 dirhams by the government of King Hassan II. In 2000, to mark the Moroccan visit of Mary Robinson, then UN High Commissioner for Human Rights, King Muhammad VI bestowed additional one-time, lump sum payments of 1 million dirhams or more. While a full list of sites of forcible disappearances is still under investigation, other places gained infamy through fear and rumor, but also eventually through published accounts by survivors in the post–Hassan II era.[8]

As the most heinous violation of human rights, disappearance is also the hardest to prove, given the erased identity, the missing corpse, or the unmarked grave. It is painful, sometimes impossible, to narrate disappearance because the absent victim, the very object of the disappearance, must be recounted and kept alive through the anguished discourse of others. Specifically on behalf of the disappeared, Moroccan families were most likely to refuse the 1999 *ta'wid*, despite Zalaquett's formula that to narrate suffering is a form of healing reparation: giving money without perpetrator trials and without a corpse was buying silence. So too, the Mothers of the Plaza de Mayo, the organization of families of those disappeared during Argentina's "Dirty War," divided rancorously in 1986. The president of one splinter group, Hebe de Bonafini, rejected the exhumation of cadavers ("we will not be contented by a bag of bones") and government indemnification ("blood money") (Feitlowitz 1998: 257–8). Nassera Dutour, head of the Algerian Mothers of Disappeared Children

---

[7] In France, notably Gilles Perrault's *Notre ami le roi* (Our Friend the King) (1990) and Christine Daure-Serfaty's *Tazmamart, une prison de la mort au Maroc* (Tazmamart, a Prison of Death in Morocco). Books appeared in Morocco by survivors of Tazmamart, notably Raiss Marzouki. For a discussion about these writings, see Slyomovics (2005c: 56–66).

[8] For analyses of Moroccan prison literature, see El Ouazzani (2004) and also the remarkable bibliography by the Moroccan Documentation Center for Information and Formation of Human Rights (French acronym CDIFDH, El Yazami, Kabouss, and Akil (2004).

(*SOS Disparus*), disdainfully rejected the 2005 Algerian reparations protocols that would have given her money instead of the body or even information about her son Amine Amrouche, disappeared in 1997 at age twenty-one. She told me that the idea of Algerian reparations was "tribal," as if the Algerian regime could force a retrograde return to some imagined prelapsarian Amazigh/Berber collectivity that subsumes the individual victim's experience on behalf of the public good (interview, Paris, December 2003). Dutour exemplifies for Algeria the rights-bearing individual grounded in a conception of the autonomous individual, motivated by her own conscience, and currently unwilling to take into account the persuasiveness of moral imperatives emanating from alternative sources of authority espoused by the Algerian state such as tribal law or religion.

Reparations and Narrative

Hierarchies of victimhood presuppose that victims are not a homogeneous group. The terms used to describe them vary according to the diverse contexts mentioned so far and encompass multiple legal, historical, economic, and literary identities and categorization. For the word "victim," equally substitutable are survivor, deponent, claimant, plaintiff, militant, political prisoner, resister, witness, heir, mother, and family member. All categories produce narratives. Narratives of suffering by victims often determine the amount and duration of monetary outcomes. The complex, dynamic relationship of so many aspects of victimhood to narratives of suffering and to financial reparation partakes of Pierre Bourdieu's systems of social hierarchization, in conformity with the ways in which individuals with institutional input create distinctions. Such narratives also create distinctions among the various cultural or "symbolic capitals" possessed by victims (Bourdieu 1986). In turn, the victims' power to narrate self-definitions broadens the way the law and humanitarian organizations think about reparation. This too involves a Bourdieuvian struggle for control over history and memory. French historian Henri Russo delineates clear ideological and practical boundaries deployed by survivors in France after World War II:

> [H]undreds of associations were formed establishing what amounts to a veritable hierarchy of suffering: the volunteer resistance fighter did not wish to be confused with the "racial" deportee; the deportee did not wish to be mistaken for a prisoner of war; the prisoner of war was careful to distinguish himself from ... the laborer "deported" to work in Germany for the Reich. (Russo 1991: 24)

I maintain that the impetus for finding the point of intersection between reparation and narration emerges first and foremost because of the need to determine what is called "non-economic loss." The 9/11 Fund payment schedules followed the precedent of previous cases of death benefits to police officers, a system that offered one template for calculations of non-economic loss that resulted in $250,000 for pain and suffering per person killed and $50,000 for "emotional distress" for spouse and dependents. Perennial questions faced by truth commissions and torts cases are: how could anyone put any monetary value on a life, and how can one predict what the victim would have earned had he or she lived? Kenneth Feinberg asked himself: "What could I say about a mother determined to write a dead daughter's future, a future that would never be?" (Feinberg 2005: 89). In addition to assessing known economic worth (home ownership, assets, current salary, and so on) in order to narrate the value of the dead, another section of the 9/11 Fund claim form provided space "to explain what the numbers could not convey, the uniqueness of the husband, wife, daughter, son or parent" (Feinberg 2005: 94). Feinberg recounts that for many claimants, completing the written questionnaire was insufficient. During hearings requested by surviving family members of 9/11, a stenographer was present to record the ways in which families orally narrated the story of their dead. These accounts were frequently supplemented by visual images (photographs and albums) and memorabilia supplied by kinfolk. Feinberg believes that those who chose orally narrated hearings, in addition to the mandatory written documentation of claims, needed the optional public narration afforded by an official setting to effect what Feinberg therapeutically terms some kind of psychological "closure" (2005: 114). Moreover, since the worth of the lost loved one is incalculable, Feinberg noted, families were forced to ask for more money, and found themselves deploying oral testimony to articulate the irreplaceable qualities of a parent, a child – understood by Fund managers in economic terms. Yet everyone, narrators and listeners alike, was implicated in telling the story.

I have discussed here victims claiming reparations whose narratives of suffering are historically, legally, and geographically disparate: Jewish victims of the Nazis, Moroccan and Algerian subjects of their respective murderous regimes, Argentine mothers of the disappeared, and 9/11 families. Equating the Nazi project with states' abuses of power, or with European colonial domination, is of course deeply problematic. Nonetheless, arguments surrounding monetary payments articulate recurring themes and contradictions that invite limited comparisons. They form part of the "Faustian predicament" (Barkan 2000: 3), a term coined by historian Elazar Barkan to refer to Jews taking money from Germans, an act in which contradictory emotional and symbolic statements are articulated: taking money is an affront to the memory of the dead; no amount of money compensates for suffering; hush money guarantees that individuals will not pursue investigations further; even those perpetrators who acknowledge crimes cannot pay off the debt of genocide and massive human rights abuses (Bazyler 2003: 286). Accusations directed against victims echo the aversion to the legitimacy and legality of equating money to suffering: victims are black-mailing or shaking down governments; victims are never satisfied; victims' lawyers steal or siphon off reparations; victims are man-ipulated by transnational organizations that act as intermediaries and pocket the bulk of the money; or victim sufferings are exaggerated, or numbers and definitions of victims are enlarged to increase payments (Bazyler 2004: 3–4).

Monetary accounting for gross human rights violations, uneasily interposed between victim and perpetrator or gingerly mediated between claimant and commission, is characterized as the apotheosis of com-modification and objectification of suffering. Financial reparations are hush money, blood money, tainted, driven by greed, undeserved, unworthy, and insufficient. The 9/11 Fund asked the question, as do many mass tort claims, how much is a life worth? In contrast, I claim that financial reparation programs for human rights violations (granted that the 9/11 Fund may be exceptional) in Morocco, Algeria, and Germany are not about asking "how much?" or primarily "what hap-pened?" but rather seek and elicit answers to the question "how does it feel?" Human rights commissions and reparations committees attach conditions to reparation funds they disburse. These conditions are both implicit and explicit. Witness testimony is a prime example of an explicit condition directly relevant to the variety of subsequent remedies available or offered. Reparation and restitution case studies represent the triumph of two intertwined notions: financial reparation is made to an individual for harm suffered, which in turn is proven through repre-sentative individual narratives of suffering. Perpetrator culpability, in contrast, also presented as a matter of individual guilt through careful judicial examination, did not, in the Moroccan and Algerian cases, result in accountability, for example by naming torturers or through trials.

Shahada (Testimony) versus *Ifada* (Statement/Declaration)

The Moroccan 2004 IER commission deliberately selected the term *ifada*, "statement," to characterize the official deposition by a witness to the commission as a claim for indemnification, whether delivered in the form of an oral or a written submission. Driss Benzekri, 2004 IER commission president, informed me that *ifada* was preferred to replace the historically and legally resonant word for "testimony" in Arabic, *shahada*, and in French, *témoignage* (interview, Rabat, January 2005).

Shahadat min al-sijn, "prison testimonies," came to characterize the productive genre from inside closed prison walls, wherein thousands of communiqués, letters, prison newspapers and manuscripts were created and circulated to the outside world by political prisoners, the most vocal and literate human rights activists. Under extreme conditions, narrative acts of *shahada* that appeared as writing, witnessing, and speaking, originated as a last resort – not as a way to communicate with disparate audiences but seemingly into the void. *Shahada* presupposes that the very idea of a literate act of witness is initially produced without an audience and with only bare prison walls as company, unless the torturers and prison guards are counted. Smuggled from prison, disseminated to supporters in Morocco, and sent abroad to international human rights organizations, testimonies describe one passage of political prisoners' pain and torture into the realm of shared public discourse beyond the ideas prisoners espoused (Beverley 1989; Gimaret 1997: 201).

The goals of *shahada* were to retrieve the political climate and memory of what had been a powerful refusal on the part of thousands of Moroccans who posed questions in the immediate post-independent years about political and economic outcomes that served merely to "Moroccanize" the former colonialist hegemony and exploitation. Indeed, the post-1999, post–Hassan II period – an era of research, public debates and testimonies, and publications in mass-circulation newspapers about the contingent truths about past histories of repression – has generated new ways to narrate the story of past opposition to human rights violations. Events surrounding years of repression, interpreting them over decades and through successive modes of communication, include testimonies by surviving actors as well as the quest for knowledge by the current generation of Moroccans about the dark periods of the past that live on in the present. Between any scholarly historical reconstruction of that past and the history of its retelling in the context of current Moroccan politics, it is *shahada* that embodies its two meanings of "to testify" and "to witness." But these are two kinds of speech activities implying different messages and audiences. *Shahada* narrates personal witness; its register is situation specific. This is quite different from bearing witness in the form of the *ifada* (statement) sought by Morocco's commissioners. How do judgments of facts enter into the Moroccan discussion, especially for a claimant in front of an indemnity commission where the requirement is to produce clear statements leading to cash awards?

Communication channels have shifted from speaking to prison walls to imagining various audiences, to the actual creation of appropriate venues of performance in many different registers, to making claims against the state, individually and collectively, for money. As of this writing, both Morocco and Algeria are in the midst of collecting information and determining disbursement. Questions for further study are: what genre of expression are reparation forms; who are the commissioners' and claimants' imagined audiences; who is now doing the judging; what is the social repair work made possible by private claims for financial remedies; what is the relationship between the narrative of suffering and pecuniary reparation; and what are the ways in which the conditionality of witnessing continues to activate, shape, distort, and create the acts of giving testimony about past human rights abuses? Thus far, reparation examples are necessarily concerned with how to talk about money, the ways in which talk brings material results, and the process undertaken to secure reparation, but less concerned about what exactly does one get or recover after embarking on the production of narratives of suffering that seek financial reparation?

One clear conclusion is that some form of witnessing is a condition for monetary indemnification protocols. Claims, money, testimony, and human beings are intertwined in financial reparations: the worth and value of a man or a woman can be provisionally quantified. This means that financial reparations since World War II beg for comparative analysis, because the way in which we scale human value to any kind of monetary grid offers a seemingly neutral and objective external marker. Following social science theories (as in Simmel 1978) about wealth and the sacred nature of humanity, the growth of individualism and the value of individual human rights testimony, another conclusion is that the monetary evaluation of death and injury means that money is now associated with the sacredness of human beings. Money is sacralized, and reparation takes on symbolic values apart from and more powerful than its utilitarian values. Institutional state-mandated reparations emerge as a new foundational ritual, one that is associated with transnational legal mechanisms based on the speaking survivor whose testimony produces the narrative of suffering with which to determine the seriousness of human rights remedies.

REFERENCES

Algeria, Ministry of Foreign Affairs. (2006). National Charter. *Journal Officiel de la Republique Algerienne*, vol. 11, February 28, at http://193.194.78.233/ma_fr/stories.php?story=05/09/06/3612066.

Baker, T. (2001). "Blood Money, New Money and the Moral Economy of Tort Law in Action." *Law and Society Review*, vol. 35, no. 2, pp. 275–319.

———. (2002). "The Blood Money Myth." *Legal Affairs*. At www.legalaffairs.org/issues/September-October-2002/review_baker_sepoct2002.msp.

Barkan, E. (2000). *The Guilt of Nations: Restitution and Negotiating Historical Injustices*. Baltimore, MD: Johns Hopkins University Press.

Bazyler, M. J. (2003). *Holocaust Justice: The Battle for Restitution in America's Court*. New York: New York University Press.

———. (2004). "Suing Hitler's Willing Business Partners: American Justice and Holocaust Morality." *Jewish Political Studies Review*, vol. 16, nos. 3–4 at: http://www.jcpa.org/phas/phas-bazyler-f04.htm.

Benayoub, A. C. (2004). *Hay'at al-Tahkim al-Mustaqillah*. Rabat: Ministry of Human Rights, Center for Documentation on Human Rights.

Beverley, J. (1989). "The Margin at the Center: On *Testimonio* (Testimonial Narrative)." *Modern Fiction Studies*, vol. 35, pp. 11–28.

Bourdieu, P. (1986). *Distinction: A Social Critique of the Judgment of Taste*. London: Routledge.

Caruth, C. (1996). *Unclaimed Experience: Trauma, Narrative and History*. Baltimore: Johns Hopkins University Press.

Cherry, R. (1890). *Lectures on the Growth of Criminal Law in Ancient Communities*. New York: McMillan.

Clapham, A. (2001). "Revisiting Human Rights in the Private Sphere: Using the European Convention on Human Rights to Protect the Right of Access to the Civil Court." In Craig Scott, ed., *Torture as Tort*. Oxford: Hart Publishing, pp. 513–36.

Daure-Serfaty, C. (1992). *Tazmamart: Une prison de la mort au Maroc*. Paris: Stock.

Douglass, A., and T. Vogler (2003). "Introduction." In *Witness and Memory: The Discourse of Trauma*. New York: Routledge, pp. 1–53.

El Ouazzani, A. (2004). *Le récit carcéral marocain ou le paradigme humaine*. Rabat. El Ouazzani.

El Yazami, A., A. Kabouss, and J. Akil. (2004). *D'ombre et de lumière*. Rabat: CCDH and CDIFDH.

Essaid, M. (1994). "Le conseil consultative des Droits de l'Homme: Representations des courants politiques au sein du CCDH." In D. Basri, M. Rousset, and G. Vedel, eds., *Le Maroc et les droits de l'homme*. Paris: L'Harmattan, pp. 409–48.

Feinberg, K. R. (2005). *What is Life Worth?* New York: Public Affairs.

Feitlowitz, M. (1998). *A Lexicon of Terror: Argentina and the Legacies of Torture.* Oxford: Oxford University Press.

Frei, N. (2002). *Adenauer's Germany and the Nazi Past: The Politics of Amnesty and Integration.* New York: Columbia University Press.

Gimaret, D. (1997). "Shahada." *Encyclopaedia of Islam,* new edn., vol. 9, Leiden: Brill.

Girard, R. (1977). *Violence and the Sacred.* Baltimore: Johns Hopkins University Press.

Hayner, P. (2002). *Unspeakable Truths: Facing the Challenge of Truth Commissions.* New York: Routledge.

Human Rights Watch. (2005). "Impunity in the Name of Reconciliation: Algerian President's Peace Plan Faces National Vote September 29." At Http://hrw.org/backgrounder/mena/algeria0905/index.htm.

Kleinman, T. (2002). "Did the Holocaust Play a Role in the Establishment of the State of Israel?" Available at http://www.history.ucsb.edu/projects/holocaust/Research/Proseminar/tomerkleinman.htm#_ftn30.

Otterbein, K. F., and C. S. Otterbein (1965). "An Eye for an Eye, A Tooth for a Tooth: A Cross-Cultural Study of Feuding." *American Anthropologist,* vol. 67, no. 6, pp. 1470–82.

Perrault, G. (1990). *Notre ami le roi.* Paris: Gallimard.

Posner, R. A. (1981). *The Economics of Justice.* Cambridge, MA: Harvard University Press.

Russo, H. (1991). *The Vichy Syndrome: History and Memory in France Since 1944.* Cambridge, MA: Harvard University Press.

Simmel, G. (1978). *The Philosophy of Money.* London: Routledge & Kegan Paul.

Slyomovics, S. (2001). "A Truth Commission for Morocco." *MERIP/Middle East Report,* vol. 218, pp. 18–21.

———. (2003). "No Buying Off the Past: Moroccan Indemnities and the Opposition." *Middle East Report Online,* available at: http://www.merip.org/mer/mer229/229_slyomovics.html.

———. (2005a). "The Argument from Silence: Morocco's Truth Commission and Women Political Prisoners." *Journal of Middle East Women Studies,* vol. 1, no. 3, pp. 73–95.

———. (2005b). "Morocco's Justice and Reconciliation Commission." *Middle East Report Online,* available at: http://www.merip.org/mero/mero040405.html.

———. (2005c). *The Performance of Human Rights in Morocco.* Philadelphia: University of Pennsylvania Press.

Sznaider, N. (2000). *The Compassionate Temperament: Care and Cruelty in Modern Society.* Boulder, CO: Rowman & Littlefield.

Torpey, J. (2006). *Making Whole What Has Been Smashed: On Reparation Politics.* Cambridge, MA: Harvard University Press.

Wievorka, A. (1998). *L'ère de témoin.* Paris: Plon.

Waltz, S. (1999). "Interpreting Political Reform in Morocco." In R. Bourqia and S. G. Miller, eds., *In the Shadow of the Sultan,* pp. 282–305. Cambridge, MA: Harvard University Press.

Weschler, L. (1990). *A Miracle, a Universe: Settling Accounts with Torturers.* New York: Pantheon.

Zalaquett, J. (1995). "Confronting Human Rights Violations Committed by Former Governments: Principles Applicable and Political Constraints." In

N. J. Kritz, ed., *Transitional Justice*, Washington, DC: United States Institute of Peace Press, pp. 3–31.

Zelizer, V. R. (1979). *Morals and Markets: The Development of Life Insurance in the United States.* New York: Columbia University Press.

———. (1997). *The Social Meaning of Money.* Princeton: Princeton University Press.

13. Remnants and Remains: Narratives of Suffering in Post-Genocide Rwanda's *Gacaca* Courts

LARS WALDORF

Urwishe abandi ntirukwibagiwe
(The death that has killed the others does not forget you)
Rwandan proverb

And the last remnants memory destroys
W. G. Sebald, *The Emigrants*

Introduction

The middle-aged woman who guided me around Nyamata's desecrated church, now a genocide memorial, narrated its history in garbled fragments of Kinyarwanda, French, and English, which she punctuated with mimicked sounds of gunfire and explosions. Towards the end of our tour, she scratched "35000" on her forearm to show me how many people had died here in April 1994. That onomatopoeic of violence and silent enumeration of victims underscored the limits of language in communicating and comprehending mass suffering.[1]

Those limits have been explored every week for several years as Rwandans come together in 11,000 community courts (*gacaca*) for the trials of lower-level genocide suspects. There, perpetrators offer confessions, victims level accusations, rescuers give testimonies, and bystanders keep silent. In many *gacaca* sessions, emotion is rarely on display, and remorse and forgiveness are conspicuous by their absence. Nor is there much dramatic arc to *gacaca*'s narratives of suffering. Further, in an eerie echo of the 1994 genocide, those narratives have engendered little in the way of empathy or humanitarian responses.

---

[1] See Whitehead (2004) for more on the "poetics of violence."

I want to express my gratitude to the United States Institute of Peace for generously funding my research on *gacaca*. It goes without saying that USIP is not responsible for any of the views expressed here. I also want to thank Richard Wilson for his incisive comments on an earlier draft.

I want to explore the construction and meaning of local *gacaca* narratives using ethnographic material that I have been collecting since *gacaca* started in 2002. I begin with an overview of the genocide and the current regime's instrumentalization of the genocide. Next, I discuss *gacaca* and its resulting narratives. I then compare the local narratives coming out of *gacaca* with the state's legitimating narratives on ethnicity and genocide. Finally, I explore the extent of humanitarian responses to *gacaca*'s narratives of suffering, looking at reconciliation, reparations, and international support.

Background

The Rwandan Genocide and Humanitarianism's Limits

On April 6, 1994, President Juvénal Habyarimana was returning to Rwanda after having been pressured by other African leaders to implement a peace agreement, when his plane was shot down. Hutu extremists quickly seized power and unleashed an extermination campaign against the Tutsi minority. The 1994 Rwandan genocide was remarkable for its speed, intimate violence, and widespread participation: an estimated 200,000 killers massacred at least half a million Tutsi in a mere 100 days.[2]

The Rwandan genocide was not the atavistic outbreak of African "tribalism" that many journalists first reported. Rather, it resulted from a very specific confluence of political and economic factors. First, like most twentieth century genocides, it took place in the context of war. In October 1990, the Rwandan Patriotic Front (RPF), a mostly Tutsi rebel group based in Uganda, had invaded Rwanda. In response to the RPF insurgency, President Juvenal Habyarimana's regime and its extremist allies militarized society, portrayed the Tutsi as a racial enemy, and committed local massacres against Tutsi civilians. Second, in the context of Rwanda's land scarcity and over-population, the RPF's demand for the right of return for all Tutsi refugees stoked fears among the Hutu peasantry that they would be dispossessed. Third, the country experienced drastic economic decline as a result of imposed structural adjustment programs and falling prices for export commodities. Finally, under pressure from the international community and the RPF insurgency, Habyarimana reluctantly introduced multi-party democratic reforms in the context of civil war and economic decline. The resulting intra-Hutu political discord sparked the emergence of Hutu Power, an extremist movement that sought to unite all Hutu against the Tutsi.

---

[2] The two best books on the Rwandan genocide are by Des Forges (1999) and Straus (2006). The estimates of victims and killers are taken from these books, respectively.

The genocide ended after three months with the RPF's military victory. While the RPF portrays itself as having saved Rwanda, the reality may be somewhat murkier. Evidence has come to light suggesting the RPF may have shot down Habyarimana's plane, thus (inadvertently) triggering the genocide. A French investigating magistrate charged the RPF's political and military leadership, including now President Paul Kagame, with Habyarimana's assassination (Bruguière 2006).[3] Once genocide broke out, the RPF placed its own military and political victory ahead of rescuing Tutsi civilians. General Romeo Dallaire, the head of the UN peacekeeping mission in Rwanda, remembered Kagame telling him, "If the [Tutsi] refugees have to be killed for the cause, they will be considered as having been part of the sacrifice" (Dallaire 2003: 358).

In 1994, the international community once again became a bystander to genocide – as it had fifty years earlier during the Holocaust.[4] The story is now familiar and has been popularized by films such as *Sometimes in April, Hotel Rwanda,* and *Shooting Dogs.* At the start of the genocide, the Rwandan army tortured and killed the ten Belgian peacekeepers guarding the moderate prime minister. This had the desired "Somalia" effect: Belgium withdrew its soldiers and got US backing to reduce the UN peacekeepers to a rump force. The US government also strenuously avoided using the term "genocide" for six weeks for fear that, as one internal memo put it, a "Genocide finding could commit it to actually 'do something'" (quoted in Power 2002: 359). After the genocide was safely over, a cholera epidemic killed thousands of Rwandans in refugee camps in northeastern Zaire, many of which were controlled by former *génocidaires.* Televised images of that suffering prompted a sudden wave of humanitarian action that had been so absent during the genocide.

Post-Genocide Rwanda

Since the genocide, the RPF-controlled government has accomplished the extraordinary task of rebuilding Rwanda, providing security, and spurring economic growth. Yet, for all its rhetoric of "national unity and reconciliation," the RPF has grown increasingly authoritarian and intolerant: it banned or co-opted opposition parties, silenced independent media, and restricted space for civil society (Front Line 2005; Human

---

[3] In his 2007 speech commemorating the genocide, President Kagame challenged the French without directly rebutting the magistrate's allegations: "What could have been in that plane that was worth a million lives, and gives the French the right to judge us? ... Moreover these accused [the RPF] happen to be the very people who put a stop to the 1994 genocide" (Kagame 2007).

[4] See Marrus, Chapter 7 in this volume.

Rights Watch 2003). These efforts paid off when President Kagame won 95 percent of the popular vote in the 2003 elections – amid credible reports of intimidation and fraud (EU Election Observer Mission 2004).

The RPF has instrumentalized the genocide to bolster its political legitimacy and to attack perceived opponents as *génocidaires*, proponents of genocidal ideology, or ethnic "divisionists."[5] Perhaps the most telling example was the accusation of genocidal ideology against a leading opposition MP, Dr. Leonard Hitimana, who was well known for saving Tutsi during the genocide and testifying against accused *génocidaires* at the United Nations International Criminal Tribunal for Rwanda.[6] President Kagame has reacted angrily to criticism from human rights NGOs and a few donors over the RPF's use of the term divisionism: "No one has the right to come and talk about divisionism when they kept quiet as people carried on with politics of divisionism that culminated in the death of a million people" (Kagame 2006).

The RPF not only targeted Hutu opponents, it also politically marginalized the Tutsi survivors. This seems surprising given how much of the RPF's moral and political legitimacy is derived from having stopped the genocide, but the RPF's Anglophone Tutsi leaders, who grew up in exile in Uganda and Tanzania, have an uneasy relationship with the Francophone Tutsi survivors (Prunier 1999: 358–9; Reyntjens 2004: 180). In the late 1990s, Tutsi survivors publicly opposed the RPF over the reintegration of suspected *génocidaires* into the government and military, the failure to create a reparations fund, and the RPF's manner of commemorating the genocide (Vidal 2001). The RPF reacted in 2000 by accusing prominent Tutsi elites of corruption and plotting the return of the Tutsi king from exile. Some fled, others were arrested, and one was assassinated under mysterious circumstances. That same year, the RPF installed one of its central committee members as the president of the leading survivors' organization.

Gacaca and Narratives of Suffering

Gacaca

Gacaca is a self-consciously Rwandan alternative to truth commissions and international criminal tribunals. The government rejected the idea of a

---

[5]   An overly broad definition of "genocide ideology," along with numerous examples, is presented in Senate Commission (2007: 16–17). As of April 2008, the Rwandan Parliament was debating a bill that would criminalize "genocidal ideology."

[6]   Dr. Hitimana disappeared in April 2003 as he was preparing to rebut the allegations against himself and his opposition party.

South African-style truth commission while also voting against the UN International Criminal Tribunal for Rwanda (ICTR). Instead, the Rwandan government arrested massive numbers of genocide suspects. By the end of 2000, the national courts had managed to try only 5,000 of some 120,000 detainees. In an effort to speed up trials and reduce the prison population, the government created 11,000 community courts named for *gacaca*, a largely moribund, "traditional" dispute resolution practice. *Gacaca* offers reduced sentences – including community service – to lower-level perpetrators who plead guilty.[7]

Gacaca is often portrayed as indigenous and restorative justice, much as the South African Truth and Reconciliation Commission (TRC) was depicted as an authentic expression of African harmony (*ubuntu*). President Kagame has promoted *gacaca* as a "traditional participatory system" (Kagame 2004a) to "dispense restorative justice" (Kagame 2005c) that "had served us well before colonialism" (Kagame 2005a). In fact, modern *gacaca* bears no resemblance to pre-colonial dispute resolution – other than the name. First, it is a state institution applying codified, rather than customary, law. Second, *gacaca* courts are judging serious crimes, whereas "traditional" *gacaca* mostly involved minor civil disputes. Third, *gacaca* courts impose prison sentences on individuals, whereas, in the past, customary *gacaca* awarded restitution against a wrongdoer's family or clan. Finally, the "main difference between the traditional and the new systems is probably the destruction of the social capital that underlies the traditional system" (Reyntjens & Vandeginste 2005: 118).

Gacaca is also not nearly as restorative as its proponents suggest. Unlike the South African TRC, truth-telling in *gacaca* results not in amnesty, but in criminal punishment (albeit with reduced sentences). Also, in contrast to the TRC, *gacaca* is one-sided victor's justice: it cannot hear allegations of war crimes committed by the RPF. Finally, *gacaca* is highly coercive: people who do not attend or participate are threatened with fines or imprisonment.

Following a lengthy pilot phase, *gacaca* was launched nationwide in January 2005 and trials finally got under way throughout the country in July 2006. *Gacaca* started with a lengthy pretrial stage, where elected lay judges heard accusations and confessions and then compiled local histories of the genocide. The judges eventually ranked the accused according to the severity of their crimes and sent their dossiers to the appropriate jurisdictions for trial: the national courts for those who allegedly planned the

---

[7] For detailed descriptions of *gacaca*, see Avocats sans Frontières (2005), Penal Reform International (2005), and Waldorf (2006).

genocide; the upper-level *gacaca* courts for those accused of murder, manslaughter, or assault; and the lower-level *gacaca* courts for property crimes.

Gacaca's Narrative Constraints

Gacaca was supposed to produce public narratives of suffering, repentance, and forgiveness on Rwanda's hills. In reality, however, the production of those narratives was inevitably constrained by culture, politics, coercion, and fear. *Gacaca's* insistence on public truth telling is deeply at odds with Rwanda's "pervasive" culture of secrecy (De Lame 2005: 14–15).[8] One anthropologist described Rwandan society as "administrative groupings of nuclear families, devoid of a collective spirit and rife with suspicion" (Pottier quoted in Eltringham & Van Hoyweghen 2001: 218). Hypocrisy and deception are considered admirable and prudent traits in Rwandan culture for maintaining good social relations (Overdulve 1997: 279–80, 282).

Gacaca narratives are especially shaped by what the legal anthropologist Sally Falk Moore once termed "the micropolitics of local standing" (1992: 11). In small communities, people are most concerned with demonstrating loyalty to kin and patrons. On Rwanda's hills, these micropolitics play out against the backdrop of pervasive secrecy, mutual suspicion, and occasional denunciation. A team of Rwandan researchers found that during *gacaca* sessions, "the sentiment of not wanting to attract enemies (*kutiteranya*) prevailed within the general population" (Karekezi, Nshimiyimana, & Mutamba 2004: 79). For example, a woman refused to answer questions about her son in *gacaca*, saying, "If my son participated in the genocide, it is his affair. Me, I cannot be a traitor to the family which gave me milk" (Gitarama *gacaca*, October 2002).[9]

The Rwandan government has also imposed political constraints by insisting that *gacaca* can only hear narratives of suffering from genocide survivors. Local officials and *gacaca* judges cut off or disregard testimonies about the suffering of Hutu refugees in the Democratic Republic of the Congo, Hutu suspects in overcrowded prisons, and Hutu victims of RPF killings. In a *gacaca* I attended in 2002, two judges described how a family member had been "disappeared" by RPF soldiers. When they asked why *gacaca* could not handle their loss, an official explained, "*Gacaca* treats

---

[8] "Traditional" *gacaca* normally involved community elders and family heads, not the entire community.

[9] Quotes from *gacaca* proceedings and interviews were collected by me or my research assistants. In order to protect my research assistants and our informants, none of those quotes have been attributed (or labeled precisely by date or place).

uniquely the question of genocide and massacres" (Gitarama *gacaca*, July 2002). In 2004, the government amended the *gacaca* law and removed *gacaca*'s jurisdiction over war crimes, which the population had understood to mean RPF killings. Not surprisingly, many Hutu resent *gacaca*'s one-sided focus on genocide victims (Longman & Rutagengwa 2004: 176).[10]

Though meant to be participatory, *gacaca* has been deeply unpopular.[11] In one *gacaca* session, a participant plaintively observed, "Let me point out that this number here in *gacaca* is small compared to the number of people who used to go for attacks [during the genocide] when an alarm was made" (Gitarama *gacaca*, January 2003). On one occasion, I saw farmers running into banana groves to hide from local officials who were rounding people up for *gacaca* (Kibuye *gacaca*, September 2005). Even when people were forced to show up, there was no guarantee they would speak up – despite sanctions for witnesses who kept silent. During a *gacaca* session, a local official chastised the assembled crowd: "These people died during the day. These people did not commit suicide. No one says anything" (Butare *gacaca*, September 2002). Silence is a means of self-preservation. Survivors and perpetrators often live side by side, and they fear retaliation, one from the other.[12] Perpetrators also feared their former accomplices. One confessed *génocidaire* told a *gacaca* court: "Is it really possible that I participated in the massacres alone! Why am I threatened by the people who accompanied me in the massacres?" (Byumba *gacaca*, August 2006).

Perpetrator, Survivor, and Rescuer Narratives in *Gacaca*

Gacaca narratives tend to be resolutely parochial, highly elliptical, and thus largely incomprehensible to outsiders (Wilson 2001: 49; 1997: 139). The contextualized, historicized social actors in these narratives are a far cry from the universalized individuals depicted in human rights and refugee reporting for whom a reader can feel immediate empathy (Dudai, Chapter 11, & Sandvik, Chapter 10 in this volume; Malkki 2002; Wilson 1997: 145–53). Furthermore, *gacaca* narratives are rarely intended to evoke sympathy or empathy in listeners. The absence of drama and sentiment (ality) is partly cultural as Rwandans consider public displays of emotion to be shameful (Overdulve 1997: 279–80, 282).

[10] See also Penal Reform International (2004: 44–7).
[11] The vast majority of Rwandans are subsistence farmers who would rather spend their days working their fields or doing itinerant labor to survive. Furthermore, many Rwandans (including Tutsi survivors) do not foresee any benefits from *gacaca*.
[12] Survivors, witnesses, and even *gacaca* judges have been killed or intimidated, and, in a few instances, that provoked violent reprisals (see Human Rights Watch 2007).

Perpetrator narratives in *gacaca* mostly evoke what Hannah Arendt famously and controversially called "the banality of evil." Their testimonies are often a chronology of comings and goings, the mundane rhythms of everyday life punctuated by episodes of extraordinary violence. As one confessed perpetrator testified:

> It was the 11th of April, 1994, very early in the morning. I went to my paternal aunt at X. Towards 2 pm, my aunt gave me some food and I returned. . . . Towards 4 pm, I went out walking and I went into the banana plantation of BK and I took 4 bananas. Towards 5:30 pm I saw an attack composed of [list of names] – those are whom I remember. G came to find me at my house to go on the *irondo* [night patrol]. We went to the house of T. T came out of his house and saw us. N, K, TW entered in the house and came out with 2 girls . . . hitting them while demanding to know where the others were who had hidden with them. They responded they did not know where they were. The attack got larger. . . . We continued to S's house. There, the attack made other persons leave the house. A in the company of her small son asked TW that, before killing them, it was first necessary to protect a [Hutu] child. She continued to demand pardon but in vain. . . . N killed them all with a blow and T and V finished them off with *massues* [nail-studded clubs]. We took them and threw them in a trench. (Byumba *gacaca*, September 2006)

This narrative is quite typical: ordinary perpetrators generally explain their participation in terms of group conformity, describing how neighbors came to get them to join patrols, barriers, and massacres.[13] In addition, these perpetrators "often referred to the violence around them in a detached fashion and often portrayed it as violence without agents" (Straus & Lyons 2006: 21–22). For example, one confessed génocidaire told the assembled community in *gacaca*, "if God wants, then people die" (Byumba *gacaca*, October 2002).

Survivor testimonies are usually more fragmentary than perpetrator testimonies. Typically, they were not eyewitnesses because they were in hiding or on the run. As one survivor plaintively demanded: "There were many people by then when my child died. I was in hiding and I was able to learn of this from friends. Why can't these people speak the truth?" (Butare *gacaca*, September 2002).

Survivor testimony sometimes comes from Hutu who lost Tutsi family members, especially Hutu widows, who are often rejected by their Hutu family members and shunned by their surviving Tutsi in-laws.[14] Other times, survivor testimony comes from Hutu who were attacked because

---

[13] This is consistent with Straus' findings in his studies of confessed and convicted *génocidaires* (Straus 2006; Straus & Lyons 2006), as well as with Browning's account of a German police battalion in Nazi-occupied Poland (Browning 1992).

[14] See Aghion (2002).

they resisted the genocide. In one *gacaca*, a would-be rescuer testified: "They told me to show that I am Hutu by killing M. I refused. I threw the *massue* in front of them. They counted three times for me to kill M and, if not, they would kill me. S hit me with blows from a machete. K hit me and the others tortured me." Such local narratives complicate and implicitly challenge the RPF's representations and the international community's understandings of the 1994 genocide, which characterize the Hutu as collectively guilty.

Legitimating Narratives and *Gacaca's* Counter-Narratives
State Legitimation
Post-genocide Rwanda, like many other post-authoritarian and post-conflict states, does not fit the teleological transitional paradigm, in which successor regimes are assumed to be democratizing (Carothers 2002). Consequently, *gacaca* and other transitional justice mechanisms need to be seen as important elements of the new regime's legitimation strategies. As Wilson emphasized in his study of the South African TRC, "We should ... examine how the politics of punishment and the writing of a new official memory are central to state strategies to create a new hegemony in the area of justice and construct the present moment as post-authoritarian when it includes many elements of the past" (2001: xv–xvi). Such an examination is particularly important when it comes to Rwanda, as the RPF regime has proved so adept at "converting international feelings of guilt and ineptitude [over the 1994 genocide] into admissions that the [Rwandan Patriotic] Front deserves to have the monopoly on knowledge construction" (Pottier 2002: 202).

The new Rwandan regime's moral and political legitimacy is founded on a compelling narrative comprised of five key themes: Tutsi suffering and sacrifice from the 1959 "Hutu Revolution" to the 1994 genocide; Hutu collective guilt for the genocide; the RPF's defeat of the genocidal forces; the international community's betrayal; and the RPF's commitment to non-ethnic "national unity and reconciliation."[15] President Kagame sounds these themes again and again in his speeches, especially those given each April to commemorate the genocide.

At the national level, *gacaca* has reinforced the state's legitimating narrative by imposing collective guilt on the Hutu, which justifies authoritarian minority rule and a high degree of social control. As a result of *gacaca*, the number of genocide suspects has increased seven-fold – from

---

[15] These themes are eloquently repackaged by Gourevitch (1998).

120,000 in 2000 to 818,000 by late 2005 (National Service of *Gacaca*
Jurisdiction 2006).[16] To put it more starkly, a quarter of the adult Hutu
population stands accused of genocide. *Gacaca* has wildly inflated the
number of genocide suspects by including 300,000 persons accused solely
of property crimes and an untold number of bystanders.[17] Furthermore,
gacaca is beset by false accusations, which serve as "weapons of the weak" in
Rwanda's impoverished and divided communities. As a prominent
Rwandan academic acknowledged, "There are survivors who visibly lie and
other survivors say so. . . . Family members denounce their own kith and
kin over land – the demographic pressures come into play."[18] Although
gacaca has legitimated RPF rule, it has not created a hegemonic discourse.
For, at the local level, *gacaca* has produced counter-narratives and revealed
"hidden transcripts" (Scott 1992).

Suppressing and Reinscribing Ethnicity
Seeking to create a new foundational myth for post-genocide Rwanda, the
RPF hearkens back to an imagined, pre-colonial Rwandan unity and
blames Belgian colonizers and the Catholic Church for creating ethnic
divisions between Hutu and Tutsi (Eltringham 2004: 12–27; Longman &
Rutagengwa 2004: 164–6; Pottier 2002: 110–23). President Kagame makes
this point repeatedly in his speeches:

> . . . the most characteristic feature of Rwanda and Rwandans is that, before
> colonialism, we had always been a united people for over five centuries.
> . . . This harmonious coexistence was disrupted by the advent of the colo-
> nialists, who deliberately chose to divide us . . . In Rwanda, this policy had a
> devastating effect because, for the first time, the notion of one nation was
> shattered, as the idea of ethnic groups was introduced . . . . (Kagame 2004b)

Yet, this account conveniently ignores the fact that "ethnic polarization, and
more generally the politicization of ethnicity, was instituted under [the Tutsi
king] Rwabugiri" (Pottier 2002: 112). The RPF's revisionist history is meant
"not only to mask the *pre-colonial origins of ethnicity in Rwanda*, but also to
intellectually justify a system of leadership by Tutsi minority rule" (111).

---

[16] By contrast, Straus (2006: 116–18) estimated that 175,000 to 210,000 perpetrators were
responsible for most of the killing – an enormous number to be sure, but not one that
justifies collective guilt.

[17] The *gacaca* law defines accomplice liability broadly and makes bystanders criminally liable.
Thus, someone who was merely present (perhaps under duress) at a roadblock where
Tutsi were killed can receive the same sentence as those who did the killings there.

[18] Alice Karekezi, then Director of the Center for Conflict Management, National University
of Rwanda (Butare), CLADHO Conference on *Gacaca*, Kigali, February 14, 2003.

The RPF's stated goal is a non-ethnic society that will usher in the harmony that existed before colonialism and so prevent future ethnic violence. Under the RPF, ethnicity has become a taboo subject, with references to Hutu and Tutsi seen as "divisionism" or even "genocidal ideology." As President Kagame made clear, "We are calculating a new outlook that is Rwandan, and not ethnic" (Kagame 2004a). This denial of ethnicity also serves the legitimating needs of a minority (Anglophone Tutsi) regime anxious to portray itself as "a government of national unity and reconciliation" for the "Rwandan people." Thus, when the RPF's first post-genocide president (a Hutu) resigned and then criticized the RPF for favoring a small Tutsi clique and turning Hutu into "second class citizens" (Bizimungu 2001: 27), he wound up in prison for five years.

The suppression of ethnicity in the RPF's historical and reconciliation narratives is contradicted by the RPF's genocide narrative, which rein-scribes a polarized ethnic identity by largely treating Tutsi as collectively victimized and Hutu as collectively guilty (Eltringham 2004: 75–6; Eltringham & Van Hoyweghen 2001: 226; Pottier 2002: 150). Obviously, it would be difficult to talk about the Rwandan genocide without mentioning the targeted Tutsi ethnicity,[19] but what is problematic is the tendency to conflate all Tutsi with victims and all Hutu with perpetrators.[20] To a large extent, the RPF has replaced the ethnic labeling of the past (Hutu-Tutsi) with new labels (*génocidaire*-victim) that further reinforce ethnic difference (Eltringham 2004: 72–99).

The ascription of collective guilt to the Hutu majority is most evident in the RPF's use of the term "Hutu moderates." As Eltringham observes, "The phrase 'Hutu moderates' is only used *retrospectively* .... It is solely an epitaph and may imply that the only 'moderate' (or 'anti-genocide') Hutu are dead" (2004: 75–6). While the RPF has been more willing to acknowledge (living) Hutu rescuers and genocide opponents in recent years,[21] this is undercut by attacks on the best-known rescuers. The most prominent example is President Kagame's repeated denunciations of Paul Rusesabagina, the Hutu hotel manager who saved Tutsi at the Hotel des Milles Collines and who was por-trayed in the feature film *Hotel Rwanda*. In his genocide commemoration speech in 2007, President Kagame extended his critique of Rusesabagina to

[19] On some occasions, however, President Kagame elides ethnicity by describing the genocide in terms of Rwandans: for example, in a 2006 speech, he stated that "the citizens of the country" were mobilized "into killing their fellow Rwandans" (Kagame 2006).

[20] Pottier (2002) has also shown how humanitarian actors and journalists after the genocide bought into, and further reinforced, the notion of Hutu refugees as collectively guilty.

[21] Compare Kagame (2006) with Vidal (2001).

the international community (and implicitly to George Bush, who awarded Rusesabagina the Presidential Medal of Freedom):

> I wish to request foreigners who use Rwandans harbouring negative ideology to stop meddling in our history and cease trying to distort it. ... It is sad to see foreigners taking a self-seeking person like Rusesabagina, who did not save a single soul, and making him a hero of the genocide – and, of course, he has other greedy people who follow him. (Kagame 2007; see also George 2006)

When confronted with an opposition parliamentarian like Dr. Leonard Hitimana, who saved Tutsi during the genocide, the RPF resorted to accusations of "genocidal ideology."

Gacaca narratives undermine the simplistic dichotomy of Tutsi victims and Hutu perpetrators. They show how individuals (more often Hutu, but sometimes Tutsi) could be (simultaneously or sequentially) perpetrators, victims, bystanders, *and* rescuers. Some Hutu lost close family members, while others were targeted directly because they opposed the genocide or tried to save Tutsi. Some individual Hutu killed Tutsi strangers, while rescuing or losing their Tutsi friends and relatives. This is less surprising once we recognize the extent of interethnic social and economic relations (including intermarriage) on Rwanda's hills before 1994.

Explaining Genocide

The RPF explains the genocide by reference to six key factors: ethnic hatred sowed by colonialism; multi-party democracy; hate media; "bad leadership"; an uneducated peasantry inculcated in habits of obedience; and the international community's "betrayal" in 1994. The RPF repeatedly deploys this official narrative to legitimize the RPF's monopoly of power and information, justify reeducation of the population through solidarity camps and sensibilizations, and encourage penitent generosity among international donors.

The RPF's account of the genocide conveniently ignores the importance of the civil war and Habyarimana's assassination, which, as Straus (2006) convincingly argues, made it much easier for Hutu extremists to seize power and opt for genocide. By contrast, most people on the hills – even Tutsi survivors – use the Kinyarwanda terms for war and killings.[22] For

---

[22] Kinyarwanda has no word for genocide, so the RPF has promoted three neologisms: first, *itsembabwoko* (extermination of an ethnicity), then *itsembabwoko n'itsembatsemba* (extermination of an ethnicity and extermination here and there), and, most recently, *genosidi* (genocide) (Twagiramungu 2006). This shift in terminology may reflect an official repudiation of *ubwoko* (ethnicity), but it also may be linked to a misunderstanding among some Rwandans that *itsembatsemba* referred to RPF killings (Twagiramungu 2006).

example, one confessed perpetrator told the *gacaca* court: "In 1994, there was the war (*intambara*). I participated in the killings (*ubwicanyi*) and I pillaged" (Byumba *gacaca*, August 2006). For many Rwandans, the genocide is not a short historical rupture of three months in 1994, but rather the culmination of the civil war that began in October 1990 with the RPF invasion from Uganda (Longman & Rutagengwa 2004: 162, 172). But the reference to the war is politically charged for it implicitly lays some of the blame for the genocide on the RPF.

Gacaca narratives also make clear that much of the genocidal violence at the local level was not driven by ethnic hatred or obedience. Rather, perpetrators often took opportunistic advantage of the genocide and war to settle personal scores and local disputes that had little to do with anti-Tutsi ideology (Straus 2006). Furthermore, these narratives contest the notion that Rwandan peasants are steeped in habits of obedience – a view that would deny individual agency and so contribute to collective Hutu guilt. Rather than obedience, the *gacaca* narratives suggest that group conformity and duress were the key factors driving participation of ordinary Rwandans.[23] A Belgian anthropologist, who did extensive ethnographic fieldwork in Rwanda before 1990, termed Rwanda a "conformist country" (De Lame 2005: 474).

Humanitarian Responses to *Gacaca* Narratives

Reconciliation

Gacaca was meant to generate reconciliation through public truth telling accompanied by expressions of remorse from perpetrators. Those expectations were unrealistic given Rwandan culture, which privileges secrecy and guarded emotions. *Gacaca*, like the South African TRC, leaned heavily on the modern (and largely Western) notion that truth telling is therapeutic for individuals as well as local and national communities. Yet, there is scant empirical evidence that (truthful) narratives of suffering help (re)humanize the other, producing empathy and humanitarianism across communities divided by past conflict (Wilson 2001; Stover & Weinstein 2004).

Hutu and Tutsi often have different attitudes towards the genocide, civil war, justice, and reconciliation (Longman & Rutagengwa 2004: 170–8), and both groups have difficulty seeing past their own notions of collective victimization to comprehend the suffering of the other group. In one

---

[23] This dovetails with Straus' findings (2006).

gacaca proceeding, for example, a Hutu witness evinced little empathy for genocide victims and talked about his own suffering instead:

> *Witness*: On returning to Kigali, I learned they were dead, but I was busy repairing my house. . . .
> Gacaca *Judge*: That shows disinterest. You could have informed yourself about the death of your neighbors.
> *Witness*: If you find your house in ruins, the first preoccupation is to rebuild it. (Kigali *gacaca*, September 2006)

Gacaca also seems to reinforce each group's feelings of victimization. Many survivors consider *gacaca* a disguised amnesty for those who killed their family members, while many Hutu fear being accused and resent *gacaca*'s one-sided focus on genocide victims. On a few occasions, Hutu witnesses justified their lack of empathy for genocide victims by making reference to the unacknowledged victims of the RPF:

> Gacaca *President*: Why did you not have pity to know about his death?
> *Witness*: There also were other assassinations in our region. That of X was not the only one.

Such statements, in turn, increase the bitterness of Tutsi genocide survivors.

The government has tried to make perpetrator confessions more meaningful to survivors by requiring public apologies, but most apologies are "formulaic" (Karekezi, Nshimiyimana, & Mutamba 2004: 79). Occasionally, they even sound more like demands than pleas for forgiveness. For example, one confessed prisoner became testy with the insistence that he show remorse, saying "I've already confessed what I did, so I don't understand what other things you want from me" (Byumba *gacaca*, October 2002). Klaas de Jonge, an anthropologist who monitored *gacaca* for several years, told me: "The accused think because they ask for forgiveness, they are entitled to forgiveness. You hear these people confessing as if they are describing a movie. There's absolutely no compassion" (Interview, Kigali, September 2002). In many cases, survivors have reacted to the lack of sincerity and remorse by challenging the truthfulness of confessions.[24]

Some government officials have blamed untruthful testimonies for *gacaca*'s difficulties, but the problem goes deeper than that. After the genocide, it was hard enough for survivors, perpetrators, bystanders, and rescuers to remain living together in small communities, bound together by

---

[24] *Gacaca* courts usually imposed the maximum sentence (25–30 years) on perpetrators whose confessions were judged incomplete.

mutual impoverishment, but even that *modus vivendi* has been disrupted by accusations and counter-accusations in *gacaca*. Hutu and Tutsi survivors do most of the talking in *gacaca* sessions, while their Hutu neighbors remain silent or defend the accused – a dynamic that only reinforces mistrust between the two groups. *Gacaca* proceedings have caused a worsening of interethnic social relations in several communities. During some sessions I attended, survivors sat apart from their neighbors. One *gacaca* president warned, "Many people don't want to talk of what they saw in *gacaca* but talk of it at beer places. . . . I don't want you to open *gacaca* in the beer places where you end up fighting" (Gitarama *gacaca*, January 2003). From February through April 2005, an estimated 19,000 briefly fled Rwanda, mostly in response to rumors that they would be accused in *gacaca* or killed in revenge after being named in *gacaca*.

Reparations

While the government and international donors have spent millions of dollars incarcerating and trying genocide suspects, there is still no compensation fund for genocide survivors.[25] *Gacaca*'s accumulating narratives of suffering have not pressured the Rwandan government or the international community into providing monetary or in-kind compensation to the survivors. This reflects the government's lack of political will and resources, the weakness of the survivors' organizations, and the resistance of *gacaca* narratives to easy media representations.

High-level government officials insist the country cannot afford a reparations fund. As the head of the National Unity and Reconciliation Commission explained to me, "The will from the government is there, but the challenge is funding for that . . . because Rwanda is a poor country." This does not convince leaders of the survivors' organization. One told me, "There's no money and there's no will." Another stated, "The government says it is poor. That doesn't satisfy us. It is being killed two times" (Interviews, Kigali, June 2006).

The government, however, has increased symbolic reparations to genocide survivors by making *gacaca*'s reduced sentences for confessed perpetrators dependent on locating the remains of those they killed. During the genocide, many victims were tossed into pit latrines and anti-erosion ditches or left scattered on the hillsides. What genocide survivors want most, apart from compensation, is to find the remains of their loved ones and to rebury them with dignity. The largest survivors' organization, which has an

---

[25] The government does contribute 5% of its budget to a rehabilitation fund for needy survivors, who are provided with free education and health care.

understandably ambivalent stance toward *gacaca*, has credited it with helping survivors to locate their dead.

At a September 2006 *gacaca* trial, the presiding *gacaca* judge told an accused "For you to be innocent, it is necessary that the bodies be found." The accused had overheard other detainees talking about where they had thrown the bodies of a Tutsi family. After being provisionally released, he informed the local authorities and survivors. After days of digging, the bodies were not found, and the survivors then accused him of complicity in the family's murder. The accused apologized, but continued to maintain his innocence: "You are sad about what happened. I understand you, but it is not a reason to accuse me of everything. . . . It's me who said to continue digging. And that hurt the family. I take this occasion to demand pardon . . ." (Kigali *gacaca*, September 2006). This exchange demonstrated how the suffering of survivors is often intertwined with the suffering of those who may be falsely accused.[26] Here, in a rare moment of empathy, the accused was able to look past his suffering and recognize that of the survivors.

International Support for *Gacaca*

International donors – particularly Belgium, the Netherlands, and the European Union – have given Rwanda millions of dollars for *gacaca* partly on the humanitarian grounds that *gacaca* promised to reduce prison overcrowding, bring justice for survivors, and further reconciliation. Yet, even as it became apparent that *gacaca* would swell the ranks of the accused and worsen ethnic tensions, donors continued financing *gacaca*. This partly reflects what one Rwanda scholar has called the "genocide credit" (Reyntjens 2004: 199). The RPF constantly reminds donors that they have no moral standing to second guess government policy or question its human rights record given their lack of humanitarian intervention in 1994.

> So there are human rights violations, but it is still not right for outsiders to pass judgement on Rwanda today. If the international community had acted [to stop the genocide], the Human Rights violations of 1994 would not have taken place. (Former justice official, quoted in Pottier 2002: 177)

> Rwanda is a special case and deserves special consideration. Obligations under international law have not been respected in regard to Rwanda. (Kagame 2004b)

The genocide credit, however, does not fully explain why *gacaca* has garnered so much international acclaim.

---

[26] I do not mean to suggest, however, that these sufferings are comparable.

Gacaca has been touted as a possible transitional justice model for other post-conflict states by a wide range of policymakers, including such odd bedfellows as the International Criminal Court Prosecutor and the Bush Administration's first Ambassador-at-Large for War Crimes. The United Nations praised *gacaca* in 2006 for having "helped bring Rwandan society together to rebuild trust, share the truth about the genocide and provide access to justice to the public" (UN 2006: 130). These plaudits reflect the international community's disillusionment with expensive and inefficient international criminal tribunals, a romanticizing of the "traditional," and wishful thinking about an "African renaissance." President Kagame has skillfully played on these themes in some of his speeches:

> First of all, we must recognise that ... there can never be a "one-size-fits-all" prescription for conflict resolution. ... Second, any approach to conflict resolution must be locally driven, people-centred and people-owned. ... Third, we Africans must learn to find African solutions to African problems, and only invite the international community to complement our own efforts. (Kagame 2005c)

Gacaca's failings underscore the need to look past such pan-Africanist rhetoric and distinguish clearly between "locally driven" conflict resolution and state-imposed informalism designed to expand the state's reach into local communities. In fact, *gacaca* looks awfully familiar to other disappointing experiments with modernized village courts in many post-colonial states in Africa and Asia.

Seen in this light, *gacaca*'s problems are similar to those encountered in other state efforts to modernize local, informal justice mechanisms: increased formalism, decreased popular participation, and increased state coercion. Though, of course, *gacaca* faces considerably more hurdles given the widespread destruction of people, property, and social capital in the genocide and civil war.

Conclusion

Gacaca was meant to produce public narratives of suffering about the genocide, but that necessarily presupposed the willingness of people to show up, speak up, *and* tell the truth.

The narratives are mostly banal, fragmentary, parochial, and, in keeping with Rwandan culture, unsentimental. While, at the local level, *gacaca* narratives revealed hidden transcripts and contradictions in the state's legitimating narratives, the government has used *gacaca* to impose collective guilt on the Hutu majority and suppress accountability for war crimes against Hutu civilians. Donors who funded *gacaca* thus became complicit in an authoritarian regime's legitimation strategies. Furthermore, *gacaca*'s narratives of suffering have not provoked humanitarian responses, whether in the form of reconciliation or reparations.

Gacaca narratives illuminate the larger debate over the communicability of suffering and its concomitant ability to provoke humanitarian responses. Scarry has argued that torture and pain destroy our very ability to communicate (1987). Nordstrom challenged that notion based on fieldwork in Mozambique: "terror-warfare is employed precisely because pain is communicated, that one victim can victimize a community at large" (1997: 170–1). For Nordstrom, pain's communicability not only enlarges the scope of suffering, it also offers a way to transform it. She has described how Mozambican victims and communities used discursive traditions to redefine violence for peace-building (xviii, 6). If Scarry is overly pessimistic about the communicability of suffering, then Nordstrom is overly optimistic about the redemptive possibilities of narratives of suffering to remake individuals and communities after mass violence. *Gacaca* sadly demonstrates how public narratives can communicate suffering without remaking communities or attracting humanitarian attention.

REFERENCES

Aghion, A. (2002). Gacaca, *Living Together Again in Rwanda*. Documentary film.

Avocats Sans Frontiéres (2005). *Monitoring des Juridictions Gacaca, Phase de Jugement, Rapport Analytique, Mars-Septembre 2005*. Available at: http://www.asf.be/FR/FRnews/rapport_monitoring_gacaca_mars_sept_2005.pdf.

Bizimungu, P. (2001). "Je suis prêt à payer le prix fort." *Jeune Afrique/L'Intelligent*, no. 2112, July 3–9.

Browning, C. R. (1992). *Ordinary Men: Reserve Police Battalion 101 and the Final Solution in Poland*. New York: Harper Perennial.

Bruguière, J.-L. (2006). "Délivrance de mandats d'arrêt internationaux," November 17. Available at: http://www.medias.lemonde.fr/mmpub/edt/doc/20061127/838957_rwanda-rapport-bruguiere.pdf.

Carothers, T. (2002). "The End of the Transition Paradigm." *Journal of Democracy*, vol. 13, no. 1, pp. 5–21.

Dallaire, R. (2003). *Shake Hands with the Devil: The Failure of Humanity in Rwanda*. Toronto: Random House.

De Lame, D. (2005). *A Hill among a Thousand: Transformations and Ruptures in Rural Rwanda*. Madison: University of Wisconsin Press.

Des Forges, A. (1999). *Leave None to Tell the Story: Genocide in Rwanda*. New York: Human Rights Watch.

Eltringham, N. (2004). *Accounting for Horror: Post-Genocide Debates in Rwanda*. London: Pluto Press.

Eltringham, N., and S. Van Hoyweghen (2001). "Power & Identity in Post-Genocide Rwanda." In R. Doom and J. Gorus, eds., *Politics of Identity and Economics of Conflict in the Great Lakes Region.* Brussels: VUB Press.

European Union Election Observer Mission (2004). *Rapport Final: Rwanda, Election Présidentielle 25 août 2003, Elections Legislatives 29 et 30 septembre.* Available at: http://europa.eu.int/comm/external_relations/human_rights/eu_election_ass_observ/rwanda/index.htm.

Front Line (2005). *Front Line Rwanda: Disappearances, Arrests, Threats, Intimidation and Co-option of Human Rights Defenders, 2001–2004.* Dublin. Available at: www.frontlinedefenders.org/pdfs/1965Front%20Line%20Rwanda%20Report.pdf.

George, T. (2006). "Smearing a Hero: Sad Revisionism Over 'Hotel Rwanda.'" *Washington Post,* May 10.

Gourevitch, P. (1998). *We Wish To Inform You that Tomorrow We Will Be Killed With Our Families.* New York: Farrar, Strauss & Giroux.

Human Rights Watch (2003). *Preparing for Elections: Tightening Control in the Name of Unity.* New York. Available at: http://www.hrw.org/backgrounder/africa/rwanda0503bck.htm.

Human Rights Watch (2007). *Killings in Eastern Rwanda.* January. New York. Available at: http://www.hrw.org/backgrounder/africa/rwanda0107/.

Kagame, P. (2004a). "Speech by His Excellency President Paul Kagame at the University of Washington." April 22. Available at: http://www.gov.rw/government/president /speeches/2004/17_04_04_us_speech.html.

———. (2004b). "Speech by His Excellency Paul Kagame, President of the Republic of Rwanda, at the Woodrow Wilson International Centre for Scholars." April 21. Available at: http://www.gov.rw/government/president /speeches/2004/18_04_04_us_speech.html.

———. (2005a). "The Challenges of Human Rights in Rwanda after the 1994 Genocide. Speech by His Excellency Paul Kagame, President of the Republic of Rwanda at the University of Connecticut." September 19. Available at: http://www.gov.rw/government/president /speeches/2005/19_09_05_connect.html.

———. (2005b). "Managing Ethnic Relations and National Reconciliation in Post-Genocide Rwanda: Lessons for Conflict Resolution in the Great Lakes Region. Speech by His Excellency Paul Kagame, President of the Republic of Rwanda, at California State University – Sacramento." April 14. Available at: http://www.gov.rw/government/president /speeches/2005/14_04_05_califonia.html.

———. (2005c). "Prospects for peace in the Great Lakes Region: A perspective from Rwanda. Speech by His Excellency Paul Kagame, President of the Republic of Rwanda, at the National War College." April 18. Available at: http://www.gov.rw/government/president /speeches/2005/18_04_05_war_college.html.

———. (2006). "Address by His Excellency Paul Kagame, President of the Republic of Rwanda, at the Twelfth Commemoration of the Rwandan Genocide." April 7. Available at: http://www.gov.rw/government/president /speeches/2006/07_04_06_genocide.html.

———. (2007). "Remarks by His Excellency Paul Kagame, President of the Republic of Rwanda at the 13th Commemoration of the Genocide of 1994." April 7. Available at: http://www.gov.rw/government/president/speeches/2007/07_04_07_murambi_genocide_.html.

Karekezi, U. A., A. Nshimiyimana and B. Mutamba. (2004). "Localizing Justice: *Gacaca* Courts in Post-genocide Rwanda." In E. Stover and H. Weinstein, eds., *My Neighbor, My Enemy: Justice and Community in the Aftermath of Mass Atrocity.* Cambridge: Cambridge University Press.

Longman, T., and Rutagengwa, T. (2004). "Memory, Identity and Community in Rwanda." In E. Stover and H. M. Weinstein, eds., *My Neighbor, My Enemy: Justice and Community in the Aftermath of Mass Atrocity.* Cambridge: Cambridge University Press.

Malkki, L. H. (2002). "Speechless Emissaries: Refugees, Humanitarianism, and Dehistoricization." In A. L. Hinton, ed., *Genocide: An Anthropological Reader.* Oxford: Blackwell.

Moore, S. F. (1992). "Treating Law as Knowledge: Telling Colonial Officers What to Say to Africans about Running 'Their Own' Native Courts." *Law & Society Review,* vol. 26, no. 1, pp. 11–46.

National Service of *Gacaca* Jurisdictions. (2006). *Report on Data Collection in Gacaca Courts.* Kigali.

Nordstrom, C. (1997). *A Different Kind of War Story.* Philadelphia: University of Pennsylvania Press.

Overdulve, C. M. (1997). "Fonction de la langue et de la communication au Rwanda." *Nouvelle Revue de Science Missionaire,* vol. 53.

Penal Reform International (2004). *Report on Monitoring and Research on the Gacaca: The Righteous: Between Oblivion and Reconciliation? Example of the Province of Kibuye.* London/Kigali.

————. (2005). *Rapport de Synthèse de Monitoring et de Recherche sur la Gacaca: Phase Pilote Janvier 2002-Decembre 2004.* London/Kigali.

Pottier, J. (2002). *Re-imagining Rwanda: Conflict, Survival and Disinformation in the Late Twentieth Century.* Cambridge: Cambridge University Press.

Power, S. (2002) *"A Problem from Hell": America and the Age of Genocide.* New York: Basic Books.

Prunier, G. (1999). *The Rwanda Crisis: History of a Genocide.* New York: Columbia University Press.

Reyntjens, F. (2004). "Rwanda, Ten Years On: From Genocide to Dictatorship." *African Affairs,* vol. 103, no. 411, pp. 177–210.

Reyntjens, F., and S. Vandeginste (2005). "Rwanda: An Atypical Transition." In E. Skaar, S. Gloppen, and A. Suhrke, eds., *Roads to Reconciliation.* Lanham: Lexington.

Senate Commission (2007). *Genocide Ideology and Strategies for Its Eradication.* Kigali.

Scarry, E. (1987). *The Body in Pain: The Making and Unmaking of the World.* New York: Oxford University Press.

Scott, J. C. (1992). *Domination and the Arts of Resistance: Hidden Transcripts.* New Haven: Yale University Press.

Stover, E. and H. Weinstein, eds. (2004). *My Neighbor, My Enemy: Justice and Community in the Aftermath of Mass Atrocity.* New York: Cambridge University Press.

Straus, S. (2006). *The Order of Genocide: Race, Power, and War in Rwanda.* Ithaca: Cornell University Press.

Straus, S., and R. Lyons (2006). *Intimate Enemy: Images and Voices of the Rwandan Genocide.* New York: Zone Books.

Twagiramungu, N. (2006). "Naming the Unspeakable: How Do Rwandans Understand and Call Their Genocide?" Unpublished draft manuscript.

U.N. Office of the High Representative for Least Developed Countries, Landlocked Developing Countries and Small Island Developing States & U.N. Development Program (2006). *Governance for the Future: Democracy and Development in the Least Developed Countries.* New York.

Vidal, C. (2001). "Les Commemorations du Genocide au Rwanda." *Les Temps Modernes.*

Waldorf, L. (2006). "Mass Justice for Mass Atrocity: Rethinking Local Justice as Transitional Justice." *Temple Law Review,* vol. 79.

Whitehead, N. L. (2004). "On the Poetics of Violence." In N. L. Whitehead, ed., *Violence.* Oxford: James Curry.

Wilson, R. A. (1997). "Representing Human Rights Violations: Social Contexts and Subjectivities." In R. A. Wilson, ed., *Human Rights, Culture & Context.* London: Pluto Press.

Wilson, R. A. (2001). *The Politics of Truth and Reconciliation in South Africa: Legitimizing the Post-Apartheid State.* Cambridge: Cambridge University Press.

Index

abolitionism, and problem of slave redemption, 118–36. *See also* slavery
Abu Ghraib prison (Iraq), 78
Acuña, C. H., 184n7, 188n12
Adenauer, Konrad, 270
Advisory Council on Human Rights (ACHR Morocco), 267–8
aesthetics, and humanitarian narrative, 39–40, 45
agency: different views of in human rights and humanitarianism, 8; global humanitarianism and changes in understanding of personal, 211; limits to children's, 208
Aitken, Stuart, 207
Akhmatova, Anna, 245–6, 262–3
Alfonsín, Juan Cabandié, 194n18
Algeria, financial reparations and witness testimony in, 265–82
American Antislavery Society (AASS), 123–4, 130, 133
American Colonization Society (ACS), 121–3
American Revolution, conflict between slavery and values of, 120, 122, 133
amnesty, and financial reparations in Morocco and Algeria, 269–70
Amnesty International, 24, 65–6, 81n32, 225, 247, 250, 255–6, 260, 261
Anguita, E., 189n13
animal rights movement, 16

anti-Semitism, and post–World War I settlement in Europe, 171
Antislavery International, 119n3
Appiah, K. Anthony, 90, 104, 105
Arendt, Hannah, 21–2, 292
Argentina: and narratives about "disappeared" victims of state repression, 177–200, 276; and truth commission report, 184, 261–2
Aristotle, 101
Armenia, and genocide of 1915–1916, 35, 140–54, 165
Armitage, David, 17n28
Arntz, E. R. N., 162
artifacts, and refugee resettlement, 237–9
Asad, Talal, 1
Asociación de Abuelas de Plaza de Mayo (Association of Grandmothers of Plaza de Mayo), 181, 188, 189–91
Ataturk, Mustafa Kemal, 153–4
Atkinson, Clarissa, 204
Austro-Sardinian War (1859), 93
authenticity: and credibility of narratives in refugee resettlement, 229, 231, 232, 239–41; and human rights reports, 251; and impact of narratives of suffering, 22, 24
Avery, Gillian, 203, 218
awareness, and international bystanders to Holocaust, 169–70

CPSIA information can be obtained at www.ICGtesting.com
Printed in the USA
LVOW10s1105030214

372090LV00010B/145/P